ALIEN NATION

Dear Lisa,

It has been so great getting to know you as a student and a real person too.

Keep crossing borders!

Abrazo,

Elliott

ALIEN NATION

CHINESE MIGRATION IN THE
AMERICAS FROM THE COOLIE ERA
THROUGH WORLD WAR II

ELLIOTT YOUNG

The University of North Carolina Press / *Chapel Hill*

The paper in this book meets the guidelines for permanence and durability of the
Committee on Production Guidelines for Book Longevity of the Council on Library
Resources. The University of North Carolina Press has been a member of the
Green Press Initiative since 2003.

Cover illustration: Frederic Remington,
Chinese Immigrant Dying of Thirst in the Mohave Desert, 1800s.
Hand-colored woodcut. Used with permission of North Wind Picture Archives.

Library of Congress Cataloging-in-Publication Data
Young, Elliott, 1967–
Alien nation : Chinese migration in the Americas from the coolie era through World War II /
Elliott Young.
pages cm. — (The David J. Weber series in the new borderlands history)
Includes bibliographical references and index.
ISBN 978-1-4696-1296-6 (paperback : alkaline paper) — ISBN 978-1-4696-1340-6 (ebook)
1. Chinese—America—History—19th century. 2. Chinese—America—History—20th
century. 3. Immigrants—America—History. 4. Foreign workers, Chinese—America—
History. 5. Transnationalism—History. 6. Community life—America—History.
7. Ethnicity—America—History. 8. China—Emigration and immigration—History.
9. America—Emigration and immigration—History. 10. America—Race relations. I. Title.
E29.C5Y68 2014
304.8′951073—dc23
2014017584

18 17 16 15 14   5 4 3 2 1

For

Reiko and Zulema

And for the alien, the border crosser,

the *clandestino illegal*

Of all the specific liberties which may come into our minds
when we hear the word "freedom," freedom of movement is historically
the oldest and also the most elementary. Being free to depart for where
we will is the prototypical gesture of being free, as limitation of freedom of
movement has from time immemorial been the condition for enslavement.
Freedom of movement is also the indispensable condition for action, and
it is in action that men primarily experience freedom in the world.

—Hannah Arendt, *Men in Dark Times* (1967)

Contents

Table, Figures, and Illustrations

Acknowledgments

My paternal grandfather, Jack Cung, arrived in New York City in 1913 as a stowaway on a boat from Warsaw. He ran away from home hidden in a hay cart and made the journey across the Atlantic when he was just thirteen years old. My orphaned grandmother followed in 1923. As Jews from Lithuania, they turned their backs on the Old Country, which had never welcomed them, and spoke to their children in English; they used Yiddish and Polish to speak to each other. My mother arrived in New York City in 1963 from India to marry my father. She also turned her back on her native land, where women had few opportunities. It wasn't until a few years ago that she finally relented and became a U.S. citizen. The history of the stranger or the alien is close to me, and yet also far away, since I grew up enjoying all the benefits of citizenship and whiteness. But the price of becoming American was losing connections to distant homelands. May the aliens of the future not have to make that choice.

When I started this project in 2000, my daughter, Zulema, was just a year old; now she is in high school. Books mature more slowly than people. This project has taken me to Madrid; Havana; Mexico City; Washington, D.C.; and Victoria, B.C., and on the way I have accumulated many debts, far too many to fully acknowledge here.

I owe most to the Tepoztlán Institute for Transnational History of the Americas, a weeklong seminar outside of Mexico City that my friend and comrade Pam Voekel and I started in 2004 as a crazy utopian alternative workshop/conference/summer camp. The conversations over the past decade in Tepoztlán turned this book from a project about the Chinese in Cuba into a transnational history of Chinese migration in the Americas. Not only have the Tepoz folks provided me with my best ideas, but, just as important, they helped to build an intellectual home where many worlds fit and where I too can be a cabaret star for a night. I would like to especially acknowledge Jossianna Arroyo, Nicole Guidotti-Hernández, Frank Guridy, David Kazanjian, Devi Mays, Ana Minian, Josie Saldaña, David Sartorius, Micol Seigel, and Julie Weise for their critical eyes and generous spirits. To the Tepoztlán Collective, that ragtag band of outlaw academics, I raise my glass.

I have also been fortunate to have had an intellectually stimulating and supportive community at Lewis & Clark College. Thanks especially to colleagues Bruce Podobnik, Juan Carlos Toledano, Freddy Vilches, Blair Woodard, and the late Franya Berkman, who provided comments on a chapter from the book in a Mellon-funded seminar on the Caribbean diaspora. My students, including Paloma González, Daniela Jiménez, and Paul Weideman, have helped me to sort through the massive quantity of documents and do archival research in far-off places.

I could not have survived in Cuba without the help of many people who wrote letters, bribed officials, obtained hard-to-find books, and did what needed to be done to get me access to the Archivo Nacional de Cuba and the Biblioteca Nacional. Without Tomasito Fernández Robaina, Nora Gámez, Julie Portela, Abel Sierra, and other people helping me to navigate the Cuban bureaucracy, I may very well have jumped onto a raft to escape the island. I have benefited a great deal from the young Cuban scholars Mario Castillo and Miriam Herrera Jérez, whose work on the Chinese in Cuba is ground-breaking.

One of the greatest aspects of embarking on a new project is getting to know all of the wonderful people in that field. Evelyn Hu-DeHart, a pioneer in the study of the Chinese in Latin America, has been an inspiration and a supporter. I have learned from a great crew of scholars working on Asians in the Americas who have been helpful and generous interlocutors, including Jason Chang, Kornel Chang, Grace Delgado, Fredy González, Madeline Hsu, Erika Lee, Kathleen López, and Julia Maria Schiavone Camacho.

This project has been generously funded by the Millicent McIntosh Fellowship from the Woodrow Wilson Foundation, a grant by the Mellon Foundation for a sabbatical extension, and numerous research grants by Lewis & Clark College. My colleagues in the history department at Lewis & Clark have always had my back, especially when we faced headwinds. I also had the good fortune to be an Oregon Humanities Chautauqua lecturer and to bring my ideas about the Chinese diaspora to an eclectic mix of Oregonians all over the state. That experience helped me to keep my academic jargon in check. The David Sartorius living room couch fellowship made possible various research trips to the National Archives.

This book has received amazing critical feedback from many readers. Susan Ferber at Oxford University Press encouraged me along the way and gave me invaluable advice for how to shape the manuscript. The insightful reviews by readers for Oxford University Press, Duke University Press, and the University of North Carolina Press forced me to rethink parts of my argument and made this a much better book.

I was fortunate to find Chuck Grench, my editor at the University of North Carolina Press, who came so well recommended that I am still convinced he has a publicist. Lucas Church, Sara Cohen, and the rest of the UNC Press folks have kept this project on track. And then I had the luck that the dynamic duo, Andy Graybill and Benjamin Johnson, were just about to start the David J. Weber Series in the New Borderlands History at UNC Press, which they graciously invited me to launch with this book. Knowing that they, along with my friend and colleague Sam Truett, would be in my corner made easier my decision about which press to hitch my wagon to. Their astute comments, sense of humor, and fine-tooth-comb editing of the manuscript were a gift. It is an honor to be part of a series named for David Weber, a man who has done so much for the field of borderlands history, helped me personally when I was looking for a job, and was such a decent human being.

In all of my endeavors, Ramón Gutiérrez has been a steadfast mentor who has always been willing to write letters for me and provide critical feedback. To him I owe more tequila than I can afford. My friend Napoleón Landaeta accompanied me from Havana to Tepoztlán to New York City, spent many days with me in Portland cafés as I worked on this *chino* book, and helped me to enjoy *la mala vida* between visits to the archives. Finally, my partner, Reiko Hillyer, has read, edited, and given me more ideas than I can ever fully acknowledge here. It is thanks to her and my daughter Zulema that I was able to complete this book and still have a life, *la buena vida*.

Note on Language and Terminology

Some readers may object to my use of terms like *alien, illegal alien,* or *coolie.* I am sensitive to the politics of trying to refashion our language so that we do not legitimize the dehumanization or denigration of migrants. However, since my aim in this book is precisely to understand the meaning of terms like *alien, illegal alien,* and *coolie,* using them is essential to understanding their genealogy. *Alien* and *illegal alien* are legal terms that were used in the United States and Canada. *Alien* referred to anyone who was a noncitizen, including permanent residents, and *illegal alien* denoted those noncitizens who were in the country without proper authorization. I am interested, however, not only in the legal definitions but also in how people popularly used these terms to refer to Chinese and others who may in fact have been citizens. There is not an exact equivalent to the term *alien* in Spanish. *Extranjero* (foreigner) is the closest translation. Since the mid-twentieth century, Spanish speakers tend to use the English word *alien* when referring to extraterrestrials. In Latin America, Chinese migrants were referred to as *colonos asiáticos* (Asian colonists) or *extranjeros asiáticos* (Asian foreigners) or simply as *chinos* (Chinese).

Coolie is also a pejorative term, referring to low-status workers, usually from China or India. Unlike *alien,* however, *coolie* has no legal definition. The term was employed by politicians, journalists, and anti-Asian activists to describe servile and indentured laborers. My point in using this term is not to ascribe these characteristics to the Chinese migrants who were thus labeled but to more accurately represent how certain Chinese laborers were viewed.

Legally there is a distinction between an immigrant and other visitors, that is, foreign students, tourists, and temporary workers. The term *immigrant* implies an intention for permanent settlement and possibly even naturalization as a citizen. I prefer to use *migrant,* unless I am referring to a specific legal status, because the people involved often did not know whether or not they were going to settle permanently, and whatever their intentions, circumstances often changed their plans. Given the book's focus on mobility and movement, *migrant* is the term that best refers to the lives of the people I am studying.

The term *Asian* is so broad as to have no meaning, except for the fact that it was used as a way to lump together vastly different kinds of people with different languages and cultures. Governments sometimes made distinctions between Asians, favoring Japanese over Chinese migrants, for example, and at other times all "Asians" were discriminated against equally. Similarly, *Chinese* is a crude instrument for describing the vast cultural and linguistic differences that comprised nineteenth- and early twentieth-century China. The fact that most nineteenth-century immigrants to the Americas came from Guangdong and spoke Cantonese should not be forgotten, and yet government bureaucracies saw the world through national lenses, and so these migrants were seen as Chinese. The goal of my book is not to sanitize the language of the past but to explore and explain its meaning.

I employ the romanized versions of Chinese names as they appeared in the sources. For place names, I have used the more standardized and recent pinyin system. I refer to Chinese biographical names using the Chinese convention, in which the family name is placed first. For some names, which have clearly been Hispanicized or Anglicized, I assume that the family name has been placed at the end. Many of the people in this book used two or more names, both to help Westerners pronounce them more easily and to evade immigration restrictions when using fraudulent papers. When possible, I have tried to use the Chinese rather than the Anglicized or Hispanicized names.

ALIEN NATION

Aliens and the Nation

Do not deport the Chinese caught to be unlawfully within our
jurisdiction; have the law amended and put the Chinaman in prison,
make it a felony to come into the United States clandestinely.
—Marcus Braun, "Undercover Report on Illegal Chinese Migration" (1907)

People moving across oceans and land borders are both visible and completely invisible to us. Governments have sought to track such movements
since the nineteenth century, and yet millions managed to cross borders undetected by state authorities. These are the strangers, the aliens in our midst,
who are excluded, and in their exclusion they give meaning to citizenship
rights. The alien has been constructed as isolated, marginal, anxious, and
deviant by sociologists, anthropologists, and historians, but this is the view
of the alien as seen through the lens of the nation. From the vantage point
of the migrants themselves, we begin to see a transnational community that
fits poorly in the national boxes to which historians too often consign their
subjects.

On 2 January 1907, U.S. immigration inspector Marcus Braun witnessed
the Chinese Commercial Steamship Company ship, the *Alabama*, land in
Salina Cruz, Mexico, with 450 Chinese from Hong Kong. Braun had come to
Mexico to investigate the clandestine migrant networks that funneled Chinese into the United States. His undercover operation began in Havana, one
of the hotspots in a global network for clandestine migration. Trailing migrants on a ship bound for Veracruz, Mexico, he found 700 Spaniards looking for work in Mexico and 250 Syrians seeking clandestine entry into the
United States, some of whom had already been rejected because they suffered from trachoma.[1] Immigration inspectors had long suspected that Chinese and others crossed illegally into the United States from Canada, Mexico,
and Cuba, but the secretive nature of smuggling made it difficult for them to
fully appreciate the size and inner workings of these networks. Braun's investigation cracked open a window on the transnational world of illegal migration that had been barely visible to state authorities.

This book is about new ways of seeing—making visible trajectories, path-

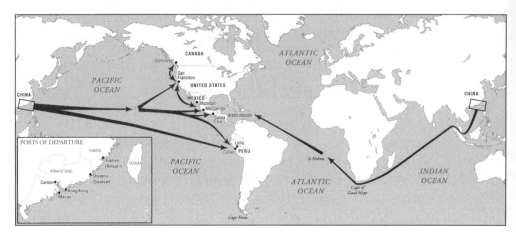

Chinese migration to the Americas, mid-nineteenth and early twentieth centuries.
Drawn by Erin Greb.

ways, and networks that have eluded and, at the same time, been the object of the gaze of the nation-state. Nation-states are better at tracking the flow of people and goods within their boundaries, but their ability to see the action at ground level, especially beyond their borders, is limited. Historians who mostly work in the archives and the framework of single nation-states have been hindered by the same double blindness, their vision at once too wide to see the details of how individuals move on the ground and too focused to see beyond the boundaries of the nation. In following the migrant trail across multiple borders, Braun unconsciously redrew the map according to clandestine transnational regional connections. Following the Chinese migrant trajectories rather than the predetermined boundaries of the nation-state maps the Americas in new ways.[2] Migrants who crisscrossed national boundaries outside of sanctioned channels made their own meanings and reconceptualized space, not the way a cartographer maps a nation or city but in unexpected and often prohibited ways that eluded legibility. Uncovering these hidden networks, trajectories, and pathways allows us to see beyond the nation and remap history. Some of the migrant trails that Chinese forged in the nineteenth century are still being used today, while others have shifted, allowing their travelers to take advantage of new opportunities. Unlike the national map, which imagines itself as static and timeless, the diasporic migrant mapping I propose is always transient, shifting, and unstable.[3]

My effort to tell a history of Chinese migration in the Americas that is not centered on the nation thus focuses on the intervening spaces, the border-

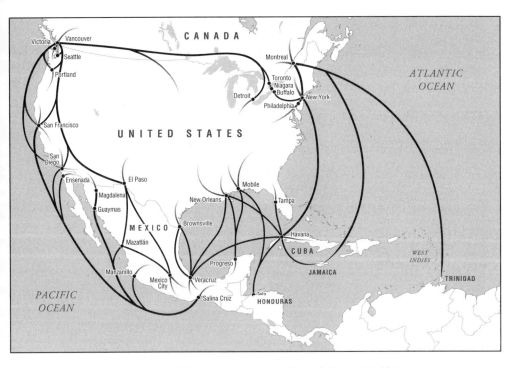

Some of the clandestine Chinese migratory routes through Greater North America.
Drawn by Erin Greb.

lands and seas through which Chinese passed on the way to some other place. Like Paul Gilroy, who in *The Black Atlantic* used the image of the ship to highlight the transactions among black people in the space between Europe, the Americas, and Africa, I emphasize the literal and metaphorical spaces in which Chinese moved between nations.[4] I am interested in capturing the moments of movement when Chinese found themselves on ships, in barracoons on the China coast, walking along rail lines or in freight cars along the U.S.-Mexican and U.S.-Canadian borders, caught on bridges between countries, pushed back and forth through border fences, and stowing away in the holds of ships in Havana's harbor. The glare of the nation-state burned intensely in these moments of border crossings, with inspectors, customs and sanitation agents, and border patrol officers focused on interdicting clandestine entries. However, the bright lights of the nation could never fully make visible the clandestine migrant pathways or the transnational networks that sustained the migrants. In spite of the dramatic increase in resources and personnel devoted to securing the borders of the United States and heightened regulation of migration more generally in the other countries, Chinese

Exhibit K from Marcus Braun's report on Chinese smuggling from Mexico depicts Chinese traveling on a steamer up the Pacific coast of Mexico en route to the United States. Marcus Braun Report, 12 February 1907, NARA, RG 85, entry 9, 52320/1.

were remarkably successful in evading state controls. This is, therefore, not just a story of invincible state power crushing and disciplining subaltern migrants; rather, it is a story of creative migrants outwitting the state. To paraphrase Marx, Chinese migrants made history, but not under circumstances chosen by themselves.

After being quarantined for two weeks in Salina Cruz, the 450 Chinese from Hong Kong were permitted onshore. José Chang, their "padrone," sent 300 of them to Torreón to pick cotton and sent the rest on a steamer up the Sonoran coast to Guaymas. Braun's blurry photograph of the Chinese is one of the only images we have that captures the Chinese in the midst of their clandestine journey to the United States. In Mazatlán, a Chinese delegation came onboard and took fifty migrants on a U.S. steamer bound for San Francisco. These fifty got off the boat in Ensenada, Baja California, just a few miles south of the border and San Diego. By the time Braun arrived in Guaymas, he had befriended Chang and witnessed him distributing hundreds of letters from relatives in the United States to the remaining migrants. These were not isolated Chinese just off the boat trying to make their way to the United States. They were part of a well-coordinated transnational network with highly sophisticated transportation and communication channels that moved them from China through various points in Mexico and finally to the United States. Braun followed the 100 remaining migrants on a train they took from Guaymas to Magdalena, a small town near the Arizona border. Of the 450 migrants who landed, 300 went to Torreón, 50 to Ensenada, and 100 to Magdalena. The majority may have temporarily remained in Mexico picking cotton or working in Chinese restaurants and stores, but many of them ended up crossing into the United States. Although the United States maintained nine examining stations along the Mexican border at railroad junctions, Braun explained that Chinese could easily cross the Rio Grande in a rowboat, or walk along the many "carriage roads, pathways, highways, [and] mountain trails." As he put it, "there is a broad expanse of land with an imaginary line, all passable, all being used, all leading to the United States."[5] The "imaginary line" was the border between the United States and Mexico.

Braun's report is one of the few descriptions we have of Chinese migrants in their border-crossing journey. The reflection of these cross-border movements can be seen in the state responses to them: fortification of borders and the development of immigration bureaucracies. This book seeks to explore not only the state construction of the Chinese as aliens but also the transnational networks of Chinese that enabled them to evade border controls and construct an alternative community that overlapped but was not synchronous with the nation-state. The narrative will thus shift focal lengths to allow us to see state attempts to solidify national borders and identities and to enable us to see the transnational diasporic networks of Chinese migrants that superseded the nation. These two elements developed in tandem and often helped constitute one another. Exclusionary laws forced the Chinese to cross the boundary clandestinely, which in turn made the "imaginary lines" Braun referred to into the policed border zones and physical barriers that we know today.

Establishing the border was more complicated than just erecting barriers and inspection stations. Given the race-based exclusion laws, immigration officers had to become protoanthropologists, evaluating race based on dubious physical and cultural markers. The large numbers of Mexicans who crossed the border daily made it especially difficult for inspectors to catch Chinese who blended in with locals. In 1905, Broughton Brandenburg published an article in *Harper's Weekly* about the hundreds of thousands of alien contract laborers who arrived each year in the United States "aided

"Coolie Disguised as a Mexican Peon to Be Smuggled into the United States," *Harper's Weekly*, 5 August 1905.

and abetted by relatives, employment agents, padrones and employers." "The immigration agents stand very nearly helpless," declared Branden-burg, "against the gigantic conspiracies that operate against them." Under the evocative headline "The Stranger within Our Gate," a large photograph prominently featured a "coolie disguised as [a] Mexican peon to be smuggled into the US," suggesting how difficult it would be to distinguish a Mexican from a Chinese laborer.[6] In 1907, Inspector Braun included twenty photo-graphic portraits in a report to his superiors to show "how exceedingly diffi-

Exhibit J from Marcus Braun's report on Chinese smuggling from Mexico.
Marcus Braun Report, 12 February 1907, NARA, RG 85, entry 9, 52320/1.

cult it is to positively state whether these are pictures of Chinamen or Mexi-cans."[7] Braun knew that Chinese tried to blend in with Mexicans by speaking Spanish, cutting their queues, and wearing Western-style clothing. What is most interesting about Braun's befuddlement is that it directly contradicted the racist notions of biological and phenotypical difference among races. If trained inspectors could not tell a Chinese from a Mexican when they wore the same clothes, then perhaps racial difference was not biological but rather a matter of clothing, language, and customs. Nonetheless, the idea of Chinese sneaking into the country disguised as Mexicans evoked a fear that the nation was being overrun by aliens who could not be identified by physical examination.

The idea of the "illegal alien" today has political power throughout the Americas, but nowhere more so than in the United States. The preeminent image of the illegal alien in the United States for the last eighty years has been the Mexican. However, as many other scholars have noted, the Chinese were the first illegal aliens in the United States, and indeed in the world. And they were the first group to be restricted by immigration laws based on their ethnicity. However, this is not just a story about the rise of the U.S. immigration bureaucracy and the ways Chinese and other immigrants were restricted, criminalized, and exploited. Mae Ngai, Erika Lee, and others have ably recounted the history of how the illegal alien was produced in the United States and thus became an "impossible subject."[8] Moving beyond the frame of the nation-state, I try to understand how the Chinese became aliens throughout the Americas in the mid-nineteenth to mid-twentieth centuries. Rather than focusing solely on the back and forth migration between China and the Americas, I also examine the zigzagging between countries in the Americas. Before the passage of the Chinese exclusion acts in the United States, before modern immigration legislation, Chinese were recruited as contract laborers to work on plantations and in mines in Cuba, Peru, the United States, and Canada. Whether they were called "coolies" or free laborers, the Chinese were viewed as strangers and regulated by laws as a distinct group. Unlike other immigrant groups, the Chinese were not expected, or allowed in the case of the United States, to become naturalized citizens and incorporate themselves into society. They were perpetual aliens.

The idea of Jews, Chinese, or other marginalized groups as aliens, strangers, or sojourners has a long and controversial genealogy. In 1908, sociologist Georg Simmel invoked the Jew as the quintessential "stranger," who, he argued, is not "the wanderer who comes today and goes tomorrow, but rather . . . [is] the person who comes today and stays tomorrow. He is, so to speak, the potential wanderer: although he has not moved on, he has not quite overcome the freedom of coming and going."[9] Although Simmel recognized some positive qualities of the stranger, he viewed the stranger as pathological. In 1928 the influential Chicago sociologist Robert Park adapted Simmel's idea of the stranger, asserting that the "marginal man" was usually of mixed race and lived between two cultures, being comfortable in neither. The marginal man was described by Park as being prone to "spiritual instability, intensified self-consciousness, restlessness and *malaise*." In 1952 Park's student Paul Siu further adapted the idea of the stranger by describing the Chinese laundryman as a sojourner, whom he defined as "a stranger who spends many years of his lifetime in a foreign country without being assimilated by it." Although Siu differentiated Park's "marginal man," who suffered from maladaptation because of biculturalism, from his "sojourner," who was isolated because he remained tied to his home culture, in both cases the subject was seen as "deviant."[10] The notion of the alien as deviant comes from a perspective that imagines national identity as normative.

More recently the idea of the sojourner has been critiqued as an orientalist idea because it implies that Asian migrants were prevented from integrating into another culture by either the culture's racism and discrimination or their own clannishness.[11] Scholars pushing for Asian American civil rights highlighted Asian migrants' desires to integrate into U.S. culture and become citizens, but in so doing they overlooked Asians' continued nationalist affiliations to their home countries and other diasporic identities not based on the nation.[12] The nationalist lens only sees the possibility of attachment to or estrangement from this or that nation and categorizes everything else as deviant. The transborder world of the Chinese migrant cannot be understood outside of the context of discrimination and racism in the Americas, but to reduce this non-nation-based identity to a reaction to racism assumes that national assimilation and integration is a universal goal. The complex alien identity of Simmel's "stranger," Park's "marginal man," and Siu's "sojourner" deserves to be recovered as a viable alternative to national identity and not merely described in terms of what it is not.[13] A Frederic Remington drawing published in *Harper's* in 1891 titled "Dying of Thirst in the Desert" is one of the rare depictions of Chinese crossing the U.S.-Mexico border illegally (see cover art). The emaciated and skeletal body that crawls across the desert graphically illustrates that Chinese migrants were imagined by some as zombie-like aliens.[14] Today we are haunted by similar images of Mexicans and others dying as they traverse the very same sun-scorched desert.

Making Aliens Illegal

This book tells the broader history of the making of the alien in the Americas by following the story Chinese migrants from ports in the Pearl River Delta in China to various destinations in the Americas, principally Cuba, Peru, Mexico, the United States, and Canada.[15] The time frame for this study is the 1840s, when the coolie trade to the Americas started, through the 1940s, when the geopolitics of World War II forced Cuba (1942), the United States

(1943), and Canada (1947) to end their exclusion of Chinese laborers.[16] The Chinese were constructed as aliens during a century-long process, as immigration bureaucracies throughout the Americas formed and strengthened. From the 1910s through the 1930s, communists, Mexicans in the United States, and others became the preeminent excluded others. The Chinese, however, were the model aliens around whom immigration restrictions were developed and the legal category of the alien was built.

The time frame of my study purposefully straddles the late nineteenth-century divide that characterizes the historiography of Chinese in the Americas. Most scholars who study Asians in Latin America either focus on the coolie period (1847–74) or examine the twentieth century.[17] Scholars of Asians in the United States or Canada have mainly treated the exclusion era as a contained unit, studying either the exclusion era or the post-exclusion era.[18] Doing a transnational history with multiple countries makes neat periodization bracketed by national immigration acts impossible, but the global phenomena of the coolie trade and World War II provide transnational bookends. The end of the coolie trade (1874) and beginning of U.S. exclusion (1882) were watershed moments in the history of Chinese in the Americas, but the continuities between the two periods have been obscured by scholarship that assumes a radical break. My point in bridging the nineteenth-century coolie era and the period of modern immigration restrictions is precisely to show the continuities over time and place in the way in which Chinese were produced as aliens, politically, socially, and sexually. Although Chinese continued to face legal discrimination and immigration restrictions in the Americas after World War II, restrictionists increasingly focused their energies on other groups.

In addition to bridging the chronological divide, I adopt a hemispheric and global perspective by following the paths of Chinese migrants from the southern coast of China to the Americas. In other words, instead of predetermining a national frame and examining people only as they enter that frame, I allow the migrants to determine the parameters of the study. I do, however, narrow my focus to a broad transnational region, what I call Greater North America, comprising Cuba, Mexico, the United States, and Canada, and including Peru because of the large Chinese migration there during the coolie era. If significant numbers of Chinese migrated from California to Australia or Mexico to the Philippines then I would have included those locales in my study; they did not. Following the paths of Chinese migrants as they cross borders, legally and illegally, within Greater North America provides a transnational scale that is at once global and yet small enough to highlight the stories of individual migrants. As other scholars have noted, Chinese migrants did not just stop when they arrived in the Americas, they continued to move and migrate between various countries, looking for work and more hospitable environments. Given the pervasiveness of anti-Chinese violence throughout the Americas, this search continued for quite some time.

The alien is not a stable or fixed category. Just who is an alien is a matter of perspective, geography, power, and time. Aliens in one place may be citizens in another. Powerful outsiders, like the Europeans, can turn indigenous people into aliens in their own land. Time can also erase the stigma of foreignness and allow someone to become a neonative or a naturalized citizen. The legal definition of an alien is someone who is a noncitizen. Therefore, even legal residents are aliens until they become naturalized citizens. However, the broader label of *alien* refers to foreigners, outsiders, and strangers regardless of their legal status. My use of the term encompasses both the strict legal definition and the broader cultural notions associated with strangers and foreigners. Although British migrants in the United States may have been aliens according to the law in the United States and Spanish migrants may have been aliens in Cuba in the early twentieth century, neither of those were aliens in the manner of the Chinese. The Chinese suffered from a double alien status, being outsiders both legally and culturally.

The title of this book, *Alien Nation*, brings together the concepts of alien, nation, and the related idea of alienation. Aliens are literally those who are not part of a nation while at the same time being inside of it. They are included as an excluded class. The word *alien* derives from the Latin *alienus*, meaning "of, or belonging to another person or place."[19] *Alien* was also used to refer to plants that came from another district or country and then became naturalized and rooted in a new territory. All of these meanings highlight the outsider status of the alien, as someone or something that comes from somewhere else and does not quite fit, even though, in the case of plants or migrants, they may thrive in the new environment and develop roots there. In the United States, the idea of aliens as threats to the nation-state stretches back to the Alien and Sedition Acts of 1798, which cast aliens as potential enemies of the state and not just guests. Over the course of the late eighteenth through mid-nineteenth centuries, the term *alien* became increasingly linked to notions of citizenship rather than merely settlement.[20] The most extreme version of alien foreignness was articulated by science fiction writers in the 1940s to refer to extraterrestrials.

The term *alienation* in psychology refers to emotional estrangement or the feeling of being an outsider in a society. In 1959, sociologist Melvin Seeman defined *alienation* with a fivefold classification: powerlessness, mean-inglessness, normlessness, isolation, and self-estrangement.[21] Migrant aliens may be viewed as psychologically estranged from the society in which they live because they are relatively powerless and appear isolated, at least from the perspective of dominant society. It is important to remember, however, that while society at large may view migrants as alienated, the migrants may not conceive of themselves in that way. Their power and community ties often remain invisible to outsiders. Furthermore, migrants may be willing to endure hardship and isolation from the dominant society in order to maintain familial and community bonds at home.[22]

There have been many kinds of aliens in the Americas, beginning with indigenous people and African slaves. Throughout the colonial period and up through the end of the nineteenth century, governments generally encouraged people to come to work on plantations and to settle vast and sparsely populated territories. Most of these people were African slaves who were brought in chains to the Americas. Latin American countries were especially interested in promoting European immigration to whiten their populations, but by the mid-nineteenth century Cuba and Peru began to recruit Chinese. Although the United States also generally encouraged immigration, Irish and other foreign paupers faced deportation by state governments in the mid-nineteenth century. Still, even as the federal government developed ship passenger regulations to limit the entry of poor people, no federal bureaucracy had the power to exclude a particular ethnic or national group until the Chinese Exclusion Act of 1882. Thus, the Chinese became the first group not only to bear the stigma of aliens but to be enmeshed in a federal bureaucratic and legal system that produced them as "illegal" as well. The development of the category "illegal alien" in the late nineteenth century produced a double alienation for Chinese as cultural foreigners and outlaws.

Immigrant Inspector Marcus Braun, who spent so much of his time uncovering the clandestine migrant networks, advocated criminalizing Chinese aliens. After reporting on the many ways Chinese clandestinely crossed borders, Inspector Braun made one recommendation: "Do not deport the Chinese caught to be unlawfully within our jurisdiction; have the law amended and put the Chinaman in prison, make it a felony to come into the United States clandestinely; put him in prison to earn his passage home, and after having spent two, three or more years in prison, deport him with the money he earned in the workhouse."[23] Braun defended the criminalization of Chinese aliens by blaming them for taking advantage of the country and breaking the law. "We are not harsh, we are not cruel, we are not unjust, when we say to the Alien, 'You came here clandestinely, you cheated our Government when you came here without subjecting yourself to our enacted law; therefore, back you go.'" Braun continued, repeating his plaintive cry, "You misused our confidence in you, you are a convicted felon, back you go."[24] Braun's hysterical declaration thus absolved the state of having enacted the very laws that made the migrants criminals in the first place, and instead shifted culpability to the migrants for having taken advantage of the innocent and trusting nation-state.

Gender, Race, and Sex

The strangeness of Chinese was articulated in terms of their race, gender, and sexuality. In addition to fearing homosexuality and effeminacy among Chinese men, anti-Chinese activists condemned heterosexual relationships with Chinese men as a threat to women and to the vitality of the nation. Chinese men in Louisiana married Creoles, blacks, whites, and Indians, and in Mexico they married Mexican women frequently.[25] These sexual relationships provoked vituperative attacks that mobilized eugenics discourse to link the offspring of such unions to the decay of the nation. Anti-Chinese activists, politicians, and journalists throughout the Americas characterized Chinese in strikingly similar ways as thrifty and hard workers, on the one hand, and as conniving, diseased, dirty, and uncivilized, on the other. Both the positive and negative traits were seen as threats to the working class, merchants, and the biological health of the nation. Although similar negative stereotypes about Chinese circulated in Cuba, the disproportionate participation of Chinese in the Cuban wars of independence (1868–98) helped mitigate the most virulent expressions of racism.

Chinese may have been seen as racial others throughout the Americas and beyond, but they were categorized differently in different countries and regions depending on the particular history of racial structures in those places. In the white settler societies of the United States, Canada, Australia, South Africa, and New Zealand, Chinese were seen as nonwhite and as "totally unfit" for the nation.[26] As part of his effort to win passage of the Johnson Act in 1924, Lothrop Stoddard published a book, *The Rising Tide of Color against White World Supremacy*, in which he remarked on the "instinctive and instantaneous solidarity which binds together Australians and Afrikanders [sic], Californians and Canadians, into a 'sacred union' at the mere whisper of Asiatic immigration." Although Stoddard was concerned that the white immigrant would "gravely disorder national life," he proclaimed that the "colored immigrant would doom it to certain death." "Black blood" may not present an "immediate danger," but Stoddard raised the alarm of "the very imminent danger that the white stocks may be swamped by Asiatic blood."[27] White solidarity thus helped define all Asians as aliens and threats to the white man's nation. The alien was a question of race.

Although the Asian versus white color line was starkly drawn in California and British Columbia, in states bordering the Gulf of Mexico, where a more Caribbean-inflected racial order prevailed, the lines were more blurred. In Louisiana, for instance, the offspring of Chinese and white parents could be categorized as white or Chinese. And, in at least one case, the child of a Chinese man and a black woman was classified as mulatto, thus recognizing an intermediate category between white and black. By 1900, however, children of mixed-race Chinese heritage in Louisiana began to be categorized as either white or black. Nonetheless, even then the Mexican or Indian classification allowed some to pass for white or black depending on the circumstances.[28] The rigid color lines that anti-Asian activists were so eager to draw were often difficult to enforce on mixed race populations, especially in the borderland regions where different racial understandings overlapped.

Chinese were also constructed as racial others in Latin America, but, again, their position in the racial hierarchy varied over time and place. In Mexico, ideas about *mestizaje*, racial mixing between Indians and whites, and white supremacy had worked in tandem since the late nineteenth century. *Mestizaje* provided the foundation for national unity, but the assumption and goal was always that the Indian would be assimilated and modernized.[29] Chinese, Jews, blacks, and others were not a part of this mestizo national project and easily became the targets for nationalist xenophobia, especially during and immediately after the 1910 Mexican Revolution. In Cuba, where the indigenous population had been wiped out early in the colonial era, national unity in the late nineteenth century was built on the mythical notion of a racial democracy for blacks and whites.[30] Like in Mexico, Chinese remained outside of the foundational myths of Cuban unification, even as they were incorporated as patriots who fought valiantly during the wars of independence. Even Cuban independence hero José Martí's antiracist writings on equality between blacks and whites did not seem apply to Chinese, whom Martí characterized in crudely racist terms. Similarly, in Peru, the Marxist José Maria Mariátegui argued for unification of the Peruvian working class, especially Indians and whites, but his portrayals of Chinese and blacks were racist caricatures. As Mariátegui put it, the Chinese has "inoculated his descendants with the fatalism, apathy, and defects of the decrepit Orient."[31] In both Latin and Anglo America, therefore, Chinese, and Asians in general, remained outsiders and threats against whom national identity could be forged; however, the tempo, dynamic, and ferocity of the hemispheric Sinophobia differed according to time and place. Although this book does not focus on the links among the anti-Chinese movements in the Americas, the outlines of these networks emerge in the broader discussion of Chinese migration.

Chinese ethnic and gender nonconformity, their queerness in other words, coincided with a legal and cultural definition that marked them as aliens or foreigners. The varieties of nonnormative relationships only became visible when the state brought charges of sodomy or "gross indecency" against migrants, when interracial relationships were outlawed, or when anti-Chinese activists wrote books and pamphlets warning about these dangers. Histories of migrants have tended to privilege the lives of migrants when they settle down, establish nuclear families, buy property, and incorporate themselves, even as subalterns, into the social fabric of dominant society.[32] In contrast, I try to uncover the largely hidden transient and clandestine lives of Chinese migrants as they moved across borders in the Americas.[33] Rather than focus on the formation of communities in any particular nation, this diasporic approach recognizes that migrants often maintain multiple homes in different countries throughout their lifetimes. Assimilation to one particular nation is not the end point of serial migration. Mobility and transience opened up possibilities for Chinese to escape from normative relations and to strategically accumulate capital and power in what Aihwa Ong calls "flexible citizenship."[34] Nevertheless, we should not romanticize the resiliency of Chinese in the context of their marginalization. Chinese who entered a country as aliens also struggled to gain legal recognition as citizens and, just as important, social recognition as a part of the nation. Middle-class and elite Chinese, especially merchants, translators, and labor brokers, were in a better position to achieve this status than laborers.[35] Chinese, as a group, however, remained perpetual aliens throughout the Americas until the mid-twentieth century.

Methodology, Sources, and Organization

How the Chinese were made into perpetual aliens in the Americas is largely a tale about state power that has been recorded in state-generated sources, court records, diplomatic correspondence, and immigration reports. Thanks to the fastidious surveillance and undercover investigations by state authorities, part of the history of clandestine cross-border smuggling has been preserved in state archives. Letters by Chinese that were intercepted by state agents and articles from Chinese-language newspapers also helped me reconstruct a clandestine world of cross-border smuggling. My broader hemispheric view allows me to fill in some of the gaps in national archives. While the voices of Chinese coolies and labor migrants have rarely been preserved, Chinese merchants, translators, and labor brokers left a more substantive record. Thus, the transnational networks formed by Chinese merchants, secret societies, political groups, and hometown associations allowed me to understand how Chinese communicated and survived as they shuttled across the Americas. I have worked in archives in Spain, Cuba, Mexico, Canada, and the United States and used mainly English- and Spanish-language sources. The Chinese-language letters and newspapers that I examined were translated by immigration officials; the testimony given by Chinese laborers to the 1874 Cuba Commission was published in English and Chinese. Although there are limits to using such translations, they provide important glimpses into the world of Chinese migrants.

This book is organized by following the Chinese migrants, starting with the coolie ships leaving the coast of southern China and ending with Chinese being expelled from northern Mexico in the 1930s. The chapters are organized not by country but by theme, although each chapter may highlight some countries more than others depending on the topic. Part 1, "Coolies and Contracts, 1847–1874," examines debates over the coolie trade and the difficulty of establishing national sovereignty on the high seas and in Chinese port cities. While European, American, and Asian governments fought with each other to regulate and control Chinese labor, the emigrants pushed for their own freedom through violent mutinies. For the advocates of the coolie trade the contract was a symbol of an individual's freedom to enter into an agreement with others, while for its critics the contract was a mechanism of bondage. Debates over the meaning of the coolie contracts and over who was a coolie helped define the free immigrant. In part 1, I argue that there are more continuities than differences between the coolies in Cuba and Peru and the free immigrants in Mexico, Canada, and the United States.

Part 2, "Clandestine Crossings and the Production of Illegal Aliens, 1882–1900," turns to inter-American border crossings between Mexico, Cuba, Canada, and the United States and to the birth of immigration bureaucracies. In these chapters, I explore the tensions and cooperation between neighboring countries as they each developed immigration policies in conjunction with one another. While Canada helped the United States restrict Chinese migration, Mexico defended the absolute right of anyone to travel and reside in his or her country, regardless of race or nationality. Mexico's liberal migration policy, based on notions of the inviolable "rights of man," would shift in the 1920s and 1930s, when Mexico banned foreign workers from entry and expelled nearly all Chinese from its northwestern states. By the 1920s, the enforcement of Chinese restriction legislation throughout the Americas had produced the "illegal alien." In the United States, despite dramatic expansion of the immigration bureaucracy's personnel and budget, officers proved incapable of stopping clandestine entries. As soon as officers managed to shut down one pathway, smugglers would find a new route to evade capture. I examine the various ways Chinese entered the United States clandestinely through "back doors" and open windows, by train, by car, by boat, or on foot. Migrants' ability to stay one step ahead of the immigration officers reveals the ingenuity of the migrants and labor brokers and the impossibility of securing thousands of miles of land and sea borders.

Part 3, "Competing Revolutionary Nationalisms, 1900–1940," explores the concurrent rise of xenophobia and nationalism across the Americas and in China, and its effect on immigration restrictions. In these chapters I focus on anti-Chinese violence in Mexico, which resulted in the expulsion of Chinese from the northern states of Sonora and Sinaloa in the early 1930s. Although I highlight the anti-Chinese movement in Mexico, I also put this movement in the context of Sinophobia throughout Greater North America. In spite of the hostile environment in the Americas, Chinese migrants survived by shuttling through transnational networks developed by merchants, secret societies, political parties, and hometown associations, which allowed them to move across national boundaries, find jobs, and establish communities in strange new places. The rise of a nationalist movement in China at the beginning of the twentieth century briefly united overseas Chinese, but divisions within that movement also led to bitter fights within this diasporic community in the 1920s.

This book invites you to see Chinese migration to the Americas without the blinders of the nation-state. This does not mean that nations, national legislation, and national identity are not an important part of the story. Even without the blinders the nation is still in full view, but something else comes into focus as well: the transnational world of Chinese migrants. When the Chinese came to Gold Mountain (Gam Saan in Cantonese), they were coming not to any particular country but rather to the Americas, a place where they hoped to find streets paved with gold. Instead they found a continent divided by boundaries, border patrol agents, restrictive laws, and mobs who wanted to kick them out. The Chinese transnational networks allowed them to evade those barriers, find jobs, establish families, and keep them mobile, ever on the search for the elusive Gold Mountain. This book is about their journey.

PART 1

Coolies and Contracts, 1847–1874

CHAPTER 1

Contested Sovereignties

Coolies on the High Seas

Would our American Consuls have winked at this trade had it the
slightest approximation to Slavery? Where are all of the British and American
ships-of-war on the East India station if this is modern or new-fashioned Slave
trade? They too must be blinded or else they would long ago have seized these
Cooly-carrying ships and sent them into port for trial and condemnation.
—"Commerce in Coolies," *New York Times*, 12 March 1856

The thing has been carried far enough, and it is time for the civilized nations
of the world to interfere. If the slave trade of Zanzibar is a disgrace, then the
coolie trade is a disgrace; if the slave trade of Zanzibar is an iniquity and a
crime against civilization, then the traffic in coolies is likewise.
—"The Coolie Trade," *New York Times*, 19 July 1873

The epigraphs above indicate a radical shift in how the coolie trade was
viewed by the *New York Times* from 1856 to 1873. In 1856 the newspaper
doubted that U.S. and British consuls would permit the trade if it came close
to slavery, but by 1873 the same paper called the trade an "iniquity and a
crime against civilization." What accounts for such a radical shift in less than
twenty years? Humanitarian impulses aside, continual rebellions of Chinese
coolies both on ships and in barracoons, along with protests by Chinese
townspeople and merchants in coastal cities, forced politicians and journalists around the world to see the coolie trade as equivalent to slavery. In
doing so, however, abolitionists portrayed emigrant laborers as unwitting
victims of powerful and conniving labor brokers and thereby rendered them
as passive. Although the Chinese were branded, sold at auction blocks, and
renamed by employers in a manner very similar to slavery, they clung to the
rights afforded them by the contracts and often claimed the more fundamental right to liberty. Not having rights as citizens, they claimed their rights as
men. This chapter explores the similarities of the coolie trade to slavery, but
it also tries to understand the ways coolies resisted and were active agents

in their own migration stories. In between the poles of free and voluntary emigrant and slave, there was a vast complex gray zone. That is the space the coolies occupied.

In 1859, the 3,000-ton ship *Norway*, sailing from Macao to Havana with 1,037 coolies, erupted in mutiny. The ship had come from New York loaded with coal for the U.S. naval squadron in the China seas, and it was making the return trip filled with Chinese coolies by way of Cuba. There were just sixty crew members on hand to keep the emigrants subdued. Five years later, in 1864, the mutiny was memorialized in *Harper's New Monthly Magazine* in an article by Edgar Holden titled "A Chapter in the Coolie Trade."[1] Although there are many newspaper accounts and government reports of coolie muti-nies, Holden's article provides a rare, detailed, firsthand narrative along with dramatic drawings that brought to life the scenes he witnessed. Holden por-trayed a brutal coolie system that echoed the African slave trade, but he also demonstrated the tenacity and resistance of Chinese emigrants.

Although the *Norway* looked like a slave ship, it was not clear if all of the emigrants were being taken against their will. The ship was outfitted like a slaving vessel with iron gratings over the holds and armed guards. However, when a government official boarded the ship prior to departure to ask if any of the passengers were unwilling emigrants, only one stepped forward, and he was released.[2] Holden made it clear that coercion and misrepresentation were used to recruit the coolies, but the emigrants' unwillingness to leave the ship also suggests that they were somewhat willing participants in the endeavor. Whether coerced or not, conditions in Macao's barracoons were dreadful, leading many Chinese to die of disease or commit suicide before they even left port.

Subduing more than 1,000 coolies with just 60 crew members required more subtle and sophisticated means of control than simply posting armed guards at the hatches and using iron shackles. Coolie ships depended on interpreters to facilitate communication and head off rebellions. The *Nor-way* had two half-Chinese, half-Portuguese interpreters who, Holden noted, were "nowise friendly to the mass of Coolies on board." Bicultural Chinese often played middlemen roles, helping recruit Chinese and also overseeing them on ships and on plantations. On the *Norway*, the crew encouraged Chi-nese to play dominoes and music that Holden dismissed as "barbarous" and "ingeniously discordant." Toward the end of the voyage, coolies even per-formed "rough theatricals" to keep themselves entertained. Nonetheless, the cramped conditions below decks often led to fights among the emigrants. Even before the *Norway* set sail, two coolies had committed suicide and an-

Edgar Holden, "Coolies Embarking," *Harper's New Monthly Magazine*, June 1864.
Courtesy of Reed College Library.

other was found strangled to death.[3] Although Holden exhibited some sympathy for the emigrants' plight, he narrated and illustrated the story not from the coolies' perspective but from that of someone above decks.

On the third day of the voyage, a fight broke out among the coolies, leaving one man seriously wounded from a blow with a cleaver. The crew descended to the hold to break up the fight. The wounded coolie confessed to the interpreter that a group of "desperadoes" had gone to the barracoons with the intention of staging a mutiny and killing the entire crew. The captain

Edgar Holden, "The Interpreters," *Harper's New Monthly Magazine*, June 1864. Courtesy of Reed College Library.

refused to believe the story, but three days later at midnight, the emigrants rebelled, lighting fires below decks and trying to pry the hatches open. As the coolies attempted to push their way through the gratings, the seamen shot at them and fired indiscriminately below decks. The crew attempted to pump water below decks to extinguish the fires and eventually threw tarpaulins over the hatches to trap the smoke in the hold and suffocate the coolies. Several coolies who were chained on the upper decks were beaten and shot to death. One of the coolies tried to escape by jumping into the hole in the grating. While he was swinging from the grating, he too was shot, his body dropping thirty feet to certain death.

Although Holden condemned the coolie trade, he also referred to the Chinese emigrants as "barbarians," and the accompanying images suggested they were savages. A drawing of the "enraged coolie" holding a cleaver and a fire torch depicted the unbridled anger of the Chinese. Other illustrations portrayed the kinds of discipline that were meted out on the ship, including whippings, firing below deck, and holding a tarpaulin over the hatchways to suffocate the Chinese. The ship's crew members were always drawn

Edgar Holden, "Enraged Coolie" (left) and "A Providential Mischance" (right), *Harper's New Monthly Magazine*, June 1864. Courtesy of Reed College Library.

Edgar Holden, "Firing down the Hatchway" (left) and "Preserving the Peace" (right), *Harper's New Monthly Magazine*, June 1864. Courtesy of Reed College Library.

fully clothed, a mark of civilization, while the Chinese were depicted with bare torsos, a signal of barbarism to readers. Many of the Chinese faces were drawn in a crude style that made them look almost simian, with their queues (ponytails) freely floating in midair or grabbed by the crew in attempts to subdue the emigrants. Holding the Chinese by their queues was a way to physically overpower them, but graphically it also represented cultural domination. Although the story portrayed the coolie trade as barbaric,

Edgar Holden, "A Vain Attempt" (left) and "Chained to the Hatch" (right),
Harper's New Monthly Magazine, June 1864. Courtesy of Reed College Library.

the visual representations rendered the Chinese in stereotypical ways as un-civilized and threatening.

The Chinese were at this point trapped in the ship's hold, choking on the smoke from the fires they had set, with scores of Chinese corpses lying around them. They were in no position to make demands, and yet one of the Chinese dipped a stylus in the blood that had pooled on the decks and wrote a note demanding that the captain bring the ship to Siam and allow them to leave. If the captain failed to comply, the mutineers wrote, they would burn the entire ship. The captain sent a terse reply: "Burn and be——." The situation above deck was also growing desperate. In addition to the threat of fires, the crew was running out of potable water, most of which was stored in the hold. The crew members managed to condense some steam and produced enough water to keep themselves alive. After a full day and night with the coolies rushing "with demoniac shrieks along the decks, burning their 'josh paper' and waving torches or clubs about their heads," the emigrants sued for peace. By the time the *Norway* reached Havana, 130 coolies had died, 70 of them killed during the mutiny.[4]

The mutiny on the *Norway* illustrates the willingness and ability of Chinese coolies to organize themselves and rebel, even under the most desperate circumstances. However, this mutiny and many others like it appear to have been not spontaneous uprisings but carefully planned revolts led by Chinese pirates who signed up as coolies so that they could take over the ships.

Edgar Holden, "The Writing in Blood," *Harper's New Monthly Magazine*, June 1864.
Courtesy of Reed College Library.

No amount of preparation could safeguard a ship when the emigrants below deck outnumbered the crew by more than sixteen to one and when they were willing to set fire to the ship to achieve their goals. Holden's story, circulating in a popular New York–based magazine at the height of the U.S. Civil War, highlighted the vulnerability and dangers of slave labor systems. On the ships as on the slave plantation those above lived in fear of those below.

At first glance, these tragedies aboard a coolie vessel can be understood as an international incident occurring on the high seas. The ship and its captain were U.S. citizens, Macao was a Portuguese territory, Cuba a Spanish colony, and the coolies were Chinese subjects. But the way this division of sovereignties over territories and people according to nation-states and empires does not recognize the complex borderlands that existed on the ground and in the sea. The coolie trade existed within and between nations and empires, in borderlands where the nation-state or imperial government did not exercise complete control. Although they were being recruited as part of state-

Edgar Holden, "On the Lower Deck," *Harper's New Monthly Magazine*, June 1864.
Courtesy of Reed College Library.

sponsored migration, coolies were viewed as aliens, outsiders who would never enjoy the same rights as citizens. In fact, their contracts specified in great detail the limitations on their rights (a subject discussed in the next chapter) and they were expected to remain indentured or return to China. Their departure from ports in China against the official wishes of the Qing government turned them into stateless people without the protection of any nation and exposed to exploitation by all. Nevertheless, coolies fought back by joining with each other to mutiny or simply committed suicide as a desperate but effective means of depriving the masters of their labor.

Although coolies were the most vulnerable to the whims of more powerful recruiters and traders, nation-states also had difficulty asserting sovereignty in these borderland ports. In 1858, William Reed, representing the American Legation to China, complained about his inability to prevent U.S. citizens from engaging in coolie trafficking. Reed believed the U.S. Slave Trade Act of 1818 applied to the coolie trade because the Chinese were "people of color," but his protestations to Spanish and U.S. captains were simply rejected.[5] Even though U.S. commissioner Peter Parker had pushed for restricting U.S. involvement in the trade since 1855, four years later U.S. citizens had become the chief carriers. With no legal authority to stop it, U.S. diplomats were relegated to issuing ineffective complaints.[6] Meanwhile, the Spanish consul general responded to U.S. entreaties by claiming that the trade was "allowable, just and legal, seeing that it consists of a contract made by one free man with another free man." Furthermore, he argued that it was up to the United States to enforce its laws on its own citizens, and not to expect the Spanish to do so.[7] In the end, Reed recognized his impotence to stop the trade, although he did mention as an aside that a coolie vessel was within "musket shot" of the U.S. warship *Minnesota* anchored in Hong Kong's harbor, implying that exercise of military force was one way to stop the trade.[8] Short of using military force, nations had a difficult time asserting themselves beyond their own borders. The *Norway* existed in a liminal space between and betwixt national sovereignties, and there was a lot of money to be made by keeping it that way. The thousands of Chinese coolies who were killed in mutinies or drowned on ships that sank were part of a human drama that cannot be wholly understood in terms of competing nationalities or empires.

Mutinies, Disease, and Death

Mutinies and tragedies aboard coolie ships like the one that occurred on the *Norway* happened regularly, in one out of every eleven such voyages. Using a variety of newspapers, books, and British and U.S. government sources, historian Arnold Meagher has compiled a detailed list of all of the mutinies that occurred on coolie ships. While there was one mutiny on a U.S. ship bound for San Francisco, another on a British ship en route to Sydney, Australia, and a third on a French ship heading toward Pondicherry, India, the sixty-five remaining revolts took place on French, British, and U.S. ships heading toward Cuba, Peru, and British Guiana.[9] These mutinies often turned bloody, resulting in Chinese emigrants' killing the captain and crew and taking possession of the ship or setting fire to the vessel. Many more Chinese than Europeans and Euro-Americans died as a result of these rebellions, but the mutinies fomented fear in ship captains. In all, more than 4,000 Chinese emigrants, 12 captains, and at least 200 sailors were killed during mutinies on the high seas.[10] In 1858, the notorious U.S. slave captain Francis Bowen, known as the Prince of Slavers, covered the hold after coolies set fire to the *Bald Eagle*, suffocating a number them to death. Bowen was held responsible for the coolie deaths, imprisoned in Peru, and sentenced to be hanged, but he managed to escape before the sentence could be carried out.[11] Bowen stopped transporting coolies and returned to the comparatively safe illegal African slave trade. Other slave traders like the Zuluetas quickly became the leading importers of Chinese coolies into Cuba to fuel the family's vast sugar plantation, railway, and shipping empire.[12] After the end of the legal slave trade, shipping Chinese contract laborers became a lucrative business. In spite of the ample and detailed documentation of dozens of mutinies and the horrors of the coolie ships, few historians have studied in detail the degree of resistance by Chinese emigrants onboard because it falls outside of the histories of China or the countries where the emigrants landed. There is a growing literature on the "many middle passages" of forced labor around the world, but for the most part the story of the thousands of Chinese who struggled and died on the open seas has simply dissolved into the vast oceans between national histories.[13]

Mortality on the passage from China to the Americas during the coolie trade rivals that of the infamous Middle Passage of African slaves. Occasionally it surpassed 70 percent. In addition to the thousands of Chinese killed in mutinies, many more died from disease. Although the statistics for mortality on the Middle Passage are just estimates, roughly 12 percent of Africans died in transit as part of the Atlantic slave trade; the death rate increases significantly if one includes those who perished en route to the coast in Africa and in barracoons on the coast.[14] About the same percentage of the Chinese who set out from China for Latin America during the period of the coolie trade (1847–74) died at sea (12%). However, if one compares roughly the same time period in the nineteenth century, the death rate for Chinese to Cuba and Peru (12%) was almost twice as high as for enslaved Africans to the Americas (7%). Chinese mortality was so high in part because their journey to the Americas was longer (almost three times as long as that of Africans). But whatever the cause, the death rate for Chinese indentured labor to these two destinations was astronomical.[15] In comparison, the mortality rate for European emigrants to New York or South Africa was only 1–1.5 percent.[16]

Death rates on coolie ships fluctuated over time and depending on destination, but conditions on ships heading to Cuba and Peru were by far the most dangerous, especially in the case of the latter country. In the early 1860s, the annual death rate for Chinese coolies fluctuated between 22 and 42 percent for Peru as compared to 20 percent for Cuba. In contrast, ships carrying Chinese to the British West Indies during the same period (1852–73) had comparatively low average mortality (5.6%).[17] Given the high death rates and the frequency of mutinies, ship owners took out insurance policies in New York, London, Amsterdam, and Paris that covered "all risk."[18] In 1854, the Manhattan Life Insurance company paid out $408 to cover a quarter of the "loss" of fourteen coolies, three of whom committed suicide and another eleven of whom died from disease, who were being transported on the *Sea Witch* from Swatow, China, to Panama; each coolie was valued at $120.[19] Insurance agents' cold calculations about potential losses caused by disease, mutiny, and shipwreck turned death and disease into a profitable business. However, average statistics mask the human tragedy that occurred on individual ships where hundreds of coolies died of disease, drowned, or burned to death. The Chinese coolie vessels, like the African slave ships, consumed bodies like a great death machine.

The principle cause of death on the coolie ships was disease resulting from a lack of sanitary water and food. On one voyage to Havana, a captain abandoned a group of sick coolies on a deserted beach because he decided that giving them medical attention would be too expensive. Most of them starved to death; others were devoured by wild dogs and pigs. On two journeys, death rates on coolie vessels to Havana reached nearly 70 percent.[20] It was in the economic interest of the contracting agents to assure a modicum of hygiene onboard because high mortality rates would cut into their profits. Skippers and doctors reportedly had their bonuses cut by up to 50 percent if mortality exceeded 5 percent on a voyage.[21] Elaborate regulations were issued in Macao for maintaining hygienic conditions on ships, including recipes for sulfuric acid disinfectants to wash the coolies' quarters and instructions for disposal of soiled bedding and dead bodies. "Great care shall be taken," Regulation 16 stated, "that the corpses of the dead be not thrown into the sea in too hasty manner; at the same time, it should not be done too slowly, so as not to prolong the painful sight to the other passengers."[22]

In response to the high death rates, the Spanish Crown issued a new set of regulations in 1854 that covered all aspects of the trade, from the moment of contracting in China to coolies' treatment on plantations in Cuba. Article 10 focused on making hygiene and medical care aboard the ships more rigorous. Ships were required to have minimum space allowances, sufficient bathrooms, and ventilation, and to provide a doctor and medical dispensary. Once they arrived in Havana, the ship had to submit to the local sanitary rules and deliver a list of Chinese who had died during the journey along with the causes of death.[23] If the authorities feared contagious illnesses, they could demand quarantine of the ship and its passengers. These regulations led to improved conditions and reduced mortality. On ships carrying coolies from China to Havana from 1853 to 1859, there was a 16 percent mortality rate; after 1860, the mortality rate dropped to around 10 percent.[24] It remains unclear, however, whether shippers simply changed their manifests to lower mortality rates and thereby avoid penalties or whether the rates actually declined. Nonetheless, even the improved shipboard conditions for Chinese coolies transported to Cuba were worse than those of African slaves and Chinese shipped to the British West Indies during the same period.

"La Trata Amarilla"

In the mid-nineteenth century (1847–74), at least 1.5 million Chinese left from the southeastern coast of China for destinations in Southeast Asia, Australia, and the Americas.[25] Over half a million Chinese had come to the Americas by 1882, half of these to Latin America as coolies and the other half to Anglo North America, mainly the United States, as putatively free laborers. The end of the coolie trade in 1874 and U.S. exclusion of Chinese labor in 1882 reduced but by no means ended Chinese arrivals. Almost 400,000 Chinese arrived in the United States and Canada during the exclusion period (1882–1940s). Taking these periods together, there were at least 670,000 individual Chinese entries to Anglo North America from the 1840s through the 1940s, and almost 340,000 Chinese entries to Latin America (see figure 1).[26] After the coolie era, most Chinese migrated to Anglo North America rather than to Latin America. This does not necessarily mean that Chinese were freer in the United States and Canada, where they entered under the credit-ticket system, but the wages and opportunities there were greater than in Latin America. Once in the Americas, most Chinese headed north from Mexico and Cuba to the United States, but traffic also flowed in the opposite direction, including a significant migration of California Chinese to Cuba in the 1870s. And when job opportunities in the sugar industry opened in Cuba from 1917 to 1921, thousands of Chinese headed there instead of the United States.

Internal strife in China, long-term demographic pressures and British forced opening of Chinese ports to trade prompted the massive emigration of the mid-nineteenth century. Wars in China, especially the Christian-inspired Taiping Rebellion (1851–64) that resulted in as many as 20 to 30 million deaths, created starvation conditions.[27] China's population doubled in the eighteenth century to 300 million; by the 1850s, the start of the period of mass external emigration, it had grown to 380 million. The population explosion resulted in extreme land pressures, especially in the southern and

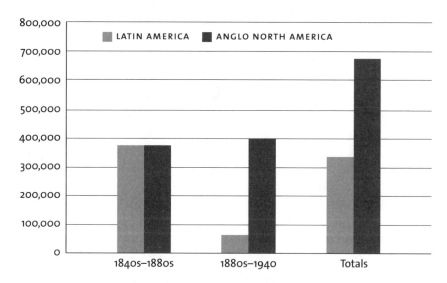

FIGURE 1. Chinese Arrivals in the Americas, 1840–1940. Figures for indentured Chinese to Latin America from Meagher, *Coolie Trade*, table 3, p. 99. Figures for Chinese to United States before 1882 from Yung, *Unbound Feet*, p. 22. Chinese in Cuba and Mexico estimates from Chang, "Chinese in Latin America," table 4-5, pp. 25–29. Mexico estimate, 1902–21, from Hung-Hui, *Chinos en América*, p. 112. Estimate for Chinese in British Columbia in 1867 from Anderson, *Vancouver's Chinatown*, p. 35.

southeastern coastal regions. Poor farmer families and merchants responded to the crisis by sending male family members to other parts of China to work for short periods. When the Spanish, Portuguese, and British coolie traders showed up in the late 1840s on China's coast to recruit laborers, this extended the pattern of internal migration. But now the migrations were controlled by foreigners.[28]

Given that almost all Chinese migrants to the Americas spoke Cantonese and came from the Pearl River delta region of Guangdong Province, it is more accurate to call it a Pearl River Delta Cantonese migration rather than a Chinese one. In addition, approximately 10,000 Hokkiens from Fujian province had left for Latin America by 1858.[29] The vast majority of the Cantonese left as so-called free emigrants to places like California. Chinese coolies were principally directed toward Cuba and Peru, and almost all of them left from the Portuguese outpost in Macao. Although there is some disagreement about the numbers, and some Chinese were undoubtedly smuggled illegally, making it hard to obtain an accurate count, approximately 150,000 Chinese arrived in Cuba, and 100,000 in Peru in the quarter century between 1847 and 1874, the year the coolie trade was finally ended. An additional 14,000 Chinese coolies were brought to British Guiana (1850–74).[30] The three-quarters of a million Chinese who signed indentured contracts with European employers during the coolie era represents a small fraction of the much bigger migration of 19 million Chinese who traveled to other parts of Asia and the South Pacific between 1840 and 1940.[31] Chinese migrants to Southeast Asia traveled under a range of labor agreements, some paying their own passage and others borrowing money from relatives to pay for transportation, but many served under onerous contracts, were kept in bondage beyond the term of their contracts, and were physically punished.[32]

Chinese Opposition to the Coolie Trade from Above and Below

Beginning in the early seventeenth century, the Manchus of the Qing dynasty (1644–1912) tried to regulate maritime trade and emigration as a means of political control. One early statute prohibited clandestine emigration for trade or work and punished offenders with beheading.[33] A 1728 imperial edit against unauthorized migration complained about ignorant commoners' being deceived by recruiters and emphasized the need for paternal protection. "Rustic people have limited understanding. They can realize the truth only when instructed by their superiors. Local officials should keep them under control at all times and should take special pains to instruct them in difficult times. . . . Protecting them as if they were children, officials should teach them to feel attached to their home villages and realize the disadvantages of migrating."[34] In spite of these prohibitions and efforts to arrest and kill Chinese recruiters, hundreds of thousands of Chinese emigrated in the mid-nineteenth century. The fact that Chinese officials referred to the coolies as "pigs," even in diplomatic letters ostensibly defending their rights, suggests the extent to which the emigrants were devalued and dehumanized.[35]

The ineffectiveness of Chinese prohibitions can be attributed in part to European control over coastal ports and to Chinese officials' complicity with the trade. Harry Parkes, a British interpreter in Canton, put it this way: "Emigration to any region, in all vessels, whether native or foreign . . . has their [Chinese officials'] complete connivance though not their expressed sanction."[36] Faced with a virtually absent Chinese imperial presence in Canton, local Chinese officials collaborated with a British commission in developing a series of regulations for the coolie trade. The Imperial Court maintained its prohibition on all emigration, but local Chinese officials who felt they could not afford to antagonize the British decided it was best to work with them rather than allow the trade to continue unregulated. In 1859, local Chinese officials established the Canton system, legalizing voluntary emigration, establishing British government coolie depots, and setting up a joint Chinese and British team to investigate abuses. The enforcement of the Canton policy that was legitimated in the British Treaty of Tientsin (1859) and the French Treaty Convention (1860) fell to the Chinese government in Guangdong.

After issuing the Canton system edict, the governor general in Guangdong sent a cruiser to Whampoa to prevent kidnapped Chinese from being boarded on ships. The governor immediately arrested twenty-nine crimps (kidnappers of laborers), beheaded eighteen of them, severely punished another eleven, and released seventy-seven coolies. According to the British plenipotentiary in China, depositions of the released coolies "reveal[ed] a system of fraud and violence which ought to startle the Europeans whose gold, acting on Chinese cupidity, has been the primary cause of these criminal acts."[37] The U.S. consul flew into action, boarding U.S. ships in Whampoa and releasing scores of Chinese who claimed they had been kidnapped. An investigation by the American Legation in China concluded that examinations supposed to guarantee the free will of coolies were a farce. "Men are forced to answer in the affirmative, when asked if they are willing to emigrate; an answer in the negative exposes them to being severely beaten."[38] In spite of the Chinese governor's and the U.S. and British consuls' efforts to prevent the unregulated coolie trade, Europeans and North Americans continued to anchor their ships offshore and arranged for recruiters to bring coolies to them.[39]

The efforts of the governor general in Guangdong might have had some chance of success if the imperial government had helped enforce it, but the Imperial Court viewed the collaboration of local Chinese officials with the British as a contravention of the long-standing prohibition on emigration. Therefore, when the Allied forces withdrew their troops in 1861, the Tsungli Yamen, the imperial foreign office responsible for overseeing the coolie trade, declared that nontreaty powers would be unable to go into the interior, thereby prohibiting them from setting up emigration agencies. This prohibition inadvertently led to the rise of the illegal and unregulated coolie trade that had already begun in Macao, a de facto Portuguese territory that became a center of the global coolie trade, gambling, and prostitution.[40]

The Qing sought to regulate and limit emigration through treaties, but their weak position and the European powers' control of the coastline limited their success.[41] In 1860, a "mob" murdered several known kidnappers on the streets of Canton, leading local merchants to call for foreign governments to restrain their citizens from engaging in the trade. Given the complicity of European consuls, it was impossible for the Chinese to stop the trade. The Dutch consul, for example, was an agent of the main coolie trader to Havana.[42] In 1866, Prince Kung developed the Peking Regulations to regulate the trade and protect coolies. However, the British and French refused to ratify the regulations because the British West India Committee objected to a provision forcing employers to pay coolies' return passage. Ultimately, the British rejected the Peking Regulations, and as a result the British were denied permission to establish coolie houses in Guangdong until 1873. The Chinese attempted to stamp out the coolie trade by themselves, issuing orders to decapitate kidnappers and strangle accomplices. None of these policies were very effective, and the coolie trade not only continued but grew, with Macao becoming the principal port of embarkation. The number of barracoons in Macao mushroomed from 5 to 200 between 1856 and 1872, and the rate of emigration from that port reached 20,000 per year.[43] Historian Robert Irick claims that Chinese officials did more to stop the coolie trade than others have acknowledged, issuing prohibitions, forcibly releasing coolies from depots, and even beheading kidnappers.[44] Nonetheless, despite such efforts, the coolie trade continued unabated for a quarter of a century.

The inability of Chinese imperial and local authorities to stop the abuses of the coolie trade inspired the ire and wrath of Chinese inhabitants of port cities, who occasionally erupted in riots that targeted foreign merchants. News of the slave-like conditions for Chinese in Cuba and of frequent mutinies on coolie ships filtered back to China and incensed the populace against the coolie traders and especially the recruiters. In December 1851, a rebellion broke out on the *Robert Browne*, a vessel carrying 410 Chinese under contract from Amoy to San Francisco. After the captain ordered the queues of the Chinese onboard to be cut off and their bodies scrubbed with hard brooms as a hygiene measure, the coolies rose up, killing the captain and several other crew members.[45] The British governor of Hong Kong, John Bowring, worried that the violence and international publicity would interrupt the well-managed coolie trade.

> Such horrors, miseries and atrocities of all sorts, such frightful mortality, such acts of piracy and murder have been associated with the transfer of coolies from foreign regions, that common humanity forbids the looking with indifference on what is taking place; and I see with deep regret, instead of a quiet, steady, and progressing system of well-digested emi-

gration, giving time for the fit selection and becoming organization of proper bodies of Chinamen, we have a sudden fleet of ships whose united presence is, I apprehend, likely to be eminently prejudicial to such arrangements as would be most beneficial to the honest interests of those concerned.[46]

Governor Bowring thus contrasted a system of "well-digested emigration" that would yield "proper bodies of Chinamen" to an unregulated free-for-all that would provoke anger and violence and ultimately threaten the whole trade. Bowring's job was to manage and regulate the trade to insure its long-term viability, but by August 1852 coolie passage to South America had become so dangerous that it was hard to find ships willing to undertake the journey.[47] It was in this context of coolie mutinies that a riot broke out in Amoy demonstrating the weakness of both the Chinese and British governments to regulate the coolie trade and revealing the impunity of foreign merchants.

The riot was precipitated when Francis Darby Syme, a British merchant and coolie trader in Amoy, marched into the local police station to release a Chinese broker who had been accused of kidnapping coolies.[48] In the days following Syme's intervention, placards began to appear all over Amoy that condemned the coolie trade, and in particular blamed the British merchant houses of Tait and Co. and Syme, Muir and Co. These British merchants were the same ones hired by the Zulueta family to recruit the first group of Chinese coolies sent to Cuba in 1847.[49] The Spanish consul was supposed to guarantee that the emigrants leaving for Cuba did so voluntarily, but the fact that James Tait was the Spanish consul at Amoy and also the largest coolie trader represented a colossal conflict of interest.[50] A group of Chinese scholars and merchants issued a proclamation condemning the "barbarians" for buying and selling people and taking advantage of the lonely and destitute:

From the time the barbarians began to trade at Amoy, they have had the practice of buying people to sell again; subjecting those guiltless of crime to cruel treatment, and employing evil-disposed and traitorous natives to entice away peaceable people. . . . By the prospect of minute advantage they drew away lonely and destitute persons, while they held out alluring baits to seduce the younger members of settled families. Their tricks were innumerable, and they would dexterously conceal their real designs.

The men being inveigled to the barbarian houses and ships are publicly sold. When amongst them they cannot understand their gibberish, and they are kept in close confinement. They may implore Heaven, and their tears may wet the earth, but their complaints are uttered in vain. When carried to the barbarian regions, day and night they are impelled to labor, without intervals even for sleep. To advance or retreat is equally impossible to them; death is their sole relief.

The authors of this declaration thus criticized not only the process of recruitment but also the act of selling people and the terrible conditions of labor in the places where they ended up. They warned their compatriots, "Let fathers caution their sons, and elder brothers their younger brothers, for seeing the evil, and guarding against it. Let none misguidedly lend themselves to promote the schemes of wicked traitors."[51] The willingness of elite scholars to speak up on behalf of migrant laborers and label recruiters as "wicked traitors" suggests an incipient national identity.

Another proclamation declared, "We, the people of the eighteen wards (the town of Amoy)," constructing the document's authors as townspeople but interestingly not as Chinese more broadly. This proclamation not only warned people to stay away from the coolie traders but also insisted that everyone boycott the merchants involved in it and threatened to kill those who continued to trade with British merchants Syme and Tait and other coolie brokers.

The barbarians are ungovernable in the extreme, and their only motive of action is desire for gain. We the people of the eighteen wards (the town of Amoy) have now agreed that we will have no dispute with the barbarians, but will concert measures for the regulation of our conduct amongst ourselves. From this time, if any persons transact business with the Te-ki and Ho-ki hongs (Tait and Co., and Syme Muir, and Co.), they shall be put to death, their property seized and their houses destroyed without mercy. None shall be permitted to establish firms for foreign trade. Any brokers who are caught shall not be carried before the authorities, but shall be at once killed.

The stridency of the message and the warning that brokers would be killed by vigilantes rather than brought before the authorities suggested that the Chinese were also frustrated by the ineffectiveness and complicity of local government officials with the coolie trade. They were taking matters into their own hands, and they promised to "concert measures for the regulation of our conduct amongst ourselves." The proclamation ended by promising to allow

Tait and Syme to conduct business again, but only if they were willing to turn over the coolie broker for punishment.[52] For the next three days business in the town came to a standstill as everyone obeyed the vigilante warning.[53]

The voice of Chinese emigrants is noticeably absent in the British, Spanish, and Portuguese archives. European governments documented in precise detail their correspondence with other governments and with coolie traders, and they issued increasingly complex regulations to manage the trade and prevent abuses. They also kept precise logs of the ships engaged in the coolie trade, the numbers of coolies, their sexes, ages, and occupations. Rare, however, in the thousands of pages dedicated to the coolie trade is a comment by a Chinese emigrant. The anonymous petitions, though not authored by coolies themselves, provide a brief glimpse into the views of the coolie trade by Chinese residents in the port cities where the trade thrived.

When British troops arrived to confront a group of Chinese who had gathered in front of Syme's hong (warehouse) in protest, the Chinese pelted them with stones and brickbats. Eventually the marines started firing their weapons, thus forcing the crowd to disperse. By the time the melee was done, seven or eight Chinese had been killed and another ten or twelve wounded. An additional four other bystanders were killed by stray bullets, including one baby who had been suckling at her mother's breast.[54]

The British inquiry into the matter exonerated the British troops for their actions. As the report concluded, "the fury of the mob was then at its height, the foreign hongs were in absolute danger of pillage and destruction, and it became necessary to act in self-defence by firing on the assailants."[55] Nonetheless, Syme and his clerk were convicted by the Consular Court of violating the treaty between England and China by harboring his coolie broker from the Chinese authorities; Syme was fined $200 and his clerk $20.[56] Four separate Chinese petitioners testified that their relatives had gone to Syme's hong to try to rescue relatives or friends who had been kidnapped, not to plunder it as had been claimed by the British merchants. The Chinese demanded that responsible parties be brought to justice for the death of their relatives and that they be compensated for their losses.[57] The Chinese received nothing.

Beyond fining Syme for violating the treaty, a British consular court found no direct evidence that he was aware of the illegal activities of his coolie brokers, and it decided that he could only be tried for false imprisonment, rather than for violating the Slave Act. The determination that the coolie trade was a violation of the Slave Act could have authorized the British to seize coolie ships on the open seas as they had during the slave trade. Nonetheless, even the lesser charge was not pursued because none of the Chinese witnesses could be produced in court. The vice consul thus resolved the matter by reading a stern warning to Syme in court: "I must also warn you that you are responsible for the acts of those employed by you as coolie brokers, so far as respects those coolies accepted by you as emigrants."[58] This warning that Syme would be held responsible for acts of his coolie brokers was clearly an empty threat, since he had not been held responsible in this very public case. Nonetheless, the Amoy riot struck fear in the hearts of the British merchants, leading James Tait to move his operations from Amoy to Swatow.[59]

The actions of the townspeople frightened not only the British consular officials and merchants but also local Chinese authorities, who witnessed their own inability to keep order. The Chinese subprefect of Amoy attempted to gain control and bring calm to the town by declaring that he would arrest any brokers who "delude poor people to make a traffic of them." He also called on everyone for calm and warned of severe punishment "should any vagabond raise a commotion of any kind." His third edict prohibited the posting of anonymous placards, which were blamed in part for having caused the riots.[60] The subprefect's edicts thus took aim at the coolie brokers and the "vagabonds" for having incited people to riot against Syme. Noticeably absent was any prohibition on British merchants' engaging in the coolie trade. Nonetheless, the vigilante actions of the Chinese and resistance by the coolies themselves seemed to have put a stop to the trade in Amoy. By February 1853, three months after the disturbances, the governor of Hong Kong, John Bowring, reported that the coolie trade had ended in Amoy: "The interference of the mandarins; the state of public opinion; the difficulty of finding emigrants; all growing out of the abuses to which I have so often referred, have for the present become an end to the export of coolies." Even Mr. Jackson, one of the coolie traders for Syme, decided to get out of the business after the Chinese on one of his shipments of coolies to Australia mutinied against the captain and crew and killed the mate.[61]

Six years later in 1859, a similar riot to the one in Amoy erupted in Shanghai when Chinese locals objected to coolie traders' kidnapping and deceiving victims. The French ship *Gertrude* had been anchored in the Huangpu River for three months, collecting coolies by sending out squads of four or five sailors, who would grab Chinese off the street and cut off their "'celestial tails' to disfigure them." On the afternoon of 29 July, a squad of French sailors was in the midst of capturing a Chinese man when they were attacked by "hundreds of infuriated coolies." One of the sailors was killed on the spot when his head was smashed open with a large stone. Two English men in the vicinity were stabbed and stoned, and another European was killed near the race-track. Sixty English marines and forty French marines took up positions on the Bund, leading Europeans to send their families to ships during the night for safety. During the disturbance, there were reports of Chinese servants' being shoved into bags and dragged to the *Gertrude* and having their teeth knocked out. One account accused a group of sailors of running a bayonet through the cheek of a young Chinese boy "merely for amusement."[62] The disturbances brought trade to a standstill and threatened negotiations with European powers until the Imperial Court finally issued an edict: "In order that neither reason nor law be stretched, let orders be immediately issued to search out the culprits who kidnapped the barbarians and execute them on the spot."[63] In the end, direct action by Chinese townspeople in Amoy and later Shanghai and Canton forced the end of the coolie trade from these ports. However, the coolie trade did not end. It merely shifted to other ports, principally Hong Kong and Macao. Chinese resistance continued as well.

Crimps, Kidnappers, and the Coolie as Victim

Although the Chinese emigrants were certainly manipulated and deceived by Chinese recruiters, European traders, and Cuban and Peruvian bosses, the image of Chinese coolies as pure victims does not account for their in-volvement in the trade or their resistance to it. Few Chinese emigrants fit the extreme ends of the spectrum from completely free and voluntary migrants to totally defenseless kidnapped victims. Most found themselves somewhere in the middle, coerced into signing contracts because of debts and hopes of providing for their families. Historians who have unconsciously accepted the abolitionists' claims have tended to focus on broker violence and coolie vic-timhood. Arnold Meagher concludes that in the recruitment process "per-suasion gave way to deceit, fraud and violence."[64] Historian Philip Kuhn writes that, "dragged onto ships by kidnapping or lured by fraud, these vic-tims of unequal treaties were forced to sign indenture contracts under physi-cal threat."[65] The testimony of coolies in Cuba and that of Chinese who were rescued from barracoons in China corroborate the stories of kidnappings. A firsthand account by Sai Qui Wing, a customs agent in Canton, also sug-gests that not all the "coolies" were poor and illiterate. Sai explained that after being kidnapped he was flogged with others for not agreeing to ship out. He also noted that among the captives were "men of family and men of literary pretensions" who had houses and land, and "no need to labor."

"These were most reluctant to go and were most flogged." Some of the men, Sai recounted, were nearly whipped to death, while others committed suicide with opium.[66]

Although kidnappings of propertied family men occurred as Sai's story attests, and coercion and deception were rife in the recruitment process, most emigrants were also motivated by the eight-dollar advance and the prospect of earning three to four dollars a month. Therefore, Chinese emigrants were not just unwitting victims of sinister European officials and devious recruiters, called *chu chai tau* (swineherds) in Cantonese, *corredores* in Spanish, and "pig-brokers," "runners," and "crimps" in English. Rather, Chinese themselves participated in subterfuge, deception, and lies to try to extract money from recruiters without intending to work as coolies. Some Chinese pirates pretended to be coolies to get aboard the ships, where they would launch rebellions, kill the crew, and pillage whatever they could from the vessel.[67] Historians have all too often overlooked Chinese emigrants' complicity with the coolie trade in an effort to portray them as innocent victims. However, it is precisely their survival strategies—including deception, mutinies, and piracy—that demonstrate their full range of humanity. The general depiction of Asians as forced rather than voluntary migrants also contributes to the orientalist stereotypes of Asians as slavish in contrast to voluntary and plucky European immigrants.[68] The great nineteenth-century migration of Europeans to the Americas is more akin to Asian migration than the Asian migration is like the African slave trade. To the extent that the Chinese were victims, it was of a global economic system that left them few options but to migrate.

The Cuba Commission reproduced these same paternalistic views, providing testimony of thousands of coolies who said they were tricked and deceived by crimps.[69] For example, Hsein Tso-Pang and fourteen other coolies stated that "'the foreigners of Macao sent out vicious Chinese in order to kidnap and decoy men and to place these in barracoons and on board of ships from which they cannot escape, chastise them there without restraint, and conveying them against their will to Havana, after removing their queues and changing their clothing, offer them for sale in the men-market.'" Others claimed they were induced by "'offers of employment abroad at high wages'" and only later discovered they were "'sold as slaves.'"[70] The commission's report focused on abuses by traffickers, recruiters, and plantation owners in Cuba, but it completely avoided the issue of the conditions in China that may have pushed Chinese to want to emigrate. The commission insisted, "industrious men who work willingly and well, can support themselves at

Edgar Holden, "Baraccoons at Macao," *Harper's New Monthly Magazine*, June 1864. Courtesy of Reed College Library.

home, and do not emigrate voluntarily."[71] Thus, according to the commission's logic, either the coolies lacked a work ethic and chose to leave China or they were the victims of kidnapping. While the testimony of the Chinese certainly suggests that recruiters misrepresented their intentions, there is also evidence that the emigrants themselves were complicit in evading the regulations of the trade. We should remember that the Chinese government went to Cuba to look for abuses in the coolie trade and to provide ammunition to stop the Portuguese and Spanish trade. The *Cuba Commission Report*, more than anything else, paints the Chinese government as a benign protector of the coolies.

The image of recruiters plying the countryside of China, seizing young Chinese men, and trapping them in barracoons in Macao does not do justice to the complex reasons why some Chinese chose to emigrate. The report divided coolies into those who were kidnapped, decoyed, entrapped, snared, or emigrated voluntarily. The entrapment category was used for those who signed contracts believing they were doing so in the place of others who were temporarily absent. The ensnarement category was for those Chinese whose gambling debts forced them to sign up as coolies. Decoying involved some kind of fraud and deception to lead Chinese onto coolie ships. The report concluded that eight or nine out of every ten Chinese emigrants to Cuba were taken against their will. However, the vast majority of these were either decoyed (72%), entrapped (5%), or ensnared (10%). Only 7 percent indicated that they were kidnapped, the same percentage who said they emigrated voluntarily.[72] Philip Kuhn notes that although some Chinese emigrants paid for their own passage and some were coerced into signing contracts, most fell somewhere in between, having indebted themselves to merchants, brokers, shipping companies, or relatives to pay for their passage.[73] Kidnapping and voluntary emigration were the extreme ends of the spectrum from total coercion to free choice, but most Chinese fell somewhere in the middle.

The testimony of five of the surviving emigrants of a mutiny on the coolie ship *Don Juan* in 1871 provides a rare glimpse into the recruiting process and the conditions aboard the ships from the perspective of the Chinese themselves. However, we should not be naive and believe that their testimony provides access to their innermost thoughts. The Hong Kong consular court proceedings were set up to indict the abuses in the coolie trade, and the Chinese were called as witnesses for that specific purpose. The picture that emerged from their testimony is one of desperately poor Chinese looking for any opportunity they could find to escape the starvation conditions in China. The emigrants also presented themselves as naive and argued that they were tricked and coerced by acquaintances or family members into becoming coolies. Of course, the British needed the Chinese to be unwitting victims to bolster their arguments that the Portuguese and Spanish were to blame for the abuses in the coolie trade and to justify their own putative protection of the Chinese emigrants. The British were not against the use of Chinese coolies on British colonial plantations, only against others' use of Chinese labor.

On 4 May 1871, the *Don Juan* sailed from Macao with 655 Chinese coolies, seven Chinese servants, a crew of forty-seven Europeans, a Chinese doctor, and a Chinese translator.[74] After three days a mutiny broke out, leading to a fire on the ship. By the time it was over, 500 coolies had died, suffocated from the smoke, burned alive below decks, or drowned when the ship sank.[75] One of the coolies who managed to escape had the left side of his face burned into a "mass of roasted flesh." As he swam away from the burning ship, he saw "blood ooze out from the sides of the vessel, from the hold where the coolies were lodged."[76] These kinds of well-publicized mutinies helped end the coolie trade, but they also served another function: justifying the paternalistic protection of Chinese emigrants by British authorities.

Of the five *Don Juan* coolies who gave testimony in the Hong Kong court, all fell into the entrapped or ensnared categories, and none claimed to have been kidnapped. In all of their cases, a friend or family member brought them to Macao with the promise of employment or making money. Wong Ahfaht, a twenty-three-year-old barber and a native of Kwai-shin, had worked for about a year in Hong Kong before a shoemaker encouraged him to go to Macao, where he could make three dollars a month. The shoemaker brought him to Macao and deposited him in a barracoon. When Wong protested, he was told that if he left he would be imprisoned. He was also instructed to tell the authorities that he was there voluntarily, and the acquaintance promised to rescue him with a *sampan* (flat-bottomed boat) once he was aboard the coolie vessel. When the Portuguese authorities questioned Wong, he agreed to the stipulations of the contract, accepted the advance of eight dollars, and declared that he had not been kidnapped. In his testimony, Wong claimed that he gave these answers because of the threats he had received. Although it appears that most of the proper procedures were followed in his case, Wong said that his contract was not read to him, which was a violation of the regulations.[77] The three other Chinese coolies who were rescued from the *Don Juan* and testified in court admitted to lying to officials about their willingness to join the voyage, but all of them claimed that the contract was never read aloud to them. One claimed to have not even signed the contract, and another said he was given a piece of paper but he could not read it.[78] The *Cuba Commission Report* contains evidence that Chinese were hired without contracts, that they were forced to sign documents they could not read or that had others' names on them.[79] Those who claimed another person's name was on the contract were most likely participating in fraud by trying to collect the advance for others too ill to pass inspection. In other words, they were conned while engaging in a con.

Four of the five coolies who were rescued and gave testimony in court in Hong Kong admitted to participating in a subterfuge and lying when asked by Portuguese authorities if they were going willingly. Nonetheless, even though the coolies were asked by Portuguese officers whether they had been kidnapped and deceived, they did not understand the terms of the contracts, and the ones who attempted to leave the barracoon were forcibly held there. There was a gray area between complete coercion and full complicity. This explains why after the initial shock had worn off, the coolies on the *Don Juan* began to play games to pass the time, seemingly accepting their fate. The coolies who were desperately poor had an incentive to play along with the ruse: anywhere from eight to thirty dollars for joining up. After they realized they had been deceived and were being held and sold like slaves, some committed suicide, others staged violent revolts, but the vast majority sought to survive their bondage by working hard and waiting for the day when their contracts would end. Years later, after toiling away like slaves on Cuban sugar plantations, the vast majority of coolies described themselves to Chinese officials as having been kidnapped. Whether they initially signed up willingly or under coercion, once in Cuba and Peru they found themselves trapped in a system that looked and felt more like slavery than free labor.[80]

Coolies versus Free Immigrants

Although there were differences between the contract labor system in Cuba, Peru, and the British West Indies, and the credit-ticket mechanism employed in the United States, Canada, and Mexico, these were distinctions of degree and not kind. Furthermore, in the mid-nineteenth century, Chinese were also imported to California under multiyear contracts. In 1851, for example, the *Robert Browne* carried several hundred Chinese to San Francisco bound by five-year contracts. And in the early 1870s, hundreds of Chinese contract laborers were imported to Louisiana from Cuba as well as directly from China.[81] In spite of the 1862 Anti-Coolie Bill and the 1885 Alien Contract Labor law (known as the Foran Act) banning immigration of aliens under labor contracts, such practices continued well into the twentieth century. In contrast to the coolie trade in Cuba and Peru, which was overseen and regulated by the governments, the credit-ticket system and its internal means of discipline were largely invisible to state authorities.[82] The U.S. government could therefore wash its hands of the coercion exercised by the Chinese Six Companies (aka the Chinese Consolidated Benevolent Association, discussed further in chapter 7) and maintain the illusion that Chinese migrants were all voluntary free laborers.

The distinction between a coolie and a free laborer was ideological. *Coolie* was not a legal term but rather a vague notion of cheap and easily exploitable labor that was almost inextricably linked to Asians, and particularly to Chinese and Indians. In the popular imagination, all Chinese in California were seen as "coolies," whether or not they were contract laborers. In 1882, when the steamer *Belgic* landed in San Francisco from Hong Kong, the *New York Times* referred to the passengers as "590 coolies."[83] The United States, Canada, and Mexico, in particular, have used this distinction to mark themselves as more liberal and modern than the backward countries that permitted the coolie trade. As the logic went, the fact that "they" enslaved the Chinese made "us" look that much more liberal. Although there are elements that separate the state-sponsored coolie trade from the credit-ticket system used in the United States, where transportation was paid by a mutual aid society and then paid off over time, there are also many similarities. Coolies were not just coerced and credit-ticket workers were not entirely free.[84] Understanding the complexities of the different labor arrangements for Chinese migrants to the Americas as a whole allows us to see the similarities and differences, and highlight the continuities over time and space.

The diplomatic debate over the coolie trade centered on whether the Chinese were slaves or free laborers. In spite of the ambiguities, the branding of Chinese coolies in Peru made the system look a lot like slavery. On 10 June 1868, the Peruvian newspaper *El Comercio* reported that an agriculturalist had branded a large C shape on the faces of forty-eight Chinese laborers with a hot iron so that they he would be able to identify them if they escaped.[85] *El Comercio* denounced the act as a "crime," and the British ambassador in Lima, William Stafford Jerningham, protested the deed as "contrary to Christian civilization, and to the ideas of a Republican country." The Portuguese consul general in Peru, Narciso Velarde, complained to the Peruvian government about the branding and the "immense number of Chinese mutilated in the service of their masters and abandoned by them when they are unable to work." The incident caused such a scandal that the governor general of Macao temporarily suspended all shipments of Chinese to Peru. Peru's minister of foreign relations investigated, finding the allegations to have been "inexact," but the damage to Peru's reputation had been done.[86]

The press focused on the hot-iron branding in Peru, but coolies were also treated like slaves and marked, albeit with paint, from the moment they landed in barracoons in coastal China. John Bowring, the British governor in Hong Kong, described the pitiful scene in Amoy, where hundreds of coolies "gathered together in barracoons, stripped naked, and stamped or painted with the letter C (California), P (Peru), or S (Sandwich Islands), on their breast, according to the destination for which they were intended."[87] In the barracoons, such letters were the only distinction between the Chinese going to Peru and those headed to California. Whatever the legal distinctions between the free Chinese laborers and African slaves, the way Chinese emigrants were handled from the barracoons in China to the auction blocks in the Americas echoed slavery.

The British and U.S. governments focused their strongest condemnation on the coolie trade being operated in the Portuguese controlled port at Macao. In response, José Tavares Mondo, acting director general of the Portuguese Department of Marine and Colonies, argued that Chinese leaving Hong Kong for California were in a more vulnerable position than those leaving from Macao. The Macao emigrants, he insisted, got an advance that they left with their families, and they determined the terms of their contract before leaving. Meanwhile, the emigrants to California received no advance and had to negotiate their contracts once they arrived, at which point "it [was] not so easy for them to reject the conditions imposed upon them, being at a great distance from their homes." Furthermore, he insisted, "these passengers, whom they call free, are put into separate places, and are watched by armed men." Tavares also condemned the practice of agents in Hong Kong who paid for the emigrants' travel and then presented them with the bill once aboard the steamers, forcing them to work off the debt in California. In the previous year, he asserted, two revolts had occurred on a Belgian ship in Hong Kong's British port that was set to sail to Peru with coolies aboard.

Tavares pointed to the hypocrisy of the British and U.S. governments, which condemned the coolie trade yet engaged in similar practices on their own ships. He argued that their regulations protected the Chinese more than did British controls on indentured labor to their colonies and U.S. rules governing free emigration to California. Although Tavares admitted that Chinese in Macao were marched onto ships by armed soldiers, he explained that "all these precautions are taken for the purpose of preventing the coolies from being robbed in the boats which convey them on board, and also of preventing any articles being sold to them at a higher price than is lawful, or their being ill-treated, or emigrants being clandestinely admitted on board the vessels, as has sometimes happened."[88] In other words, he claimed, the armed escort was not there to enslave the Chinese but rather to protect them. Tavares noted that the English and North Americans also had armed guards onboard their ships sailing between Macao, Hong Kong, and Canton. On those daily steamers, he said, Chinese passengers were set apart from others, and armed guards watched over them to prevent pirates who had snuck aboard as passengers from commandeering the ships.[89] If the British and the United States complained about Macao, it was only, he protested, to shut down competition from the Portuguese.[90]

The governor of Hong Kong, Richard Graves MacDonnell, responded to Tavares's accusations by claiming that they contained factual inaccuracies and arguing that the condition of Chinese in California was grossly exaggerated. In particular, MacDonnell argued Chinese passengers were "as free and unrestricted as any European or American passengers in those vessels." The Chinese emigrants were fed "abundant, wholesome and clean food" on the ship, he said, and once in California they made lots of money. In contrast, MacDonnell pointed to the 348 Chinese who had been discharged from the Macao barracoons the previous year for sickness or physical incompetence, and who later died on the streets of Macao, as evidence of the terrible conditions that prevailed in the Portuguese port.[91] T. W. C. Murdoch, from the British Emigration Board, also responded to Tavares's assertions, pointing out that the Chinese on British and U.S. steamers were not imprisoned between decks by iron gratings as occurred on Spanish ships. Murdoch compared the behavior of the crew on a British ship to that on a Spanish one. When the British ship en route to British Guiana was destroyed by fire in 1866, the master and crew made every attempt to save the Chinese, whereas on a Spanish vessel the *Don Juan* the captain and crew left the Chinese imprisoned below deck to be burned alive by the fire.[92] Although there were occasional mutinies by Chinese on ships to California and the British West Indies, the fact that the vast majority of the violent mutinies occurred on ships to Cuba and Peru and that these ships had much higher mortality rates suggests that conditions aboard these ships were much worse. Nonetheless, the notion that Chinese on ships to North America were free while they were enslaved on ships to Cuba and Peru exaggerated the differences between them.

Protecting Chinese emigrants provided justification for all governments to intervene at every level of migration, from medical inspections to contracts to health and safety provisions on the ships. The Spanish, Portuguese, British, and U.S. governments argued that they needed to increase their regulation of the coolie trade to prevent abuses by private recruiters, ship owners, and contractors. They created procedures whereby officials would board a ship to ask Chinese emigrants whether they were leaving freely and voluntarily, and whether anyone had coerced them. Chinese almost always participated in these rituals by lying, assuring the officials that they traveled freely. However, ship captains defended the "fair and equitable manner" of these examinations. The U.S. captain of the *Messenger* said that, when questioned by Chinese officials, only 48 out of 630 emigrants on various ships in the port of Whampoa asked to be relieved of the contracts they had signed. For the captain, the fact that some coolies were able to leave even after signing contracts, and that the vast majority chose to stay, indicated that the system worked well.[93] One could also interpret the hasty change of mind of forty-eight emigrants as a sign that many were being coerced or tricked into signing contracts they did not understand. For the Spanish, Peruvians, and British, the signing of a contract of indenture was part of the ritual that guaranteed the rights of the Chinese. For U.S. officials, it was the absence of any contract, or at least one that they knew about, that signified freedom. In all cases, the defense of Chinese emigrants' rights justified control over their mobility, rarely to their benefit.

Contested Sovereignties

Although states tried to assert control, global trafficking across oceans made it difficult for any one nation to exercise absolute authority. The locales where the trade originated, places like Macao (Portuguese territory), Hong Kong (British territory), and Amoy (British treaty port), were sites of overlapping and limited state sovereignties. European and American countries criticized each other for participating in the coolie trade, but the reality was that it was hard for any country to enforce its rules on the high seas or on the coast of China. The putative nationality of ships gave nation-states some leverage over particular vessels, but the ease with which ships changed flags through short-term purchasing agreements demonstrated the limits to this expression of national power. However, the fact that the trade was beyond the reach of any one nation does not mean that particular nations did not try to control and manage it. The companies that organized and profited most from the coolie trade included Spanish, French, and Portuguese capitalists, and the ships that transported the coolies flew principally French, Spanish, British, U.S., Portuguese, Dutch, and Russian flags. For Chinese transported to Latin America (1847–73), French ships accounted for 30 percent, Spanish 22 percent, and British and U.S. ones 10 percent each.[94] This was an international trade, but it was primarily controlled by European capitalists.

By the 1870s, various governments began to challenge the right of others to conduct the coolie trade, sparking contests over sovereignty. In July 1872, a storm forced the Peruvian *María Luz*, en route from Macao to Peru with 238 Chinese emigrants aboard, to stop in the Japanese harbor at Yokohama. One of the coolies jumped overboard there and was picked up by the nearby British ship *Iron Duke*. The British handed the Chinese laborer over to Japanese authorities, who learned that the Chinese migrant had been flogged and shackled aboard the *María Luz*. The Peruvian captain was detained, charged with mistreating the Chinese, and sentenced to receive 100 lashes; he ended up not being flogged and was let off after six weeks with a severe reprimand. The Japanese sent the Chinese passengers back to China. The Peruvian government was outraged that a vessel flying its flag was seized, its cargo of coolies removed, and the captain jailed. The incident ended up prompting the Peruvians to send a representative to Japan and China to establish treaties that would permit free migration between the countries. Although China's Prince Kung refused to establish any treaty until Peru returned all coolies, China ultimately agreed to a treaty that recognized "the inherent and inalienable right of man to change his home." As part of this agreement, a commission was sent to Peru to study the conditions of Chinese there and to allow repatriation of coolies after the end of their contracts.[95] The case of the *María Luz* indicates the limits of claims to national sovereignty by ships in the territorial waters of another country. Given the large gray zone in the realm of competing sovereignties, the degree and extent of national sovereignty would have to be negotiated through treaties. The treaties' terms and thereby the degree of national sovereignty were determined by the relative strength of each of the parties. In every one of the treaties signed by the Chinese with foreign powers, the right of free and voluntary emigration was inscribed as a guiding principle, but just what constituted free and voluntary emigration was difficult to determine.

The Auction Block

If the Chinese managed not to die of disease or be killed in a mutiny during their passage over the oceans, they would most likely have found themselves on an auction block in Havana, Cuba, or Callao, Peru. Travelers, missionaries, and journalists seized on the image of the coolie auction block to show the similarities to slavery, but in the process they also rendered the Chinese as silent and mute victims of all-powerful masters. Having portrayed the Chinese as emasculated victims, observers could simultaneously condemn the coolie trade and justify intervention by civilized and Christian people to rescue the suffering Chinese. Although not off the mark, comparisons to slavery were used to bolster notions of U.S. and British superiority and to justify these nations' intervention in other countries.

Richard Henry Dana, a prominent U.S. lawyer and abolitionist who wrote about visiting a coolie auction in Havana in 1859, was sympathetic to the plight of the Chinese, but his descriptions reaffirmed the idea of the Chinese as powerless. Dana's reference to the building where the auction took place as a "Coolie jail, or market," reveals a degree of uncertainty about the liminal status of the Chinese. Were they enslaved against their will in a jail or merely selling their services in a market? His description, however, makes clear that the coolie market was like a slave auction:

> Yesterday I drove out to the Cerro, to see the Coolie jail, or market, where the imported Coolies are kept for sale. It is a well-known place, and open to all visitors. The building has a fair looking front; and through this I enter, by two porters, into an open yard in the rear where, on the gravel ground, are squatting a double line of Coolies, with heads shaved, except a tuft on the crown, dressed in loose Chinese garments of blue and yellow. The dealer, who is a calm, shrewd, heartless look-ing man, speaking English as well as if it were his native tongue, comes out with me, calls to the Coolies, and they all stand up in a double line, facing inward, and we pass through them, preceded by a driver armed with the usual badge of the plantation driver, the short, limber whip. The dealer does not hesitate to tell me the terms on which the contracts are made, as the trade is not illegal.[96]

This description suggests the openness of the Chinese coolie auction and the direct coercive force necessary to keep the Chinese in line. Even though the Chinese were ostensibly voluntary laborers, the plantation driver was there with whip in hand to insure compliance. Dana, who had also witnessed the auction of African slaves on his visit to Cuba, was a shrewd observer. "This was a strange and striking exhibition of power," he noted. "Two or three white men, bringing hundreds of Chinese thousands of miles, to a new cli-mate and people, holding them prisoners, selling their services to masters having an unknown tongue and an unknown religion, to work at unknown trades, for inscrutable purposes!"[97] The stark imbalance of power and the image of the Chinese completely cut off from their community, language, and religion rendered the Chinese almost completely subject to the whim of their owners no matter what protections their contracts ostensibly afforded them. What is missing from Dana's account are the Chinese labor brokers and translators who served as middlemen in the trade as well as the armed crew members and soldiers who maintained order in China and Cuba. From Dana's description, we have the impression that two or three white men were able to hold hundreds of Chinese as prisoners and bring them thousands of miles across the ocean, an image that portrays the Chinese as inordinately weak in relation to the powerful white men.

In Peru, Chinese were sold at a similar auction block. Peruvian newspapers advertised "just landed" coolies for sale, describing them as "models of health and sound of limb." When the ships arrived, plantation owners brought their buyers with them to size up and choose the best coolies based on their physical appearance. An *El Comercio* reporter described the auction scene: "It seems to be the correct thing to squeeze the coolie's biceps, give him a pinch or two in the region of the ribs, and then twist him around like a top so as to get a good glance at his physique generally. There is often a look of bewilderment on the Chinaman's face whilst undergoing this process— that is to say as far as his Mongolian features are capable of expressing such emotion."[98] One can only imagine the scene from the perspective of the Chinese who, having just landed in a strange country after nearly three months aboard a cramped boat, perhaps a third of their shipmates dead from disease or suicide, find themselves being poked, pinched, and prodded by people they can't understand. These public physical evaluations were described by a newspaper in Lima as "a shameful examination, which humiliates the dignity not only of the one who suffers it but also of those who witness it."[99]

The testimony of Chinese coolies in the *Cuba Commission Report* provides rare insight into how the Chinese saw their arrival in Havana and their sale in the "men market." The Chinese described their experience as humiliating and complained that they were treated "like pigs and dogs" in the Havana barracoons. In particular, they were upset at being disrobed and prodded like oxen and horses by potential masters who divided them into three classes based on their strength. Chinese focused on the "shame" of being manhandled like animals. However, their testimony also reveals attempts to resist and maintain some dignity. One coolie refused to have his queue removed and, for such an act of defiance, "was almost beaten to death."[100]

In addition to purchasing the Chinese laborers on an auction block, plantation owners renamed their coolies like masters did with slaves. The renaming was not done simply to use more common names but also to cut slaves and coolies off from their prior identities and lives and bind them to their new status as dependents on their masters, the givers of new names. As sociologist Orlando Patterson notes, "a man's name is, of course, more than simply a way of calling him. It is the verbal signal of his whole identity, his being-in-the-world as a distinct person."[101] One correspondent for *El Comercio* described the scene of Chinese coolies being incorporated into a plantation, noting the owner's central role as a giver of names:

One is called forward through the interpreter, who enquires his name, and he answers Afo, Asau, Atere, Achin & c. & c., as the case may be; his paper is then examined, and returned to him, when the grave question arises as to his name.

"Oh! Call him Calisto," says the owner.

"No Sir," breaks in one of the stewards, "we've got one already."

"Have we got a Samuel?"

"No Sir."

"Then call him Samuel."

I have never seen the name giver pause a moment (knowing well that such vulgar names as Juan, Pedro, Manuel, José, &c. were out of stock), then as if seized by a brilliant idea as for a calendar, and select such an out-of-the-way name as Calisto, Pancrasio, Ticiano, Zenon, Mimerto, Protasio, &c.; and the knotty point having been settled, down went the lucky *chinee* in the book as Protasio Asin—Age, 29 years—Stature, medium—Colour, yellowish-white—Forehead, high——Eyes, small—Mouth, wide (muttered ejaculation: plenty of room for rice!).[102]

This satirical description of the master as name giver suggests the extent to which the master hoped to wipe out the Chinese person's prior life. U.S. railway magnate John G. Meiggs, who in 1872 employed up to 25,000 people in Peru and was lauded for his benign treatment of his workers, simply referred to his Chinese laborers by numbers in the same way that prisoners of war and domestic inmates are labeled.[103]

Many travelers' and journalists' descriptions highlighted not only the brutality of the coolie labor system but also what they perceived as the racial and sexual inferiority of the Chinese. One U.S. historian and pastor, John S. C. Abbott, wrote in his 1860 travel account, "I find it to be the universal impression that in Cuba the Coolie trade is merely a Chinese slave-trade under the most fraudulent and cruel circumstances." His own impression upon seeing "several hundred of these wretched Coolies in the blazing sun" focused on their nakedness and filth and the omnipresence of the overseers whip. As he put it, "such a spectacle of misery I never saw, or conceived of before! Nearly all of them were naked to the waist. They were excessively filthy in person, and their countenances of the most abject debasement and joylessness. Several overseers with limber whips in their hands, were standing beneath shade trees, watching them and directing their work." Abbott's Christian-inspired critique of the coolie trade contained a hierarchical view of race in which the Chinese were portrayed as weak, dirty, and feminized victims of virile, superior whites. "What is to be the doom of these debased and fallen races?

How are they to be rescued from the tyranny of pride and avarice, and elevated to the dignity of manhood?"[104] In a similar vein, an 1873 *New York Times* article reasoned that although the "'heathen Chinee,' taken as a moral fixture, may not be all that we could wish in the matter of manhood and honesty," he was still a "creation of God's formation" and therefore had the right to liberty.[105] In these cases, the sexual and racial hierarchies worked together to make the coolie into a feminine subject who needed to be defended in the name of liberty and Christianity.

Travelers and local observers frequently compared the fate of Chinese laborers in Cuba and Peru to that of African slaves. In some ways, material conditions in terms of housing and wages were better for the Chinese, but in other ways, the Chinese were less integrated into Cuban society than Africans. Plantation owners expended more energy to Christianize African slaves than they did with the Chinese contract laborers, and unlike the Africans, there was no plan for the Chinese to become a lasting presence in Cuba or Peru. In Cuba, the 1861 regulations made clear what had always been assumed, that the Chinese were expected to leave the island once their contracts were finished. Frederick Trench Townshend, a captain in a senior regiment of the British Army, visited Cuba in 1874 just as the coolie trade was coming to an end. Townshend noted that, "in quarters, the Chinese were considerably better off, occupying separate huts at some distance from the negro barracks, and living entirely by themselves." In other ways, however, he found the Chinese to suffer under the same work conditions as the African slaves. "Nominally, not subject to the lash, in reality they experience the same treatment as the African, and are compelled to work the same time, eighteen hours a day in the busy season—a fearful task in such a climate."[106] Even though the Chinese were subjected to the same work routine and beatings as the African slaves, Townshend felt worse for the Chinese, whom he felt had an "inborn sense of freedom."

> Though the fate of the poor African slave in Cuba is horrible, that of the
> unfortunate Asiatic, who is serving under contract, struck me as even
> more pitiable. The wan face, feeble frame, and dejected looks of the
> wretched Chinamen were absolutely painful to see. Having enjoyed the
> blessings of freedom up to the hour when his evil fate led him to quit his
> native country, the poor Chinaman is ill-treated on board ship in a fearful manner, and on reaching Cuba, is bought, sold, subjected to the lash,
> and compelled to work like the negro slaves. Against such treatment his

natural intelligence, and inborn sense of freedom rebel, and he either runs away and engages himself in some trade in the large towns, or goes about a miserable and heart-broken wretch.[107]

Traveler and journalistic accounts of Chinese coolies often depicted them as both passive and potentially threatening. Townshend recognized their "inborn sense of freedom" and rebelliousness but also focused on the coolie's "wan face, feeble frame, and dejected looks."

In Peru, Chinese coolies first arrived after the passage of the 1849 legislation that came to be known as the Chinese Law. At that point African slavery still existed in Peru, but the number of slaves was small and dwindling. By the time emancipation was decreed in 1854, there were only 17,000 slaves in the country.[108] The Chinese therefore worked alongside African slaves for the first five years, and after that they labored with the newly emancipated free blacks. In 1873, one Peruvian writer compared the rights enjoyed by black slaves under the Civil Code to the more limited rights of the coolie under the immigration regulations. In a long list, the writer asserted that under the Civil Code masters owed slaves food, protection, and healthcare, could not transport slaves without their consent, had to feed them when they became useless, and were required to provide slaves with an education. According to the writer, Chinese coolies had none of these protections. If the master had no use for the coolie, he would "abandon the Chinese in the field or in the streets begging public charity." Furthermore, while slaves could gain their freedom if the master "refrain[ed] one year from feeding, clothing and educating him," or by saving his master's life, no equivalent possibilities for freedom existed for the Chinese. Some of the writer's assertions about regulations governing Chinese emigrants were technically incorrect, but the writer's point was that African slaves had more paternalistic protections than the Chinese coolies, and that the Chinese were therefore in a "worse condition than slaves."[109]

The Peruvian writer's conclusion that Chinese coolies were in a worse condition than African slaves notwithstanding, comparing the conditions of free wage laborers and slaves was potentially very explosive. As Patterson notes, the existence of slavery in capitalist societies undermines the ideological myth of free labor. "The use of personally dominated individuals for the production and reproduction of wealth exposed the reality behind the so-called free labor. The laborer came to see his work for others for what it really was—alienation from the means of production and exploitation by the employer." He goes on to explain, "the free laborer became dangerously radicalized by the presence of slavery. Nonslave workers universally tended to despise work for others in all societies where a critical mass of slaves was used."[110] In the context of a slave society Chinese free laborers could see through the thin veil of free labor ideology to the reality of extreme alienation, not only from their labor but from all aspects of their life. Chinese laborers became "dangerously radicalized" not by confronting slavery but by coming face-to-face with the reality of free wage labor exploitation in its most naked form.

Conclusion

The debate over the morality of the coolie trade was at its heart an argument about the merits of slavery over free wage labor. Those who condemned the trade showed how similar it was to African slavery, with branding of bodies, corporal punishments, auction blocks, and the masters' almost total domination. Defenders of the trade argued that Chinese contract laborers agreed to the terms of their indenture and chose to sign up. Both of these Manichean views ignored the large gray area in between, where the Chinese emigrants actually lived. They were neither abject slaves nor completely free agents making rational economic choices. Although some were kidnapped, most laborers chose to enter into the contracts to relieve their dire economic circumstances in China. Coercion was exercised more by the market than by guns and shackles. Once onboard the ships, however, coolies were shocked to discover that they were being chained, whipped, and generally treated like slaves. Given that situation, some chose to mutiny, killing the captain and crew and claiming their liberty, and others simply committed suicide. Some signed up for the journey with the intent to overtake the crew and pillage the ship.[111] Abolitionists who tended to portray the Chinese as dejected and feeble victims of all-powerful whites flattened and obscured the range of Chinese responses. In their condemnation of the coolie trade, such abolitionists reinforced stereotypes of Chinese as effeminate, weak, and ineffectual.

The port cities from which coolies departed and the ships on which they traveled, although ostensibly under the legal jurisdiction of a particular nation, were in fact borderlands where nation-states had limited control. The treaty ports like Amoy were particularly complex borderlands given that Europeans exercised extraterritorial jurisdiction over their nationals in these multinational zones.[112] Furthermore, the Qing government in the mid-nineteenth century had limited control over its coastal ports or the regional governments that operated there.[113] Unable to rely on protection from the

Qing or other governments, Chinese emigrants often resorted to attacking their captors. Although most mutinies aboard coolie ships were either subdued or ended with the entire ship burning, there were remarkable cases when coolies managed take control of the ship, such as occurred in 1868 when fifty coolies seized the Prussian bark *Cayaltil*, murdered the crew, and sailed the ship back to China.[114] Since the archives have only recorded faint traces of such successful rebellions, we are left to imagine an alternative narrative to the stories of failed mutinies and enslaved coolies. Coolies who made it to the Americas alive found their lives regulated by contracts. The next chapter turns to those contracts and Chinese efforts to claim freedom within and against them.

CHAPTER 2

Contracting Freedom

A society based on contract is a society of free and independent men.
—William Graham Sumner, *What the Social Classes Owe to Each Other* (1903)

The origin of every contract also points toward violence.
—Walter Benjamin, "Critique of Violence" (1921)

In the late eighteenth and nineteenth centuries, free wage labor distinguished modern capitalism from more primitive and backward economic systems that relied on slavery. Notwithstanding the fact that slave plantation economies in Brazil, Cuba, and the U.S. South were highly integrated in the world capitalist market, in the mind of nineteenth-century liberals, free wage labor was synonymous with capitalism. The Chinese laborers who began to be recruited in the middle of the nineteenth century were at the epicenter of the debate between free wage labor and slavery. British and U.S. pressure to end the slave trade pushed up the cost of slaves as new imports became scarcer and the supply of slaves dwindled. Planters throughout the Americas began to search for an alternative cheap labor supply, and Chinese coolies seemed to fit the bill. Journalist Whitelaw Reid summed up the solution to having free blacks in the U.S. South following emancipation, a sentiment shared by planters in Cuba and Peru: "We can drive the niggers out and import coolies that will work better, at less expense, and relieve us from this cursed nigger impudence."[1] In addition to bringing them relief from such "impudence," planters and government officials argued that free wage labor was more efficient, productive, and enlightened. Contract labor seemed to solve the problem of maintaining a cheap and controlled labor force after slavery.

Chinese contract laborers were imported into the United States throughout this period, and they were referred to by slavery advocates, abolitionists, and government officials as coolies. Notwithstanding the Congress's 1862 prohibition of the coolie trade, Chinese contract laborers continued to be imported into the United States. In *Coolies and Cane*, historian Moon-Ho Jung argues that the distinction between "coolies" in the Caribbean and "immigrants" in the United States was a false one. "The habitual assertion of this false binary—coolies versus immigrants," Jung argues, "not only reifies coolies and American exceptionalism but ironically reproduces the logic and rhetoric of nineteenth-century debates on whether Asians in the United States were, in fact, coolies."[2] I also want to highlight the similarities between the labor exploitation of Chinese in Cuba, Peru, Mexico, Canada, and the United States and to show the degree to which free labor was an ideological smokescreen to cover workers' continued bondage after emancipation. In none of these countries did the government explicitly import "coolies." Rather, each insisted that they were importing free wage laborers, which the governments in Cuba and Peru referred to simply as "colonos" (colonists). Journalists used the term *coolie* indiscriminately to refer to Chinese or Indian laborers, but they also made distinctions between conditions in Peru and Cuba versus those in California. Even as late as 1891, seventeen years after the coolie trade officially ended, Frederic Remington still referred to Chinese laborers in Havana as coolies. As one *New York Times* article put it, "the term 'coolie' is very elastic. In Peru it meant a bond slave; in California it means a Chinese laborer."[3]

Enterprising plantation owners sought out laborers from a transnational market. In the wake of emancipation, planters from Louisiana began to import Chinese coolies from Cuba. Mr. Bullitt of Nachitoches Parish went to Cuba in 1867, hired Chinese whose contracts were expiring, and brought them to New Orleans on two steamers. An article in the *New York Times* outlined the advantages of coolie labor over free black labor, including coolies' lack of women and children to support, their good work habits, the strength of the young Chinese men, and their familiarity with the "severe discipline of their Cuban masters." However, the greatest advantage of coolies' labor was that, since they were not citizens, they had no rights except those explicitly set forth in their contract.

> The coolies come to this country under contract for a term of years. The interest of their employer will be theirs. He alone pays them, he alone can direct or discharge them. They are not citizens, consequently they can have no votes and will not trouble themselves about matters outside of their plantation. They are intelligent enough to make a contract which amply satisfies them, and no interloping politician can unsettle their minds on the subject of status. Neither Congress nor Bureaus will feel the least interest in them for they come simply in pursuance of an agreement, which binds them to do "so much for so much." They and the other party to the contract being the only ones who are to be satisfied.[4]

Frederic Remington, "Chinese Coolies Loading a Steamer at Havana,"
Harper's Weekly, November 1891.

For the *New York Times*, as well as many politicians and planters, the coolie was the solution to get cheap labor without the stain of slavery. In postemancipation societies like the United States (after 1865) and Peru (after 1854), Chinese contract labor provided a means to achieve control over the labor force and avoid contending with a newly emancipated black population. Given their status, Chinese were unprotected by the government, outside the reach or interest of politicians, and only regulated by a private contract. As noncitizens and perpetual aliens, the coolies could not make claims on the nation and would be completely at the disposal of their private employers.

Not everyone was so enamored of the coolie solution. The idea of importing "aliens" to do farm labor in the U.S. South in the wake of emancipation unsettled some people in the North who believed that coolie labor would perpetuate the evil of slavery. In 1867 *Harper's Weekly* condemned the practice in a strongly worded editorial: "These people are the lowest and in every way the least desirable portion of nations the most alien to us and our civilization. They are not needed as laborers; and their introduction into a section of the country in which the traditions and habits of slavery are still

"Chinese Coolies Smuggled into the United States, Disguised as Mexicans, at Work on a Southern Farm," *Harper's Weekly*, 5 August 1905.

fresh could result only in establishing a new form of slavery, and infinitely perplexing and delaying the natural and desirable consequences of emancipation."[5] The fact that the Chinese laborers were seen as the "least desirable portion" of the population made them unfit as immigrants. In the 1850s through 1870s, the coolie debate was a hemispheric concern. Although some Brazilian planters attempted to import Chinese contract laborers, they were consistently rebuffed by the contention that Chinese were degenerate aliens. One influential coffee planter, who published his ideas frequently in the Rio de Janeiro newspaper *Jornal do Commercio*, argued that that the Chinese were "stationary, from a doubtful civilization, inert from progress, [and that China] must cede its place and be exterminated by the nations of Europe and America who are obeying a providential mission, marching, armed like evangelical gladiators with the light of civilization."[6] The otherness of the Chinese emerged as a constant theme in the calls to limit or prevent further Chinese migration. While their proponents and detractors could not agree on whether coolies helped or hurt the transition to a postslavery society, both sides agreed that Chinese laborers were aliens who could be easily exploited.

Although there are many similarities between the racial constructions of

Chinese laborers across the Americas, the legislation and degree of government control over the trade in Cuba and Peru was far greater than in the United States or Mexico. This chapter will focus on the ways regulations and contracts in Cuba and Peru developed in tandem, and in the context of Chinese laborer recruitment to the United States, Canada, and Mexico. In the mid- to late nineteenth century, Cuba and Peru were very different. Cuba was still a colonial slave society until the late nineteenth century. Peru was an independent republic that had abolished slavery in 1854. The particular contexts in each nation influenced the ebb and flow of the coolie trade, including foreign and domestic wars, diplomatic relations, and the timing of the abolition of slavery, but nonetheless recruiting, contracting methods, and labor legislation for Chinese laborers were strikingly similar in Cuba and Peru during this period. Although nations like Peru, colonies like Cuba, and empires like Portugal, Spain, and Britain established their own rules and regulations for Chinese emigrants, the recruiters, ships, and insurance companies were part of a vast transnational plantation economy that wrapped around the entire globe, from the Americas to Europe and across to Asia. Reading the national laws and regulations regarding coolies through a broader transnational lens reveals the similarities of the coolie system in the Americas, how it developed and why it ended, or was transformed, less than three decades after it began.

Slavery versus Free Wage Labor

The debate about free wage labor and slavery stretched from Europe to the Americas in the nineteenth century. If ever there was a transnational debate, this was it. Liberal ideas about freedom had developed in relation to slavery, and thus it should not be surprising that many reasoned that systems not based on slave labor must ipso facto be free. It also helps that liberal thinkers hijacked the term itself, labeling this particular labor relation "*free* wage labor." In 1767, long before Karl Marx criticized wage labor as slavery, or was even born, the French journalist Simon Linguet asserted that so-called free laborers were in fact less free than slaves. "They live only by hiring out their arms. They must therefore find someone to hire them, or die of hunger. Is that to be free?"[7]

This notion of "wage slavery" was criticized by Northern abolitionists in the United States as a spurious Southern claim to defend slavery by comparing the situation of slaves to the dire conditions faced by Northern factory workers. However, the *New York Times* in 1854 also defended southern slavery as more humane than the British exploitation of coolie labor on Peru's Chincha Islands:

> The labor of the Southern negro is light and his lot is happy in comparison to theirs. The negro of the South is under the protection of laws; he is the property of his master, and self-interest, if not humanity, will deter that master from working him to death, or subjecting him to treatment that would make life intolerable. But the unfortunate Coolies of the Chincha Islands are under the protection of no law; they are the property of no master. . . . Hence there is no check to the cruelties of the Peruvians—no end, save death, to the sufferings of the Coolies.[8]

Although the assertion that the southern slave's lot was "happy" and "light" is absurd, the *Times* was highlighting the hypocrisy of the British press, which was quick to condemn U.S. slavery and turned a blind eye to Britain's own slavelike labor regimes. Coolie labor was an extension of slavery through the free wage labor system. Both systems dehumanized and exploited labor and both were bitterly resisted. While it may be true that particular slaves in a relatively privileged position had more opportunities than the most unfortunate factory workers, my point is not to argue which was crueler but to suggest that neither was free in any meaningful sense of the word.

Traditional definitions of slavery hold that a person who is owned and can be sold to another person is a slave. A slave, according to this view, is subject to the will of the owner and is made to labor by coercion or threats of violence. Orlando Patterson finds this basic definition of slavery lacking, arguing that property guides many different kinds of human relations, including those within the family. Although the question of property is important for understanding slavery, Patterson focuses on what he calls "social death." For Patterson, therefore, slavery is "the permanent, violent and personal domination of natally alienated and generally dishonored persons."[9] In particular, he focuses on the ability of slave masters to separate families and the inability of slaves to legally marry, raise children, and form families as central to their "social death."[10] Chinese coolies fit many of Patterson's descriptions of what it was to be a slave: they were subject to violent and personal domination, owners attempted to alienate them from their families and communities, and they were generally dishonored. However, none of Patterson's descriptions speak to the lived reality of coolies, or slaves for that matter. Historian Vincent Brown takes issue with Patterson's description of slaves as socially dead, citing the voluminous social histories that have documented slave communities, families, African cultural retentions, and resistance.[11] In this chapter, I argue that laws and regulations in Cuba and Peru governing Chinese coolies rendered them as socially disabled but not completely dead.[12] Chinese could and did reconstruct a social world through marriage, raising families, hometown associations, secret societies, and political parties (see chapter 7). Even in the most desperate of situations when Chinese committed suicide, they undermined the attempt to render them socially dead by taking control over their deaths and giving them meaning.

Regulations in Cuba and Peru granted the owner almost total control over Chinese laborers, but the laws also recognized some degree of Chinese autonomy. In both places, coolies were obligated by the contracts to do whatever work the plantation owner ordered. Their mobility was also severely curtailed; they could not even leave the plantation without the written permission of the master.[13] However, after harsh criticism from inside and outside Peru about the conditions for Chinese laborers working in the guano mines on the Chincha Islands off the coast of Peru, contracts with Chinese specifically stated that they would not work extracting guano.[14] The "Chinese Law" of 1861 in Peru also forbid the transfer of contracts without the "consent of the contracting colonist."[15] It seems that these legal limitations on the owners' power were rarely enforced; a contract from 1868 even states in contradiction to the 1861 law that the Chinese emigrant was bound to anyone to whom the contract was transferred.[16] Furthermore, given that an estimated two-thirds of Chinese emigrants to Peru were illiterate, and that the different dialects in China made it hard for interpreters to convey the precise meaning of the contracts, it is likely that the Chinese did not understand the provisions either. To make matters worse, many of the contracts did not bear the signatures of either the employer or the Chinese laborer.[17] The contracts were tiny fig leaves covering the shame of the conditions of coolie labor, but these were extremely important fig leaves.

Cuban regulations recognized that Chinese men had some right to patriarchal control, but they could only marry someone if the owner agreed. Nonetheless, owners were not allowed to separate families, and Chinese men were granted *patria potestad* (fatherly power) over their children and *potestad marital* (husbandly power) over their wives.[18] In this way, there was some formal recognition of Chinese family life and male patriarchal privilege. However, given the almost complete absence of Chinese women, and therefore recognized families, these acknowledgements did not mean much in practice. If these laws do not fit Patterson's definition of being socially dead, they also fail to match traditional definitions of slavery. While it is true that Chinese laborers could be bought and sold and transferred from one person to another, the contracts also had a time limit, usually of five to eight years. Although this term could be extended, the Chinese laborer could look forward to freedom once he fulfilled his contractual obligations. In short, the Chinese coolie exhibits elements of being like a slave, and elements of being a low-status but free man. At least on paper, the Chinese coolie had legal rights.

The completely skewed power relations that typify the master-slave relationship and the near total domination of the slave's life are echoed in coolie labor. It is almost impossible to come up with a universal definition for master-slave relations across space and time because slavery has existed in so many different forms. The Virginia Slave Code of 1705, for example, allowed anyone to kill a runaway slave, while the French Code Noir in 1685 Louisiana prohibited torture of slaves, although "when their slaves will have merited it," owners could "have [the slaves] chained and whipped with wooden switches."[19] However, even a brief survey of some of the quintessential slave societies suggests that slaves were often granted the right to form and maintain families, and even a method by which to gain their freedom. The Cuban Slave Code of 1842, for instance, forbid masters to prevent marriages of slaves and required the husband's master to purchase the wife and her children if she lived on a different plantation. The Cuban code also required masters to allow slaves to purchase their freedom.[20] Although slaves were still considered property, they were regarded as people in the law. As Patterson writes, "As a legal fact, there has never been a slaveholding society, ancient or modern, that did not recognize the slave as a person in law."[21] The slave, however, was a particular type of person, one that was at the whim of his master, just like the coolie.

Contracting Freedom

The contracts that guided the Chinese coolie trade were emblematic of the nineteenth-century liberal ideal of individual parties entering into a voluntary and mutually beneficial agreement, but their provisions enslaved the Chinese emigrant. The U.S. sociologist William Graham Sumner summed up the centrality of contracts to nineteenth-century notions of freedom: "A society based on contract is a society of free and independent men."[22] Spanish defenses of the trade repeatedly stressed that the Chinese emigrant freely chose to enter into an agreement to provide labor at a particular salary for a given number of years. Furthermore, the contracts specified in painstaking detail the clothes, the food, and the health benefits that emigrants would receive in exchange for their services. So, in the sense that the Chinese agreed to the terms, and that the term of indenture was limited, this was qualitatively different from chattel slavery, in which no agreement was necessary and no limits were placed on the period of service.

A letter to the editor of the *New York Times* in 1856 defended the coolie trade to Peru as both a relief from the overpopulation and danger in China and a boon to Peru's economy. After listing all the provisions of a Peruvian coolie contract, the writer asked rhetorically, "Is there aught in this that is inhuman or unchristian? Is it not, in the providence of God, one of the means by which Slavery may be annihilated, and free labor introduced over the world?" The coolie trade, therefore, was not only not "inhuman and unchristian" but God's way of ending slavery and extending free labor around the globe. "May it not be one of the grand means God is using for opening China to foreigners?" the writer asked. The coolie trade thus also served as a wedge to open the closed Chinese society. And finally, the writer quoted Dr. Peter Parker, a U.S. medical missionary and government envoy in China, who declared that when the coolies returned to China, "these men do not come back Chinamen, but Republicans!" Rescuing Chinese from their homeland's backwardness and turning them into liberal citizens, "republicans," enabled them to lose their Chineseness. In this writer's crude calculus, republican citizenship was antithetical to being Chinese.[23]

Notwithstanding the existence of the contract and liberal ideas about freedom and republican virtues, the almost total domination of Chinese coolies by their owners echoes Patterson's definition of slavery. One of the most egregious imbalances of the contracts was the unlimited nature of the laborers' obligations and the very specific duties of the employer. One typical contract for work in Cuba obligated the emigrant to do "whatever kind of work they assign to me in the plantations or in other farms during the customary hours." The job description was completely open-ended. The obligations for the employer were much more specific: "eight ounces of salted meat: one and a half pounds of bananas, sweet potatoes, or other root foods, medical and nursing care, two changes of clothes and a blanket every year and a woolen shirt." The medical care that would be provided to the Chinese also came with a catch. If a coolie's illness lasted longer than fifteen days, the salary would be suspended until he was able to return to work. The contract also specified that the advance received by the coolie would be discounted from the salary.[24] In Peru, the contracts also provided for healthcare, but the coolie would have his salary docked if the illness was deemed to be his fault.[25] These contracts therefore resembled free wage labor agreements in form, but the precise details provided for a system of forced labor in which the owner controlled nearly every aspect of the laborers' lives, including food, healthcare, work, mobility, and family relations. Like slaves, Chinese coolies could be sold to other people, although technically it was their contracts that were being transferred.

Rather than a bright line, what separates a slave from a free laborer is a range of practices on the continuum from bondage to freedom. The Cuban historian Manuel Moreno Fraginals has pointed out that slaves labored under a variety of conditions in late nineteenth-century Cuba; some slaves earned wages, some were exempt from physical punishment, and some paid their owners for the right to the status of semifreedmen so they could sell their services.[26] The fact that Chinese contract laborers worked alongside African slaves on Cuban and Peruvian sugar plantations only adds to the confusion.

The Contract

The existence of a contract was supposed to guarantee freedom for Chinese laborers, who had supposedly chosen to enter into such agreements with certain obligations and rights, but for laborers, the contracts' terms were heavily weighted toward the former and short on the latter. Contracts in Cuba and Peru varied depending on the employer and the years in which they were written, but the basic outlines remained the same, providing virtually unlimited powers to the masters and very limited rights to the laborers. One contract in Cuba gave the "master" complete discretion as to the number of hours worked per day, only providing that workers be allowed an unspecified number of "consecutive hours of repose" each day. Even the clause that ostensibly provided for a break on Sunday stated, "I cannot be compelled on Sundays to execute more labor than that which, of necessity, must be performed on such days." In terms of discipline, the laborer agreed to submit "to the system of punishment which in those places is adopted for lack of application and industry, for disobedience of the master's or of his representative's orders." As if this did not grant the employers enough coercive force, the contract also explicitly stated that the laborer could "for no reason, and under no pretext, . . . during the eight years for which I am bound in this contract, refuse my services to the master who will take me, nor escape, nor attempt to do so, for any cause whatever."[27] Essentially the contracts put the laborer under the complete control of the master for eight years.

The typical rate of pay for Chinese contract laborers in Cuba and Peru was four dollars a month, in addition to the eight dollars they received as an advance in China. The eight-dollar advance and the cost of the clothes and other provisions (four dollars) provided to the emigrants on the voyage were discounted from their wages at a rate of one dollar a month.[28] Furthermore, all Cuban contracts included a clause that had been developed as part of the 1854 regulations, indicating that the emigrant was aware "that the wages earned by other free laborers and the slaves in the Island of Cuba [were] much higher," but that the difference was compensated by other advantages.[29] In general, labor salaries in Cuba were three to four times higher than in Europe in the mid-nineteenth century, and even accounting for purchasing power, a common laborer could earn double in Cuba what he could in Europe.[30] In the late nineteenth century, the historian Juan de Arona estimated that in Peru, accounting for the $500 cost of the contract, the monthly wages, and upkeep, the Chinese coolie cost about the same as a free unskilled worker: about sixty cents a day. Plantation owners sought Chinese labor in both Cuba and Peru, however, because labor was scarce and they could control Chinese more effectively.[31] Chinese labor also made economic sense in the United States. In 1870, Andrew Hynes Gay argued that the monthly fourteen-dollar salary for Chinese contract labor, even considering the seventy-dollar transportation charge from California to his father's Louisiana plantation, would be cheaper than bringing in black labor from Virginia. And unlike the free black laborers, who signed yearly contracts, the Chinese signed three-year contracts.[32] The salary of four dollars a month in Cuba may have seemed like a lot for Chinese emigrants, but the high cost of living in Cuba meant that in real terms the salaries did not allow the coolies to save much of anything at all.

British officials relentlessly criticized the Spanish contracts as illegitimate expressions of a free labor agreement, and they pointed to the differences between their own indenture contracts to highlight the coercive elements of the Spanish ones. In 1858, T. Chisolm Anstey, the attorney general of Hong Kong, argued that the Spanish contracts for coolie labor in Cuba were akin to slavery.

The indefinite power of coercion; the want of reciprocity with respect to complaints on the score of wages and food; the sordid calculation of *horae non* of sickness, no matter how necessarily incident to the nature of the employment; the arbitrary power to transfer and assign the servant; the arbitrary denial of all power to the latter to exchange mas-

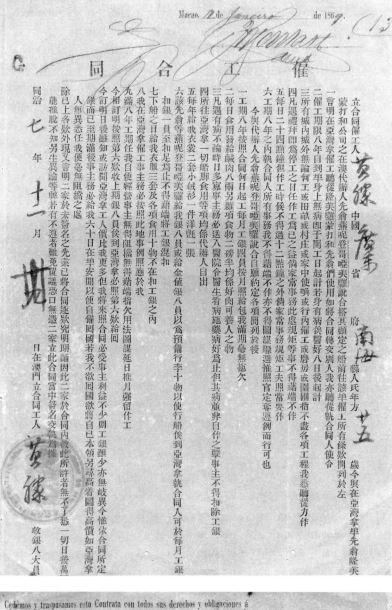

同 合 工 催

立合同催工人 黃綠 中國 廣東省 南海縣人民年方 廿五 歲今與在亞灣拿埠先翁隆美

一言明在亞灣拿催工聽從隆美驪打和公司之在澳代辦人先翁燕呢登哥嚁美驪說合搭其顧定之船前往該半催工所有條欵開列於左

二催工期限八年目到半身上無病即于開工日起計若身有病俟醫好八日後起計

三所有城內城外無論何工或用猷或村庄或家中使喚或行內催工或磨房或園圃皆指不盡各項工程我悉聽從力作

四凡退禮拜日任作工爲已之益倘家常事務此處規矩等事亦不得藉端不作

五每日二十四點鐘但作工時候不得過十二點鐘之外倘家事務規矩工夫照常要件

六工期八年之內倘合同人所有事務我不得藉端不作亦不得圖謀墜避惟照官定等遵例而行可也

一工期八年按照合同每月工銀四員按月照給包我滿期毫無拖欠

二每日食用發給鹹肉八兩另雜項食物二類半均係好肉可養人之物

三凡遇有病不論時日多寡事主務必送入醫院令醫生看病施藥病好爲止但其病薑非自作之孽事主不得扣除工銀

四所往亞灣拿一切船脚食用等項均係代辦人自出

五每年給我衣裳二套小絨衫一件洋氈一張

六該先翁等燕哥嚁美驪給我銀八員以爲預備行李十物以便行船俟到亞灣拿執合同人可於每月工銀

七下扣除我衣服三套及各項食用十物不在扣工銀之內

八我在亞灣拿催工事主務必按照此地事例應於我

九滿八年工期任我自便經營事主無得阻撓指欠用法圖謀延日推月強留作工

今訂明日後離如或訪問亞灣拿工人償比我更多但我將來照合同必受事主利益不少則工銀離少亦無岐異今惟依合同所定

銀而已至期滿後事主務必給我六十日在半安期以便自僱回國若我不欲回國欲將自已本領另尋高着圖得高價如亞灣拿

人無異悉任我便亳無阻攔之遏

除已上各欵外現又言明二家於合同內彼此所許者無不悉一切日後萬...

同治 七 年 十一 月 卅 日 在澳門立合同工人 黃綠 收銀八大員

No. 29

CONTRATA.

Martín

"NADESDA."

Conste por este documento que yo *Nong Sing* natural del pueblo de *Namai* en China, de edad de **25** años, he convenido con el Señor **N. TANCO ARMERO**, Agente de los Señores **LOMBILLO, MONTALVO y Cª.** de la Habana en embarcarme para dicho puerto en el buque que se me designe bajo las condiciones siguientes:

1ª.—Me comprometo a trabajar en la Ysla de Cuba a las ordenes de dichos Señores ó de cualquiera otra persona a quien traspase este Contrato, para lo cual doy mi consentimiento.

2ª.—Este Contrato durará ocho años, que principiarán á contarse desde el dia que entre á servir, siempre que el estado de mi salud sea bueno; pero si me hallare enfermo ó imposibilitado para trabajar, entonces no será hasta que pasen ocho dias despues de mi restablecimiento.

3ª.—Trabajaré en todas las faenas que alli se acostumbra ya sea en el campo ó en las poblaciones, ya en casas particulares para el servicio doméstico, ó en qualquier establecimiento comercial ó industrial; ya en ingenios, vegas, cafetales, sitios, potreros, estancias, &c. Enfin, me consagraré á qualquiera clase de trabajo urbano ó rural á que me dedique el patrono.

4ª.—Serán de descanso los Domingos que podré emplear en trabajar por mi cuenta si me conviniere, siempre que no sea destinado al servicio doméstico en cuyo caso me sujetaré a la costumbre del pais.

5ª.—Las horas de trabajo no podran pasar de 12 por término medio de las 24 del dia, salvo siempre el servicio doméstico y el interior en las casas de campo.

6ª.—Bajo ningun concepto podré durante los ocho años de mi compromiso negar mis servicios á la persona a quien se traspase este Contrato ni evadirme de su poder ni siquiera intentarlo por causa alguna, á no ser la de redencion obtenida con arreglo a la ley.

El Señor Dn. **N. TANCO ARMERO**, se obliga a su vez a lo siguiente:

I. A que desde el dia en que principie á contarse los ocho años de mi compromiso, principie tambien a correrme el salario de cuatro pesos fuertes al mes, el mismo que dicho Agente me garantiza y asegura por cada mes de los ocho años de mi Contrato.

II. Que se me suministre de alimento cada dia ocho onzas de carne salada, y dos y media libras de boniatos ó de otras viandas sanas y alimenticias.

III. Que durante mis enfermedades se me proporcione en la enfermeria la asistencia que mis males reclamen, asi como los auxilios, medicinas y facultativo que mis dolencias y conservacion eesijan por qualquier tiempo que duren. Y mis salarios continuarán asi mismo, salvo que mi enfermedad hubiese sido adquirida por mi culpa.

IV. Será de cuenta del mismo Agente ó por la de quien corresponda mi pasage hasta la Habana y mi manutencion a bordo.

V. Que se me den dos mudas de ropa, una camisa de lana y una frazada anuales.

VI. El mismo Señor me adelantará la cantidad de ocho pesos fuertes en oro ó plata para mi habilitacion en el viage que voi á emprender, la misma que satisfaré en la Habana a las ordenes de dicho Señor con un peso al mes que se descontará de mi salario por la persona á quien fuese entregado este Contrato, entendiendose que por ningun otro concepto podrá hacerseme descuento alguno.

VII. A darme gratis 3 mudas de ropa y demas utensilios necesarios el dia de mi embarque.

VIII. A que se me conceda la proteccion de las leyes que rijan en la Ysla de Cuba.

IX. A que transcurridos los 8 años estipulados en esta Contrata, tendré libertad para disponer de mi trabajo sin que pueda servir de pretesto para prolongar esta Contrata contra mi voluntad, qualquiera deudas, empeños ó compromisos que hubiera contraido.

DECLARO haber recibido en efectivo segun se espresa en la ultima clausula la suma de pesos ocho mencionados que reintegraré en la Habana en la forma establecida en dicha clausula.

DECLARO tambien que me conformo con el salario estipulado aunque sé y me consta es mucho mayor el que ganan otros jornaleros libres y los esclavos en la Ysla de Cuba; porque esta diferencia la juzgo compensada con las otras ventajas que ha de proporcionarme mi patrono y las que aparecen en este Contrato.

QUEDO impuesto que al concluir el presente Contrato se me conceden 60 dias para volver a mi pais de mi cuenta si me conviniere, ó para buscar acomodo con el patrono que me sea mas util y con el mayor salario que se dice en el anterior articulo ganan los trabajadores en Cuba, segun mi capacidad ó aficion al trabajo ú oficio que me pueda proporcionar.

Y en cumplimiento de todo lo espuesto arriba, declaramos ademas ambos contratantes que antes de poner nuestra firma hemos leido por la ultima vez detenidamente todos y cada uno de los articulos anteriores, y que sabemos perfectamente los compromisos que hemos contraido mutuamente, afin de que en ningun tiempo, ni por ningun motivo pueda arguirse ignorancia ni haber lugar a reclamos, escepto en el caso de faltar a qualquiera de las condiciones estipuladas en esta Contrata.

Contract for a Chinese laborer hired in Macao to work in Cuba, 1867.
Courtesy of Kathleen López.

ters; the enormous duration of service, if taken in combination with the probable nature thereof; and the bold avowal of a right of chastisement not recognized even by Cuban law: these are surely ingredients whose compound is nothing else than unadulterated slavery.[33]

The basic idea of a free labor contract was that a person could agree to work for another person for a specified period of time in exchange for a particular wage. Anstey took issue with the Spanish contracts, not only because they allowed corporal punishment and did not pay for sick days but also because they bound the emigrants to work for unspecified masters. As Anstey put it, "The contract is not one of hiring and service at all; and all the laws of 'master and servant' are entirely out of place. It is a contract with A by B to work not for A alone, but for all the other letters of the alphabet."[34] The fact that a contract could be bought and sold, and transferred from one master to the next, Anstey argued, made the coolie into a piece of property like a chattel slave.

The contracts themselves were signed in a carefully scripted ritual that was supposed to ensure the legitimacy of the agreement and the free will of the emigrants. In 1854, new regulations in Cuba required contracts to be written in the emigrants' native language and stamped by the Spanish consuls, presumably to assure that proper procedures were being followed; copies of the contracts were supposed to be held by the emigrants.[35] There were instances when Chinese emigrants indicated that they did not desire to travel to Cuba and were then released. In one case in 1859, the Spanish consul in Amoy released thirty-five prospective emigrants who indicated their unwillingness to go to Cuba.[36] While it is difficult to determine to what extent these safeguards actually functioned in practice, the British press continually asserted that the emigrants were being kidnapped and brought forcibly to Cuba. In 1857, the *Hong Kong Daily Mail* condemned the Spanish for having "kidnapped 50,000 Chinese [who were] seduced by contracts that are only an illusion, led by blacks and kept working under the whip."[37]

The *Cuba Commission Report* also suggested that the voluntary contracts were more of a legal fiction than a reality. After taking testimony and depositions from 2,841 Chinese laborers in Cuba in 1874, the Cuba Commission concluded that "8 or 9 of every 10 have been conveyed there against their will." The report further asserted that the Chinese and Spanish officials were not present, as had been demanded by the Chinese and Spanish Emigration Convention, when the emigrants signed their contracts. In the vast majority of cases, the report continued, the Chinese were coerced to sign. One typical statement, by Ku Ch'iao-hsiu, asserted, "I was beaten with great severity, and the suffering being unendurable I could not but accept the contract."[38] Two pages of similar testimony corroborated these assertions.

The focus on whether the emigrants signed these papers willingly distracts our attention from the fiction at the center of nineteenth-century liberal ideology, namely, the mythology of autonomous individuals entering into voluntary contracts with each other. Whether or not the Chinese were beaten, tricked, or voluntarily signed the contracts, they were not in a position to negotiate the terms of the agreements, which were printed in boilerplate fashion and written in Madrid, Havana, or Lima. The signing of the contract, rather than exemplifying mutual agreement and freedom, is, in fact, the greatest moment of violence. In his essay "Critique of Violence," Walter Benjamin argues that the legal contract is the epitome of violence: "We are above all obligated to note that a totally nonviolent resolution of conflicts can never lead to a legal contract. For the latter, however peacefully it may have been entered into by the parties, leads finally to possible violence. It confers on each part the right to resort to violence in some form against the other, should he break the agreement. Not only that; like the outcome, the origin of every contract also points toward violence."[39] For Benjamin, even if there is no mention of violence in the contract, the power of enforcement behind any contract is always violent force. In the coolie contract, the violence is quite explicit, granting as it does the right to discipline the emigrant for refusing services to the master or even seeking to escape. Although the labor contracts were heralded by European governments as a modern form of freedom quite distinct from the brutal coercion of slavery, the contracts themselves were the tools of enslavement, less visible yet more effective than shackles and whips.

Subordination, Discipline, and Hegemony

Regulations for Chinese coolies changed over time as the Spanish and Peruvian governments responded to international and domestic pressures and sought mechanisms to manage and control laborers. Although the regulations provided more protections for Chinese laborers and asserted a paternalistic state power over the coolies, such measures were designed to prevent Chinese revolt. After the first group of Chinese was brought to Cuba in 1847, plantation owners ran into trouble trying to discipline workers in the same manner as they had African slaves. For the government the issue was a technical one because introduction of Asians represented "a new and unknown element in the country." With this in mind, the government developed a series of rules "that while protecting the rights of the colonists also assure subordination and discipline, without which agriculture could be hurt rather than producing benefits." The two elements were related, protecting the rights of the colonists and assuring "subordination and discipline" in order to make agriculture more productive. However, there was also another goal in laying out rules for Chinese laborers, namely, limiting the private powers of plantation owners and clearly marking the line where governmental authority took over. The rules were therefore designed to "make them [plantation owners] know the limits of domestic corrections to avoid the excesses of the private faculties, and mark the boundary where the intervention of the public authority begins."[40] While the regulations seem to indicate a desire for a clear divide between public (government) and private (employer) interests, the reality was that the plantation owners were intimately linked to the governing bodies that developed these regulations.

The coolie trade to Peru occurred in two phases, 1849–56 and 1861–74, with a five-year suspension between the two. The first Chinese Law was passed in Peru in 1849, followed by subsequent decrees in 1853 and 1854 that were meant to improve conditions for Chinese. Facing strong international as well as domestic pressure, particularly in response to reports of harsh conditions in the guano mines, Peru's government suspended Chinese immigration to Peru in 1856. The suspension decree reasoned that because the "Asiatic colonists" were a "degraded race," the trade was "degenerating into a kind of Negro slave trade." The government further blamed the cramped conditions on ships for high mortality rates and for introducing immigrants with "dangerous diseases" into Peru.[41] As one newspaper, *El Peruano*, argued in March 1856, "Our population with the passage of time will perhaps come to assimilate the repugnant and unpleasant Asian race. Without providing the services we expected in favor of agriculture, we have filled ourselves with a multitude of corrupt men, who unfortunately (as it seems very probable) mix with our common folk, producing degraded offspring, whose dire consequences our grandchildren will suffer."[42] Fear of racial mixing and disease were frequently cited by Peruvian newspapers as reasons to stop importing more Chinese, but landowners were less worried about the effects of the Chinese on Peruvian society than they were about having their crops planted and harvested.

By the early 1860s, plantation owners in Peru pressured their government to reopen Chinese immigration, especially in light of their opportunity to expand cotton production given the U.S. Civil War. The new Chinese Law in 1861 passed by the Peruvian congress over the veto of President Marshal Castilla provided a little more guidance about the kind of labor to which the coolies could be compelled, namely, agricultural and domestic labor on coastal plantations; the law also gave guidelines to prevent overcrowding on ships and prevented the transfer of contracts without the consent of the Chinese.[43] Over time, government regulations in Peru curbed plantation owners' most egregious abuses.

Government intervention and control over coolies was much more elaborate in Cuba than in Peru. In part, this may have resulted from the colonial state's greater ability (compared to the relatively new and weak state in Peru) to administer labor regulations and limit the power of large landowners. In the twenty-seven years that the trade lasted (1847–74), three sets of regulations were issued in Cuba (1849, 1854, and 1860), and two new instructions amending these were also deemed necessary (1868 and 1872). With each new set of regulations, the number of articles and clauses grew in number, as did the specificity of the controlling mechanisms. The regulations, along with elaborate residency documents and census measures, were designed to help the government control the expanding and increasingly rebellious Chinese population. In addition to the new regulations, the colonial government built jails to incarcerate runaway Chinese and those who had fulfilled their contracts but had not yet been recontracted. The label used for the runaway Chinese, *cimarrón*, was the same one used for escaped African slaves. However, the new regulations also provided more protections for the Chinese laborers and limited the powers of the plantation owners.

So why would plantation owners develop rules that limited their own power and affirmed state power? The answer lies in the interest of both the state and plantation owners in reducing the risk of rebellion by the Chinese and improving productivity. Plantation owners understood that the coolies needed some protections, or at least they needed to feel that they were being protected and represented by some benign power to legitimize the labor system as a whole. Regulating the disciplinary functions of the plantation owners and protecting the rights of the Chinese helped construct hegemony for the Spanish colonial authorities and the Peruvian state. When one looks at the precise terms of these protections, it is clear that the employers' interests were privileged over those of the Chinese, but the state is still configured as a benign and protective arbiter between the Chinese and the employers. This framework was designed by state officials and plantation owners, who were often the same people, to channel Chinese complaints through legal channels rather than allowing them to explode in violent rebellion.

The regulations, like the contracts, stipulated wages, medical care, and holiday time. In Peru, newspapers criticized a contract clause that only allowed Chinese three days of vacation on Chinese New Year, arguing that Peruvian law granted all workers the right to rest on Sundays and legal holidays. Some employers even argued that providing these holidays would make Chinese workers more productive. In the middle of 1873, the government issued a decree forbidding coolies to labor on Sundays except for domestic service. A few days later, another decree adjusted the prohibition, allowing coolies to work on Sunday until 10:00 a.m. as long as they were paid eighty cents extra.[44] The debates in both Peru and Cuba over vacation days and sick leave raised the question of whether Chinese enjoyed the same protections as other workers. The fact that they developed elaborate decrees and regulations specifically for Chinese labor indicates that the Chinese were a special case.

The most detailed and extensive rules in Cuba addressed the issue of discipline. For every ten Asians, employers would have to provide a white overseer "who cares for and watches over them." The dual function of the regulations, caring for Chinese and watching over them, was present in almost every clause. The rule that most explicitly echoed slave codes was the one that gave precise instructions on how many lashes to mete out for each infraction by the laborer: "The colonist who disobeys the voice of his superior, whether it be by resisting work, or any of his obligations, will be corrected with twelve lashings; if it persists, with eighteen more, and if he still doesn't get on the path of obligation, shackles will be placed on him and he will have to sleep in the stocks." Punishments by plantation owners could last only two months; after that time the matter would have to be referred to the state authorities. In establishing these procedures, the state both empowered plantation owners to beat their laborers for disobeying them and limited the number and duration of beatings. The number of lashes increased if more than one laborer "resisted work"; if the number of laborers resisting was large local authorities would be called in to administer punishments. Attempted escape would be punished by wearing shackles for two months; if the laborer tried to escape a second time, shackles would be imposed for six months and the laborer would be forced to sleep in stocks. Anyone who helped the laborer escape was fined four *reales* a day and forced to cover the expense of capturing the escapee. These rules reproduced almost verbatim the regulations for escaped slaves—*cimarrones* and *apalencados*—that had been issued in December 1845.[45]

Blacks and Chinese and the Cañete Valley Massacre in Peru

The potential for black solidarity with the Chinese frightened state officials, but blacks and Chinese were at least as likely to attack one another as to join forces against the white elite in Cuba and Peru. The Cuban government worried about how precisely calibrated beatings and use of shackles and stocks would affect the Chinese and Africans and the relations between these two groups. Cuban regulations insisted that overseers were the only ones who could carry out the punishments and that the beatings could never occur within "sight of the blacks."[46] Why insist on hiding the disciplining of the Chinese from the "blacks?" One explanation was that it was more insulting for the Chinese to be whipped in front of a black person, and thus the government was protecting the Chinese from humiliation. Another possible reason for punishing Chinese separately from blacks is the government's fear of Chinese and black solidarity in the face of common exploitation and suffering under the white lash.

The Cuban government worked hard to manage Chinese and black tensions and to promote a hierarchy that divided one group from the other. In 1864, the Administrative Council in Cuba decided that a Chinese contract could not be sold to black people. Their reasoning was based on maintaining the racial hierarchy and thereby preserving social order.

> Although today there is no special provision that prohibits the black
> race from having superior races in its service, the political and social
> order, in harmony with nature itself, . . . repudiates the disciplinary
> dependence of superior races under the power of the inferior ones. . . .
> It has been constantly observed on the Island that if the immigration
> of Asian colonists has not yet produced all of the advantages that one
> could have hoped for, one of the most notable obstacles has been the
> constant concurrence of black bondage, looked at with repugnance
> by the Asians, who naturally resist the idea of equality.[47]

The council tautologically argued that in order to preserve political and social order, the government had to reaffirm "nature itself." Since Asians were naturally superior to blacks and inferior to whites, the government could not allow Chinese to be owned by blacks, or to be beaten in front of them. The "natural" racial hierarchy helped justify the social order, with whites on top, Asians below them, and blacks on the very bottom.

In 1881 in Peru, black and *cholo* (mestizo) peasants brutally attacked Chinese in what would become the single-worst massacre of Chinese in the Americas. The only detailed account of the massacre in the Cañete Valley was published by Peruvian historian Juan de Arona in 1891. Arona was no neutral observer. His real name was Pedro Paz Soldán y Unanue, a writer, diplomat, and the owner of a plantation where the killing occurred. Arona highlighted the barbarity of Afro-Peruvians, as well as the indigenous people and the *cholos*, all of whom he believed were incapable of becoming respectable citizens and improving Peru's economy. Instead, Arona argued for Asian immigration, believing that the Chinese had proved themselves by becoming successful merchants and storeowners.[48] Arona contended that free blacks and slaves lashed Chinese "with the same whip that so many times had macerated the meat of their own flesh." According to Arona, blacks had no pity on the Chinese, and their religious training "made them firmly believe that the Chinese were not people." For Arona, Chinese suffered double oppression, from both whites and blacks. As he put it, "The blacks in slavery did not have any other tyrants than the whites; the Chinese have the whites and the blacks."[49] It is hard to know whether Arona's description of conflict between blacks and Chinese was generally true, but the assertion that they treated each other with suspicion is corroborated by the Cañete Valley massacre.[50]

The attack occurred in the midst of the War of the Pacific (1879–83) with Chile. The Chileans recruited some of the Chinese in the Cañete Valley during their march toward Lima, a move which fed xenophobia against the Chinese, seen as unpatriotic enemies of the nation. When the Chileans left the valley, the local black and mestizo peasantry attacked the Chinese. It is unclear whether they blamed the Chinese for having sided with the Chileans or for being economic competitors. One theory posits that the conflict was rooted in class tensions and that black peasants killed Chinese merchants, not peasants, to free themselves from debt.[51] The large numbers of Chinese killed, however, indicates that this was a broader attack on Chinese, even if class resentment was the initial motivation.

In his account, Arona notes that the Peruvian newspaper *El Orden* ignored the massacre of Chinese, during which the "mob of mounted blacks and armed *cholos*" rampaged through each plantation in the valley one by one.[52] His description of the killings was graphic. The basic outlines of Arona's story were corroborated by Chilean military reports and newspaper articles as well as diplomatic correspondence. Although sources differ on the numbers killed, with numbers ranging from 500 to 1,700 (most of whom were murdered in one day), even if the lowest estimate is taken, the Cañete Valley massacre was the most devastating attack on Chinese anywhere in the Americas.[53] Arona described Chinese being dragged from their dormitories and killed with "sticks, machetes, stones, [and] knives."[54] The manner in which the Chinese were murdered and their bodies desecrated suggests that the killings were a ritualized and sexualized form of humiliation.

> The cadavers of the Chinese were strewn around the middle of the stately patio . . . which served as a Bacchanalian and cannibalesque desecration for women and boys. The same black women who had shared in the conspiracy gifted by the victims ridiculed the bodies by mutilating them and putting them in their open mouths as a mockery, forming a cigarette out of the bloody and palpitating members that they had amputated. "Leave this one for me!" shouted the black women fighting over the victims, drunk with blood like the women who had dismembered Pentheus.[55]

The mob burned down haciendas and set fire to 40,000 pounds of sugarcane. A group of sixteen Chinese returning on a boat from a shopping trip in Lima were met by a group of attackers in the middle of their journey. They were tied by their hands and feet, then dumped overboard to drown. Arona commented that the "black and the cholo hordes celebrated their agony."[56]

Although the Chinese seemed to suffer the brunt of the violence, this outbreak was directed more generally against the sugar estates. As Arona put it, "The uprising of the Cañete mob was not only directed against the Asian but also against whites, property, and civilization." A group of 1,000 Chinese barricaded themselves inside the walls of the Casa Blanca plantation and fought off assaults by the mob for four months. In the end, a Chilean military force arrived to put down the rebellion. When the Casa Blanca was opened, the Chinese who walked out looked like a "procession of ghosts, livid bogeymen, a simulacrum of men who have been disfigured by hunger, suffering, and terror." Reliable estimates indicate that at least 1,000 and perhaps as many as 1,700 Chinese died in this attack on Chinese in the Cañete Valley.[57]

Corporal Punishment

Beatings of Chinese coolies, by blacks or whites, always threatened to upset the social order and often led to revenge attacks by the Chinese. Cuban exiles and travelers to Cuba pointed to the legality of corporal punishments as a violation of the rights of free men. In 1850 the newspaper *La Verdad*, published by Cuban exiles in New York, declared its opposition to the "punishment of whipping (lashes) the colonists or laborers," arguing that no "moderately civilized government violated the rights of free men like this."[58]

Chinese laborers themselves resisted the beatings. Jacques Ampère, a French traveler in Havana in 1852, noted "that the Chinese denied receiving lashings from anybody other than a boss chosen among them who was charged with giving beatings (blows with a stick) and that they accepted these because it formed part of their tradition."[59] While we may question the existence of the "tradition" to which Ampère refers, the idea that Chinese were more willing to accept beatings from their own people suggests that being beaten by foreigners, black or white, was perceived as a greater humiliation. The U.S. journalist Richard Dana noted among the Chinese a similar resistance to beatings by foreigners: "Idolaters as they are, they have a notion of the dignity of the human body, at least as against strangers, which does not allow them to submit to the indignity of corporal chastisement. If a coolie is flogged, somebody must die; either the coolie himself, for they are fearfully given to suicide, or the perpetrator of the indignity, or some one else, according to their strange principles of vicarious punishment."[60] Numerous rebellions, suicides, and international condemnations led the Spanish to prohibit corporal punishments in new regulations issued after 1854. In spite of the legal prohibitions, testimony from travelers and the Chinese themselves suggests that the beatings continued unabated. In 1874 a British visitor to Cuba noted that although the law prohibited selling and whipping Chinese contract laborers, "the Cuban buys and flogs his Chinese slave openly and with impunity."[61]

The frequent rebellions led plantation owners in Cuba to fear the Chinese they had imported. One of the first plantation owners to import Chinese coolies, Alejandro Fusté, wrote to the Board of Development in June 1849, complaining about living in a "continuous anxiety of fear." He imagined "that in one plantation or other some misfortune would happen, [the Chinese] being very daring would join together as one ferocious mob. From the time they visited a comrade of theirs, who is said to be a doctor, they have shown more insubordination and rashness. . . . Right now there are seven in stocks, who the writer does not dare to remove to work."[62] Fusté lived in such dread of his Chinese laborers that he asked the authorities for permission to sell them to someone else. These kinds of experiences led the government to reform the regulations regarding Chinese laborers, both to eliminate abuses that might incite the Chinese to rebellion and to provide for more strict controls on their movements.

Patria Potestad, Patria Marital, *and Mixed Marriages*

In response to the frequent rebellions by Chinese and the high death rates both on the ships and in plantations, the Spanish Crown passed a set of regulations in 1854 that made the governor the "natural protector of the colonists." The Chinese agreed in their contracts to "renounce the exercise of their civil rights that are not compatible with the accomplishment of the obligations to which they have agreed." However, the government gave Chinese men control over their children and wives, while at the same time limiting their intimate relationships. Chinese were only allowed to marry with the consent of their employer; if their employer disagreed they either had to purchase their own freedom or look for another employer who could purchase them. In spite of these restrictions, Chinese men continued to exercise *patria potestad* (fatherly control) over their children and *potestad marital* (husbandly control) over their wives. Like children born to slaves, the children of Chinese women would acquire the condition of their mothers until the end of their contracts or eighteen years of age. Although these provisions gave the owner almost complete control over the Chinese, their marriages, and their offspring, the owners were not allowed to separate families.[63]

In her book *From Bondage to Contract*, Amy Dru Stanley argues that the issue of marriage was always at the center of the debate over slavery, which called into question a man's right to control his wife. The logic was that if a slave owned nothing, not even himself, then he was not in a position to enter into a contract with anyone, not even with a wife. The Louisiana Code made it clear that a slave owned nothing: "A slave is one who is in the power of the master to whom he belongs. All that a slave possesses belongs to his master; he possesses nothing of his own." Some U.S. abolitionists who condemned patriarchy nonetheless criticized slavery for undermining patriarchal rights of male slaves over their wives. Angelina Grimké, the U.S. abolitionist and women's suffragist, in her 1836 *Appeal to the Christian Women of the South*, declared that "slavery is a violation of the natural order of things." It "robs the slave of all his rights as a man: wages, wives, children."[64] Emancipation would restore the male slave's freedom to earn wages and, significantly, to rule over his wife and children as a patriarchal master. In Cuba, however, the slave code of 1842 allowed and even encouraged formal marriages among slaves, recognizing the importance of keeping such unions together. This provision can be seen as way to ameliorate slavery for men by allowing them patriarchal control within the household that they could not exercise in their work lives. Although Chinese males were granted *patria potestad* and *patria marital*, the fact that the owner had to consent to the marriage and could demand work from coolies' children severely limited Chinese patriarchal control.[65] The almost complete lack of Chinese women made this provision moot. Nevertheless, the expansion of black and Chinese men's freedom came at the expense of their spouses.

There is anecdotal evidence that Chinese men in Cuba and Peru married or had sexual relationships with white, black, mulatto, and Indian women. The extent of this intermarriage is hard to determine.[66] The *Cuba Commission Report* noted a few marriages of Chinese men to white women, mulattoes, and "negresses," but suggested that these were very few in number. One Chinese man who amassed some wealth and married a white woman twice tried to leave the island but was arrested each time.[67] A *New York Times* article pointed to the lack of Chinese women in Peru to explain the lack of Chinese families there, but it hinted at mixed marriages. "Now and then," the article contended, "he [the Chinese man] becomes enamored of the charms of some sombre-hued chola or samba, and is converted and joins the Church, so that may enter the bonds of wedlock with the dusky señorita." His conversion and marriage would apparently cancel his contract, but rather than being liberated, the article asserted, he became subjugated to his wife. As the reporter put it, the "'weaker vessel' becomes emphatically the 'better half.'" Although the article described a Chinese man as a "model husband, hardworking, affectionate, faithful and obedient," it also portrayed him as feminine and servile. The reporter thus turned the question of *patria marital* on its head, arguing that when Chinese men married black or Indian women, it was the women who ruled the household and the Chinese men who were submissive.[68] In contrast, in Mexico, Chinese men were criticized for enslaving their Mexican wives, a point that we will explore more fully in chapter 6.

The new regulations also reformed the section on discipline, omitting the articles on corporal punishment and the use of shackles but providing more detail on the obligations of laborers to follow the orders of their employers. Even though they could not be beaten, laborers could still be jailed and docked wages for a variety of infractions, including "lack of subordination," "resistance to work," escape, drunkenness, and "any kind of offense to good customs." If the laborer believed his employer was unfairly punishing him, he could appeal to the local government "protector," who would bring the case before a tribunal. The maximum fine for the employer was fixed at 100 pesos. The employer was also authorized to use force to put down a collective rebellion by laborers on his plantation. The local "delegate protector" would decide whether the gravity of the insubordination required the guilty parties to be publicly punished in front of the other laborers.[69] The reforms tried to balance out the interests of the laborers and the employers, giving the government "protectors" a role in mediating conflicts and also curbing the authority of the employers to some degree.

If the laborer gained more protection under the 1854 regulations, he did so at the expense of his freedom of movement, which the new rules severely restricted. They also implemented a documentation system that allowed the government to track Chinese not on plantations. Article 34 prohibited laborers from leaving their farms without their employer's written permission; those found without such a document would be arrested and returned to the farms at the employer's expense. Article 51 gave employers the task of teaching "the dogmas and the morals of the true religion" to their non-Catholic workers but only by using "persuasion and convincing."[70] The strict control over the intimate and work lives of the Chinese and efforts to influence their spiritual lives demonstrated the state's desire to manage and control the island's Chinese population.

Manumission, Escape, or Suicide

Chinese had two options for gaining their freedom while serving out their contracts: manumission or escape. Chinese attempted the latter frequently, which led to provisions requiring them to carry documents at all times so that their movements could be better controlled. Manumission, or purchasing one's own freedom, was an option open to African slaves and Chinese contract workers. However, plantation owners were not happy to concede this right to the Chinese. On 10 March 1852, a Chinese laborer in Matanzas named Pablo went to the local authorities with seventy pesos and tried to buy his way out of his contract, five years of which he had already served. At first Captain General Cañedo agreed that Pablo should be freed, but the master who owned the contract complained that it was unfair to deprive him of Pablo's labor given how much time and energy he had invested in his "education and discipline." Cañedo referred the matter to the Development Board and the Real Audiencia (Appeals Court). The Development Board refused to give its opinion, and local authorities decided to return Pablo to the plantation. Upon hearing the news, Pablo unsuccessfully tried to kill himself by cutting his throat with a glass bottle. The Appeals Court finally ruled on the case in terms of contract law, deciding that the primary issue was "a bilateral contract in which one of the parties obliged himself to work for a specific amount of time and the other to pay this price." The court reasoned that having agreed to work for eight years, Pablo could not evade his responsibilities. Cañedo ratified the decision on 25 October and ordered Pablo to return to work on the plantation. When he received word of the decision, Pablo hung himself.[71]

Suicide in barracoons, coolie ships, and on plantations was a desperate means for Chinese to escape bondage. The *Cuba Commission Report* contains dozens of testimonials of Chinese who witnessed suicides by coolies "by hanging on trees, by drowning, by swallowing opium, and by leaping into the sugar cauldrons."[72] As a result, Cuba earned the dubious distinction in the mid-nineteenth century of having the highest suicide rate in the world, more than twenty-two times higher than Spain's. In 1862, Chinese accounted for 173 of the 346 suicides on the island. Controlling for the population of each group, Chinese killed themselves 100 times more frequently than whites, and 14 times more frequently than African slaves. Most Chinese committed suicide by overdosing on opium or hanging themselves. There were several cases of mass suicides, including one in 1870 in which fourteen coolies killed themselves on a sugar estate, thus depriving the owner of all his remaining workers.[73]

Although suicide should not be romanticized, there is compelling evidence that observers interpreted it as a political act. In 1860, a traveler from the United States, Julia Ward Howe, commented that the Chinese propensity for suicide forced the plantation owners to improve conditions for the coolies. "So many of them emancipated themselves from hard service by voluntary death, that it became matter of necessity to lighten the weight about their necks, and to leave them that minimum of wellbeing which is necessary to keep up the love of life."[74] The Cuban abolitionist José Antonio Saco viewed Chinese suicide as a direct attack on the plantation owners, claiming that the "corrupt and perverse race" (Chinese) committed suicide as "pure vengeance" against their bosses.[75]

There can be many different interpretations of suicide, and ascertaining the intent of those who choose to kill themselves is almost impossible. Louis Pérez Jr., in his book *To Die in Cuba*, interprets the high rate of Chinese suicide in Cuba, the manner in which most suicides were carried out, and the cultural meaning of suicide in China as evidence that Chinese who killed themselves were not simply victims. As Pérez notes, "It is important to stress, again, that suicide was not necessarily a deed of hopelessness. On the contrary, under certain circumstances it was undertaken as an affirmation of hope. It could suggest agency, a willingness to act, to take one last measure in the expectations that the act of suicide as symbol or as solution offered a response to the problem of living."[76] Colonial authorities often blamed the "little attachment to life and addiction to opium" for the high rate of suicide among the Chinese.[77] However, missionaries tried to understand suicide in its cultural context, noting that those who were seen as the cause of suicide were held legally liable in China. In 1860, one missionary observed, "The conduct of a man who destroys his own life, to avenge himself on an enemy whom he has no other way of reaching, is regarded as heroic and magnanimous."[78] Therefore, Chinese coolies may have seen their suicide as an act of vengeance and retribution against their masters. The fact that Cubans like José Antonio Saco and other travelers to Cuba also interpreted Chinese suicides as acts of revenge and attacks on plantation owners and that there were so many collective suicides lends credence to the notion that these suicides were sometimes political acts.[79]

In Peru, there were similar reports of large numbers of coolies throwing themselves off cliffs on the Chincha Islands. One *New York Times* reporter, describing the backbreaking mining of guano on the dusty and hot islands, wrote that it was no "wonder that numbers of these unfortunate people should rush to the precipices, and seek refuge in a watery grave from the torments of that terrestrial hell which their fellow men have prepared for them."[80] Whether as revenge against their bosses or to escape from bondage, Chinese suicide proved an effective weapon in the struggle for liberation. The fact that so many Chinese coolies committed suicide highlights their desperate situation. With few opportunities to reshape their lives, suicide provided a counterweight to employers, who were forced to consider whether overwork and brutal treatment of their laborers would lead to loss of their investment. Ultimately, the suicides, widely publicized by traveler accounts, newspapers, and the Chinese commissions sent to Cuba and Peru, helped lead to the termination of the coolie system in 1874.

The outcome of Pablo's case highlighted the absurdity of a situation in which "free laborers" had even less ability to purchase their freedom than slaves. The 1854 regulations in Cuba addressed this anomaly, including a new provision for manumission. Article 28 allowed Chinese to purchase their own freedom by paying the owner the cost of his contract, any other expenses incurred, as well as the cost to replace him with another laborer. Given the difficulties Chinese encountered earning enough money to buy their freedom, this was an infrequently exercised option, but even this right was restricted to nonharvest periods.[81] In spite of these obstacles, Chinese used this provision to purchase their freedom when they could. According to the 1872 census 24 percent of the 58,400 Chinese in Cuba were free; the rest were in jail or still under contract. In that same year, 38 percent of Africans were free.[82] As one Chinese coolie put it bluntly, "Niggers bad enough in Cuba, but China-man worse. Some chance nigger be free, but none for Chinaman."[83]

In spite of the small numbers of free Chinese, government authorities worried about an increasing population of Chinese not under the control of anyone else. The 1860 regulations explicitly forced laborers to either pay for their return to China or sign a new contract upon completion of their eight-year indenture. If the Chinese did not contract themselves within two months of the end of their previous indenture, the government would force them to work on public projects until such a time as they had earned enough money to pay for passage off the island.[84] In 1872 the government clarified that Chinese who had finished their contracts would be placed in municipal jails while awaiting contracting or to earn enough money to pay for their return passage. The goal was to "prevent the evils of this mass of people, and . . . to make these workers useful at the same time in agriculture and indus-try."[85] Given that few Chinese were able to pay for their return, this provi-sion condemned most Chinese to a permanent state of indenture. In 1872, for example, only 134 Chinese obtained their passports to leave the island. The *Boletín de Colonización*, a Cuban bimonthly magazine published by the De-velopment Board, argued that this low number proved that the vast majority of Chinese voluntarily chose to renew their contracts.[86] Another, more likely explanation is that very few Chinese could gather the resources necessary to buy their freedom and obtain a passport. The Chinese had for all intents and purposes contracted their lives away.

Seeing Like a Census

Beyond regulating contracts, the state employed many mechanisms to re-strict the mobility of Chinese migrants once they reached Cuba. These new technologies allowed the state to make the contract labor population legible as well as to keep the laborers as perpetual aliens. When high modernist states narrow their focus and attempt to capture complex phenomena in one synoptic view, as is done in a census, they produce an abstract view of the world.[87] The census, for example, helps a government design its immi-gration policy to provide a steady supply of cheap labor. While gathering this information may be harmless (though it often requires coercion), the policies that may be implemented based on this information can be dev-astating for the people being abstracted.[88] In the Cuban case, the colonial government's desire to track and count the contract laborers was motivated by the need to maintain enough laborers on hand to cut sugarcane and run the mills. Government leaders were also worried about the possibilities for political upheaval if large numbers of Chinese were able to escape the control of their employers and work freely. Finally, the government kept tabs on the racial makeup of the island to try to prevent being overwhelmed by a nonwhite population. The census was one of the tools to manage and limit Chinese mobility.

In the government's ideal world, every Chinese laborer would be individually tracked from the time he left China until he died. In 1854, the government ordered an annual survey of the Chinese on the island with name, age, sex, marriage status, time of contract, and information about their employers. This data was then collated and summarized according to a range of factors.[89] It was also expressly forbidden for the Chinese to be moved from their place of residence without informing the government, and the government had to be notified within twenty-four hours of the completion of their contacts.[90] The point of the census was not only to track individuals but also to be able to view the population as an aggregate and divide it according to categories that would help the government control the labor supply and maintain political order.

The desire to manage the labor supply from a strictly utilitarian viewpoint led to repeated demands by the Colonization Board and other government officials that a certain percentage of Chinese women be imported to ensure reproduction of the labor force and to prevent "immorality."[91] The "immorality" referred to here may have meant homosexuality among the Chinese or racial mixing between Chinese men and non-Chinese women in Cuba.[92] The Cuban government attempted but failed to recruit Chinese women. One Spanish government report suggests that it was difficult to find Chinese women willing to emigrate and that the ones who were willing were unlikely to settle down and form families. That the policies to bring Chinese women to Cuba generally failed and only a handful of Chinese women arrived illustrates the limitations of the colonial government's power to control its labor population rather than a conscious policy of exclusion.[93] Cuban authorities also advocated reproduction for African slaves, even proposing on one occasion that slave owners be given prizes for having the highest rate of slave procreation.[94] The desire to increase the population of Chinese women and to push African slave procreation demonstrates the government's efforts to control the most intimate bodily functions of bonded laborers.

The 1868 regulations expanded the kinds of information gathered for the census of the Chinese and set forth a more aggressive procedure for surveying Chinese not under contract or in prison. The preamble to this legislation suggested that the new rules were necessary because the 1860 decree had been abused, and the government desired "the establishment of perfect order in all matters connected with Asian immigration."[95] Instead of only surveying the Chinese under contract, the new census ordered tables to be established for deserters, prisoners, and free Chinese. While the information for most of these could be obtained from employers or jail administrators, the counting and inspection of domiciled or free Chinese required a door-to-door survey, thus opening the way for direct intervention into their lives. Article 16 of these new regulations called for an officer to visit the houses of free Chinese, "personally inspect them, and call for the production of their Letters of Domicile and Licenses." The officers were then to take these documents for verification, and if valid they were to be returned to the Chinese sealed and stamped "Registered." If the Chinese presented licenses that had been issued to someone else, they were to be arrested. It appears as if this census was not carried out, at least until 1872, when a new decree called for its preparation.[96] Onerous as the official procedures were, the *Cuba Commission Report* suggests that the real situation was far worse, with officials charging exorbitant prices for licenses and inspectors simply seizing or destroying identity documents to force the Chinese to spend more money acquiring new papers.[97] The Cuban procedures for identifying and tracking Chinese foreshadowed the regulations that would be implemented in the United States in the 1890s to enforce Chinese exclusion laws.

After the outbreak of an independence movement on the island in 1868, colonial authorities were concerned with tracking and counting those who may have joined the rebels or could potentially support them. The change in the categories of the census immediately made free Chinese vulnerable to regular inspections by state authorities, who could incarcerate them if not satisfied with the authenticity of their papers. Administering the census was not a neutral task of counting the population but an exercise of state power to abstract and categorize the Chinese population. The fact that the census also suggested measures for tracking the movements of Chinese after the census was completed and for dealing with deserters indicates that the census was a mechanism of surveillance more than anything else. In 1873 new legislation was issued requiring that Chinese deaths be reported to the authorities and the licenses and contracts returned for cancellation.[98] The colonial government hoped it could track and regulate the movements of every Chinese laborer from the time he signed a contract in China to the moment he died in Cuba. All of these administrative procedures were meant to keep the Chinese separate from the rest of Cuban society, to keep them as aliens in the nation.

Tracking Coolies in Peru

By 1873 the Peruvian government followed Cuba's lead, seeking to tighten controls on plantation owners, further regulate coolie labor, and keep track of coolies in the country. The first two decrees in June and July 1873 set limits for work on Sundays and national holidays and established the length of the normal workday. The third decree in October established a new agency in the Prefecture of Callao called the Registry of Contracted Asiatics. This registry was almost identical to the census ordered in Cuba the previous year. The prefect in Callao was named chief officer of the registry. Under him were two Chinese invested with police powers and authorized to act as interpreters. Their job was to make sure that the contracts with the Chinese were being faithfully carried out, and to register and track each coolie from the moment he arrived in Peru until his death. The decree therefore interposed the state between the coolie and the employer. If a coolie was going to be transferred to a different plantation, the original contract would have to be remitted to a subprefect, along with the information about the new employer. If a coolie was moved to a different province, the subprefect of that province would have to be notified and the coolie registered there. The master was also required to notify the subprefect if the coolie escaped, when his contract ended, and when he died. When a coolie completed his contract, he could present himself at the Registry Section in Callao to be returned to China at the state's expense. To ensure enforcement of these new rules, one of the articles declared that if any of the provisions were not complied with, the coolie would be considered free.[99]

In spite of the government's efforts to reform the coolie trade, most plantation owners simply refused to comply with the decrees. Six months after the October decree was issued, Toribio Raygada, head of the Registry Section in Callao, reported, "little has been done by the private individuals who have Asiatic colonists in their service." The frustrated Raygada complained that only 1,236 colonists had been registered, a fraction of the number in the country, and that subprefects in only two provinces had submitted their registry lists.[100] Plantation owners must have been aware that only two months after the October decree, the governor in Macao had issued an edict ending the coolie trade from that port. Instead of worrying about registering their coolies, plantation owners were more concerned with the bigger question of who would continue to supply labor for their operations.

In 1876, just two years after the last coolies arrived in Peru, the government's annual *Memoria* described the agricultural sector as devastated by a lack of labor. It warned of impending doom when the remaining coolies fulfilled their contracts. As the report put it, "The exploitation of many large estates is reduced today for this reason to half, or perhaps even less, of what their plantings and machines should produce." The ending of the coolie trade in Peru had an immediate impact on plantations, which had depended on thousands of new Chinese laborers coming in each year. More worrying for the government and plantation owners was that the contracts for coolies in the country were coming to an end. The report declared that the end of the contact labor system would bring "ruin of not only agriculturalists but of the whole country."[101]

The government feared not only the lack of Chinese labor to work on plantations but also the dangers posed by a growing number of liberated Chinese who freely roamed city streets. According to the *Memoria*, "Thousands of Chinese swarm the towns giving themselves over to vagrancy and their entourage of forced vices, damaging themselves and the towns." The government called for 20,000 new workers for the agricultural sector, but without the influx of new coolies they had to develop novel ways to coerce Chinese laborers. Like the authors of U.S. postemancipation laws, they recommended curbs on "laziness and vagrancy" that would force Chinese to work on plantations after their contracts had expired.[102]

"What Constitutes a Free and Voluntary Emigrant?"

The U.S., Canadian, and Mexican governments did not manage and finance the recruitment of Chinese coolie labor as their Cuban and Peruvian counterparts had, but Chinese laborers were recruited under private contracts and various forms of apprenticeship arrangements that reproduced many of the features of coolie contracts. Before Congress outlawed U.S. participation in the coolie trade in 1862, planters in Louisiana imported Chinese coolies from Cuba. During and after the Civil War, Chinese laborers became even more important as replacements for emancipated slaves. On one vast Louisiana sugar plantation that had been decimated after its slaves had rebelled and left en masse in 1862, the new Boston-based owners hired 140 Chinese migrant laborers.[103] In 1867 the U.S. consul in Havana reported that a shipment of 80 coolies had left on a French steamer to work on plantations in Louisiana. In one year, an estimated 2,000 coolies left Cuba for Louisiana. The traffic had become so regular that a direct steamship line had been established from Matanzas in Cuba to New Orleans.[104] Historian Moon Ho-Jung argues that after the Civil War, it was the free labor advocates and not the proslavery ideologues who pushed for government-sponsored "apprenticeship" and "immigration" of Chinese labor to help maintain the plantation economy in the South without the labor of African slaves.[105]

Even if it was not government-sponsored, the importation of Chinese laborers to the U.S. South was more than a scattershot attempt by a few entrepreneurial planters. In July 1869 a convention with 500 delegates from all over the South came to Memphis to jumpstart recruitment of Chinese laborers. Cornelius Koopmanschap, a Dutch-born recruiter of Chinese laborers, assured the gathering that he could provide thousands of workers on contracts of two to five years and for wages of eight to twelve dollars a month. The delegates at the convention had an almost religious faith that the Chinese were the answer to their Reconstruction-era labor problems. In the euphoria of the meeting, they organized the Mississippi Valley Immigration Labor Company, with a capitalization of $1 million. The company's goal was to bring "the largest number of Chinese agricultural laborers in the shortest possible time, "while at the same time respecting laborers' rights and all local and federal laws."[106]

The northern press, including *Harper's Weekly* and the *New York Evening Post*, condemned the Memphis proposal, arguing that it violated the 1862 law prohibiting the importation of coolies. This debate raised once again the issue of just who was a coolie. The proponents of Chinese immigration argued that the recently signed Burlingame Treaty guaranteed the free migration of Chinese, but opponents noted that the treaty specifically demanded that only Chinese who gave their "free and voluntary consent" would be allowed into the United States. The debate centered on the question of what constituted "free and voluntary consent." For those who cited the 1862 prohibition on coolie importation, the existence of the contract was a sign of coercion, while for others the contract was itself proof of consent. It is important to remember that the quintessential coolie trade in Cuba and Peru was also based on the idea that Chinese laborers were entering into free and voluntary contracts. Spanish and Portuguese officials were supposed to certify that all Chinese coolies signed contracts of their own free will and without any coercion. In spite of attempts by the proponents of Chinese importation to distinguish their scheme from the coolie trade in Cuba and Peru, the bad reputation coolie labor had earned in those countries undermined political support for the Mississippi Valley Immigration Labor Company. In November 1860, the Tennessee legislature voted to prohibit the importation of Chinese into the state, but Koopmanschap and other promoters simply moved their operations to Louisiana, where they found a more amenable climate for their labor importation scheme.[107]

The issue of what constituted a free immigrant versus a coerced contract laborer finally came before a U.S. government official when George W. Gift, one of the aspiring recruiters at the Memphis convention, asked the U.S. consul in Hong Kong to certify that the Chinese he intended to bring to Louisiana were in fact free and voluntary immigrants. Consul C. N. Goulding put the question to the U.S. secretary of state: "What constitutes a free and voluntary emigrant?" Two months later, the assistant secretary of state replied that a contract was compatible with the notion of a free and voluntary emigrant, "if the contract is not vitiated by force or fraud." The assistant secretary of state offered no further instructions on how to make this determination, but five months later the State Department ruled that importation of any Chinese from Cuba would violate federal law. Gift and other recruiters managed to send a few shiploads of several hundred Chinese to New Orleans, after getting Consul Goulding's certification, but by June 1870 the British shut down the trade from Hong Kong to non-British destinations after several well-publicized coolie ship mutinies.[108] Although most contract labor experiments in the United States happened in the South, in September 1870 the *New York Times* reported the arrival of 150 of 500 "coolies" supplied by Koopmanschap to the builder of the Midland Railroad in New Jersey. The coolies were under five-year contracts and received nine dollars per month. Only 2 of 150 of them spoke English, and they all "dressed in the Chinese costume, with wooden shoes, loose trowsers [*sic*], blue blouses and broad hats."[109] In addition to the international and domestic pressures against Chinese contract labor, Chinese laborers themselves frequently rebelled, refused to do work not stipulated in the contract, or simply walked off the job. Although the U.S. recruiters managed to import Chinese contract laborers, international pressure to end the trade together with Chinese labor resistance ultimately undermined their efforts. Faced with such resistance, Southern planters turned to sharecropping agreements rather than direct payment of wages to contract laborers.[110]

Importing Chinese contract laborers into Mexico and Canada did not require the legal maneuvering that it did in the United States. In the first decade of the twentieth century, the China Commercial Company and the

Eng Hock Fong Company each brought in a ship of 200–700 Chinese every month to Salina Cruz, a port on the southern Pacific coast of Mexico. The Chinese had signed contracts to work on plantations or in mines, but 75 percent of them reportedly jumped their contracts within two months.[111] The labor conditions may have been onerous, but unlike in Cuba and Peru, the Chinese could easily escape to another place in Mexico or cross the border into the United States. Contracts for Chinese laborers were legal in Canada, where Chinese were required to have offers of employment to be able to immigrate. The issue was not really contract labor versus free labor but rather how to guarantee that slavery would not be reintroduced under a new guise. The term *coolie* was synonymous with slave-like labor conditions, and therefore changing the name was one way to evade the question of labor conditions. The free and voluntary immigrant was seen as beneficial to the economy and the nation, while the degraded coolie was viewed as a threat and a step backward. After the end of the official coolie trade in 1874, Chinese laborers throughout the Americas were still constructed as aliens, and they continued to be called coolies in the popular press and by politicians. It was their alien status that prepared the way for Chinese laborers to be excluded and expelled from countries that had just a few years earlier recruited them in the thousands to do hard labor. Just a few years after the coolie trade ended, a new form of exclusion emerged, that of the illegal alien.

Conclusion

The title of this chapter, "Contracting Freedom," refers to the two different and contradictory meanings of *contracting*. Chinese signing of contracts was supposed to insure their freedom, but those very agreements contracted, as in shrunk, their freedom. Rather than liberating workers, contracts were tools used to continue bondage in the postslavery era. The increasingly complex and detailed regulations for contract laborers in Cuba and Peru provided some protections for Chinese and curbed abuses by plantation owners, but such mechanisms merely transferred the power to punish, incarcerate, and force Chinese to work from employers to state authorities. The census, residency documents, and other papers became bureaucratic means of state control meant to be more efficient and effective than shackles and whips. These new technologies of state power would be employed throughout the Americas in the late nineteenth century to regulate entry and keep track of immigrants inside a country. These techniques of state power kept Chinese as aliens far beyond the end of the coolie trade.

Chinese coolies were key in the transitional moment from slavery to free labor. However, Chinese contract labor, touted by abolitionists as the answer to labor shortages, looked and felt too much like African slavery. International press reports, travelers' accounts, and the 1874 *Cuba Commission Report* exposed the dreadful conditions on the coolie ships and the auction blocks, where coolies were sold like slaves, and it provided the evidence that the Chinese were free laborers in name only. The coolie trade ended officially in 1874, but the end of the coolie period, like the end of slavery, did not end bondage for laborers.

By the close of the nineteenth century, the Chinese laborer had become an immigrant and a free laborer, but he was not just any kind of immigrant. The legal and social constructs that isolated and discriminated against Chinese workers continued beyond the coolie period, as new laws and methods of surveillance targeted the Chinese. Public health, housing, labor, antimiscegenation, naturalization, and immigration laws all worked to keep Chinese as perpetual aliens at the same time as they became voluntary and free immigrants. The press and government officials often referred to Chinese laborers as coolies well into the twentieth century because the image of the easily exploitable Chinese laborer had become so ingrained in popular consciousness that the two were often seen as synonymous. This slip revealed the continuities that linked mid-nineteenth-century Chinese coolies to twentieth-century Chinese immigrants, and slavery to free labor.

The distinction between coolie and immigrant labor was also a way for certain countries (the United States, Canada, Mexico, and Britain) to distinguish themselves from other countries (Cuba, Peru, and Spain). Condemning coolie labor in other places bolstered the sense that one's own country was modern and enlightened, and the degree to which it had moved beyond slavery. In 1877, the British Reverend Williamson published *Criticism of the Cuba Report*, a bilingual pamphlet in English and Chinese in which he worried that the critique of coolie labor in Cuba would tarnish other countries that employed Asian labor. Williamson's point was that Britain, the United States, and Holland had been enlightened, abolishing slavery and providing food aid to starving Indians, in contrast to the Spanish in Cuba, who enslaved and brutalized Africans and Chinese.[112] However, just as the coolie trade was ending for Cuba and Peru, new immigrant laws began to be developed in other parts of the Americas, a movement led by U.S. legislators, who perpetuated and deepened the idea of Chinese as permanent outsiders and aliens.

PART 2

Clandestine Crossings and the Production of Illegal Aliens, 1882–1900

CHAPTER 3

The Rights of Man and of the Citizen, 1882–1900

All men have the right of entering and leaving the Republic, of traveling
through its territory, and of changing their residence without the necessity of
letters of security, passports, *salvo-conducto*, or other similar requisite.
—Article 11, Mexican Constitution of 1857

By reason of its natural liberty it is for each Nation to decide
whether it is or is not in a position to receive an alien.
—Emmerich de Vattel, *The Law of Nations*, 1758

The Declaration of the Rights of Man and of the Citizen during the French
Revolution in 1789 held certain "natural" rights to be universal across time
and place. The declaration, however, also recognized that national citizenship was the mechanism through which to guarantee such rights. The ten-
sion between the universal inalienable rights of man and the rights of citizens
came to the forefront in the late nineteenth century as nation-states began to
restrict the rights of aliens. The question of whether aliens enjoyed universal rights of mobility was debated in the Americas. The United States stood
at one end of the spectrum, enacting the most draconian migration restrictions in the hemisphere, while Mexico was at the other end, defending the
absolute right of migrants to travel through its territory. By the early twentieth century, all countries in the Americas were increasing restrictions on
migration in general and against Asians in particular. The rights of citizens
eclipsed the rights of man, a trend that would continue into the twenty-first
century around the globe.

The modern nation-state was the form through which liberal freedom was
supposed to be made real. The nation-state, after all, is the guarantor of individual rights and civil liberties. The political theorist Hannah Arendt understood that the "right to have rights" depended on citizenship in a particular
nation; she understood that the universal rights of man could not be guaranteed in any meaningful way outside of national belonging.[1] The division

of the world's political map into nation-states, each with its brightly colored flag, gives a sense of equality to a deeply unequal world. Everyone is ostensibly protected by some nation-state, unless one is a pirate and remains literally an outlaw or is a stateless refugee. Almost all emigrants from China in the mid-nineteenth century were de facto stateless because the Qing government did not officially recognize the right to emigrate and was itself besieged by foreign and domestic enemies. Even if it had wanted to, the Qing government could scarcely protect its subjects if they chose to leave China. Despite the prohibition on emigration, the Qing rulers began convening treaties with various countries—Britain in 1842, the United States in 1868, Spain in 1877, Mexico and Peru in 1899—to protect Qing subjects abroad and to try to regulate the coolie trade. In 1893, the official ban on emigration from China was rescinded, and in 1909 all children born to Chinese fathers (or mothers, if paternity was unknown) were recognized as Chinese nationals, a measure designed to tie overseas Chinese to the homeland.[2] Without a robust diplomatic corps abroad, however, Chinese representation of emigrants remained weak through the nineteenth century and into the early twentieth. As quasi-stateless people, Chinese migrants did not enjoy the right to have rights.

The rights of man were supposed to be universal, but defending some men's rights often meant taking rights away from other men. In the United States, the 1882 Chinese Exclusion Act was designed to protect the rights of white working-class men who felt threatened by economic and sexual competition from Chinese workers. The legislation sought to keep Chinese laborers out and to reduce the existing Chinese population. At stake was not merely the economic well-being of the white working class but also the racial integrity of the nation itself. As the sociologist R. D. McKenzie of the University of Washington wrote in 1927, "The exclusion movement is an index of the rising tide of national and racial consciousness. The recent development of communication has not only made for a greater fluidity of peoples of the world, but has also given rise to a highly sensitized spirit of nationalism, everywhere reflected in the modern tendency of nations to erect barriers to regulate the international movements of commodities and peoples."[3] By the mid-1920s, the rising tide of national and racial consciousness led to similar kinds of immigration policies toward Chinese, but in the late nineteenth century there were significant differences across the Americas. While in 1882 the United States declared the most stringent exclusion of a particular racial and national group to have ever existed in the world, the neighboring countries of Mexico and Cuba continued to receive unrestricted Chinese immigration. Cuba stopped recruiting Chinese contract labor in 1874, but it was not until 1902 that Chinese laborers were prohibited from the island, when the U.S. military issued Order 155.[4] In Peru, Chinese continued to trickle in after 1874, but in 1909 the government signed the Porras-Wu Protocol, in which China agreed to voluntarily restrict emigration.[5] When the provincial government in British Columbia tried to stop Chinese immigration in the late 1870s, Canada's federal government frustrated these efforts. By 1885, however, Ottawa gave in to pressure and passed restrictionist legislation designed to slow and regulate Chinese immigration. Meanwhile, in the late nineteenth century, Mexico began a period of recruiting Chinese laborers, both under specific contracts and as free workers. For the Porfirian government, permitting unrestricted Chinese migration upheld one of the fundamental rights of man.

For a long time, histories of the Chinese in the Americas have been written as part of national narratives, even when these histories reveal strong connections among Chinese across the Americas. In the past decade, scholars have begun to examine the circular networks of migrants between China and various countries in the Americas, and to focus on Chinese cross-border movements in the U.S.-Mexico and U.S.-Canadian borderlands.[6] My book continues this trajectory, but rather than focus on a particular binational region or country, my frame is hemispheric and global.[7] I follow Chinese migrants across the oceans to multiple sites in the Americas and continue to track them as they circulate within the Americas and back and forth to China. From this hemispheric perspective, a web of Chinese migrant pathways comes into focus rather than a line from point A in China to point B in the Americas.[8]

"All Men Have the Right of Entering and Leaving the Republic"

The fact that neighboring countries sharing thousands of miles of land and sea borders had such different immigration policies led to conflict. Although each country was ostensibly able to assert its sovereignty over its territory, in reality the economic and immigration policies of one country directly impacted the others. In an increasingly interrelated world, defending national sovereignty required international cooperation as well as more robust policing power to guard the boundaries of the nation. Ever since the 1882 exclusion act, Mexico and Canada were used as backdoor entryways by Chinese. In 1888, U.S. congressional representatives began to clamor for a treaty with Britain and Mexico to enlist their help in preventing Chinese from crossing the northern and southern borders into the United States. In response, the

Mexican ambassador to the United States, Matías Romero, cited a clause in Mexico's 1857 Constitution to explain why his government would not enter into such a treaty: "All men have the right of entering and leaving the Republic, of traveling through its territory, and of changing their residence without the necessity of letters of security, passports, *salvo-conducto*, or other similar requisite." The next sentence of Article 11 reserved the right of judicial and administrative review in criminal and civil cases, but the right of immigration and emigration, and transit, was absolute.[9]

The Mexican response was striking, not just in its rebuff of a friendly neighbor but also for heralding a radical principle enshrined in the 1857 Mexican Constitution: the absolute freedom of movement into, through, and out of the country regardless of race or nationality. In a detailed interpretation of the Mexican Constitution, the lawyer Y. L. Vallarta laid out the legal reasoning for not helping the United States prevent Chinese entry from Mexico. In addition to citing Article 11, which clearly prevented the Mexican government from obstructing the passage of people through its territory, Vallarta referred back to the discussions at the constitutional convention in 1856 to show that the intent of the framers was to prevent any limitation on the rights of free movement. Vallarta cited deputy Zarco's argument in the constitutional debates that Article 11 was a true right of man and "not a police question; because it deals with the right to transit freely that is granted to as many men as arrive in Mexico."[10] Vallarta indicated that the framers of the constitution wanted to allow all races and nationalities into their country, and therefore, he argued, "it would be perfectly unconstitutional to expel the Jew from their domains as the Tsar of Russia is doing today, and for the same reason we cannot pass the same laws as the North Americans have against the Chinese. Our Constitution respects the rights of man as much in a Chinese as in a Jew, a European or an Asian."[11] By way of comparison, Vallarta was showing that Mexico guaranteed the rights of man more fairly and universally than either Russia or the United States. Vallarta's radical defense of the rights of man was tempered only by the right of a nation to close its doors to foreign criminals and vagrants, and to expel them if necessary. However, even in these cases, Vallarta argued, it had to be individual acts by specific foreigners that resulted in exclusion and not a blanket prohibition against an entire race or nationality.[12]

Vallarta's argument rested on a long-standing principle of unrestricted rights to travel and sojourn stretching back to the Spaniard Francisco de Vitoria, who in 1539 articulated the most expansive notion of the right to migrate freely.[13] As Europeans became more concerned with regulating international relations, they gave more weight to national sovereignty and less to the right of the foreign traveler. Samuel Pufendorf explained in 1688 that anyone passing into another's territory would be understood to have given up "his natural liberty, and to have subjected himself to the sovereignty of that state." States thus had a right to exclude foreigners who "were not upright, or were not able to pay for their own lodging."[14] In 1758 the Swiss jurist Emmerich de Vattel advocated a middle path between the right of states to exclude foreigners and the absolute right of free mobility. Vattel argued that "by reason of its natural liberty it is for each Nation to decide whether it is or is not in a position to receive an alien." Vattel also recognized that a state's right to exclude was limited and should not be abused.[15] Therefore, by the mid-eighteenth century, European thinkers tried to balance the rights of free migration with the rights of a state to control migration. The justification for exclusion, however, was open for interpretation, and, increasingly in the late nineteenth and twentieth centuries, the rights of the state to exclude trumped the rights of individuals to migrate. In the late nineteenth century, the United States stood at the exclusionist side of this spectrum, while Mexico was at the other extreme. Peru, Cuba, and Canada lay somewhere in between, neither prohibiting nor encouraging Chinese immigration.

U.S. Exclusion of Chinese Labor

Up until the late nineteenth century, the United States generally encouraged immigration and had few laws regulating entry into the country. The 1798 Alien and Sedition Acts empowered the government to deport alien enemies of the state, but this was less an immigration policy than an effort to expel foreign enemies. Beyond that the federal government only indirectly regulated immigration by requiring ships to deliver passenger lists and insuring that ship passengers had a modicum of comfort and safety. Aristide Zolberg shows how most early efforts at regulating immigration happened at the state level and did not distinguish between aliens, that is, noncitizens, and people from other states within the United States. As early as 1794, Massachusetts passed a pauper removal law based on English poor laws that allowed the state to "remove or convey by land or water" immigrants or people from other states who had become paupers. Although the law did not distinguish explicitly between citizens and aliens, provisions of the law made it clear that it was, at least in part, an effort to track and control immigrants in the state.[16] In the mid-nineteenth century, the commonwealth government of Massachusetts, responding to the mass migration spurred on by the Irish famine, began to centralize its efforts to prevent poor Irish immigrants from entering the country.[17] The federal government also enacted legislation that indirectly affected the kind of immigrants who arrived on U.S. shores. The 1819 Passenger Act, for example, mandated a minimum amount of space per passenger and other safety guidelines for ship passengers, thereby protecting the rights of immigrants but also making it uneconomical to transport paupers. The various state regulations, together with the federal passenger acts, Zolberg argues, "created a rudimentary system of 'remote control' whereby the United States sought to select immigrants by projecting its boundaries into the source countries."[18]

In 1862, Congress passed an Anti-Coolie Act that prohibited U.S. citizens and foreigners residing in the United States from participating in the Chinese coolie trade and importing Chinese subjects "known as 'coolies' to be held to service or labor." Nonetheless, the right of "free and voluntary immigration of any Chinese subject" was explicitly protected.[19] Historian Moon-Ho Jung argues that the 1862 anticoolie statute was simultaneously the last slave-trade law and the first immigration law. As Jung writes, "coolies bridged the legal and cultural gap between the national exclusion of slaves and immigrants, liminal subjects that were neither yet both in this age of emancipation."[20] In 1875, Congress passed the Page Law forbidding the entry of involuntary Chinese, Japanese, and other "Oriental" laborers, particularly women prostitutes.[21] The Page Law was part of a longer effort to prevent Chinese "coolie" or contract labor in the United States that stretched back to debates over slavery in the mid-nineteenth century. State efforts to control paupers and federal laws to limit Asian migration developed over the course of the nineteenth century into a more robust federal immigration policy.[22]

The drumbeat of anti-Chinese sentiment and discriminatory legislation in California foreshadowed national immigration policy. In 1878, the federal circuit court in San Francisco ruled that Chinese were not eligible for naturalization because they were of the "Mongolian race" and were not white. The court concluded that the naturalization statute only referred to "a free white person" or a person of "African descent" and therefore did not include Asians. In 1879, the new California constitution denied Chinese the right to vote in state elections, authorized towns to remove Chinese or establish ghettoes, and empowered the state to kick Chinese out of California. Although most of California's discriminatory laws were struck down in federal courts for violating the U.S. Constitution's equal protection clause of the Fourteenth Amendment and the provisions of the Burlingame Treaty with China (1868), the effort to reduce the size of the Chinese population and strip it of power continued unabated.[23] Anti-Asian court decisions and legislation both at the state and federal level set the groundwork for the eventual passage of the Chinese Exclusion Act in 1882.

In the exclusion debates, congressmen pointed to what they considered to be the inferior racial status of the Chinese, their economic competition with white laborers, and the detrimental effect that Chinese would have on the white American family. Senator John F. Miller of California compared Chinese to "machines" and warned that if forced to compete with thrifty Chinese workers, white men and their families would be reduced to "misery, want, self-denial, ignorance and dumb slavery." Miller also asserted that white women would be forced outside the home and children taken from school, all to work to keep up with the Chinese laborer.[24] Restriction of Chinese immigration in 1882 was cast, just like the 1862 prohibition on "coolie labor," as a measure to end slavery and promote freedom for white workers. Although the exclusion act was based on racist ideas about the Chinese, it only applied to laborers. Chinese diplomats, merchants, and students were exempt from the prohibitions, although they often also faced informal discrimination for being Chinese.

Chinese exclusion was opposed by free trade merchants, who feared its impact on trade with China, and committed liberals, who believed in free migration. Antirestrictionists in congress, representing northeastern commercial and religious interests, argued that over time Chinese laborers would demand higher wages and that white workers would be pushed up the labor ladder as Chinese occupied the lower rungs. Some senators worried that Chinese exclusion would dampen commerce between China and the United States and strain diplomatic relations. Senator George Frisbie Hoar of Massachusetts, who led the antirestrictionists, argued that the Chinese Exclusion Act moved away from the tradition of liberal immigration policy and the principles of equality enshrined in the Declaration of Independence. None of these antirestrictionist arguments swayed Congress, and in 1882 the act passed by a wide margin, becoming the first immigration law to ban immigrants based on their race and nationality as well as their class status.

Anti-Chinese activists throughout the Americas had strikingly similar reasons for opposing Chinese immigration, including protecting national workers from economic competition, defending the nation against dangerous racial mixing, and rescuing women and children from diseased and lecherous Chinese men. Although immigration policies were national, they were created in a transnational environment. In 1884, a royal commission charged with investigating Chinese immigration in Canada conducted field research in Portland and San Francisco because, its members argued, the experiences there were "analogous to those existing in British Columbia."[25] In 1909, Senator William Dillingham's U.S. immigration commission studied the situation in Canada, comparing the legislation there and in the United States. Anti-Chinese immigration policies in various countries in the Americas developed in relationship to one another. Given U.S. domination of the hemisphere, it is not surprising that eventually all countries followed the U.S. lead in excluding Chinese.

Canada's Act to Restrict and Regulate Chinese Immigration

Although Canada followed the same trajectory as the United States regarding Chinese immigration, the Dominion government opted for restriction rather than outright prohibition of Chinese laborers in the 1880s. As a result of this policy, Chinese numbers steadily increased at a time when the U.S. Chinese population declined. In 1858 Chinese began arriving in large numbers in British Columbia, attracted from San Francisco and China by a gold rush in the Fraser Valley. Most Chinese worked in canneries or coal mining, and later in building railroads. As in California, the local white population reacted to these newcomers with hostility. In March 1859, the first colonial newspaper in British Columbia, the *Gazette*, expressed the racist antipathy toward the Chinese: "They are with few exceptions, not desirable as permanent settlers in a country peopled by the Caucasian race and governed by civilized enactments."[26] One of the commissioners in Victoria who witnessed the "Mongolian invasion" in the 1850s emphasized that they could never assimilate: "The great objection to a large influx of Chinamen, or of any other extremely foreign element, is that it is an indigestible mass in the midst of a society with which it can never amalgamate in a political and general sense."[27] The combination of the end of the gold rush and anti-Chinese legislation led to a slowing of Chinese migration in the 1870s. When British Columbia became a province of Canada in 1871, Chinese gained the right to vote, but they were quickly disenfranchised and as a result lost their right to serve on juries. Between 1876 and 1880, Chinese entries to British Columbia fell to just 2,236 in five years. Between 1881 and 1884, however, more than 15,000 Chinese arrived from San Francisco and the Puget Sound, the majority recruited by the Canadian Pacific Railway to build its treacherous mountain section.[28]

Throughout the late 1870s and early 1880s, the provincial government in British Columbia passed many anti-Chinese laws, but the federal Canadian government struck each one down as unconstitutional. As in California's case, however, the discriminatory legislation that began at the state level eventually became national policy. A select committee in British Columbia that investigated Chinese immigration in 1879 concluded that Chinese "slave labour has a degrading effect as it causes an inconquerable and not unreasonable prejudice on the part of the free members of a community." In addition to fearing that Chinese labor would drive down wages and introduce slavery, British Columbian politicians worried that Chinese would bring disease and racial degeneration. The provincial governor William Smithe complained to the prime minister that "the hordes of Chinese . . . surge in upon the country and carry with them the elements of disease, pestilence and degradation over the face of the fair land." In 1884, Smithe passed the Act to Prevent the Immigration of Chinese and the Act to Regulate the Chinese Population of British Columbia. The first act prohibited all Chinese entries and the second established an annual ten-dollar tax for all Chinese over fourteen years of age. Within six weeks, the first act was disallowed by the governor general in council; the provincial Supreme Court eventually declared the second act unconstitutional. When the railroad track was completed in 1885, thousands of unemployed Chinese workers flooded Vancouver's labor market, leading Smithe to reenact the disallowed tax on Chinese; he was overruled once again. Nonetheless, in 1885 the federal government finally acceded to the pressure from British Columbia by passing the Act to Regulate and Restrict Chinese Immigration, which levied a fifty-dollar head tax on Chinese immigrants, and limited the number of Chinese passengers on each ship.[29]

When the Canadian government enacted its immigration law in 1885, it had the benefit of being able to study and learn from the impact of exclusion on California. The 1885 Royal Commission recommended a more gradual restriction of Chinese immigration than the draconian exclusion in the United States. "If restrictive legislation were considered opportune," the commission's report stated, "it should aim at gradually-achieved results, and the history of the question, as well as the evidence, shows that by legislation regulating, not excluding Chinese laborers, every purpose can be effected which those who apprehend evils from Chinese immigration could, and actually do desire."[30] The 1885 head tax succeeded in drastically reducing Chinese immigration to less than 300 in a seven-year period (1885–92), but in 1892, 3,000 Chinese entered. Given the increasing willingness and ability of Chinese to pay the head tax, the government kept raising the amount, from $50 in 1885, to $100 in 1898, and finally to the exorbitant $500 in 1903.[31] The average yearly salary for workers in Canada in 1900 was $375.[32] The 1885 Restriction Act also allowed Chinese in Canada to obtain a "return certificate," visit

China, and return without paying the tax. In 1892, after it became clear that many return migrants simply sold their return certificates in China, Chinese were required to prove their identities through lengthy interrogations in a manner similar to U.S. procedures. In the 1890s Chinese also became subject to stringent public health inspections and health quarantines for new immigrants. In spite of increasing head taxes and restrictionist legislation, the Chinese population in Canada grew throughout this period, from 4,383 in 1881 to 85,548 in 1931; the decline to 74,064 in 1941 was more the result of the economic depression than immigration laws.[33] The growth of the Chinese population was not simply a result of natural growth; between 1885 and 1949, there were over 97,000 individual Chinese entries to Canada.[34] Given the concentration of Chinese in British Columbia, reaching more than 12 percent of the total population by 1916, the influx of Chinese was seen as a deluge by restrictionists.[35] In 1917 Rev. John Mackay gave a fiery speech to the Kiwanis club in Vancouver in which he declared the influx of "Orientals" as a "menace" to the entire "civilized world." Mackay argued that "Orientals" had proved themselves incapable of assimilating and that they stuck together in Canadian cities like "festering sores."[36] Such anti-Chinese sentiment gathered steam, leading to the 1923 Chinese Immigration Act that, like the U.S. 1882 exclusion, prohibited all Chinese immigration except for merchants, diplomats, and students. The law went into effect on 1 July, the day Canadians celebrate as Dominion Day. For the Chinese in Canada, 1 July is remembered as Humiliation Day.[37]

Porfirian Mexico's Recruitment of Chinese

Canada's immigration policy represented a middle ground between U.S. exclusion and the Mexican open border. In the late nineteenth century, the modernizing regime of Porfirio Díaz (1876–1911) attempted to recruit foreign laborers to come to Mexico. Shortages of labor in the agricultural and mining sectors, especially in the north and along the coast, spurred this recruitment effort. The government sought European laborers, but these efforts were crippled by Mexico's lack of incentives and relatively low salaries. The first effort to recruit Chinese laborers as railroad workers began in 1865, when the emperor of Mexico, Maximilian, granted Manuel B. da Cunha Reis the exclusive privilege to import contract workers from Asia and Egypt for ten years to work on Cunha Reis's plantations in Veracruz.[38] However, it was not until the mid-1870s that Matías Romero, finance minister and later ambassador to the United States, sought to solidify and expand Chinese immigration to shore up the labor supply along the coast. In 1875, Romero made his case in the Mexico City press, arguing that Chinese were used to hot climates similar to Mexico's, that they were accustomed to earning low wages, and that China's coast was relatively close. It is not clear what kind of map Romero was consulting. He proposed sending a government agent to China to study the question of Chinese immigration, establishing diplomatic relations with China, and promoting commerce.[39]

The contrast between the Mexican and U.S. policies could not have been starker. The United States was trying to block the entry of Chinese and reduce the population in the United States, while the Mexican government was encouraging immigration. A Canadian newspaper, the *Ontario Times*, explained the Mexican position bluntly: "Mexico refuses to engage in an anti-Chinese crusade—in fact, encourages the immigration of the Mongolian population. Employers of labor find the Chinamen much more tractable than the ordinary 'greaser,' as willing workers are hard to get, especially in the mining and agricultural districts, there is a disposition to give the almond-eyed toiler full swing, however objectionable his presence may be in some social respects." The contrast between the two countries' policies was not just an academic point because, as the *Ontario Times* pointed out, the U.S. prohibition would be ineffectual if Chinese could simply enter Mexico and then cross the border into the United States. The only way to prevent such fraudulent entries would be by establishing a patrol along the 2,000-mile-long border. And even then, agents would be faced with the difficulty of determining the Mexicans from the Chinese. The *Ontario Times* warned that given "a peculiar resemblance existing between the Chinaman and the 'greaser,' there would be a daily danger in the driving back of the unwelcome visitors that outrages on Mexican citizens would be committed by mistake."[40] In the end, whether any country liked it or not, U.S., Canadian, and Mexican immigration policies toward Chinese were intimately linked by two very long and porous land borders.

The Mexican government pushed for direct steamer lines from China to propel Chinese immigration and develop trade with China.[41] Without a direct line, Chinese wishing to enter Mexico needed to first land in San Francisco and then transfer to another ship heading south to Mexico. The need for a direct line to Mexico became especially urgent after restrictionists in the United States made it harder for Chinese to transfer through U.S. ports. In 1884 the Mexican Pacific Navigation Company signed a contract with the Development Ministry to establish regular service between Asia and Mexico to increase commerce and aid in transportation of laborers. The contract privileged European over Asian immigrants, and men over women. The company would receive a subsidy of sixty-five pesos for each European immigrant and only thirty-five pesos for each Asian. The fact that the contract referred to Europeans as "immigrants" and Asians as "laborers" indicated that the Europeans were expected to settle and form part of Mexican society while the Asians were needed as cheap labor. The contract also stipulated that women should not outnumber men on these voyages.[42] The main goal was to import cheap manual labor.

The Mexican Pacific Navigation Company needed British permission to ship Chinese from Hong Kong, but the British kept denying such requests. The British had just fought a two-decade-long battle against the Spanish and Portuguese to end the "coolie" trade from Macao, and this new effort to ship Chinese to Mexico seemed like the same kind of operation to them. A Mexican special envoy was sent to London to respond to the British belief that "immigrants are in the condition of slaves in Mexico" and to insist that the Chinese would be "entirely free."[43] The Mexican diplomat, Ignacio Mariscal, met with the Chinese representative, Marquis Tseng, in London to outline guarantees for the Chinese in Mexico. Mariscal declared to his Chinese counterpart, "Slavery is not even possible, nor even peonage in this case."[44] The lack of diplomatic relations between China and Mexico, however, impeded establishment of the steamer line. The Mexicans agreed to allow Chinese agents in Mexico to oversee Chinese immigration, but the Tsungli Yamen declined, citing the lack of a diplomatic treaty. The only way the Chinese would agree to any further shipments was by establishing a formal treaty with Mexico, or by putting the Chinese under British protection. The Mexicans refused to allow the Chinese to be formally represented by the British, and the effort to establish a direct steamer line from Asia faltered. In May 1885 the Chinese government conceded to allow just one shipment of Chinese from Hong Kong.[45] By that time, however, the Mexican Pacific Navigation Company had disintegrated, and the journey was never completed. Another steamship company, the Compañía Marítima Asiática Mexicana (Asian Mexican Maritime Company), managed to ship 500 Chinese from Macao to the Mexican port at Salina Cruz in 1890, but this effort was short-lived as well.[46] The treaty between China and Mexico that had been the precondition for establishing direct steamer lines was not signed until 1899. The treaty eventually granted Mexico most-favored-nation status, extraterritorial rights for its citizens, and declared emigration to be "free and voluntary.[47]

Most Chinese who came to Mexico arrived not under a regulated contract labor system, as had prevailed in Cuba and Peru until 1874, but as free laborers. Nonetheless, there were particular areas where Chinese laborers were brought in under contracts to work on plantations or on railroads. In 1908, Harrison Gray Otis, of the Times Mirror Company based in Los Angeles, wrote to the U.S. consul in Hong Kong to ask him for assistance in recruiting Chinese workers and transporting them through San Francisco to work on the Colorado River Land Company plantation near Calexico, a California border town across from Mexicali.[48] Although the workers would be on plantations in Mexico, the advertisements gave the impression that they would be living and working in the United States. These "coolies," as immigration inspector F. H. Larned called them, were required to sign five-year contracts, earning twenty-four Hong Kong dollars per month, and guaranteed return passage to China at the end of the contract. They were eligible for vacation time during Chinese New Year's and festival days along with European holidays, and they would be allowed to gather wood for free and to cultivate and gather vegetables. The contracts also required laborers to comply with U.S. laws and mandated that the laborers receive consent from their families before leaving.[49] This scheme sought to evade U.S. laws against contract labor by having the Chinese working on the Mexican side of the border, while at the same time trying to enlist U.S. diplomatic cooperation to facilitate the operation. In early 1909, Oscar Strauss, the secretary of commerce and labor, advised the U.S. government not to facilitate this scheme, arguing that even if the Chinese completed their five-year contracts, it would be impossible to prevent them from crossing over the border into the United States afterward.[50]

Even though the efforts to establish direct shipping lines from Asia to Mexico failed in the nineteenth century, and treaty negotiations dragged on for almost two decades, Chinese continued to be recruited to work in Mexico. In 1902, a group of twenty Chinese businessmen from Hong Kong formed the China Commercial Steamship Company. The line between Hong Kong, Yokahoma, Manzanillo, and San Francisco started operations in the summer of 1903 allowing Chinese passengers to travel directly to Mexico without worrying about passing through San Francisco and dealing with U.S. inspections. On the return trip, however, the steamer passed through San Francisco to pick up Chinese passengers who wanted to return to China. Most of the steerage passengers on these voyages came to work on the construction of the Central Mexican Railroad, especially the stretch from Manzanillo to Guadalajara.[51] As a result of the Sino-Mexican treaty in 1899 and the establishment of direct steamers between Asia and Mexico, the Chinese

Year	United States	% of Total	Mexico	% of Total
1890	107,488	0.17		
1895			987	0.01
1900	89,863	0.12	2,837	0.02
1910	71,531	0.08	13,203	0.09
1920	61,639	0.06	14,750	
1921			14,472	0.10
1926			24,218	0.20
1930	74,954	0.06	15,976	0.10
1940	77,504	0.06	4,856	0.02

Sources: Carter et al., *Historical Statistics of the United States*; Romero, *Chinese in Mexico*, 55–56. I used Table XL from the 1930 census, which compares 1921 and 1930 statistics. Dirección General de Estadísticas, *Censo general de la República Mexicana, 1895*; Dirección General de Estadísticas, *Censo general de la República Mexicana, 1910*; Dirección General de Estadísticas, *Censo general de la República Mexicana, 1921*; Dirección General de Estadísticas, *Censo general de la República Mexicana, 1930*; Dirección General de Estadísticas, *Censo general de la República Mexicana, 1940*.

population in Mexico grew. According to the national census, in 1895 there were fewer than 1,000 Chinese registered in Mexico, but by 1910 the number of Chinese had grown to more than 13,000. It maintained itself from 1920 (14,750) to 1930 (almost 16,000). By 1940, after the campaign to expel Chinese from northern Mexico, only 4,856 Chinese were left in the country. The national census probably undercounted Chinese, and other estimates put the Chinese population as high as 24,000 by 1926.[52] Mexico's Chinese population pales in comparison to that of the United States in absolute numbers, but as a proportion of the total population, Chinese in Mexico outpaced the United States since 1910, and from the mid-1920s to 1930 Mexico outstripped the United States by a ratio of almost two to one (see table). More Chinese went to the United States, but proportionally Mexico was a strong draw for Chinese in this period.

Figure 2 demonstrates that Canada and Mexico saw steady growth in their Chinese populations through the 1920s, while the United States, Peru, and Cuba saw dramatic declines from the late nineteenth century onward. By

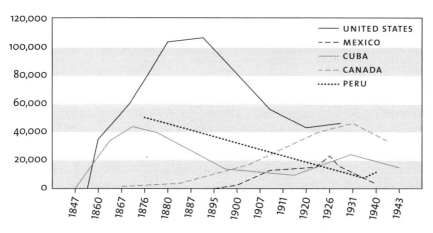

FIGURE 2. Chinese Population in the United States, Mexico, Cuba, Canada, and Peru, 1847–1943. Cuban population data from Rodríguez, *Los Chinos de Cuba*, 13, 90–92. Mexican population data from Dirección General de Estadísticas, *Censo general de la República Mexicana, 1895*; and Romero, *Chinese in Mexico*, table 3.1, p. 56. U.S. population data from Gibson and Jung, "Historical Census Statistics on the Foreign-Born Population of the US." For Canadian population, see Basavarajappa and Ram, "Origins of the Population"; and Anderson, *Vancouver's Chinatown*, 35. Peruvian population from Rodríguez Pastor, *Herederos del dragón*, 113; and McKeown, *Chinese Migrant Networks and Cultural Change*, table 5, p. 48.

the 1930s, the Chinese population in the Americas had declined to levels lower than had existed in the nineteenth century. Immigration restrictions together with an economic depression reduced the Chinese population, but they did not stop Chinese migration altogether. Although the number of Chinese in Anglo North America (the United States and Canada) in 1950 was 150,157, about double Latin America's 77,142, the proportion of the Chinese relative to total population was higher in particular Latin American countries; for example, Cuba had a proportion of Chinese six times higher than the United States.[53]

"We Are Only Workmen in Name but Slaves in Reality"

Although Chinese were not restricted from going to Mexico, their official status as "free" laborers did not prevent companies from establishing onerous contracts. Immigration policies could make access to the nation easier or more difficult, but the mobility and freedom of Chinese in each of these countries depended on local and national labor laws, as well as on Chinese ability to seek redress in the courts. Paradoxically, Chinese in the United

States, even after exclusion, had more success defending their rights in courts than Chinese in Mexico. Chinese were free to come into Mexico, but they were not really free once they arrived.

In one dramatic example of the lack of freedom in Mexico, a group of Chinese workers that arrived in Canada was kidnapped and brought to Mexico to work on plantations and to build railroads. The incident in 1899 involved more than 480 Chinese recruited from Hong Kong to work in Victoria and Vancouver, British Columbia, for thirty dollars a month. Once they arrived in Vancouver, they were locked in trains and sent to Montreal; from there they were packed off to Tampico, Mexico, where they worked for the On Wo Company owned by Ma Chok. In desperation, the workers in Tampico wrote to the Chinese consul in San Francisco, the president of the Six Chinese Benevolent Associations, and the missionary societies of the Baptist, Presbyterian, Congregational, and Methodist churches explaining their predicament and pleading for assistance.

The petition by the more than 480 workers was accompanied by a personal letter signed by a few of the workers who also complained about their ill treatment. Both letters were translated from the Chinese into English and forwarded to the Mexican government. The petition and letter are rare glimpses into the work conditions for Chinese in Mexico, and they provide a firsthand account of the recruiting process from the perspective of the workers themselves. The petition was written in the form of a legal complaint and began by identifying the authors as more than 480 Chinese subjects from various districts in China. They explained that Ma Kang-Chok of the On Wo Company had recruited them in Hong Kong to build railroads in Vancouver. They continued by listing the various ways they were taken advantage of and exploited:

> That we Chinese, being poor, fell into the trap, and were kidnaped to Tampico, Mexico;
>
> That the On Wo Company, having a secret understanding with the railroad company, caused us to be locked up in the cars and carried to the City of Montreal in such manner as to prevent communication, and then transferred in the night time so as to render all cries for rescue ineffectual to a cellar guarded by sentinels.
>
> That we were deprived of liberty, driven to desperation and intimidated with fear for our lives;
>
> That we were forced to take the cars to Tampico, Mexico and were set to work building railroads;

That our wages were fixed at only twenty-six (26) Mexican dollars per month, of which amount five dollars and twenty-five cents was deducted by the Company, twelve dollars was deducted for food, and eight dollars was deducted for clothing, boots and shoes, there being hardly anything left for us to lay up for the rainy day.[54]

After laying out in detail how they were "kidnapped," "locked up in cars," "deprived of liberty . . . [and] intimidated with fear for our lives," the petitioners begged to be rescued "from the hands of that brute Ma Kang-chok, who has sold us to the Railroad Company in Mexico, and enable us to return to our parents, our wives, and our children." The use of words like "kidnapped" and "sold" invoked the worst elements of the coolie trade and, of course, of slavery. The Mexican government had tried to persuade the Chinese officials that workers in Mexico were free and well treated, but this plea from the workers told a different story.

The letter from just a few of the workers provides a more detailed and personal account of their treatment. It began as if responding to a request by someone asking how they were doing. Given the rarity of Chinese commentary on their working conditions in Mexico, I will quote the letter in its entirety:

My dear———,

We are glad to hear from you to-day. You ask how we are. We left Hongkong last year with the understanding that we were to go to the City of Victoria and to receive thirty dollars ($30) in United States money per month for our wages. To our surprise, we were taken to Tampico, Mexico, and set to work building railroads. The weather here is hot and mosquitoes and other insects are very troublesome. The overseer of workmen is a man of violent temper. He uses his whip on the least provocation. We have to toil rain or shine, and to endure all manner of hardship without daring to raise our eyes. Some time ago, two of our number were whipped to death by the overseer, because they were sick and could not work. We are only workmen in name but slaves in reality. Some of our fellows have written to San Francisco, and told their friends and relatives the miserable plight we are in. We understand that the story has got into the newspapers. Now we hear that Ma Chok has circulated in the newspapers the statement that the Chinese workmen here receive ten dollars cash for food every month. Do not believe a word of it. Take immediate steps to rescue us from this place. Let us hear from you soon.

The authors of this letter highlight the violence of the overseer who whipped them mercilessly and ended up killing two of them who were too sick to work. Their narrative directly contradicted the owner's story about the wages workers received.[55]

The railroad company denied any wrongdoing, claiming that it complied with all its contractual obligations.[56] It even sent the government a copy of the contract between the railroad company and the labor recruiter San Hing asking for 500 or more Chinese workers. These contracts were not regularized or controlled by the state in the way that coolie contracts in Cuba and Peru had been, and they seemed to guarantee the workers a decent wage: $1 or $1.25 per ten-hour day, not bad for Mexico. However, the cost of transporting the workers, which was paid by the railway, was deducted from their wages. The other costs for housing and food that the workers claimed were being deducted from their pay did not appear in the contract. The contract also mandated that the railroad company pay an overseer $200 a month "to watch over these workers." If the workers fell ill, they could use the railway's hospitals, but they would have to pay twenty-five cents a month. And finally, the workers were expected to obey all of the railway's rules and the laws of the country.[57] It was not the contract so much as the actual work conditions, the abuse by the overseer, and the deductions from their pay for housing and food that upset the workers.

The Mexican government investigated the Tampico workers' allegations, but, unable to determine the claims' veracity, it simply referred the workers to the courts.[58] The Chinese labor contractor, San Hing, wrote to President Díaz and blamed the whole incident on unnamed Chinese who spread rumors among the workers, "causing them to believe that they are going to be sold as slaves" and encouraging them to escape. Even after the 1899 Sino-Mexican treaty, China lacked the diplomatic weight to gain redress for its subjects in Mexico.[59] Without strong diplomatic representation in Mexico, Chinese workers were at the mercy of unscrupulous labor contractors and abusive employers. Although welcome to enter Mexico as aliens, Chinese had few rights there.

"The Mongol Is the Ant of the Human Family"

As the Tampico case shows, even though the Díaz government recruited Chinese workers, it did not protect them once they had arrived in Mexico, and by the end of the nineteenth century vehement anti-Chinese sentiment began to surface more publicly. In 1899, at the same time as Chinese workers were complaining about the conditions of work in Tampico, the newspaper *El Tráfico* of Guaymas, Sonora, published a series of articles condemning Chinese immigration for bringing economic competition, miscegenation, racial degeneration, and disease.

Although *El Tráfico* depicted the Chinese as extremely hard workers, this trait was depicted in a negative light. As the newspaper put it, "The Mongol is the ant of the human family." Like the Jews, Chinese were also criticized for being successful merchants. *El Tráfico* made the comparison to Jews explicit, arguing that "the commercial talent of the sons of the celestial empire is superior to that of the Jews."[60] Some of the paper's readers apparently interpreted this article as support for Chinese immigration, but the newspaper clarified the following week that it was only commenting on the economic benefits of such immigration. It also detailed the supposed Chinese faults: "The Chinese is not exempt from vices and defects; he is a gambler, a fatalist, a smoker of opium, and he lacks patriotism. He will never gain affection for the country to which he emigrates, and he rejects the traditions and customs of his adoptive country. He is a bird of passage and of prey, and when he fills his beak, he takes flight for the Orient. If he is a bird of prey, he is a bird who leaves his fertilizing guano in his wake." *El Tráfico* thus managed to both confirm racist stereotypes about the Chinese as fatalistic, opium-addicted, opportunistic gamblers and recognize that the country needed their "fertilizing guano." The newspaper noted that the United States brought the Chinese in to build its railroads and then stopped them from coming when they began to compete in commerce. In a similar fashion, *El Tráfico* proposed boycotting Chinese businesses as the best strategy for ending their "monopoly" over small-scale commerce.[61] While it is hard to say how representative *El Tráfico*'s anti-Chinese reporting was of general Mexican popular opinion, the newspaper regularly published petitions by merchants and workers articulating similar views. One petition to Sonora's governor signed by 167 merchants and workers in dry goods stores complained about Chinese economic competition, diseases, and marriages with Mexican women.[62]

The enthusiastic plans for Chinese workers to develop the country were tempered by the perceived dangers of miscegenation for the racial makeup of the Mexican nation. *El Tráfico* explained that even the United States, which had extremely liberal laws for foreigners, made an exception with the Chinese, restricting them to certain neighborhoods, banning their entry, and finally taking away their right to become naturalized or marry anyone outside of their race, including Indians. Given the U.S. example, the newspaper proposed creating special ghettoes for Chinese, where Mexican children would remain free from the "contagion of their customs." *El Tráfico* argued against Chinese miscegenation with indigenous people who, according to the paper, "degenerated upon crossing with the Chinese."[63] It argued that Mexico needed "new blood" but insisted that immigrants should be intellectually and physically superior to Mexicans, "like the Teutonic race, the French, the Slav, the Saxon and the British." Even though people in Sonora were robust and tall, the paper explained, if the Chinese were allowed in "we will become a nation of dwarves."[64]

El Tráfico was particularly upset about Mexican women who were "sufficiently degenerate" to mix with wealthy Chinese men. The paper asked its readers rhetorically, "And what will be the good that results for the State with the propagation of that race?"[65] It portrayed women both as the victims of corrupt and diseased Chinese men and as heartless and money-grubbing degenerates. One story described how authorities in Demming, New Mexico, rescued a beautiful fourteen-year-old girl from a group of Chinese who had bought her in San Francisco for $1,500. The newspaper warned against allowing the Chinese to "introduce here the immoral customs of their land."[66] In this case, the young girl was clearly an unwitting victim, but *El Tráfico* felt that Mexican women shared part of the responsibility for engaging in relationships with Chinese men. In another story, the paper asserted that a Mexican woman had contracted leprosy in a Chinese store where she was groped. However, rather than blame the Chinese, the newspaper criticized the woman for allowing herself to be touched: "It does not surprise us that [the Chinese] groped women; what amazes us is that among these women some are sufficiently degraded that they allow themselves to be groped."[67]

The Chinese were seen as threats to the larger public because they were supposedly vectors for disease. *El Tráfico* complained that Chinese lived piled on top of one another in small houses that became "flashpoints of infection." In order to keep the general Mexican population safe, the newspaper recommended moving all Chinese to ghettoes where the police could watch over them constantly and prevent disease from spreading.[68] The doctor who concluded that the Mexican woman had contracted leprosy from the Chinese formed a commission to visit the Chinese "slums" and investigate. Unfortunately, the newspaper reported, the Chinese were forewarned, and so when the commission arrived, they hid all of their sick and cleaned their houses. The commission was therefore forced to issue a favorable report.[69]

The reporting in *El Tráfico* in 1899 demonstrates the tenor of popular anti-Chinese sentiment, at least in northern Mexico, in spite of the government's generally favorable policies toward Chinese immigration. Increasingly Mexicans began to look to the U.S. immigration policies and discriminatory laws as a model and ask why they should be accepting the Chinese who were being rejected by their neighbors. Given the porousness of the border, the two countries' immigration policies were inextricably linked. As *El Tráfico* graphically put it, "It is Mexico's turn to apply the restrictive laws for Chinese immigration in the United States; the fetid wave has overflowed us with its entourage of lepers and gamblers, opium smokers and black plague contagions, converting our cities into an immense pagoda that absorbs everything."[70] It would not be until the middle of the Mexican Revolution in the 1910s, however, that the anti-Chinese movement *El Tráfico* attempted to foment became an organized force throughout northern Mexico.

In Canada, those who argued against Chinese immigration articulated the same litany of concerns as did Mexico's *El Tráfico* and the virulent exclusionists in the United States. In 1879, a Select Committee on Chinese Labor and Immigration presented evidence to Canada's parliament. The panel's arguments against Chinese immigration were enumerated by the 1885 Royal Commission:

1st The absorption of employment to the exclusion of white labor, and consequent retardation of the settlements of the country.
2nd Absorption of domestic service and immorality engendered thereby.
3rd Personal uncleanliness and filthy habits of the Chinese, diseases, leprosy and crowding habitations.
4th Opium smoking, prostitution, slavery and immorality.
5th Secret organizations, want of truth, evasion of taxation and expense to the administration of justice.
6th Non-identity with the people of the country and withdrawal of capital resulting from their labor.

The similarity of anti-Chinese discourses in the Americas, Australia, and South Africa suggests a common racist framework that borrowed heavily from ideas of racial hierarchies used by social Darwinists in Europe and North America. These groups not only were intellectual bedfellows but also were organized transnationally. The Anti-Asiatic Exclusion League, which formed in Vancouver in 1907 and moved its headquarters to San Francisco the next year, advocated Asian exclusion in white settler societies around the globe.[71] Similar anti-Asian organizations would emerge in Mexico a few years later, a subject we will explore in chapter 6. For the politicians investigating it, this transnational phenomenon signaled not a similarity in anti-Chinese rhetoric but the certainty that Chinese must be alike in all places. In 1885, the *Royal Commission Report* declared that "the Chinaman seems to be the same everywhere, and the advocates of his advent or his restriction or exclusion use the same words whether they live in Melbourne, or London, or San Francisco."[72]

Naturalized Chinese

The politics of naturalization stood at the center of the debate over Chinese migration. Even those who advocated Chinese immigration to fill a labor need worried that Chinese would undermine the racial health of the nation. Allowing Chinese to come in as temporary laborers but keeping them from acquiring citizenship was a way for some to have their cake and eat it too. As early as 1878, the issue of whether Chinese could become naturalized citizens of the United States was settled with federal courts issuing a resounding "no." The idea that Chinese were ineligible to become naturalized citizens was written into the 1882 exclusion act; all other Asians were subsequently included in the prohibition.[73] Although Canada did not explicitly outlaw naturalization, judges routinely denied requests by Chinese for all sorts of trumped up reasons. As a result, by 1941, only 5 percent of the Chinese population in Canada had become naturalized citizens.[74] Mexico's liberal treatment of all immigrants meant that Chinese could become naturalized Mexican citizens. However, when naturalized Mexican citizens of Chinese descent arrived at the U.S. border, customs officers treated them according to their ethnic heritage as Chinese and not according to their national citizenship as Mexicans. In March 1892, the Mexican ambassador to the United States, Matías Romero, wrote to the Foreign Ministry informing his colleagues that the U.S. government would not recognize naturalization of Chinese as Mexicans for the purpose of entry into the United States. Romero noted that there was no treaty that guaranteed Mexicans' ability to enter the United States in any case and that few Chinese actually availed themselves of the privilege of naturalization after living in Mexico for two years.[75] Although Romero did not press the matter, the denial of Chinese Mexicans' entry into the United States could have been construed as an affront to Mexico.

In 1892, when three Chinese men who were naturalized Mexicans tried to cross the border into Texas at Eagle Pass, they were arrested. The Mexican consul there sided with the U.S. authorities, suggesting that the Chinese request for naturalization was not "bona fide."[76] Even though very few Chinese became naturalized Mexicans, Mexican authorities usually questioned their motives. In 1904, the *jefe político* (political boss) in Ciudad Júarez complained that Chinese who became Mexicans "do it, not for love of our country or its institutions but because once they obtain their naturalization certificate, they can penetrate U.S. territory."[77] Only a handful of Chinese had become naturalized Mexicans by 1893, and by the end of the Porfiriato in 1910, only 175 Chinese, just over 1 percent of the Chinese population, had become naturalized Mexican citizens; most of these listed their occupation as "merchant."[78] Like in Canada, although technically able to become naturalized, few Chinese could or would take advantage of this right.

U.S. courts treated Chinese Mexicans as Chinese for the purposes of immigration and even seemed to ignore provisions in the exclusion law that exempted merchants. On 13 May 1892 Wong Foon Chuck, a well-known merchant, owner of extensive ranch lands, and contractor for mines in San Felipe, Coahuila, was arrested in San Antonio for not having proper papers. The *New York Tribune* reported that Wong had assets of more than $100,000.[79] Although he was born in China, Wong had lived in the United States since he was twelve years old in the era prior to exclusion. From the mid-1870s until the time of his arrest, Wong worked in California and along the U.S.-Mexico borderlands. He managed to rise from being a cook and a railroad worker to becoming a landowner and proprietor of a hotel, restaurant, and laundry.[80] The Mexican consul in Eagle Pass noted that Wong had a good reputation for "his conduct and honorability" and provided the U.S. courts with documentation proving that he was a naturalized citizen of Mexico. Even though Wong had enough money to provide a bond, U.S. law prohibited Chinese from doing so, and thus he was forced to pay for a round-the-clock guard until he was able to appear before the commissioner.[81] The Western District Court of Texas ruled that Wong was a "Chinese person or of Chinese origin" and therefore should be excluded from the United States. The courts acknowledged that he was a businessman and had become a citizen of Mexico, both of which should have allowed him to enter the United States, even under the exclusion act. Nonetheless, the court sentenced him to one hour of forced work and then deported him to Mexico.[82]

Wong's case highlighted the vulnerability of all Chinese in the United States. If this wealthy, well-known businessman, landowner, and Mexican citizen could be arrested and summarily deported, then the future for Chinese in the United States must have seemed bleak. Following Wong's deportation, the *Washington Post* published an article that condemned the harsh treatment of Chinese in the United States and suggested a mass exodus of Chinese in the United States to Mexico as the solution.

In Mexico the Chinese would be treated with justice, even with liberality. Their industry, their skill, their frugality, would be appreciated, and they would find, not only the reasonable recompense of honest toil, but a humane and civilized spirit in their reception by the people. They have been treated here with shameful brutality. They will encounter in Mexico nothing but kindness and encouragement. We hope that the exodus will be consummated, and this we hope for their sake as much as for our own. The change will be to their advantage in every way, and it will be to ours in that it will obviate the cruelty and oppression which the new feature of the "exclusion" law provides for, and which, in many parts of the country, would infallibly be practiced. We wear already a sufficient odious stigma in the matter of our dealings with the Chinese; there is no reason why it should be made bigger and blacker and more disgraceful.[83]

Even though the *Post* seemed to sympathize with the Chinese and condemned the hostility they faced in the United States, it advocated the "exodus" to repair the damage to the reputation of the United States as much as to help the Chinese. The *New York Post* also criticized the arrest of Wong, arguing that it violated a treaty with Mexico guaranteeing Mexican citizens' rights in the United States: "Suppose Mexico were to pass a law putting a like stigma upon an Irish person or person of Irish descent, and ignore the fact that he might be an American citizen nevertheless. We fancy there would be a good deal of foaming at Washington."[84]

In the United States, anti-Chinese politicians and newspapers constantly decried the fraudulent entry of Chinese by means of false papers or clandestine border crossings. The passage in 1892 of the Geary Act, which tightened Chinese exclusion and made it mandatory for Chinese to carry certificates of residency at all times, was designed specifically to prevent fraudulent entry. U.S. newspapers reacted to reports of Chinese becoming naturalized as Mexicans with great alarm, arguing that this was a ploy to evade U.S. restriction laws. "Two years ostensible residence in Mexico is not a long period of waiting, even if endured by the wily pagan," one paper wrote. "As for other acts and proofs necessary to obtain citizenship there, the little brown man never has been found wanting when bribery and perjury were in demand. In his hands those twin resources of lawbreakers have effected much in the United States, and would accomplish much more in Mexico. Without undue derogation of Mexican officials it may fairly be assumed that the whole matter would be soon systematized and certificates of citizenship be issued by the ream and be practically for sale in the open market."[85] The newspaper thus blamed evasion of laws and corruption of Mexican officials by Chinese on their supposed propensity for lying and deceit.

Some newspapers even blamed the situation on Mexico's liberal constitution and immigration laws that did not permit "denial of citizenship on the ground of race or color." This same newspaper posed a question to its readers: "What are we going to do with John Chinaman when he presents himself at our frontier panoplied in the citizenship of the sister republic and claiming his rights as a Mexican?"[86] Given the hyperbolic warnings in U.S. newspapers, one would suspect that there were hundreds if not thousands of Chinese who had used Mexican naturalization as a springboard to jump over the restrictionist hurdles in the United States. However, Mexico's foreign minister, Ignacio Mariscal, reported to the U.S. ambassador that by July 1892, only five Chinese had become naturalized Mexicans, and that Wong was the only one of these who had crossed into the United States.[87] In the next seven years, 1892–99, only thirty-five more Chinese became naturalized Mexican citizens.[88] This was hardly an invasion.

A few months later, Ching You, a person of Chinese descent who had been naturalized as a British citizen in Vancouver, British Columbia, arrived at Port Townsend, Washington. The incident that followed became a widely reported test case, much like that of Wong Foon Chuck for the Mexican border. The collector of customs at Port Townsend warned that "if the man was allowed to enter, the authorities on the other side of the line would begin at once to make British citizens of the Chinese to evade our restriction law." Assistant Secretary of the Treasury O. L. Spaulding issued orders not to allow Ching You to enter and not to recognize naturalization of Chinese people as citizens of another country for the purposes of entering the United States. Treasury Department officials argued that it was a "debatable question" whether their actions violated a treaty with Great Britain that permitted its subjects to "enter and leave the United States at any time."[89] What the ruling by the Treasury Department makes clear, however, is that the Chinese exclusion was a racially or ethnically based exclusion, not a national one. Even Chinese merchants who were naturalized citizens of another country had to present Section 6 certificates and not just passports to gain entry. By 1895 the attorney general clarified that exclusion laws "were based on moral and racial objections" and not on citizenship status. "Under this ruling," noted historian Mary Roberts Coolidge, "the Chinese citizens of Mexico and Canada, although members of the exempt classes, were refused admission."[90] No matter what the nationality, Mexican or Canadian (British), laborers of Chinese descent would be barred from entering the United States because of the way they looked. In 1939, Juan Pangtay Tea, an ethnic Chinese Mexican citizen born in Mexico in 1917, was required to obtain a certificate indicating that he was a member of an exempt class in order to enter the United States. The stain of Chinese heritage could never be erased in the eyes of U.S. law.

Passports and Centralization in an Era of Free Mobility

Chinese faced increasing obstacles at the end of the nineteenth century, with stricter rules about who could qualify as a merchant. In 1899 a group of thirty merchants from Canton were denied admission and deported at San Francisco because the particulars of their merchant status were only indicated on the Chinese version of their certificates. In 1898 Lei Yok, a partner in a Chinese merchant firm in San Francisco, attempted to return to the United States after a visit to Cuba. Immigration officers in New Orleans denied him reentry even though he was a partner in a San Francisco firm. He presented a passport issued by the Chinese consul in Havana and a visa for the United States stamped by the British consul on behalf of the United States and also by the Spanish governor in Cuba.[91] Passports and visas did not guarantee entry for Chinese. Even for U.S. citizens of Chinese descent, passports were not sufficient to gain reentry; all Chinese legally residing in the United States were required to obtain a "return certificate" before traveling.[92] In 1905 an internal letter from the Department of Commerce and Labor to the State Department pointed out the inconsistency of requiring foreign governments to recognize the passport as proof of U.S. citizenship, yet not recognizing the legitimacy of that same document for entry into the United States. A handwritten note on the letter indicated that it had not been sent, but clearly bureaucrats in the government were aware of the hypocrisy of not recognizing their own documents as proof of citizenship.[93] Nonetheless, a court in Northern California in the Gee Hog case ruled that the passport was not proof of citizenship.[94] In 1910, when Wong Chau Pak arrived in San Francisco with passport in hand claiming to be the son of a U.S. citizen, immigration inspectors declared his passport false, arguing that consular officials had limited ability to determine citizenship.[95]

Beyond the trouble they faced returning to the United States, U.S. citizens of Chinese descent also had trouble traveling around China. Those who turned in their papers in exchange for a preinvestigation document that would allow them to return to the United States were unable to obtain a travel certificate in China because they had no passport. Given that many of them did not wear queues and wore Western clothes, traveling around

China's countryside without a passport or travel certificate presented a danger, especially in 1911 in the midst of revolutionary ferment. The U.S. consul general in Hong Kong therefore asked the State Department to change its rules to allow Chinese to obtain a travel certificate with their preinvestigation certificates.[96]

In 1896 another well-known Chinese merchant from Baja California who had become a naturalized Mexican citizen was denied entry to San Diego. The merchant, Charles Sam, had presented a letter from the U.S. consul in Ensenada attesting to his considerable real estate, livestock holdings, and good reputation; he also showed two certificates from merchants in Ensenada confirming his good character, as well as a round-trip steamer ticket from Ensenada to San Diego as evidence of his intent to only stay in San Diego temporarily to do business.[97] After the Mexican government complained, the United States agreed to allow Sam into the United States as long as he was provided with a certificate verifying he was a naturalized Mexican.[98] In this case, the United States grudgingly recognized a Chinese Mexican as a merchant, but in most other cases, Chinese Mexicans were denied entry.

As U.S. exclusion laws tightened, officials in northern Mexican states began to issue certificates testifying to the Chinese merchants' Mexican nationality to facilitate their movement so that they could travel for business to the United States.[99] On 12 February 1899 two Chinese men arrived in San Diego and presented the customs collector there with certificates issued by Manuel Choza, the prefect in Mazatlán, Sinaloa.[100] The United States complained that they were unable to verify these certificates issued by local officials. Ultimately, the Mexican federal government put a stop to local officials' issuance of certificates, arguing that only the president and federal authorities had that right.[101] Historian Adam McKeown notes that the mid-nineteenth century was generally an era of free mobility as passport requirements and internal document checks were abolished in countries around the Atlantic. However, he argues that this era of free mobility was merely an "interlude in the repositioning of the power of identification from local to central authorities."[102] In North America, not only were papers necessary to move across borders, but increasingly the only documents recognized were those issued by central government authorities.

Crossing the Border for Freedom from the United States

Although it is almost certain that most Chinese clandestine migrants went from Mexico to the United States because of greater economic opportunities there, a significant outward migration occurred as well from the United States to Canada, Mexico, and Cuba. In the early 1880s, more than 15,000 Chinese migrated northward from California and the U.S. Pacific Northwest to British Columbia to work on the Canadian Pacific Railway.[103] From 1903 to 1924 more than 23,000 Chinese migrated to Cuba, mostly from California.[104] And after U.S. exclusion the possibility of government land grants in Mexico and the hope of finding a less racist society there prompted hundreds if not thousands of Chinese to head south. In April 1886, just eight months after twenty-eight Chinese miners were killed and seventy-five Chinese homes were burned in Rock Springs, Wyoming, newspapers in the United States described a German plan to import 600,000 Chinese workers to Mexico. The German speculators, the rumors suggested, had contracted with the Mexican government to bring in the Chinese in exchange for twenty acres of land for each of them. The Mexican ambassador, Matías Romero, noted that the newspaper stories had "caused a big impression" in the United States.[105] *The World* of Philadelphia reported that Chinese had already left Portland after hearing of the colonization effort, but the newspaper worried that "if 600,000 Chinamen ever get to Mexico, a perpetual slipping over the Rio Grande will be the consequence." Given the increasing antipathy toward Chinese workers in the United States, the rumor of opportunities in Mexico may have been a ploy to get Chinese to migrate to Mexico. The *New York Herald* argued that the rumors of such a colonization effort had to be false because the Mexican government did not have such large tracts of vacant land to hand out. Meanwhile, the *Philadelphia Press* mocked the effort to bring in so many Chinese, arguing that it was a sign that Mexico was in desperate straits: "Is Mexico trying vaguely an experiment in civilization? Or is she in a state of despair over the tropical indolence of her own people, and consequently determined to resort to the heroic measure of demonstrating to these what industry in its most concentrated essence can accomplish for itself?"[106] In May Romero denied the rumors of plans for such colonization in Mexico.[107] A few years later, however, the Mexican government had entered into an agreement with the Chinese government to import Chinese workers to the hot regions of Mexico, including Tamaulipas, to work on plantations. The government-sponsored Tamaulipas colonization never came to fruition, but a small Chinese community eventually developed in that state.[108]

The idea of escaping from anti-Chinese pogroms in the United States may have been attractive for many Chinese, but it was unclear whether Mexico was any more welcoming. In 1886 there was a false report that a steamer from San Francisco was going to land at Mazatlán with more than 600 Chinese. The townspeople erupted in a riot, attacking Chinese homes and driving them out of town.[109] The *San Francisco Call* warned about the anti-Chinese sentiment in Mexico in light of "projects for the mongolization of Mexico."

> If the Mexicans really start to oppose Chinese immigration they will be likely to adopt much more extreme measures than the self-poised citizens of California. The Spanish and Chinese race conflict in the Philippines furnishes a hint of what may ensue in Mexico. The Chinese continued crowding into Manila until the people rose en masse and butchered them. This was repeated several times with intervals of many years. The possibility of similar action on the part of the ignorant, prejudiced and passionate mixed races of Mexico should be taken into consideration by those contemplating schemes of wholesale Chinese importation into that country.[110]

No matter where Chinese went in Mexico, the United States, or Canada, they faced the prospect of violence at the hands of xenophobic mobs. The difference between the three countries, however, was that after 1882 the official federal government policy in the United States was decidedly anti-Chinese, whereas it was only moderately anti-Chinese in Canada, and it was still fairly pro-Chinese in Mexico.

Although the German-backed Chinese colonization scheme in Mexico may have been just a rumor, Chinese businessmen in the United States made efforts to take advantage of Mexico's offer of land for colonists willing to settle remote and hot regions of the country. In 1892 two wealthy Chinese businessmen, Ching Wun from San Francisco and Kong Foo from St. Louis, went to Mexico City to meet with President Díaz to discuss a colonization scheme to move all Chinese from the United States to Tamaulipas. The Chinese businessmen claimed to represent a society of several thousand Chinese in the United States who had pledged to leave the United States because of the exclusion acts. News reports in the United States suggested that the Mexican government favored Chinese immigration, and they predicted that the land concession would be granted.[111] The *New York Times* wondered whether the Chinese in Mexico would "remain permanently unmolested by the somewhat lawless population in that country," but it compared the "visionary" colonization scheme to that of African Americans.[112] In 1895 William H. Ellis would undertake a similar colonization plan in Tlahualilo, Durango, to re-move African Americans from the racist U.S. South to a freer Mexico. Ellis's exodus-like experiment lasted less than six months before the bedraggled and sick black colonists returned to Alabama.[113] Like other U.S. newspapers, the *Washington Post* saw Chinese colonization across the border as a mutu-ally beneficial solution for both the United States and Mexico:

> They would prove a valuable substitute for the mixed and indolent population to be found in many parts of Mexico, and the climate condi-tions are doubtless preferable to those of the United States for the par-ticular classes of Chinamen that are used to agricultural occupations. At the same time the project may help to effect the object sought by the framers of the exclusion act, who seem to be quite as anxious to get rid of the Chinese we already have among us as they are to prevent any more accessions of the same sort.[114]

U.S. press coverage of the colonization plans in Mexico tended to malign Mexico for its "indolent" population, criticize Mexicans for their hostility to Chinese, and at the same time favor plans to send Chinese south of the border.

Conclusion

The rights of man were interpreted differently throughout the Americas. At the end of the nineteenth century, the Mexican government viewed immi-gration policy in light of the universal rights of man, which would apply to all men regardless of race or nationality. In the United States, the courts and politicians worried about protecting the rights of white men over and against the competition and perceived dangers posed by Chinese laborers, and so they advocated exclusion. The Canadian Dominion government overruled the most egregiously discriminatory laws in British Columbia and opted for a restrictionist middle ground between open immigration and exclusion by regulating the flow of new immigrants through heavy taxes on Chinese entries. Cuba's policy toward the Chinese zigzagged. In the coolie period (1847–74), it recruited and encouraged Chinese immigration, afterward it discouraged it, and in 1902, with the U.S. military occupying the island, Cuba banned further Chinese laborers. However, as the needs of the sugar industry grew in the first three decades of the twentieth century, the Cubans recruited a new wave of Chinese. Peru followed roughly the same pattern as Cuba, with

Chinese migration dwindling after the end of the coolie trade and picking up again in the early twentieth century.[115]

In all of these countries the need for cheap labor to work in mines and sugar plantations and to build railroads led the government to initially seek out and recruit Chinese laborers. Nonetheless, the Chinese, even when welcomed as workers, were always viewed as outsiders who could never assimilate to the national culture; they were aliens. And in all of these countries, competition with national (often white or mestizo) workers and racist sentiments led to anti-Chinese movements that called for limiting and controlling the Chinese population, and in the most extreme cases expelling them.

There were differences, however, in the timing and severity of the policies toward Chinese migrants. Framing the history of Chinese migration to the Americas in a hemispheric framework does not mean flattening out differences between nations but rather showing how the policies in each country related to the others. In the mid- to late nineteenth century, Peru's and Cuba's coolie systems were by far the most akin to slavery. The end of the coolie trade, however, led Chinese to migrate to other countries, principally Canada and Mexico. Chinese came to the United States from the mid-nineteenth century onward, even after exclusion laws were passed. However, exclusion laws forced many migrants seeking to enter the United States to first go to neighboring countries, like Cuba, Mexico, and Canada, from which they would surreptitiously attempt to enter the United States. Eventually all of these neighboring countries would follow the model of the United States, adopting the same kind of restrictions on Chinese immigration.

The Chinese contract laborer stood at the center of the mid- to late nineteenth-century transition from slavery to free labor. Nationalistic and xenophobic workers targeted Chinese, pushing for restrictive and discriminatory laws, organizing protests, and leading mobs to harass and kill them. As the central governments in the United States and Canada assumed greater control over immigration, popular vigilante violence slowly subsided. Rigorous inspections, constant patrols and surveillance, and the development of a deportation mechanism for illegal aliens by a more robust federal bureaucracy took over the role of lynch mobs in instilling fear and terror in the Chinese community. Given the weakness of the central Mexican government following the long and devastating Revolution, state officials and popular vigilante groups continued to harass Chinese through the 1930s. Cuba never experienced the kinds of anti-Chinese violence that occurred in the rest of North America, perhaps because of the patriotic role played by Chinese in the independence wars (1868–98), but xenophobic anti-Chinese legislation and discrimination flared up in the 1920s during a wave of heightened nationalism. Many historical narratives argue that the move from coolie to free immigrant labor was a progressive step on the ineluctable march toward freedom. Taken as a whole, however, the end of the coolie era brought not freedom but a different form of bondage. By the early twentieth century, migrants of all stripes faced increasingly strict regulations and mechanisms of control. At the same time as the state centralized and strengthened its role in regulating migration, citizenship rights supplanted the rights of man. Chinese, as people who were both legally and socially alienated from citizenship, found themselves with few rights in a brave new world marked by borders and immigration officers. In the next chapter we will examine how the immigration machine developed and inextricably tied the Chinese alien to the notion of criminality and illegality.

CHAPTER 4

The Immigration Bureaucracy and the Production of Illegal Aliens

The ways of the smuggler to defeat the law are devious, cunning and many.
—U.S. Immigration Commissioner, Montreal, 1922

Vigilantes regularly attacked Chinese along the Pacific coast of the United States, Canada, Mexico, and Peru during the late nineteenth century. There were major massacres in the Cañete Valley, Peru (1881), in Rock Springs, Wyoming (1885), and Snake River, Oregon (1887). On many more occasions mobs burned down Chinese stores and homes and chased them from town, including a whole series of anti-Asian riots along the Pacific coast from Mazatlán, Mexico, to British Columbia between 1885 and 1907.[1] Although most extreme violence occurred during the exclusion period after 1882, by the time the immigration bureaucracy grew more robust and extended its physical presence and effectiveness in the first decade of the twentieth century, vigilante violence diminished. The immigration bureaucracy took over the disciplining and punishing functions previously handled by vigilante mobs. The state had an interest in containing anti-Chinese violence because what began as a race war against Chinese could have easily turned into a class war and more generally into antigovernment rebellion. Furthermore, massacres of Chinese led to recriminations by the Chinese government and thereby threatened trading as well as diplomatic relations. By taking control of the disciplining of Chinese immigrants in the name of law and order, the state gained power. In the United States and Canada, Chinese were generally free from mob violence by the 1910s, but they found themselves confronting a more formidable enemy: the state. In Mexico, as the state disintegrated amid a chaotic revolution that began in 1911, mobs attacked and massacred Chinese at unprecedented levels. By the 1930s, although the central Mexican state had consolidated its power, regional xenophobic movements led to mass expulsions of Chinese from the northwestern states of Sonora and Sinaloa. Strong central governments more often than not mitigated popular anti-Chinese violence, but they also worked to politically and socially exclude and disenfranchise Chinese through the law.

Chinese throughout the Americas in the pre-exclusion era were viewed as aliens. Even where Chinese were recruited with the official sanction of the governments in Cuba and Peru, politicians, laborers, and merchants alike saw them as unassimilable and exotic foreigners. By 1874 the official coolie trade ended, but Chinese continued to arrive as free laborers under the credit-ticket system or under private contracts. The freeing of Chinese coolies and the creation of immigration legislation to control and manage the Chinese population occurred almost simultaneously. The coolie of the mid-nineteenth century therefore became the illegal alien of the late nineteenth century. Although regulation of Chinese immigration to the United States was conceived in the Anti-Coolie Bill in 1862 and the Page Law of 1875, the 1882 Chinese Exclusion Act gave birth to the illegal alien. The act also set in motion the creation of an entire bureaucracy to enforce Chinese exclusion, including inspectors, judges, jails, residency certificates, and interpreters. By the 1920s the bureaucracy that created illegal Chinese aliens had developed into a much more intricate machine designed to produce a greater number and greater variety of illegal aliens, including Europeans and Syrians. The 1920s also saw the creation of the quota system for immigrants, along with requirements for passports and visas, and the establishment of a robust border patrol with hundreds of agents. Canada's immigration bureaucracy grew at around the same time as it synchronized its anti-Chinese policies with those of the United States. Although Mexico, Cuba, and Peru increasingly adopted anti-Chinese measures in the twentieth century, their immigration bureaucracies remained small and ineffective.

This chapter focuses on the making of the illegal alien by examining the work of the immigration bureaucracy, the legislators, immigration inspectors, and courts that defined and implemented Chinese restrictions in the United States. The bureaucracy did not create migration, but in criminalizing certain migrants it produced the category of the illegal alien. The U.S. inspectors had a daunting task of patrolling thousands of miles of land and coastal borders for illegal entries and determining whether Chinese inside the United States were legal residents. To accomplish this task they relied on spies, informants, interpreters, and captured Chinese migrants themselves. The immigration hearing was the official forum to determine status, requiring migrants to document their identity as well as their entries and exits. Papers, legal proceedings, interrogations, and detention barracks were the tools the state used to regulate the modern immigrant. At stake was not simply the influx of thousands of new migrant workers but also the very idea of national sovereignty within a geographically bounded territory. Politicians, journalists, and intellectuals increasingly began to equate the strength of a nation with its ability to manage its borders against a seemingly everchanging and always threatening enemy: the illegal alien.

Growth of the Immigration Machine

At the time Chinese exclusion became law, the immigration bureaucracy was a jerry-rigged jalopy held together with bailing wire. The Customs Service under the Treasury Department was given the task of enforcing the law, but it had no prior experience with immigration laws or dealing with international steamship companies. The Chinese inspector position was created, but its jurisdiction, powers, and tasks were vague at best. By the 1890s, an administrative structure had been established with the secretary of the treasury at top, the commissioner general of immigration who directed the Immigration Bureau just below, and the Chinese inspectors at the very bottom. Inspectors had a great deal of latitude in interpreting the laws, and so each port tended to apply local standards. The San Francisco port under the leadership of Collector of the Customs John Wise had a reputation for being the strictest and for imposing restrictions on Chinese that were not even written into the law. In 1898, for example, 15 percent of all applicants were refused entry in San Francisco, while northeastern ports admitted everyone. Prospective migrants quickly learned that entering at ports with fewer Chinese arrivals significantly increased their chances of success.[2]

For the government, immigration went from being a financial burden to a source of revenue by the early twentieth century, thus creating an economic incentive for immigration enforcement. When Congress passed the exclusion act, it mandated a fifty-cent head tax that was deposited in an "immigrant fund" to help pay for enforcement of the new laws; the tax steadily increased, reaching eight dollars by 1917.[3] By 1904 the Immigration Bureau had become financially self-sufficient, taking in $300,000 more than it spent. In spite of the growing costs of running the immigration bureaucracy, the rising head taxes and other fees made immigration a profitable enterprise for the government.[4] In 1909 the Treasury Department did away with a separate "immigrant fund" and instead deposited head taxes as miscellaneous receipts directly into the treasury's coffers; the bureau would henceforth be funded by annual appropriations. In the two decades from 1894 to 1913, the government pocketed more $8.2 million, in spite of losses in the 1890s.[5] By 1910, the bureau made a record profit of $1.5 million. The next year the commissioner general of immigration announced proudly in his annual report, "Very distinctly has the immigration act become a revenue producer."[6]

In the nineteenth century, almost all of the costs of the immigration bureaucracy came from enforcing Chinese exclusion, but by the early twentieth century the amount dedicated to excluding Chinese became a smaller and smaller portion of the total budget as the bureau began inspections for Europeans and others. Furthermore, the bureau was constrained by Congress from spending more than half a million dollars enforcing Chinese exclusion. In 1904, for example, the bureau spent $432,000 to enforce Chinese exclusion, representing only one-third of its total budget.[7] By the early twentieth century, Immigrant Inspector Marcus Braun estimated that more than 50,000 migrants, including Italians, Greeks, Lebanese, Japanese, and Chinese, were crossing the U.S.-Mexico border clandestinely each year. Although Mexicans were not subject to specific quotas or restrictions, inspectors increasingly excluded them if they believed they were likely to become public charges. Between 1906 and 1910, 1,000–3,600 Mexicans were refused entry into the United States each year, and by 1917 rejections had reached a relatively high rate of 17 percent for Mexicans applying for entry as immigrants.[8] The bureaucracy that had been developed to exclude Chinese had by the early twentieth century become a much larger and more expensive bureaucracy whose mandate had expanded far beyond the Chinese.

The staffing, equipment needs, and physical plant of the bureaucracy mushroomed along with the increasing role of immigration enforcement. In twenty years, the personnel of the Immigration Bureau had doubled. In 1911 there were 1,600 employees working in the bureau's field service; by 1930 there were 2,263, plus another 805 in the Border Patrol.[9] Along with increasing revenues, the infrastructural footprint of the immigration bureaucracy began to grow as major inspection stations like that of Ellis Island in New York City (1892) and Angel Island in San Francisco (1910) were built. The 1904 annual report included numerous photographs of immigration inspection stations throughout the country in major U.S. cities and in remote rural outposts to demonstrate the physical presence and geographical reach of the bureau. There were even photographs of U.S. immigrant detention and landing stations in Canada, indicating the extraterritorial breadth of the Immigration Bureau.[10]

Immigration continued to generate revenue for the government through-

Immigrant detention station, Quebec, Canada. Bureau of Immigration, *Annual Report of the Commissioner General of Immigration to the Secretary of Labor* (1904).

out the 1910s, but the bureau's budget remained stagnant.[11] In 1915 the commissioner general proposed that head-tax money collected from immigrants be put toward Immigration Bureau work and not be funneled off into the general treasury.[12] This appeal was repeated the following year to no avail. In 1921 the immigration bureaucracy generated $2 million in profits for the government, but, given the passage of quota restrictions that year, the commissioner general worried about declining profits.[13] He was proved correct. Given the drastic reduction in immigration from 707,000 in 1921 to 310,000 in 1922, the Immigration Bureau collected less than half of what it had in the previous year. Increasing immigration restriction signified more work and less revenue.[14] The bureau managed to turn a profit in 1923, in part by charging aliens maintenance fees for meals, detention, and hospital care, but increased enforcement kept immigration unprofitable for the government in the long term.[15]

In 1924 Congress passed the Johnson-Reed Act, which established immigration quotas for different nationalities limited to 2 percent of their population in the United States in 1890. The 1890 date was chosen strategically to favor northern Europeans and to restrict southern and eastern Europeans. The 1924 quota restrictions, together with the establishment of the Border Patrol in that year meant that fewer immigrants paid the head tax and more employees were needed to enforce restrictions. In its first year the Border

Patrol had 450 officers and a budget of $1 million. Five years later, the Border Patrol had nearly doubled both the number of its officers and its budget.[16] In that same period, the cost of administering the immigration bureaucracy more than doubled, to over $8.4 million in 1930. At the same time, the amount of revenues collected from head taxes and fees stagnated. The result of the quota restrictions and increased cost of enforcement was that by 1930 the Immigration Bureau was a net cost to the government of $4.6 million each year, whereas in the early 1920s the government was making roughly $2 million dollars each year from immigrants.[17] The more successful the bureau became in preventing immigration, the less successful it became as a business.

Although the story of the growth of the immigration bureaucracy is dramatic and impressive, in relative terms the government devoted few resources to immigration control. Kelly Lytle Hernández, in her book *Migra!*, notes that even though the Border Patrol's budget and officers had doubled by 1932, it paled in comparison to the much larger Narcotics Division within the Prohibition Unit, which had a budget of over $11 million in 1926. The fact that the Narcotics Division had ten times more money than the Border Patrol, and that the total budget for federal liquor and narcotics control was more than $100 million, indicated the government's priorities. As Lytle Hernández concludes, "In the world of federal law enforcement, the U.S. Border Patrol and immigration control had very low priority."[18]

Nonetheless, the Immigration Bureau had established itself as a formidable bureaucratic machine in the three decades since it was consolidated under the Department of Labor. By 1930, the bureau employed more than 3,000 people, had an annual budget over $8 million, and could boast thousands of interrogations, apprehensions, and deportations every year. The Border Patrol, in particular, liked to tally up its work to justify its existence. For the six years between its creation and 30 June 1930, it reported the following statistics: 88,504 smuggled aliens and 2,384 smugglers of aliens apprehended; contraband estimated at $4,467,622 seized; 29,012,242 miles patrolled; 907,632 trains, 3,256,308 automobiles, 241,936 buses, 70,154 boats, 113,100 other conveyances, and 1,449,254 pedestrians examined; and in just four years, 101,955 aliens and citizens apprehended.[19] This bureaucracy appeared to be functioning efficiently, examining millions of vehicles and suspects, patrolling millions of miles, and arresting more than 100,000 lawbreakers. These statistics, however, mask the tens of thousands of immigrants who managed to enter the United States clandestinely and avoid detection.

Legal Landscapes

The rise of surveillance and patrols on the physical borderline and ports of entry coincided with a narrowing of the legal spaces for Chinese migrants. Although Chinese successfully exploited the legal system in the nineteenth century, their ability to do so was severely curtailed by the early twentieth century. Even before the exclusion act, Chinese pursued justice in the courts frequently and successfully. Individual Chinese and the Six Companies hired the best lawyers and paid them hefty sums. As historian Lucy Salyer shows, in California alone, by 1891, Chinese filed more than 7,000 petitions in federal courts to have their cases reviewed after being denied entry by an immigration inspector. In 85–90 percent of these cases, Chinese won reversals from the courts. Although the Northern California district court was not as lenient in the following years (1891–1905), Chinese still had a success rate that averaged well above 50 percent. The 1891 Immigration Act gave immigration officials final decision-making power over whether to allow aliens to enter, but ironically the Chinese were exempt from those provisions and were instead subject to the exclusion acts. It was not until 1903, when the Immigration Bureau consolidated its jurisdiction over both Chinese and non-Chinese immigrants, that Chinese fell under the general immigration act. Federal courts continued to frustrate efforts to enforce Chinese exclusion through the beginning of the twentieth century, but over time the courts' discretion diminished, and ultimately ended with the Ju Toy decision in 1905.[20]

As their legal channels for redress were being closed off, Chinese turned to another tactic, which was to claim U.S. citizenship and seek redress in courts where they previously had been successful. In 1904 scores of Chinese crossed the border from Canada, submitted to arrest, and claimed to be U.S. citizens while refusing to answer any further questions. Immigration inspectors ruled that they were not citizens and ordered their deportation. After choosing not to pursue an administrative appeal to the secretary of labor and commerce, Sing Tuck and thirty-one others brought their case to a district court on a writ of habeas corpus. The Sing Tuck case ended up having broad constitutional implications when the Supreme Court ruled in the Immigration Bureau's favor, indicating that its officers had the right to determine citizenship status.[21] Although the majority found that the administrative procedure was adequate for determining the citizenship status of new arrivals, it left open a small loophole for judicial review after exhausting administrative appeals. While the Sing Tuck case wound its way through the courts, more than 200

Chinese overflowed the detention center in Malone, New York, where seventeen of them died. After the Supreme Court decision, the remainder were deported back to China.[22]

The consolidation of responsibility for all immigrants under the Immigration Bureau in 1903 was the beginning of the end for Chinese ability to seek redress in the courts. The bureau had been used to acting on its own without judicial review, and once the Chinese came under its purview it was not about to let the courts interfere. As one New York federal judge explained in 1896, "If the Commissioner [of immigration] wish[es] to order an alien drawn, quartered, and chucked overboard they could do so without interference." In 1905 Ju Toy, a cook from Oakland, California, who attempted to return from a visit to China was denied entry by bureau inspectors. The district court ruled in Ju Toy's favor, but the Supreme Court upheld the bureau's decision, arguing that the decision of the secretary of commerce and labor was final. "Due process of law does not require a judicial trial" for citizens entering the country, wrote Justice Oliver Wendell Holmes Jr. From that point on, Chinese had to argue that bureau officials had abused their authority or not provided them due process; they could no longer immediately file habeas corpus writs and pursue their cases in federal courts. It was not until 1922, when the Supreme Court decided the *Ng Fung Ho v. White* case, that a constitutional right to a judicial hearing was extended to those claiming to be citizens.[23] In the meantime, with or without judicial protections, Chinese kept coming into the United States by boat, train, car, and on foot, sometimes through legal ports and sometimes through the many illegal entryways.

When U.S. immigration officers caught Chinese they suspected of entering the country illegally, it was up to the Chinese to prove that they were legal residents of the United States by showing a legitimate residency certificate and providing witnesses. If officers could show that they were using false papers, or that the story of where they lived was not true, they could be deported. While the law required them to be deported to the country from which they entered the United States, it was often not so clear whether they had come directly from China or from a neighboring country like Canada, Cuba, or Mexico. Since many of the Chinese who had entered illegally from neighboring countries claimed during their trials to have come directly from China, it became difficult for them to change their story later. Most Chinese preferred deportation to a neighboring country because it was much easier to reenter from there than from China. Although the burden of proof was mostly on the Chinese, there were limits to the immigration officers' ability to deport Chinese they picked up in the United States.

In 1914 four Chinese contested their deportations based on various anomalies in their hearings. The judge in the U.S. District Court in western New York found that one of the defendants, Ho Jung Ley, should not be deported because the immigration officers had not proved that he had been domiciled in the country less than three years. The only evidence for the government's case was that his clothing was made in Hong Kong and that he had no friends or relatives in the United States. The judge ruled against the other three defendants, arguing that even if there were minor anomalies in their hearings, they had all received a fair trial. The Chinese argued that having Inspector Wallace as prosecutor, interpreter, and judge was unfair, but the judge disagreed, saying, "his familiarity with their language no doubt secured to them a fairer trial than if a third party had had to be called in as interpreter."[24] As Lucy Salyer has argued, the "federal district court refused to impart a strict judicial notion of the concept of a fair hearing in immigration matters." Deportation hearings were held without the immigrants' having counsel or the ability to compel witnesses to testify.[25] Although Chinese used the courts effectively, the rules were stacked against them, and their right to a fair hearing was severely diminished after 1905.

Canadian Restrictions

At the beginning of the twentieth century Canada generally promoted immigration, but when it came to "undesirable immigrants" the United States and Canada had almost identical laws. Like the United States, Canadians excluded aliens they considered "physical, mental and moral defectives and delinquents." However, there were important distinctions. Canada did not exclude polygamists, anarchists, or contract laborers. In addition, the contract labor provisions in the two countries were polar opposites; a migrant arriving in Canada who did not show proof of a job offer could be excluded, while the same migrant who arrived in the United States would be excluded because a job offer suggested he was a contract laborer. In terms of enforcement, the United States was much more likely to exclude migrants than Canada. In 1908, for example, Canada rejected 1 out of 262 migrants, while the United States rejected migrants at almost four times that rate, 1 out of 72. While some of this difference can be chalked up to different laws, when subtracting contract laborers from the equation, the United States still rejected approximately three times as many migrants as Canada. Based on this data, the Dillingham Commission (1907–11), charged by Congress with investigating immigration, concluded that "the inspection of immigrants, both medical and otherwise, under the Canadian law is less rigid than under the United States law." At the same time, the commission also found that Canadians discriminated much more heavily against southern and eastern Europeans than did U.S. inspectors.[26]

Even though Canadian inspectors appeared more lax in their enforcement, they had undisputed power to determine eligibility of prospective immigrants. Unlike in the United States, where judicial review was the main avenue for Chinese immigrants to protest government exclusions, at least until 1905 in Canada the inspectors had the final word. Although there was a provision in Canada for a board of inquiry to make determinations for immigrant cases, by 1910 no board had ever been convened. In 1910, a new immigration bill in parliament proposed a permanent board of inquiry and gave immigrants the right to counsel; in the United States, courts had already decided that immigrants had no right to counsel under the Constitution.[27] Taken as a whole, immigrants seemed to be in a better position to contest immigration authorities in the United States, at least until around 1910, when it became harder for immigrants to seek judicial review in the United States and easier for them to obtain such a review in Canada. For the Chinese, however, migrating to Canada, which until 1923 did not prohibit Chinese laborers, was a much better bet than trying to squeeze through the U.S. immigration inspection gauntlet.

Deportations

Rejection at ports of entry in the United States was the most common way for immigrants to be sent back home, but arrests and deportations inside the country were also becoming more frequent in the twentieth century. Arrests of Chinese near the border often resulted in deportation, but those apprehended in the interior who claimed citizenship were usually able to win their cases on appeal to district courts. Even if the Immigration Bureau found them guilty in an administrative hearing, Chinese had a second chance to prove their citizenship in the district court. In 1911 the Commissioner of Immigration complained that "it is only occasionally that a Chinaman arrested in one of the large interior cities having a considerable Chinese population can be deported." Even though the law placed the burden of proof of citizenship on the Chinese, courts often demanded that the government prove the Chinese were not citizens. As a result, the commissioner argued, "arresting Chinese within the interior too frequently results in converting them into American citizens, usually by flagrant miscarriage of justice."[28] In 1908 the

Immigration Bureau developed a new strategy and began to arrest Chinese under the general immigration laws to prevent a judicial hearing that would have been required under the exclusion act.[29] The numbers of deportations of Chinese ranged quite a bit from year to year, as did the success of Chinese in contesting deportation in the courts. The number of deportations brought to the Northern District of California Court from 1893 to 1905, ranged from a low of 16 in 1893 to a high of 261 in 1903, but in most years only 30–40 cases were brought before the court. The success of Chinese in challenging their deportations also ranged widely, from 75 percent of cases resulting in deportation in 1893 to only 10 percent in 1901.[30] Nationally, about 500 Chinese were deported each year in the early twentieth century.[31] By 1930 the total number of deportations rose sharply to 16,631, but only 461 of those were returned to China.[32] It is likely that Chinese figured prominently among the thousands of deportees to Mexico and Canada. In 1911 the bureau began to return Chinese apprehended on the southern border to Mexico rather than ship them to China, believing that many of them purposely had themselves arrested in the hope of securing a free trip back to China.[33] Furthermore, deportation was an expensive and time-consuming process. For example, in 1904, it cost the bureau $75,000 to deport 673 Chinese, or approximately $112 for every Chinese deportee.[34] Given the thousands of Chinese who entered clandestinely or using fraudulent papers, deportation was an ineffective and expensive means to stop Chinese migration.

The Dillingham Commission viewed favorably Canada's relatively high rate of deportations. In the United States, most deportations occurred because of illegal entry or when an immigrant became a public charge within three years of arrival. In Canada, immigrants could be deported not only for becoming public charges but also for demonstrating health or mental defects like diabetes, blindness, or deafness within two years of arrival. For 1908–9, Canada deported 1 in every 193 immigrants, while the United States only deported 1 in every 544. Therefore, while Canadian inspections were relatively lax and their rejection rate lower than that of inspections in the United States, the Canadian deportation policy was relatively harsh. Deportations, however, mainly affected Europeans; the rate of deportations for Chinese in Canada was astonishingly low, only 2 out of 3,890 between 1903 and 1909.[35]

Canada seemed more open to immigrants than the United States, but U.S. immigration officials envied the more streamlined deportation process in Canada. The U.S. Immigration Bureau pushed the courts for authority to deport immigrants quickly and without judicial review. In 1912 the U.S. Supreme Court responded, issuing a ruling that would speed up deportations for the bureau and simplify its work. The Supreme Court decided against Wong You in a case that upheld immigration officials' ability to issue administrative deportations through general immigration laws and not process them through the more onerous Chinese Exclusion Act. The result was an easier and more efficient deportation process. As a consequence, the strategy of Chinese showing up on the border and submitting to arrest, claiming to be U.S. citizens, like they had in 1904 in New York, was curtailed. However, when they were arrested near the Canadian border, district courts ruled that they could not be returned to China but had to be deported to the country from which they entered. Immigration officers complained that they could not comply with the court order because Canada required a $500 head tax for every immigrant entry and the destitute immigrants either could not or would not pay the tax.[36]

In the late 1880s, U.S. immigration officers would routinely force Chinese across the Canadian border. On one occasion in 1888, the Canadians refused to accept a group of Chinese who had been denied entry into the United States in Buffalo and who could not pay their head tax to enter Canada. The group of men were trapped in limbo on the Niagara Suspension Bridge, unable to return to the United States and prevented from entering Canada. It is not clear what happened to these men, but it is likely that the United States would have had to accept the Chinese and then deport them back to China. On another occasion nineteen Chinese found to have entered the United States illegally were sent back to British Columbia, but the Canadian authorities refused to allow them in the country unless they paid their head tax. The nineteen were held in prison on McNeil Island in the Puget Sound while their case was being adjudicated. Finally, in May 1890, after the men had spent two and a half years in prison, the secretary of the treasury ordered them deported back to China in what became one of the first deportations from Washington Territory.[37] Given the difficulty and expense of deporting migrants and the political pushback it encountered, the Immigration Bureau ultimately found the strict immigration laws ineffective. The outgoing commissioner general of immigration, Daniel Keefe, summed it up succinctly in 1913: "The present immigration law has but little effect in reducing or checking the great influx of aliens."[38]

Immigration Hearings

When Chinese were caught on the U.S. side of the border, they usually claimed to be U.S. citizens. It was up to the inspectors to prove through interrogations and investigations that their stories were false. These investigations were expensive and time consuming for the Immigration Bureau. In the process, however, they produced voluminous reports about smuggling networks. It would be naive to assume that every statement by Chinese migrants was true. They were seeking to enter a country with highly restrictive laws designed to keep them out, and most received extensive coaching on what to say to immigration officials to increase their chances of entry. Many Chinese caught crossing into the United States illegally refused to provide any information and simply asked to be deported. The testimony of others, however, provides a glimpse into the shadowy world of clandestine smuggling.

Immigration hearings left little room for Chinese to maneuver, especially without access to legal counsel. In many cases, inspectors were able to solicit an admission of guilt. Given that the hearings were held with the assistance of interpreters who may not have understood the dialects of the suspects, it is not clear whether the Chinese even comprehended exactly what they were being asked. For example, in 1914, when Lum Sing was found in a Grand Trunk Freight car in Manchester, New York, hidden along with another Chinese man among merchandise, he admitted he was Chinese. Sing was asked, "Do you dispute the allegation that you are an alien![?]" His response, "I am of Chinese parentage and born in China," conveniently sidestepped the question of "alien" status and whether he had entered the country illegally. Nonetheless, this testimony was taken as an admission that he had entered the United States clandestinely, and he was deported.[39]

Immigration hearings often led to absurd questions by the inspectors and absurd answers by the Chinese suspects. Chinese migrants were generally presumed to be guilty and lying and had to prove otherwise to the inspectors. In the case of Lee Foo, arrested in Plattsburgh, New York, in 1919, his inability to speak English or explain his lack of friends or relatives in the United States doomed him. Lee admitted that he had no residency certificate, although he claimed to have been born in San Francisco and lived in New York. His story seemed vague and unconvincing. When the inspector confronted Lee with the fact that his jacket was made in China and his undershirt had a label from Canada, he responded that a friend had given him these clothes. His story kept changing; finally, when the inspector asked how it is possible to have been born in the United States and lived in New York for twenty years and be unable to speak English, Lee retorted, "Because I am stupid." The inspector recommended deportation.[40]

Given the difficulty of catching the Chinese as they crossed the border, it was up to inspectors to catch Chinese in the process of heading to the interior on foot or in trains. On 11 August 1914, Ching Hoy Soon and five other young Chinese men were arrested while walking along the railroad tracks near Odem, a small town a few miles from Corpus Christi, Texas. Ching was fifty, and the ages of the five others ranged from twenty to thirty. The six men were transferred to Galveston, where they were individually brought before an immigration inspector for a deportation hearing. The hearing consisted of a series of questions to ascertain when the Chinese men had arrived in the United States, where they had worked, and whether they had illegally entered the United States from Mexico. The Chinese men all denied having entered from Mexico, but their stories about where they had lived in the United States were vague and contradictory. In the end, the immigration inspector decided that the six men had lied and ordered their deportation.

Because Ching Hoy Soon was older and spoke "fairly good" English, the immigration inspector suspected that he was a smuggler who had gone into Mexico to ferry the five younger Chinese to the United States.[41] Unlike the other men, who gave cursory and vague accounts of their time in the United States, Ching provided an elaborate and detailed story about his multiple residences in the United States in the preceding thirty-four years, including details such as street addresses and the names of his employers. The way Ching responded to questions also suggests that he wanted to emphasize the ignorance that Anglo-Americans displayed toward Chinese names and their general obliviousness to individual Chinese identities. Ching's critique was especially pertinent given that the inspector's interrogation rested on his ability to identify individual Chinese. When asked his name in the hearing, he stated, "My name is Ching Hoy Soon, that is my Chinese name, but the Americans call me Charley Sun." Even after Ching stated his real name, the immigration inspector continued to refer to him as Charley Sun, only recognizing his Chinese name as an alias. Ching, in contrast, acknowledged two naming systems, one Chinese and the other Anglo-American, stating that the Chinese name of the ship on which he arrived was *Leon Hi Kee* but that there was also an Anglo-American name. The inspector privileged the U.S. name, rendering the original name as an alias and therefore fraudulent.[42] Inspectors would often have difficulty with Chinese names, using several different spellings of the same name in one document. One inspector acknowledged that the certificate of residency "might have been [under] quite a different name" from the one commonly used.[43] The divergence between the commonly used names and the names that appeared in the documents made the job of identifying individual Chinese very difficult.

Ching's testimony at the hearing paints picture of a highly mobile world for the Chinese worker that relied on strong friendship networks in the Chinese community on the West Coast and Southwest. According to his testimony, Ching arrived in San Francisco in 1880 when he was seventeen years old. He went into great detail about the places where he had worked and lived up and down the Pacific coast, from Southern California to Portland, Oregon. In all, Ching moved seventeen times, living for as little as a few months at a time in some locales. Rather than occupying one job, he seemed to easily move between various jobs as cook, laundryman, and gold miner. In many of these places, he found work in Chinese owned businesses, but on a few occasions he worked for Anglo-Americans. He claimed that he was visiting a friend in Portland, Oregon, in 1894 when the registry requirements began, and he provided the residency certificate number 55613. However, when the inspectors compared Ching's photograph on his residency certificate with the original in the archives, they discovered that they were not the same person, the certificate having been issued to someone twenty years his senior.[44]

Whether or not these six men knew each other before their meeting on the railroad tracks in Odem, Texas, they collectively had Chinese contacts throughout the United States and even in Mexico. The immigration inspectors kept tabs on the letters the Chinese sent while in custody, which included addresses in Lincoln County, Nevada; New Orleans; Union City, Tennessee; San Francisco; Mobile, Alabama; St. Louis; and Mexico City.[45] This suggests that even if the men had crossed the border illegally into the United States, they were not arriving in a country where they had no friends, family, or contacts.

The arrest of these six men in Odem, Texas, is just one of thousands of cases where Chinese found themselves caught in the United States without papers. This incident illustrates the kind of technologies of control that the U.S. government employed to manage its borders and enforce its immigration policies. Principal among these technologies was the residency certificate. Following passage of the Geary Act in 1892, all Chinese living in the United States had to obtain a residency certificate and were required to produce such a document upon request. The certificate system theoretically allowed the government to determine which Chinese were in the country legally and which ones had emigrated illegally after the 1882 Chinese Exclusion Act. However, this system also contained the seeds of its own destruction by opening up the possibility of creating a legal status for oneself through the use of false papers.

Illegal Entry and Fraudulent Papers

The primary means of verifying the legality of Chinese once they had made it into U.S. territory was by checking their residency certificates. However, if the Chinese claimed to have a certificate but did not have it with them when they were apprehended, the inspector would have to begin an investigation. Inspectors were also wary of Chinese who had false certificates or were simply using someone else's certificate, as apparently was the case with Ching Hoy Soon. When inspectors found Chinese near the border, they would have to decide, based on the suspects' ability to produce certificates and speak English and their knowledge of the United States, whether they should be arrested. In one case in 1915, six Chinese suspects were picked up in Elmira, New York. One of the men had with him a discharge certificate from 1902 issued by a commissioner in Plattsburgh. Judges who ruled that the Chinese were legally in the country issued discharge certificates; these discharge certificates could be used in the future to prove one's legal status. Another one of the migrants said he had a residency certificate in New York. A third, twenty-two-year-old Lee Sam, claimed to have been born in Bakersfield, California. However, given that he could not speak or understand a word of English, and had not yet become "accustomed to walking in occidental shoes," the inspector believed he was a new arrival and arrested him.[46] The Immigration Bureau was also aware that new Chinese immigrants sometimes used the certificates of legal Chinese residents who had died, so the bureau tried to keep track of Chinese deaths to cancel these certificates.[47]

Even when Chinese could produce certificates of identity that indicated they were in the country legally, inspectors still suspected fraud. In 1909 Hart Hyatt North, the San Francisco commissioner of immigration, asserted that "nearly 90 percent" of the Chinese who sought admission to the United States did so fraudulently. Some Chinese who were interviewed on Angel Island in the 1920s and 1930s corroborated this statistic, claiming that as many as 95 percent of Chinese used fraudulent papers to enter. One of the detainees, Arthur Lem, explained that when someone announced they were leaving China, people would ask, "Whose papers are you using?"[48] While both of these percentages seem extremely high, it is likely that fraudulent papers were used in a majority of Chinese entries. Inspectors therefore would attempt to verify the identities of the Chinese by requesting a copy of the certificates held by the Immigration Bureau to compare the photographs and physical descriptions. Canadian immigration inspectors ran into similar problems at the end of the nineteenth century, believing that many Chi-

Left to right: Chin Chung, U.S. Commissioner's Court, Northern District New York, 28 October 1902; Chin Chung, New York, 28 June 1911; Chin Chung, Vancouver, British Columbia, 8 October 1912. NARA-Seattle, RG 85, Port of Vancouver, British Columbia, 1905–25, Box 1, Van 12.

nese sold their return certificates to others. Suspecting fraud, they ended up moving to a system of interrogations similar to what was practiced in the United States, but the Canadian immigration bureaucracy was underfunded and the government outsourced gatekeeping to private companies like the Canadian Pacific Railway.[49]

In trying to establish the identity of Chinese, inspectors had a difficult time determining whether photographs taken years earlier matched the people who presented themselves at ports with preinvestigation papers in hand. One such case was that of Chin Chung, who departed from Vancouver on 2 August 1911 and returned through the same port on 7 October 1912. His file included a 1902 document from the U.S. Commissioner's Court in northern New York attesting to his right to remain legally in the United States. In the photograph affixed to that court document, the subject wore a traditional Chinese shirt and had his hair in a queue. In the preinvestigation document (which dated from 1911) and the landing document (1912), the subject sported more of a Western-style haircut and did not appear to have a queue. It is possible that Chin changed his hairstyle in the decade between the first and last photographs and that he gained some weight, but looking at the first and last photograph, it is not clear that they are the same person.[50] The inability of immigration officers to distinguish Chinese faces left open the possibility for Chinese to use other people's papers.

Even with the benefit of hindsight it is almost impossible to determine whether particular individuals were lying in order to gain entry. Immigration officials faced the same conundrum. Sometimes fathers would not be able to identify photographs of their children, but that might be reasonable if they had not seen them in many years. In other cases, the testimony of children and parents differed about the layout of their homes in China, but again, such minor discrepancies were not necessarily proof of deception. In fact, stories that seemed to match up perfectly were probably evidence that coaching books were used to synchronize stories between relatives or fictional relatives.

In July 1914 Quon Goon Duck landed in Vancouver, claiming to be the son of Quon Lim Chong, a native of San Francisco. Quon Lim returned to China twice, once when he was ten years old and a second time when he was thirty-three years old. After his second trip, he was arrested in Burlington, Vermont, and taken before a commissioner who found that he was legally in the country because he had been born in the United States. Quon Lim was arrested a second time in El Paso, after crossing into the United States from Mexico. He was released by the court after presenting the Vermont court's discharge papers. However, the lack of photographs on the documents made verifying the identity of the bearer almost impossible. The immigrant inspector, John F. Dunton, who noted discrepancies between the testimony of alleged son and father, the inability of the father to identify a photograph of the son, and the circuitous route of the father from Vancouver to Montreal to New York, and then on to Mexico City, Juárez, and finally El Paso, suggested that the father was not who he claimed to be. While no action was taken against the father, who had already been declared a citizen by two courts, Dunton recommended denying entry to the alleged son. If the son was allowed to enter, Dunton reasoned, this would open the door for two additional sons and a daughter to follow.[51]

Letters written by Chinese and then captured and translated by immigration authorities help us see how migrants concocted elaborate family histories and were able to convince immigration officers that they were who they claimed to be. In one instance, Foo Gwan was awaiting an immigration hearing in New York City when he was handed a pastry. Some people told him not to eat the pastry because it had been poisoned, but when he did finally bite into it, he discovered a coaching letter and photograph inside of it. On another occasion, Fong Gau wrote about the outlandishness of the whole fabricated family story he had provided to inspectors: "Wing Tong Shuk will testify as my father, although he does not even belong to the Fong family, and does not know anyone by the name of Mok Pok Yun, which is the name he gives. It is certainly funny that the father and the two sons all belong to different families, and my mother does not know the man who came to this country with me as my brother."[52] Such confessions in personal letters were used as evidence by immigration inspectors to deny entry to Chinese.

The increasing importance of the photograph, the certificate of residency, and other "papers" that Chinese needed to prove their legal status in the United States gave birth to an industry in fraudulent documents. In September 1919 Dea Kay Sing, the owner of a Chinese restaurant in Globe, Arizona, was arrested after an immigration inspector discovered a trunk full of residency certificates and large amounts of cash. The evidence suggested that Dea was involved in smuggling and selling false papers to Chinese. At the hearing, the inspector pressed Dea, asking him why he had attempted to bribe him to have the documents from the trunk returned. Dea claimed to be holding the certificates for Chinese working in the area. However, when the inspector showed him a photograph of Dea's family, including his wife and children, Dea claimed to be unable to identify them. Apparently, he had sent this photograph to China to be used by Chinese attempting to enter the United States illegally as his relatives. Dea had previously testified to immigration authorities on several occasions by identifying his Chinese relatives in photographs. The inspector interrogating Dea was exasperated by his lack of cooperation at the hearing and his unwillingness to identify his own family photograph. If Dea could not recognize his own wife and children, the inspector asked, "then how in the name of Creation have you been able to identify the photographs of dozens of Chinese persons claiming to be natives, or sons of natives, of this country when at the time of identifying them you claimed that you had only seen them once or twice in China and then only for a few moments?" Dea responded, "This photograph is too old; it has been too long ago."[53]

Fraudulent papers were similarly a problem for Canadian, Mexican, and Cuban immigrations officials. In 1930 a secret memorandum from the Mexican Ministry of Foreign Relations pointed to the main causes for clandestine immigration of Chinese to Mexico. The first on the list was the inability to prevent the use of false documents like passports and identity cards.[54] Mexican authorities only began to ask for visas from Chinese entering from Hong Kong in 1920, and there was no entry or exit annotation on identity cards by Mexican officials until the middle of 1921, making it almost impossible to determine who was legally in the country.[55] Canadian entry documents lacked photographs until 1913, and exit certificates lacked photographs until 1910, leaving ample room for fraud. Officials there pointed out that 99 percent of Chinese immigrants "lost" their entry documents, thus suggesting that they had actually been sold in China to prospective migrants.[56] Chinese were also able to purchase fraudulent Cuban passports in Hong Kong that gave them permission to travel to Cuba.[57] For the right price, prospective migrants could buy entry documents for several different countries in the Americas.

Performing as one of the exempt classes, either students or merchants, was one of the easiest ways that Chinese could gain admission to the United States. Chinese who dressed up to look like middle- and upper-class students and merchants found it easier to convince inspectors that they were who they claimed to be. As important as looking the part, papers provided documentary evidence of their status. Chinese companies also regularly sold partnerships so that prospective migrants could enter as merchants. In 1911, 100 school-age Chinese children arrived in Seattle pretending to be students. They had fraudulent letters from private schools in Seattle and San Francisco, and they arrived in second-class rather than steerage to allay suspicions. Chinese also frequently forged the signatures of prominent whites on their merchant papers to convince inspectors that their papers were legitimate.[58] In 1913 Commissioner General Caminetti wrote in his annual report on immigration that "Chinese laborers are constantly gaining admission, in the guise of 'minor sons of merchants,' 'student,' 'natives,' or 'sons of natives.'"[59] With a little bit of creativity, forged papers, and a photograph, Chinese could perform as merchants or students and gain entry into the United States. Sometimes the performances were weak and the would-be migrants were deported. Mostly, however, Chinese knew what the immigrant inspectors wanted to see and hear, and as long as they played their roles well, they gained admission.

Protesting Exclusion and the 1905 Anti-U.S. Boycott

Chinese mostly responded to increasingly stringent immigration restrictions by evading the law either through the use of fraudulent papers at legal ports or by clandestine entry. However, Chinese also resisted restrictionist policies more overtly, refusing to comply with registration requirements and challenging the Geary Act in court in 1893. These protests were highly successful, at least temporarily. The Six Companies led the movement against the Geary Act's requirement that all Chinese to carry an identification paper with a photograph that indicated their residency status and described their physical characteristics. Posting signs forbidding Chinese to register and other efforts by the Six Companies to resist the identification requirements paid off. An estimated 99 percent of Chinese refused to register by the deadline, forcing the government to extend the deadline by six months. The law was challenged by Six Companies lawyers, but the Supreme Court ruled in *Fong Yue Ting* that the Geary Act was constitutional. In fact, the ruling went farther, holding that deportation was not a constitutional violation because aliens were not protected by the U.S. Constitution. With the failure to win in the courts, the Six Companies and the Chinese government reversed their strategy in 1894 and ordered all Chinese to register. Although the government may have been exaggerating its success, it claimed that 100,000 Chinese eventually registered.[60]

The Six Companies and the Chinese government attempted to defend Chinese laborers, but they were particularly concerned with protecting the interests of merchants and maintaining the vibrant trade with China. The harsh treatment and humiliating inspections of Chinese who were supposed to be exempt from Chinese exclusion laws, including diplomats, students, merchants, and U.S. citizens, eventually sparked a boycott on U.S. goods in 1905. The exempt-status Chinese were particularly upset by the invasive measurements used in the Bertillon system, whereby inspectors armed with specialized calipers measured the skulls, torsos, ears, genitalia, and limbs of Chinese entering the country in order to better identify them. In addition to merchandise, the boycott extended to U.S. ships, schools, and employment in U.S. companies based in China. The boycott was led by Chinese merchants in Shanghai, but the effort was quickly supported in both the United States and China by students, teachers, diplomats, laborers, and women.[61] Historian Guanhua Wang shows how the boycott briefly unified a broad multiclass social movement, reflecting both growing nationalism in China and emergent Chinese merchant gentry and intellectual-professional classes in urban centers around the globe. The inability of the Qing government to negotiate effectively for Chinese in the United States signaled a crisis for the new middle classes.[62]

The Immigration Bureau tracked the efforts by Chinese in the United States to protest the new regulations, and it translated reports from Chinese-language newspapers about the boycott and other efforts to protest the new harsh examination procedures. Newspapers listed the money that had been received and expended in opposing the exclusion acts, including paying for stamps for letters to Shanghai, paying a lecturer to organize people in Canada, and hiring people to write articles in English. By August 1905 the General Society at San Francisco for the Opposing of the "New Exclusion Treaty" had more than $10,000 on hand to pursue its fight.[63] The boycott had a dramatic effect on trade with China, reducing cloth imports from the United States by half and mineral oils by one-third in 1906.[64] This transpacific organizing effort was well-organized, relatively well-financed, and savvy about the need to influence broader public opinion.

President Theodore Roosevelt responded to the boycott by demanding that inspectors respect the rights of the Chinese who were allowed to enter the United States. Although Roosevelt reaffirmed the desire to keep Chinese laborers out and noted that many of them had entered illegally, he ordered inspectors to use great restraint at ports of entry: "We cannot afford either from the standpoint of our national interests or from the standpoint of civilization to be put in the attitude of failing to do complete justice and to show courtesy and consideration to Chinese who are entitled to come here."[65] After a meeting with the president, the secretary of commerce and labor told an inspector that it was "not desired that you shall make any arrests of Chinese within your district until further notice."[66] In June 1905 the Department of Commerce and Labor issued a sternly worded directive to its inspectors to treat Chinese who did not appear to be laborers "with the same consideration extended to members of any other nationality, and they are not under any circumstances to be subjected to unnecessary surveillance." In case the message was not already clear enough, the circular emphasized that "harshness . . . will not for one moment be tolerated," and that "any discourtesy shown Chinese persons, either laborers or of the exempt classes, by any of the officials of this Department will be cause for immediate dismissal of the offender from the service."[67] The boycott thus succeeded in ending the invasive Bertillon inspections, curtailing arrests of Chinese in the interior of the country, and generally limiting the power exercised by inspectors at the border. Chinese exclusion of laborers did not disappear, but professional and upper-class Chinese and Chinese Americans had scored a significant victory.

The new orders meant that if a Chinese person was able to make it past the border, he or she would be relatively safe in the interior of the country. In 1913 the assistant commissioner general of immigration complained that "the fact that a Chinese person, once in this country, is safe from molestation is a strong inducement to successful smuggling." He recommended a more robust system of checking papers of all Chinese and arresting the ones who were in the country illegally.[68] Given the potential negative impact on U.S.-China trade relations, and the power of the 1905 boycott, such a policy was never enacted. Nonetheless, immigration authorities continued to subject Chinese to harsh inspections, and in 1910 the Immigration Bureau opened the Angel Island inspection station. The Chinese Six Companies protested the new station and the harsh examinations there to little effect. Chinese merchants and others exempt from exclusion laws continued to push for their own rights, arguing not against exclusion laws per se but the erroneous application of exclusion and inspections to themselves. In 1910 the Immigration Bureau issued new instructions to conduct inspections only on boats for officials, merchants with Section 6 certificates, citizens with return certificates, preinvestigated returning merchants, students, and teachers, and preinvestigated wives and children of returning merchants and natives. All others were to be brought to Angel Island for more intrusive and extensive examinations. Nonetheless, Chinese merchants and U.S. citizens continued to be brought to Angel Island if they were suspected of using fraudulent papers or if inspectors desired further review of their cases. The reaffirmation of the line between exempt and nonexempt Chinese served to strengthen the divide between deserving and undeserving, legal and illegal immigrants.

Conclusion

The massive militarized borders that we know today, with airplanes, drones, satellite technology, and electronic fences did not exist when Chinese exclusion became law. Chinese inspectors were few and far between in the 1880s and 1890s, and they could barely manage to process migrants arriving at established ports, not to mention the thousands who entered clandestinely through the thousands of miles of unprotected coastline and land borders. However, by the early twentieth century, the Immigration Bureau became larger and more centralized; its staffing and budgets grew as well as its authority to act independently of judicial review.

Inspectors faced the impossible task of enforcing exclusion laws against Chinese who used fraudulent papers and concocted complex family histories to get through the gates. Chinese also adeptly used the legal system to overturn immigration officers' decisions. Even as the legal venues for redress were increasingly shut off by the Supreme Court, lawyers for the Chinese found ways to bring their cases into the courts and out of the jurisdiction of the immigration hearings. Finally, the Chinese boycott of U.S. goods in 1905 secured better treatment for exempt classes but not for the masses of laborers, who faced harsher and more humiliating inspections and detentions. As more migrants crossed illegally, the bureau demanded larger budgets and more patrol agents. The ability of Chinese to evade exclusion thus justified the Immigration Bureau's existence and expansion. Failure paradoxically guaranteed the bureau's success.

The end result was the birth of a massive immigration bureaucracy that maintained detailed statistics on every aspect of immigration, including the race, nationality, age, sex, and occupation of every arrival and departure from the country. Detention and landing facilities were built throughout the United States and Canada to interrogate millions of migrants, patrol millions of miles, and apprehend and deport thousands of migrants each year. Starting in the late nineteenth century and picking up in the early twentieth century, Europeans, Syrians, Lebanese, and Japanese who had been denied entry into the United States because they appeared to be poor or diseased began to use Canada and Mexico as stepping-stones to the United States.[69] By the 1920s, when Congress passed quota restrictions for Europeans, the bureaucracy that had been developed to keep track of and exclude Chinese was put to work to restrict and manage hundreds of thousands of Jews, southern and eastern Europeans, and others. Even Mexicans, who were exempted from the quota restrictions, faced increasing difficulties trying to enter the United States, based on fears they would become public charges or carried contagious diseases. The idea of the alien that had been constructed around the Chinese was easily applied to new groups of migrants.

The tightening of legal entry through the front door for Chinese and other immigrants led to the prying open of back doors through Canada, Mexico, and the Caribbean. Given the huge expanses of unguarded land and sea borders, it was almost impossible for immigration inspectors to prevent clandestine entry, no matter how many millions of miles they patrolled and how many thousands of people they questioned. The next chapter will focus on these backdoor entryways, which became the most important channel for illegal entry into the United States.

CHAPTER 5

Clandestine Crossings to the United States

We cannot have too much immigration of the right kind, and we should have none
at all of the wrong kind. . . . I hold, Sir, that all immigrants who come to the United States
clandestinely, who are smuggled into the territory of our republic, and—of course—thus
evade subjecting themselves to the inspection demanded by our laws, are undesirable
immigrants and are "per se" immigration of "the wrong kind."
—President Theodore Roosevelt, 1903

The potential points of entry into the United States were almost limitless. Although immigration authorities and customs inspectors tried to channel entry through the front doors at seaports on the Atlantic and Pacific coasts and back doors on the borders with Canada and Mexico, migrants could simply walk across land borders or take boats through the unguarded and unfenced boundaries that connected the United States to Canada, Mexico, and the Caribbean. While immigration inspectors vigilantly poked, prodded, and fumigated immigrants coming through the front and back doors, the official ports of entry, the windows remained ajar. It is through these unofficial and illegal entryways that most Chinese came into the United States during the exclusion era. The contemporary press viewed Atlantic and Pacific coast ports as front doors and Mexico and Canada as the back doors, emphasizing a class hierarchy as well as a sexual undertone to the different forms of entry.[1] With hundreds of vessels moving through the Gulf of Mexico and landing at various U.S. ports, not to mention the Atlantic and Pacific seaboards, smugglers had ample opportunity to penetrate U.S. borders by way of the sea. As soon as immigration authorities in various countries chopped off the head of the smuggling hydra, new heads would emerge. One smuggling route would be discovered and shut down, and the hydra's many tentacles would slip around and find new entryways. In the battle between national sovereignty and the transnational smuggler, the smuggler always seemed to be winning. We must remember, however, that migrants were forced to climb through the windows at great expense and danger to themselves because the front

"And Still They Come!," *The Wasp* 5 (August–December 1880).
Courtesy of the Bancroft Library, University of California, Berkeley.

and back doors were so closely guarded. This chapter describes strategies for entering the United States, the role of smugglers and labor contractors, and efforts of immigration inspectors to close down clandestine networks.

With each new tightening of the restriction screw, migrants found alternative routes. In 1930 the commissioner general of immigration looked back on the enforcement of Chinese exclusion since 1882 and expressed the inspectors' Sisyphean task: "When, in 1882, laws were placed on the statute books absolutely excluding Chinese laborers, it was like damming up a more or less placidly flowing stream. At every point the flow sought to escape its bounds. Immigration officers were for many years kept busy day and night stopping the leaks. This flow now, after nearly half a century, has fairly subsided. Some of it, however, it should be stated in passing, has formed new channels, and is entering by way of the so-called deserting-seaman route."[2] Images of water and metaphors like flowing rivers were often used to describe migrants. Water was an apt metaphor because it could slip through the tiniest cracks and yet also had tremendous weight and power in large quantities. There was also something inevitable about the flow of water. It could be dammed up, and leaks could be patched, but water would eventually find its way to the lowest point.

An 1880 cartoon published in the San Francisco magazine *The Wasp* depicts Chinese streaming in from British Columbia and Mexico and evading the American eagle diligently attempting to regulate the entry of Chinese. The Chinese who are sneaking in the back doors are making fun of the eagle, literally thumbing their noses at him. The balloons on the smaller boats with the number "15" on them refer to the Fifteen Passenger Bill that Congress passed in 1879 to limit the number of Chinese on any ship to fifteen. The cartoon suggests that Chinese arriving on large steamers would simply break up into groups of fifteen passengers on smaller boats once they entered U.S. ports. President Rutherford B. Hayes ended up vetoing the bill, arguing that renegotiating the Burlingame Treaty was the proper way to limit Chinese immigration.[3] Nonetheless, this cartoon shows that the general public was aware as early as 1880 of the various smuggling routes that Chinese used to evade restrictionist immigration laws.

It is difficult to trace the exact amount and tempo of clandestine crossings, but the Immigration Bureau believed that Chinese illegal entries increased in the first three decades of the twentieth century and by 1930 had "fairly subsided." The combination of the Great Depression, which limited job opportunities for prospective migrants, and stricter immigration controls after the quota acts of the 1920s resulted in a dramatic decline in the foreign-born population of the United States between 1930 and 1950, from 14.2 million to 10.3 million; in comparison to the total population, foreign-born represented 11.6 percent in 1930 and only 6.9 percent by 1950.[4] Immigration restrictions had a major impact. However, the Chinese population in the United States shows growth during the period when all other foreign-born groups decline. Whereas the foreign-born Chinese population steadily declined from 1890 to 1920, it rose by almost 1,000 from 1920 to 1930. The foreign-born Chinese population fell by about 7,000 during the 1930s, but this loss was made up for by an increase in the Chinese American part of the community. Overall, the total Chinese and Chinese American population grew from 61,639 in 1920 to 77,504 in 1940, and this growth occurred in the period of strictest immigration controls, quota restrictions, and economic crisis.[5] What is even more surprising about this increase of foreign-born Chinese during the 1920s is that the number of departing Chinese far exceeded their entries. Between 1921 and 1930, there were 24,345 registered entries of Chinese to the United States and 40,376 departures, meaning a net loss of 16,031, at least according to officially recorded entries and exits.[6] During that same decade the total Chinese population grew by about 13,000, and even the foreign-born portion grew by almost 1,000. What accounts for such growth in the foreign-born Chinese population when the net migration is negative? Thousands of clandestine entries of foreign-born Chinese in this decade of heightened restriction is the most likely explanation.[7]

In April 1890 U.S. secretary of the treasury William Windom investigated fraudulent entries of Chinese into the United States and furnished the Senate with statistics on the number of Chinese entries and exits through San Francisco. Windom concluded, "The alleged violations appear to consist mainly in the use of fraudulent certificates, in smuggling across the northern and southern frontiers of Chinese laborers, and in the existence of a general system among Chinese residents in this country and Canada for the fraudulent landing of Chinese laborers within the territory of the United States." The porous borders and use of fraudulent papers allowed Chinese to evade U.S. restrictions. The statistics that the Department of Treasury collected showed greater numbers of departures of Chinese than entries from 1882 to 1886 and the reverse trend after that point until the end of the decade. Except for 1882–83, when almost 7,000 Chinese new immigrants arrived, entries in other years consisted mostly of Chinese "returning to the United States with legal certificates" and only a handful of new immigrants.[8] One explanation for the change in the pattern of entries to exits could be that as the exclusion laws tightened, Chinese were increasingly afraid to return to China for fear that they would not be allowed back into the United States. Stricter exclusion laws kept Chinese in rather than keeping them out, just as today undocumented Mexicans are less likely to return to Mexico than in the past.[9]

Taking the exclusion period as a whole (1882–1940s), however, demonstrates that restrictionist legislation in the United States and Canada impeded Chinese entry. Chinese continued to arrive as citizens, however, or claimed exempt status as merchants or students, and ultimately the growth of the Chinese female population allowed for the Chinese community to reproduce itself. The effectiveness of the U.S. exclusion laws in preventing Chinese entry has been studied by many historians, with some emphasizing that the ingenuity of Chinese allowed them to evade restrictions and others pointing to the decline in the Chinese population in the United States as evidence that the exclusion laws succeeded in slowing Chinese immigration. Both of these positions are correct. Historian Erika Lee makes one of the most convincing arguments emphasizing the agency of Chinese migrants, arguing that 300,955 Chinese, including first-time entries, returning residents, and U.S. citizens, entered the United States during the exclusion era (1882–1943), compared to only 258,210 before exclusion (1849–82). "The fact that so many managed to enter the United States in spite of the exclusion laws," Lee states, "is truly significant. It raises questions about the efficacy of restrictive immigration laws and demonstrates the power of immigrant resistance and agency."[10] While Lee is correct, the exclusion period (1882–1943) is roughly twice as long as the pre-exclusion period (1849–82). If one only looks at "immigrant" arrivals, and excludes returning U.S. citizens, transit passengers, and tourists, we find that 72 percent of Chinese arrived in the pre-exclusion era.[11] Furthermore, the total Chinese population in the United States steadily shrank from a high of 125,000 in 1882, the first year of exclusion, to a low of around 60,000 in 1920. Even though the population rose to almost 80,000 by 1940, exclusion laws were successful in reducing the growth and absolute number of Chinese in the United States.[12] Exclusionists did not get everything they wanted, but they got what they needed: fewer Chinese with fewer rights.

The Transit Problem

In the late nineteenth century, the U.S. Senate launched an investigation into reports that Chinese passengers in transit were simply escaping en route and staying in the country. Given that Chinese had to post bond and had guards accompany them on trains to their destination, the chance for escape was minimal. The Immigration Bureau reported only a handful of cases of escaped transit passengers each year, and after an investigation in 1890 the secretary of the treasury found that in six months only 100 Chinese took advantage of the transit privilege. And all of these transit passengers arrived from the Caribbean at New Orleans and left from San Francisco to China.[13] The worry over transit passengers seemed overblown.

Although the Senate's fears seem unwarranted in 1890, by the beginning of the twentieth century, the importance and size of the transit population grew exponentially.[14] Given that the transit privilege was a mark of a civilized nation that was embodied in international law and ideas about natural rights to mobility, the United States could not easily just abrogate this privilege. From 1882 the attorney general and the Department of State issued instructions that Chinese in transit were not to be restricted; subsequent court decisions at the beginning of the twentieth century upheld the Chinese right to transit even when the treaties that had guaranteed such rights had lapsed.[15] Unable to stop the transit privilege altogether, the Immigration Bureau sought to restrict it by requiring Chinese transit passengers to issue bonds and seeking cooperation with neighboring countries to track and control transit passengers. Furthermore, it became clear that the problem was not the escape of transit passengers en route to the border but the surreptitious return of passengers who transited through the United States to Mexico and the Caribbean. Up until 1901, it was estimated that 37,000 Chinese passed through the United States in transit, with none being denied entry. In 1901, however, there was an abrupt shift in policy with rigorous inspections of transit passenger baggage and increasingly frequent denials of the right to transit if immigration officers could not be convinced of the intentions of the Chinese migrants. In 1903 a record 95 of 2,493 Chinese transit passengers were denied transit based on the suspicion that they were not traveling to Mexico or would cross the border back into the United States.[16] The next year, the commissioner general of immigration stated that in all likelihood almost all of the 2,080 Chinese who transited that year through the United States to Mexico snuck back across the border. For that year, the number of possible illegal entries just from the transit population equaled almost half of the 4,309 legal entries.[17] And it was not just transits through the United States but also those through other countries that worried the bureau. Between 1907 and 1909, 8,334 Chinese transited through Canada, mostly to the West Indies (4,181), the United States (2,785), and Mexico (1,007). "There is no doubt that with these transits, as with the same class in the past, many enter Mexico and other near-by countries with the purpose, often accomplished, of eventually taking up a residence in the United States despite the provisions of law," the U.S. commissioner general of immigration argued.[18] In 1913 there were almost 3,000 Chinese transit passengers, leading the commissioner general to warn, "It may soon become necessary materially to curtail said privilege and to hedge it about with additional safeguards."[19] For example, in 1920 Gee Fong was admitted to the United States as a "transit alien" from Mexico, supposedly on his way home to China. He passed inspection in San Francisco, boarded the ship, was smuggled ashore by his relatives, and disappeared into the city's large Chinatown.[20] Many others like Gee Fong who were listed as being "in transit" ended up in the United States but remained unaccounted for by the authorities. By the 1920s the number of Chinese transit passengers more than doubled, to an average of over 8,000 per year.[21]

For my purposes of tracking clandestine entry, I am particularly interested in the number of transit passengers, which was significant throughout this period, many times exceeding the number of those admitted to the country. From 1918 to 1930, 83,034 Chinese of all kinds were admitted into the United States, while 126,562 were permitted to transit through the United States by land or by water (see figure 3). In just one year, 1918, 34,977 Chi-

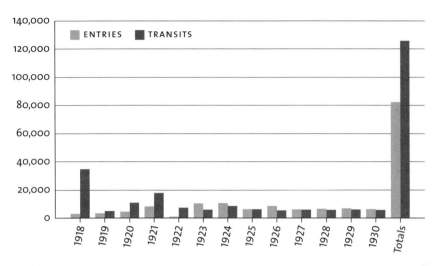

FIGURE 3. Chinese Entries and Chinese Transit Passengers to the United States, 1918–1930. Information culled from AR-CGI (1904–30).

nese passed through the United States, 28,838 of whom were destined for France for "war work."[22] Even if we exclude the anomalous group that went to France in 1918, the transit population was still larger than the regular admissions to the United States. The fact that most of the transit passengers headed to Cuba or Mexico and then returned to the United States illegally suggests that the clandestine entries may have been much larger than has been previously estimated. According to Helen Chen, close to 200,000 Chinese passed through the United States en route mostly to Cuba and Mexico from 1894 through 1940.[23] While it is not known how many of these eventually returned to the United States, immigration officials suspected that most of them returned clandestinely.

Another major source for illegal entry were the 35,000–40,000 Chinese seamen who entered the United States each year, of which several thousand were believed to have deserted on U.S. soil. Seamen of all nationalities deserted, especially after the 1920s quota restrictions. Although the Immigration Bureau did not provide a breakdown of the nationality of deserting sailors, the total number was large and growing. In 1913, 9,136 seamen deserted, and by 1925 the bureau announced that 77,917 seamen had deserted in the previous three years. What was even more alarming to the bureau was the fact the desertions did not even count the large number who entered illegally by discharging and never reshipping.[24] In 1921, the bureau report stated, "a not inconsiderable number of Chinese, not carried in the statistical returns, succeeded in entering the United States by deserting from vessels upon which they arrived as crew members."[25] Furthermore, the bureau was concerned about hundreds of Chinese who entered to participate in the Louisiana Purchase Exposition and World's Fairs and then simply stayed. In 1904, 360 Chinese "disappeared" after being admitted to participate in the Omaha Fair, and there was no record of departure for hundreds of Chinese from other fairs.[26] With a few thousand Chinese transit passengers, a few hundred Chinese participants in fairs and expositions, a few thousand deserting Chinese sailors, and thousands of additional Chinese who arrived first in Canada, Cuba, or Mexico and then crossed surreptitiously into the United States, the number of clandestine entries could easily have surpassed those of registered entries.

Most historians are reluctant to estimate clandestine entries of Chinese because there are no concrete records to back up such claims. The evidence from primary sources varies widely, contributing to the confusion. Based on the Immigration Bureau's reports, historian Erika Lee concludes that 17,300 Chinese entered the United States through the Mexican and Canadian back doors from 1882 to 1920.[27] The House Committee on Immigration in 1901 came up with a much higher estimate, concluding that 20,000 Chinese were smuggled into the United States each year.[28] The difference between these two estimates cannot be attributed to a marginal counting error. In 1928 Luther Fry published a statistical analysis of illegal entry of Asians to the United States by comparing immigration entry and exit records against census data. After accounting for anomalies in the census and immigration data, Fry estimated that between 7,167 and 21,000 Chinese entered the United States illegally between 1910 and 1920.[29] Using a similar methodology, I have calculated that anywhere from 18,000 to 29,000 Chinese illegally entered the United States between 1920 and 1930.[30] In 1908 the Mexican legation in China reported that 60,000 Chinese had entered Mexico, but it estimated that almost 48,000 of them had crossed into the United States illegally.[31] What we know about the large number of transit passengers from the United States to Mexico, many of whom presumably crossed back into the United States, suggests that the Mexican estimates were somewhat accurate. Even if we conservatively estimate that half of the 200,000 transit population (between 1894 and 1940) returned to the United States illegally, the number of Chinese who gained admittance through smuggling of various kinds through Canada, Mexico, and Cuba almost certainly outstrips the number of registered Chinese entries. Taking various estimates from different sources in different countries, it seems clear that the actual number of

Chinese smuggled into the United States is much higher than previously estimated by historians. While historians are right to highlight Chinese ingenuity and creativity in evading exclusion laws through the legal ports of entry, the use of "paper sons" (and daughters) and other legal means to challenge exclusion was probably not the most frequent means to evade exclusion. Chinese smuggling across the vast expanses of open land borders or unguarded coastline was the easiest and most often used method to gain entry during the exclusion era.

Clandestine entry into the United States was highly responsive to immigration inspectors' actions and their vigilance of particular routes and regions. Chinese did not simply arrive in a foreign port and attempt to cross from there to the United States. Arriving at Vancouver, they might first take the train to Montreal and cross at Buffalo, or they might transit through the United States to New York, New Orleans, or Tampa and then take a boat to Cuba before trying to return to the United States. Smugglers shuttled migrants through a complex network of safe houses and transportation networks to the least guarded areas. In spite of these zigzagging trajectories, three major regions of entry can be identified: Canada, the northwestern Mexican border, and the Gulf region. In 1911 Commissioner General of Immigration Daniel Keefe sought to create a "general uniformity of administration" at all the ports, but he recognized that different conditions and immigrant populations at different ports required different "modus operandi." In Canada, for example, although there was a large unguarded land border, inspectors conducted most of their work in interior and coastal points, whereas in Mexico, because inspectors did not have an agreement with railway companies, inspections had to occur only at the boundary crossing. In spite of the resources devoted to stopping Chinese illegal entries, there was a sense of resignation; the Immigration Bureau would never be able to keep up with the demand. "On both borders," the commissioner general wrote, "the smuggling of Chinese is a regular business and a very lucrative one. The intricacies of the task, in its entirety, can better be imagined than described."[32]

While immigration officers might have had a difficult job, the migrants themselves often faced harrowing journeys trekking through the desert or locked inside of freight train boxcars. In several cases, train cars were found with the corpses of Chinese migrants who had not been retrieved in time and as a result died of hunger, thirst, heat exposure, or hypothermia. On one occasion in 1904, a Chinese man was found frozen in a refrigerated car when it was opened in St. Louis. The man had been lowered into the car a few miles north of Detroit; he was supposed to be taken out just after crossing the bor-

Buggy used for smuggling Chinese aliens across the Mexican border, 1921.
Courtesy of NARA, Pacific Region.

der, but a storm prevented his retrieval. Around the same time, four Chinese were found frozen in a refrigerated car on the Mexican border.[33] As one man put it, "The poor 'chinks' were found dead when they got the boxes open."[34] The lengths to which Chinese were forced to go to cross the border often put them in dangerous situations that could end in their deaths.[35]

Braun's Investigation

New York immigrant inspector Marcus Braun was sent in 1906 on a special mission to investigate the smuggling routes of Chinese and Japanese from Cuba and Mexico. In his detailed report, more than forty pages in length, he not only documented the various smuggling networks and pathways but also outlined a new way of thinking about immigration. Braun began by dividing immigrants into two groups: the good, hardworking ones and the bad, criminal ones. "My heart and soul beats warmly for the good immigrant," Braun began. "But, to the very core of my heart I am opposed to immigration which regards the United States to be the dumping ground of the scum of European or Oriental society." Braun's idea of the good immigrant was linked to his notion of a good citizen. As he put it, "I believe with all earnestness that the United States shall gladly welcome every immigrant who adds to the wealth of the nation the value of a citizen, who is strong in body, healthy in mind, a manly, decent, law-abiding honorable man, who will make a splendid citizen." Braun's qualifications for good citizenship were markedly gendered. He also seemed to echo the eugenicists of the day when he invoked the healthy mind and body of the immigrant. Braun wanted to be clear, however, that although he was in favor of "stringent immigration laws," he wanted each person judged individually and not on the basis of their race or religious beliefs.[36]

Who were these undesirable immigrants and how could they be kept out? Braun quoted President Theodore Roosevelt's speech on the subject from 1903 to make his point.

> We cannot have too much immigration of the right kind, and we should have none at all of the wrong kind. The need is to devise some system by which undesirable immigrants shall be kept out entirely, while desirable immigrants are properly distributed throughout the country.
>
> I hold, Sir, that all immigrants who come to the United States clandestinely, who are smuggled into the territory of our republic, and—of course—thus evade subjecting themselves to the inspection demanded by our laws, are undesirable immigrants and are "per se" immigration of "the wrong kind."[37]

Roosevelt's distinction merely reinforced the racial and class discrimination already enshrined in U.S. immigration laws. Those who came in clandestinely were undesirable immigrants and therefore immigrants of the "wrong kind." Braun and Roosevelt could claim they were not targeting particular races or religions because the law already did that for them; the distinction between lawful and unlawful entry, legal immigrants and illegal aliens became an apparently race-neutral way to reinforce racist immigration policies.

Braun recognized the importance of neighboring countries' cooperation in enforcing U.S. immigration restrictions. He applauded the Canadians for synchronizing their policies with those of the United States and noted that the Mexicans had not. To explain Mexico's position, Braun quoted an "educated Mexican" who facetiously described Mexico's open immigration policy: "The slag of humanity of no country can be worse than our own Peons." Given the limited cooperation from Mexico and Cuba, Braun organized an undercover mission to learn about smuggling from these places by following migrants as they crossed borders. He began in Havana, where he boarded a steamship with 700 Spaniards and 250 Syrians bound for Veracruz. The Syrians wanted to go to the United States, but, given the strict trachoma inspections at U.S. ports, they hoped to enter clandestinely from Mexico, which did not require medical inspections of immigrants. Furthermore, in Mexico there were no restrictions on immigration unless they were Chinese coming from the United States, in which case they were limited to groups of ten. Finally, Braun noted that even if migrants were caught on the U.S. side of the Mexican border, they would be returned to Mexico rather than their home countries, making it much easier for them to attempt another crossing soon after.[38]

In Mexico, Braun found thousands of Chinese and Japanese waiting to be smuggled into the United States. As we saw in the introduction, on 2 January 1907, Braun witnessed 450 Chinese from Hong Kong land in Salina Cruz, Oaxaca; he followed them northward as they made their way to the U.S. border. After Oaxaca, Braun traveled to the Yucatán where he heard that 5,000–6,000 Chinese had been working in the hemp fields; most of them had abandoned this work and left for the United States. In Sonora, he was told that 20,000 Chinese had arrived in the previous few years, and only 4,000 were left, suggesting that the rest had crossed to the United States. In the last year and half alone, Braun was informed that 8,000 Japanese and 5,000 Chinese laborers had come to Mexico. Wherever he went, the story was the same: thousands of Asians had arrived and then headed north to the United States.

Braun gathered information from people involved in the smuggling, but he also witnessed Chinese migrants holding English-language dictionaries, Chinese American newspapers, and U.S. railroad maps, preparing themselves to cross the border. They cut their queues and changed their "blue jeans and their felt slippers to the most picturesque Mexican dress," Braun reported. "They learn[ed] to be able to say 'Yo soy Mexicano'—'I am Mexican,' in case they were stopped." The bulk of the Chinese came to Mexico as contract laborers, but whether they came under contract or not, most of them used Mexico as a jumping-off point for the United States. Given the lack of cooperation with Mexican authorities, Braun recommended sending Secret Service agents to Mexico to watch for Chinese approaching the border. He concluded that the only solution to this "deplorable condition of affairs" was to make it a felony to come into the United States clandestinely. Instead of immediately deporting Chinese caught illegally in the United States, Braun wanted them jailed for two to three years, during which they would be forced to work to earn their return passage and then deported.[39] Criminalizing clandestine border crossers was central to Braun's strategy of distinguishing between good and bad immigrants.

Braun's secret investigation was just one of many conducted by U.S. immigration agents in the next few years. Each time they discovered a smuggling route and stepped up enforcement in that zone, smugglers shifted to another area or mode of transportation. What these investigations revealed, however, was a transnational network that linked China to an underground web within the Americas, knitted together by labor recruiters, smugglers, clan associations, interpreters, and corrupt immigration officers.

The Northern Back Door

Although Canada seemed to turn a blind eye to clandestine entry of Chinese into the United States at the end of the nineteenth century, by the beginning of the twentieth century, the United States had entered into agreements with the Canadian government and the Canadian Pacific Railroad to curb illegal crossings. These new international agreements for migration issues foreshadowed the development of a global system of passports and visas in the 1920s to regulate movement across borders. A cartoon in the San Francisco magazine *The Wasp* in 1889 graphically depicts the ease with which Chinese crossed illegally from Canada to the United States. In the cartoon a Chinese migrant pays the Canadian head tax, while another Chinese migrant sneaks across the border past a sleeping U.S. immigration official. The caption reads: "The Back Door. The wily Chinese sneaking over the northern frontier." Two years later, in 1891, Julian Ralph, a U.S. journalist, traveled to Victoria, British Columbia, to report for *Harper's New Monthly Magazine* on what he referred to as the "Chinese leak." Although Ralph found it hard to obtain information about Chinese smuggling from Canada because shipping companies, Canadian immigration agents, and many others were complicit with the trade, he found "two score" men who told him that "the Chinese come here mainly to smuggle themselves across the American border." This was not the invasion of Chinese hordes that had been discussed in the U.S. Congress, but Ralph found that more than 4,000 Chinese landed in British Columbia in the preceding three years, and that 99 percent of them intended to cross illegally to the United States. Based on various informants and his own investigations, he concluded that 1,500 Chinese crossed into the United States from Canada each year. The decline of Chinese in British Columbia was noticeable to Ralph, who claimed there had been 18,000 five or six years earlier, and that there were only 7,000–8,000 in 1891. In Victoria alone, half of the Chinese population had disappeared, "the streets [had] grown deserted-looking, the theatre [was] closed for lack of support, and the Chinese themselves freely told me that at least 1,500 men had gone away,

"The Back Door: The Wily Chinese Sneaking over the Northern Frontier," *The Wasp* 23 (July–December 1889). Courtesy of the Bancroft Library, University of California, Berkeley.

principally to my country." Ralph argued that although some may have returned to China, and some migrated to eastern Canada, the "great majority of the other 11,000 have gone to the US."[40]

Ralph documented Chinese clandestine entries from Canada at the same time as he tried to put these into perspective in terms of the other kinds of illegal entries. Although he recognized that Chinese used fraud to enter at U.S. ports claiming to be merchants, students, U.S. citizens, or relatives of U.S. citizens, he asserted that the number of people who evaded exclusion in this manner was relatively small. Similarly, he claimed that the number of Chinese who crossed the southern frontier from Mexico was "very limited." Therefore, he declared, "the most serious breach of the exclusion law is that on the Canadian frontier."[41] Whether this was in fact true or not, his point was that thousands of Chinese were entering the United States clandestinely through the Canadian border.

Given growing numbers of Chinese coming to Canada, U.S. immigration authorities sought cooperation from the Canadian government to stop Chinese from crossing into the United States. In 1893, Canada allowed U.S. officers to examine passengers arriving at Canada's major ports who intended to travel to the United States, but until 1901, there were no deportations of Chinese from Canada. Whether because of lack of staffing to scrutinize incoming passengers or lack of political will, until the early twentieth century, U.S. authorities acted alone to secure their very remote and easily penetrated northern border. Ralph described the unfenced and unguarded border as a "gigantic wilderness" where "geologically and naturally there is no difference between the countries; the boundary line is an arbitrary mark." As he put it, "there are scarcely any parts of [the border] where [a Chinese migrant] may not walk boldly across it at high noon."[42]

Evidence of Chinese clandestine migration was apparent not only in British Columbia's depleted Chinese population but also in U.S. Pacific Northwest cities, which swelled with Chinese in the late nineteenth century. A headline in the *Portland Telegram* in 1899 declared "Portland a Headquarters for Smugglers of Chinese Coolies." The article asserted that "Chinese are being smuggled into Portland nearly every day and there is a Chinese firm in this city which makes a business furnishing bogus certificates for the purpose." The growth in Portland's Chinese population, and the fact that "laborers [were] constantly leaving for China," was "clear evidence" for the journalist "that Chinese [were] entering illegally." The northern border was preferred to the southern border because it cost only $50 to be smuggled in from British Columbia as compared to $450 to cross from Mexico. Portland was the best place to run smuggling operations, the *Portland Tribune* concluded, because of the large size of the Chinese community and its ability to absorb large numbers of new Chinese without raising alarm. "Hundreds have been smuggled over the border and scattered throughout the country," the reporter declared.[43] Photographs of Chinese merchants and labor contractors in Portland illustrate the tight links between these enterprises; they were literally run by the same people out of the same storefronts.

Under mounting pressure from the U.S. government, the Canadian Pacific Railway agreed in 1903 to send all Chinese transit passengers under guard to one of four entry points to the United States. In 1904 Canadian authorities began to screen the 25,000 passengers who requested passage to the United States and even deported some who failed to meet the requirements for legal entry into the United States. Given the new cooperation with Canadian authorities and railways, as well as the new administrative structure of the Immigration Bureau, which consolidated management of all immigrants under the Department of Commerce and Labor, the commissioner of immigration was optimistic that the northern border could be controlled. "No Chinese person from China can enter the United States through Canada

Wing Sing & Co. during the flood in Portland, Oregon, 1894. Chinese grocers would often also serve as labor contractors, as the sign indicates. Oregon Historical Society, 45704.

without submitting to an examination by Bureau officers," the commissioner wrote in 1904. "And only a few of those Chinese residing in Canada will resort to smugglers or to unlawful crossing, since the Dominion has imposed an admission tax of $500 per head on those who may lawfully enter her territory."[44] This prediction turned out to be wrong, as smuggling across the northern border exploded in the next two decades.

Insuring the continued cooperation of foreign governments and foreign corporations was always a difficult dance for the Immigration Bureau. In 1909 the bureau sought to change the policy of allowing Chinese merchants, travelers, and students to be examined at various stations along the Canadian border and to concentrate all operations in one station at Vancouver. The Boston Chamber of Commerce opposed the change, arguing that it would impede trade with China by annoying exempt classes and hampering their travel.[45] John R. Clark, the U.S. commissioner of immigration in Montreal, tried in vain to enlist the cooperation of the Canadian Pacific Railway, but the company stalled and refused to make a definitive agreement. Clark expressed his frustration at the limited U.S. power to force the hand of a foreign corporation. "I sincerely feel that it is humiliating for a government thus to be placed in an attitude of treating and temporizing with an alien corporation in a matter wherein it would seem more fitting for the company to be a supplicant rather than seek to be dictator." With only three weeks until the change was scheduled, Clark recommended issuing an ultimatum to the Canadian Pacific Railway that on 21 November 1909 it would cease to receive Chinese at ports in Richford, Vermont; Malone, New York; and Portal, North Dakota.[46]

From 1906 to 1915, the number of immigrants coming into Canada more than doubled from the previous decade as steamship service became more frequent. The number of Chinese also skyrocketed 1,200 percent, from only 27 between 1896 and 1906, to 32,295 from 1906 to 1915.[47] In 1908 Immigrant Inspector Babcock from Buffalo warned of increasing Chinese immigration to Canada, arguing that its ultimate goal was illegal entry into the United States. "There are many hundreds of Chinese at the present time in Toronto and Montreal," Babcock wrote, "waiting for arrangements to be made for smuggling them across the border."[48] A few years later, in 1913, the U.S. commissioner of immigration in Canada, John H. Clark, expressed similar concerns. The new arrivals were, according to Clark, "aliens of the roving, prospecting class, who are never satisfied to remain in one country until they have tried conditions in the other."[49]

Immigration inspectors and smugglers were caught in a cat and mouse game, with each side trying to outsmart the other, but smugglers always seemed to be a few steps ahead. One inspector at Niagara Falls, New York, complained that smugglers kept track of inspectors' movements, and telephoned their accomplices when patrol boats left and returned.[50] Immigration officials also blamed the Buffalo police for aiding their relatives in the smuggling business by passing information to them and firing signal flares to warn when Chinese inspectors were around.[51] In 1922 the U.S. commissioner of immigration in Montreal noted that smugglers had automobiles and boats and limitless funds, while the Immigration Bureau was understaffed and poorly equipped: "It is fully appreciated that dope, liquor, Chinese, and alien smuggling has become a lucrative business and is being carried on by international gangs in which there have been found the hardest, most daring, and cleverest criminals, backed by no limit of funds and possessed of the highest powered vehicles, boats, etc., the automobile predominating as a means of traveling."[52]

Given the vast potential entry points by land and sea, the relatively small inspection staff depended on tips from the public or infiltrators among the smugglers to obtain information. In one case, Inspector McCabe overheard a conversation indicating that smugglers moved Chinese out of Detroit on trains.[53] On another occasion, the Immigration Bureau received a tip from John Smith about four Chinese in a laundry in Iowa City whose "papers were no good." "I am a trembling American," Smith began. "I know they are not citizens of US. There [sic] papers are no good. I want you to catch them and send them back to China."[54] When the inspector arrived at the laundry named by Smith, only one of the four Chinese was able to produce a certificate; one of the three Chinese without certificates pleaded guilty and was deported, and the other two fought their case in court.[55]

The northern border was notoriously difficult to patrol. The almost 4,000 miles between the U.S. mainland and Canada, including numerous rivers, lakes, and two open oceans, made it relatively easy for smugglers to enter the United States. Trains were the most frequent form of clandestine entry from Canada.[56] In addition to passenger trains, Chinese snuck onto freight trains. One inspector noted that almost 1,000 train cars were entering the United States at Black Rock, near Buffalo, and that the empty train cars from Canada were not being inspected. Unlike the Mexican border, the train cars from Canada were not left open, making it was impossible to see what was inside.[57] U.S. immigrations officers were stationed on the Canadian side of the border, where they inspected the rail cars and then closed them with U.S. government seals. William Baldwin, the inspector in charge at Niagara Falls, noted that Chinese managed to sneak into the sealed cars, then had their accomplices affix new U.S. government seals that apparently could be "procured in almost any freight yard."[58]

Even though Canadian authorities cooperated with U.S. immigration officials and allowed U.S. Immigration Bureau officers to be stationed at ports in Vancouver, Victoria, and Montreal, it seemed as though Canada was not as diligent as the United States in enforcing immigration restrictions. The fact that Canada benefited economically from increased migration thanks to its high head taxes led some to believe that the country's inspectors turned a blind eye to smuggling across the U.S. border. The Mexican consulate in Montreal noted that 1,380 Chinese arrived in Canada in 1907 alone, netting the government $690,000.[59] In 1922 the Canadian controller of Chinese immigration reported that the government had taken in almost $22 million in receipts from the Chinese head tax since it was established in 1885.[60] In 1914 U.S. inspector S. J. Buford, stationed in Victoria, commented wryly, "Canada gets coin and we get the Chinese."[61]

The Canadian *Royal Commission Report* in 1908 found that although raising the Chinese head tax initially slowed migration, it had little dampening effect over the long term. More than 16,000 Chinese paid the $100 tax from 1900 through 1903, during which time the Chinese population doubled. After the tax was raised to $500, there was an almost "complete cessation" of Chinese immigration until 1907–8, when in eight months more than 1,400 Chinese paid the higher tax. The report concluded that the higher taxes reduced the supply of labor, and thus increased the salaries that workers could demand. One Chinese labor contractor in Vancouver, Yip Sang, testified that before the $500 tax, he paid Chinese laborers $25 to $40 a month for packing fish, and now he was "obliged" to pay $60 to $70 for the same work. According to the report, "As a result of the rise of wages consequent upon the monopoly created by the tax, Chinamen have found [that] it is possible to accumulate within half the time, the sum desired, and that thereafter the fortune from year to year is apt to be nearly, or more than double what it was."[62] After a few years, then, the increased tax actually benefited Chinese workers, who could demand a higher wage. Prospective Chinese immigrants to Canada could borrow the money to pay their hefty head tax, knowing that within a year they would be able to pay back their debt.

The Mexican Back Door

The thousands of miles of unguarded land border with Mexico also provided ample opportunities for Chinese to cross undetected, but unlike the Canadian government, Mexico refused to cooperate with U.S. immigration authorities. Before 1903 most of the Immigration Bureau's resources were directed toward the northern border, leaving the southern border largely unattended for anyone to pass through without being subject to inspection. In 1900 there were only three official ports of entry on the Mexican border, at El Paso and Eagle Pass in Texas and Nogales in Arizona, but by 1908, there were twenty-one such stations. Although historian Patrick Ettinger argues that the "locus of illicit entry shifted to the border with Mexico after 1900," there is little evidence that clandestine entry from Canada abated in the early twentieth century.[63] What shifted, however, was the bureau's attention, which began to focus more intently on the Mexican border. After the United States implemented Chinese exclusion in 1882, entry through the Mexican back door became more frequent. In many cases, Chinese simply slipped across the vast unguarded southern border and disappeared into Chinatowns in major cities across the United States. In 1908 the Mexican legation in China estimated that 48,000 of the 60,000 Chinese who had emigrated to Mexico had crossed illegally to the United States.[64] Although it is impossible to determine accurately how many Chinese crossed the border clandestinely, numerous reports from inspectors along the length of the boundary line suggest that thousands made the journey each year. In 1908 the supervising inspector in San Antonio reported that his officers had captured 500 Chinese crossing the border illegally in the El Paso district in just the past year, and he estimated that at least that many managed to cross without detection.[65] The clandestine entry of Chinese was a subject of hot debate in Congress and in newspapers, leading to proposals to beef up border patrols and to establish treaties with Mexico and Britain to help keep the Chinese out. In 1892 the *New York Times* reported that large numbers of Chinese were crossing the river from Mexico every week, and it warned that "customs officials are unable to prevent this wholesale violation of the Exclusion act owing to a lack of river guards."[66]

The U.S. government tried to pressure the Mexican government to cooperate in preventing the Chinese from crossing the border to the United States, to no avail. Not only would such acts violate Mexico's constitution, but the country lacked the resources to patrol its 2,000-mile northern border. The "Mexican leak" or the "Chinese border leak," as newspapers liked to call it, revealed the inability of the United States to guard its own borders. One typical article in the *San Francisco Examiner* in April 1890 described the arrival of a steamer from Hong Kong with 213 Chinese aboard. Of these, 74 disembarked in San Francisco, but the rest were in transit to Guaymas (87), Mazatlán (17), Havana (16), and Panama City (8). The *Examiner* declared, "All of these may be assumed to harbor the intention of bringing up ultimately in the United States. The customs officials at San Diego are now in the thick of a fight against a returning swarm of coolies that originally went to Mexico for the purpose of coming back."[67] Although the coolie trade had officially ended in 1874, in the popular imagination, Chinese laborers were still coolies and were usually imagined as "swarming," like bees or ants.

The most frequent routes from Mexico into the United States were by land, but Chinese also took advantage of the unguarded coastline. On 7 April 1890 thirteen Chinese were arrested as they tried to cross the border at San Diego just before daylight. The collector of customs at San Diego, John Berry, discovered that the thirteen were on the list of Chinese passengers who had landed in San Francisco on 25 March and transferred to another ship heading to Ensenada. He suspected that the rest of their shipmates had clandestinely entered the United States the same way. Berry pleaded with the secretary of the treasury: "Necessary to guard both harbor entrance and about 20 miles boundary line from coast inward. Additional temporary officers absolutely necessary. Can they be appointed? No deputy marshal here, and local constabulary will not assist because no pay in it."[68] Two days later ten more Chinese were arrested while entering San Diego's harbor on a fishing boat from Baja California. The officer who apprehended them wrote, "Useless to send convicted Chinamen back to Lower California. Ought to send back to China if possible under law."[69] The agents in charge of preventing Chinese entry from Mexico knew that if they deported someone to Mexico, the same person would attempt to cross again later that day or the next.

Deporting Chinese to Mexico may have been pointless, but sending them back to China was expensive. In 1910 immigration authorities captured a letter that indicated Chinese were crossing from Mexico into the United States with the intention of being arrested and deported to China, thereby garnering a free return trip. The letter written in Chinese by prisoners in a Tucson jail to the Six Companies complained that they would starve in Mexico if they were returned there.

> We people, small and insignificant as ants, are on our knees petitioning our great minister (the head of one of the Six Brothers Companies). The United States has enacted a new law, and instead of shipping our countrymen back to China, is sending them to Mexico. They have never had such a law before. It has never even been advanced in the newspapers. They did it all secretly. Over in Mexico there is still tens of thousands of our countrymen who have no work to do, and who are looking forward to smuggling themselves into the United States, submit to arrest, and be deported back to China. If this course is closed, many of them will have to commit suicide by hanging themselves or die of starvation.[70]

The desperation of the message suggested the dire situation in Mexico. The strategy of submitting to arrest in the United States in order to be deported to China was widely publicized among Chinese. A San Francisco Chinese-language newspaper even published a letter from a Chinese person in Mexico explaining how to cross the border at Nogales on foot and get arrested and sent back to China.[71]

Smuggling Chinese across U.S. borders became a profitable enterprise that involved corrupt immigration officials in the United States, Mexico, and Canada; local border police; and a multinational group of ship captains. The Chinese inspector at San Diego, Datus E. Coon, interrogated a Portuguese captain of one of the sloops that smuggled Chinese for $140 per person. "Whether Chinamen land in Mexico or British Columbia," Coon noted, "their ultimate destination is the United States, and it is almost impossible to prevent their coming over the border by night." Coon argued that the only solution would be a treaty with Mexico and Great Britain excluding Chinese from Mexico and Canada the same way they were from the United States.[72]

In the same month, April 1890, the secretary of the treasury ordered the administrator of customs in San Francisco to prevent Chinese from transferring to steamers going to Mazatlán because he suspected that they would disembark in Ensenada and then cross the border illegally into the United States.[73] That year, San Francisco customs collector T. G. Phelps reported that in less than a year, 256 Chinese had been sent in transit to Guaymas and 36 to Mazatlán. Of these, 86 disembarked in Ensenada, and the others, he believed, would enter the United States at Nogales.[74] Given this situation, Phelps informed steamship lines not to sell tickets to Chinese passengers in transit to Mexico because they would not be allowed to transfer in San Francisco and would have to return to China.[75] The *New York Herald* announced that hundreds of Chinese arriving in San Francisco "will have the pleasure of returning home again, as under no conditions will they be allowed to land."[76] When the denial of transit to Mexico was brought to the attention of Mexico's U.S. ambassador, Matías Romero, he ignored the issue, reasoning that the affected were not Mexican citizens.[77]

Smuggling Rings and Corrupt Officials

The discovery in 1892 of a transnational smuggling ring in the Mexican border area revealed the level of corruption of both U.S. and Mexican officials, and the cruelty Chinese suffered at the hands of smugglers. The smuggling operation took large groups of Chinese who disembarked in Ensenada or Guaymas and moved them clandestinely to the outskirts of Tijuana or Nogales. Any migrants who tried to escape were handcuffed or beaten. According to an article in the *San Diego Union*, U.S. marshal Thomas Smallcomb went into Mexico to ferry the Chinese across. The article suggested that U.S. officials made money for every Chinese arrested, while Mexican officials were paid to bring the Chinese across to the United States. Apparently both sides were making a profit delivering and arresting the Chinese in this operation. The newspaper article asserted that U.S. officers "entered the foreign territory of Mexico, brought the Chinamen across the line, lodged them in jail, and heralded the news that their watchfulness and activity had circumvented the heathen Chinee in his attempt to sneak into the United

States."[78] The plot was eventually discovered only because one of the smugglers, who had not been paid for two shipments, became an informant to U.S. authorities.[79]

Denials by the U.S. marshals accused of smuggling Chinese filled the pages of the *San Diego Union* in the following days.[80] After further investigation, the paper discovered a more elaborate smuggling plot involving U.S. marshals Goodrich and Marsh as well as officials on the Mexican side, including judges Ildefonso Fuentes and Donaciano Cruz and a policeman. Joaquín Fuentes, the policeman, was a brother of the judge. The U.S. officials made money by arresting the Chinese, while the Mexicans would earn money by helping them cross the border. The Chinese did not know that two groups were working together. The money-making scheme fell apart when a group of Chinese who had been employed in a Mexican mine were captured, robbed, and locked up in Inocencio Pollorena's house in Tijuana. After unsuccessfully trying to take possession of the Chinese migrants, Fuentes enlisted Governor Luis Torres of Baja California to force Pollorena to release them to him. Once Fuentes had control of the migrants, he stole their money and blankets and sold them to marshals Goodrich and Marsh, who arrested them for illegal entry into the United States.[81] The story suggests the extent to which Chinese were subject to exploitation from all kinds of criminals, from Mexican judges and police to U.S. marshals and others. The fact that Governor Torres helped Fuentes gain control of the Chinese indicates how high up the corruption ran. The saga of the five Chinese was not over yet.

When the Mexican consul tried to visit the Chinese in jail in San Diego, he found that they had been moved to Los Angeles. The commissioner in Los Angeles deported them to China before the consul could meet with them. Goodrich and Marsh must have believed that the story would end once the Chinese were thousands of miles across the Pacific. However, the Mexican consul in San Diego and the Spanish minister in China took up their cause and arranged for affidavits from the Chinese to be sent to Porfirio Díaz in Mexico City. Díaz ordered Fuentes arrested and began an investigation. The investigation found that Fuentes received twenty dollars from each Chinese and fifty dollars from the U.S. authorities for delivering the Chinese. The *Los Angeles Times* wrote, "In addition to the punishment he will deserve for his dealings with the Chinese, [Fuentes] stands a very good chance of being shot for murder and robbery."[82] Ildefonso Fuentes, who was originally from Los Angeles and presumably therefore a U.S. citizen, was held in prison in Ensenada while his case made its way through the Mexican courts. Finally, in 1897, Fuentes was found guilty of kidnapping the Chinese and sentenced to five years in prison, fined 500 Mexican pesos, and banned from ever holding a government post again.[83] Meanwhile, a grand jury in the United States exonerated Marshal Marsh.[84] The Fuentes case shows that although immigration policy was written in Washington, D.C., and Mexico City, local officials could enforce the rules to the extent they thought necessary or profitable. Estelle Lau similarly argues, in her book *Paper Families*, that although the federal government crafted immigration policy, it was implemented at the local level by officials who were sometimes sensitive to pressure from civil society and Chinese migrants.[85] Ultimately, all sides in this case used the Chinese for their own profit. Nevertheless, it was ultimately the law that rendered the Chinese as "illegals" and thereby made them susceptible to exploitation. For the five Chinese who were robbed, extorted, kidnapped, and passed along like cattle, North America was not the Gold Mountain of which they had dreamed.

Smuggling Networks in Mexico

Smuggling was concentrated along the U.S.-Mexico border, but immigration investigators discovered that smugglers operated throughout Mexico from the south to the capital city and along well-worn railroad routes leading to border towns. In September and October 1909, Immigrant Inspector Richard Taylor traveled to Mexico with a Chinese interpreter, Tang Shue Wan. Tang went in the guise of a cook who had been recently discharged from a steamer. In each city, Tang would meet with Chinese, ostensibly to organize smuggling operations to the United States. Tang discovered an elaborate network of Chinese smuggling run out of various restaurants, stores, and laundries in Salina Cruz, Oaxaca, in the south; Mexico City in the center; and Júarez, Chihuahua, in the north. In Mexico City, the smuggling was run through a store owned by Quong Fong Hai, who not only arranged for migrants' passage but also issued bonds to be paid when they arrived in the United States. This was a highly integrated clandestine migration business. Quong had even built dormitories in Mexico City to house between sixty and seventy Chinese as they awaited transfer to Chihuahua. At the time Tang visited the dormitories, there were forty Chinese waiting to be transported north. Taylor concluded that all Chinese smuggled from Mexico City were sent through El Paso. Their first stop was Chihuahua City, where they were coached by Yee Sing Lung, a former resident of San Francisco. He helped them learn street names in San Francisco and taught them basic English. Yee owned a restaurant and had accommodations for 150 Chinese. When Tang visited, at least

600 Chinese were in Chihuahua waiting to cross to the United States. Most of these Chinese already held certificates, and after wading across the river, they checked in with the Chinese Bureau in El Paso. Chinese laborers who held certificates chose to clandestinely cross from Mexico rather than enter the United States directly from China because it was easier and less expensive. Legal return had to be done within a year, and the costs associated with paying "fixers" was more expensive than the $200 they paid to cross illegally from Mexico. Those without certificates, "newcomers," were generally smuggled across the river and placed on freight cars to move them out of El Paso. They paid $450 for the service. What was surprising is that given the obstacles of going through legal channels posed by strict and dehumanizing immigration procedures, even Chinese who were legally allowed to enter the United States chose to enter clandestinely.[86]

In Salina Cruz, Oaxaca, Taylor and Tang talked to the principal smuggler who represented the Mexico City operation. There were 200 Chinese in the town, and although a few of them were being sent directly from Salina Cruz on the American-Hawaiian steamers to San Francisco and Seattle, most were being directed to Mexico City and then across the land border at El Paso. In just over a year, 539 Chinese had landed in Salina Cruz.[87] Following Taylor's report, the Immigration Bureau sent a warning to the immigration inspectors in Seattle, San Francisco, and Philadelphia, informing them that Chinese were being carried on American-Hawaiian steamers to their ports. Once in U.S. ports, Chinese would slide down ropes from the bows of the ships and disappear.[88] Another report by a U.S. citizen who had lived in Salina Cruz for ten years suggested that every month, 200 to 700 Chinese arrived there with contracts to work in mines and plantations. Within a month or two, 75 percent of these Chinese had jumped their contracts. The writer claimed that it was a "well known fact that the greater part of these contract jumpers went to the States by devious ways."[89]

The flow of Chinese to Mexico was slowed briefly when Mexican authorities began screening more rigorously for trachoma. In fact, two steamship companies that had been bringing Chinese to Salina Cruz went bankrupt because the Mexican authorities began "exercising a policy of rigid sanitary inspection," which resulted in 1,100 out of 1,600 Chinese passengers being rejected for trachoma on three ships. After a new steamship line was organized with British and Mexican capital, the rejection rates for trachoma dropped to between 10 and 20 percent. The large numbers of Chinese arriving in Salina Cruz were simply landing there as a springboard for eventual entry into the United States. While waiting for steamers northward to Guaymas, the Chinese were put into a detention camp featuring large Chinese-language posters describing the various "underground methods of entering the States." Taylor also noted that agents for U.S. railroads had come to Salina Cruz and met with prominent Chinese, ostensibly to collude on the smuggling operation. The same U.S. writer from Salina Cruz cryptically observed, "Such is the situation and I am of the opinion that it will become interesting."[90]

After landing in Salina Cruz and being transported to Mexico City, migrants would be sent by rail to either Ciudad Juárez, Nuevo Laredo, or Matamoros. In his annual report, the immigration inspector in charge in El Paso estimated that the quarters of the smuggling firms in Juárez held around 150–200 unemployed Chinese at all times. Of the 486 Chinese who had recently arrived in Juárez, only 46 found employment there, while 100 left for other border points, leaving 320 who "have disappeared near the international boundary line in the vicinity of El Paso, and doubtless gained unlawful entry." The report also noted that the best-respected and most influential Chinese businessmen of El Paso were directly involved in the smuggling rings, hiding Chinese in their cellars or in underground or attic chambers: "In fact, it is believed that the handling of Chinese coolies is the sole occupation of perhaps one-third of the Chinese population of El Paso."[91]

The South Texas border also provided ample opportunity for smugglers, given the easily fordable Rio Grande and miles of remote boundary crossings.[92] In 1909 Clarence A. Miller, the U.S. consul in the Mexican border town of Matamoros, wrote a confidential report about the prevalence of smuggling in his area. He estimated that there were more than 100 boats engaged in smuggling and making irregular trips across the border. Miller also noted the difficulty of stopping the smuggling given the dependence of Brownsville merchants on the trade. Even if immigration officials could stop it, he argued that the merchants "would raise a storm of indignation and protest." Therefore, Miller concluded, the "business has assumed such large proportions that it could only be stopped by US troops."[93]

Miller's hope for U.S. troops to guard the border would begin to become a reality a couple of years later, in 1911, after fighting broke out near the border as a result of the Mexican Revolution. Initially only 1,500 troops were dispatched to prevent violation of neutrality laws, but over the next five years the number of troops skyrocketed. Thousands more troops were sent to the border when a rebellion broke out in South Texas in 1915 called the Plan de San Diego.[94] By 1916, following Pancho Villa's raid on Columbus, New Mexico, the Punitive Expedition to catch Villa in Chihuahua, and the outbreak of World War I, tens of thousands more National Guard troops were sent to protect the Mexican border. An estimated 110,000 National Guard were stationed on the U.S.-Mexico border in 1916; they took an active role in inspecting migrants and established a measure of control over the border for the first time.[95] By 1917, however, troops already began to be withdrawn, and by the early 1920s immigration officers began to notice that an increasing number of Europeans, especially Jews, and "Hindus" were entering clandestinely through the southern border as a way to avoid more stringent passport regulations.[96] The brief mass troop deployment on the border provided a glimpse of what could be accomplished in controlling migrant crossings by militarizing the border.

Gulf of Mexico

The Caribbean gateway provided potential migrants with hundreds of miles of unprotected coastline and ports where ships landed without thorough inspections. The U.S. military occupied Cuba between 1898 and 1902 and therefore regulated its borders, but afterward the Cuban government had a hard time controlling migration to and from the island. Starting in 1904, steamship companies petitioned the U.S. government to establish inspection stations in Havana to prevent the long delays caused by processing passengers once they arrived in Tampa or Key West. Although Commissioner General Sargent originally believed that "Cuba could be regarded as a foreign contiguous territory," when he looked into the relevant immigration laws passed in 1891, 1903, and 1907, they all specifically limited inspections to the borders of Canada and Mexico, and therefore he denied permission to allow immigration inspections in Cuba.[97] U.S. inspectors had been placed at Canadian ports to determine entry eligibility since 1893, but Canada had a very specific and close relationship with the United States. When the issue came up again in 1909, Commissioner General Daniel J. Keefe argued against posting an inspector in Havana because of the legal objections to having such an inspector in a "practically independent position at a foreign port."[98] The U.S. solicitor made the case that such an inspection to distinguish between U.S. and non-U.S. citizens would not constitute permitting entry into the United States, but Keefe rejected the idea.[99] As a compromise, the assistant secretary of the treasury allowed the Marine Hospital Station in Havana to screen passengers for diseases before they departed.[100]

Havana was the central hub of Chinese smuggling in the Caribbean, not only because Cuba had the largest Chinese population in the Americas outside of the United States but also because it was ideally located in the Gulf about 100 miles from both the United States and Mexico. Over the first two decades of the twentieth century, U.S. immigration officers slowly uncovered the shadowy world of Havana smuggling rings with the help of Chinese spies, paid informants, and captured migrants. However, even with the support of immigration authorities in Cuba, smuggling continued unabated. From 1903 to 1924, more than 23,000 Chinese entered Cuba.[101] We can surmise that a good portion of these made their way into the United States as stowaways on cargo vessels or on smaller fishing boats that dropped Chinese along remote sections of the Gulf coastline.

In 1908 and 1909 federal agents intercepted two ships, the *Cynosure* and the *Axel*, carrying Chinese from Mexico's Gulf Coast town of Progreso to Gulfport, Mississippi. The smuggling ring was based in Gulfport and led by a wealthy Greek restaurant owner, Nicolas Stratakos, together with a Chinese man named Sam Hop Sing. In January 1909, the *New Orleans Daily Picayune* ran a blaring headline "Chinese Smuggling Unearthed on Gulf Coast." The article asserted that three shiploads of Chinese had already arrived and been transferred by smaller boats to New Orleans; it claimed that the "promoters of the enterprise were planning operations on an even more extensive scale when the United States officers got wise."[102] In the following months, the Immigration Bureau sent Inspector A. P. Schell to New Orleans to investigate and prepare prosecutions of the smugglers who had been captured. Schell took the opportunity to expand his investigation to Havana, where his translator, Chin Coy, went undercover. Coy learned that 3,000–4,000 Chinese were employed in restaurants, stores, and laundries in Havana. He also met with Chaw Lin Hong, a former partner of Chin Bing, who had moved to Havana to organize smuggling parties of Chinese to the United States.[103] What began as an investigation of smuggling on two ships from Mexico to Gulfport, Mississippi, quickly uncovered a much larger smuggling operation that included several points in the Gulf region, including Tampico and Progreso in Mexico and Havana in Cuba.

In the first decade of the twentieth century, the Immigration Bureau began to expand its investigation of smuggling beyond the borders of the United States. Agents were routinely sent with Chinese translators on undercover missions to gather intelligence on smuggling operations in Cuba, Mexico, and Canada. These investigations revealed that the Gulf Coast of Mexico, including Tampico, Veracruz, and Merida, was a hotbed of smuggling activity. A former U.S. deputy marshal, W. M. Hanson, who lived in Mexico's

Gulf state of Tamaulipas, identified Tom Key of Tampico and Wong Foon Chuck, the "rich millionaire of Durango," as two of the leaders. Wong had been arrested in San Antonio in 1892 on charges of illegally entering the United States. Although the courts acknowledged that he was a Mexican citizen and a very wealthy businessman, they still deported him to Mexico.[104] This bitter experience of the discriminatory laws in the United States may have prompted Wong to help other Chinese cross the border illegally, or maybe he became involved simply because it was a good business opportunity. Wong also owned several restaurants along the Mexican International Railroad line, which he used to organize smuggling through El Paso.[105] Chin Coy, the Chinese translator who went undercover in Havana, and Richard Taylor also traveled to Mexico and found scores of Chinese in Progreso, Merida, and Tampico waiting for a chance to smuggle themselves into the United States. For a $500 smuggling fee, Chinese migrants had easy access from the port in Progreso to hundreds of miles of unguarded coastline in the United States from Texas to Florida.[106]

Although Monterrey and Mexico City had been important transit points for Chinese heading to the United States, by 1908 most of the action seemed to have switched to sea entry through the Gulf Coast.[107] In December 1908 the acting commissioner general wrote to the Immigration Bureau office in New Orleans, to warn it that the improvement in preventing land entries from Mexico had pushed Chinese to seek entry by water routes in the Gulf of Mexico.[108] A few years later, it became clear that smuggling from the Gulf had not only continued but seemed to be expanding. On 13 April 1913 four Chinese were found stowing away on a Gulf Coast Fruit and Steamship Company vessel that ferried goods between Galveston, Texas, and Gulf ports in Mexico. In this incident four sailors were sentenced to six months in jail for smuggling and the Chinese were deported. The Galveston inspector praised the local Chinese who apparently refused to help the smugglers and concluded that this was an isolated case and not a smuggling ring.[109] Immigration Inspector Richard Taylor had a different perspective, believing that there was ongoing Chinese smuggling on ships from the Caribbean. In a letter to the inspector in New Orleans, Taylor wrote, "While I have no new information upon the subject, it is reasonable to suppose that the smuggling of Chinese into your District on schooners from the West Indies and Mexico is still being carried on. Operations from the latter place will doubtless be suspended for some time excepting those who may come in fishing boats from the vicinity of Yucatan." Taylor concluded that if Chinese were still being smuggled into New York on fruit steamers, then they probably were being smuggled into New Orleans as well. He therefore recommended that inspectors in New Orleans conduct periodic searches of ships.[110]

It was relatively easy to hide Chinese on the many ships sailing from the Caribbean to the U.S. ports. On occasion Chinese stowaways would be found and arrested, but it is likely that most Chinese on these ships entered the United States undetected. In October 1914 a Chinese stowaway, Chin Lee, was discovered on the SS *Minnesota* coming from Jamaica to Philadelphia. Chin was twenty-four years old and married. His father had lived in Los Angeles and then returned to China. He had gone to Vancouver the previous year, and from there to Montreal, Halifax, and finally to Jamaica, where he worked in a laundry for almost a year. The captain and ship's officers were interrogated along with a "black mess boy" and the Chinese stowaway. The ship's officers and crewmembers denied knowing that Chin Lee was on-board until he was discovered below decks and brought out in handcuffs. Before leaving Jamaica, they fired a few pistol shots into the hold below deck to scare off any stowaways, but in this case the tactic appears to have failed. Chin was smuggled onboard by a Chinese restaurant owner in Port Antonio, Jamaica, after paying a $100 fee. He remained in the hold for five days without water, urinating once and never defecating. When he vomited from seasickness, the rats ate his vomit. Chin's desperate situation became clear in his description of his time in the hold, and the fact that he had little idea of where he was headed or what he would do once he got there. He said that he planned to go to Philadelphia, where he would work off the rest of his smuggling debt, even though he claimed not to know anybody there. As he put it, "If I land I could go anywhere and in Chinatown they will help me."[111] We do not know whether Lee was hiding his contacts from the authorities, but his insistence that he expected to be taken care of if he could just make his way to Chinatown suggests that extensive informal and formal networks existed in ethnic enclaves throughout the Americas. Chinatowns tied Chinese together in a transnational diasporic community.

Chinese seamen also formed part of the smuggling network. The crews that sailed between the Caribbean and U.S. ports were a motley group of seamen of various nationalities. Given the ability to communicate and the potential for ethnic identification, Chinese crew members were perhaps more likely to help Chinese stowaways than were crew from other places. While the captains of these ships may have been in charge, they also worried about potential mutinies by their ethnically diverse crew. For example, the

British ship *Castle Bruce* landed in Philadelphia with two Chinese stowaways and a crew made up of three white officers, three white engineers, one white steward, four Malay quartermasters, and eighteen Chinese crew members. The two Chinese stowaways, Gum Tung (thirty-three years old) and Lee Dai (twenty-nine years old), claimed to be picking up a load of laundry on the ship in Curaçao when the ship unexpectedly left shore. The two men survived on the ship by begging for food from the Chinese crew. "It was common fact and common talk," the ship's captain testified, that the Chinese wanted to sneak onto the ships and that was why he conducted searches at every port. The captain explained that his crew discovered the Chinese after they had left the port at Daiquiri, Cuba, and could not turn back because it was illegal to bring Chinese into Cuba. When asked why he did not do a full inspection when one of his Malay crew reported the presence of the Chinese stowaways, the captain explained the precariousness of his situation: "Put yourself in my position. You have eighteen [Chinese] to serve you[;] they can sneak along like a rat and before you know anything you have a knife in your back, and they have ample opportunities for doing it in the night time." The captain explained that he did not let on that he even knew of the presence of the Chinese stowaways because he feared "they would make a mutiny among the crew."[112] While these statements may be seen as self-serving explanations for why the captain did not investigate and apprehend the Chinese earlier, if his story can be believed it suggests that ship captains were well aware of the possible solidarity between Chinese crew members and Chinese stowaways, and that they feared reprisals by the crew if they enforced regulations too stringently.

Although ship captains usually claimed that Chinese found aboard their ships were stowaways, there is evidence that some ship captains were involved in smuggling. In 1920 a Cuban schooner, the *Sunbeam*, foundered 130 miles east of the Virginia capes with a cargo of molasses and nineteen Chinese. Seventeen of them drowned when the schooner went down. The inspector in Norfolk, Virginia, J. E. Williams, reported that "the master and his four Spanish crew members testified under oath that the Chinese were stowaways, but the two surviving Chinese testified that they and the other Chinese were being smuggled into the United States by some other Chinese, the one being in charge of the party on board having been lost." Even though the inspector believed that the ship's captain was involved in the smuggling operation, he argued that it was "useless to try to take action against the master," given that it was the word of the Chinese against four Spaniards. In this case, the captain and his crew along with the two surviving Chinese were sent back to Cuba. Inspector Williams warned that they should look out for Captain Rivera in the future, "as he is likely to try the same trick again."[113]

Even if there was not an overt attempt to smuggle in Chinese as seemed to be the case with the *Sunbeam*, Chinese who signed on as crew members could simply disappear after they landed in the United States. In 1920, when a Dutch vessel was seized, forty Chinese landed in Virginia, "and were not heard from again."[114] Reports of Chinese crew on Cuban sugar ships landing in the United States, never to be located again, came in from all points along the eastern seaboard and the Gulf Coast from Gloucester, Massachusetts, to Mobile, Alabama.[115] In 1889 a cartoon in the magazine *The Wasp*, titled "And Now They Come as Spaniards," depicts a Chinese migrant dressed as a caricatured bullfighter who claimed to be Spanish when he arrived at the customs house in New York City. The dialogue below the cartoon reveals the incredulity of the customs agent, but also the ability of Chinese coming from Cuba, then still a colony of Spain, to enter the United States with papers attesting to their Spanish citizenship.

> N.Y. Customs Officer: What! You are a Spaniard!
> Don John: Paper say so, so be.
> N.Y. Customs Officer: That's so; pass in.

The increasing presence of Chinese in U.S. towns and cities even after restrictionist legislation was passed suggested that borders were not being adequately guarded. One inspector in Richmond, Virginia, reported that every so often "I see a strange Chinaman or a Jap (they all look alike to me) passing through this town from one depot to another." He had also seen new Chinese restaurants and oriental art stores sprouting up all over the place. "You can figure this matter out any way you like, but it looks to me like there is a chain of these places extending from the Mexican border right into New York."[116] These stores and restaurants not only were symbols of Chinese smuggling but also acted as distribution points for the Chinese being transported to major U.S. cities. Merchant networks doubled as an underground railroad for smuggling operations as migrants were moved across borders and from city to city.

In 1916, after the Immigration Bureau had some success against Jamaican smugglers of Chinese, its agents noticed increasing numbers of Chinese passing through Canada to Trinidad. While there may have been a growth in opportunities for Chinese in Trinidad, inspectors believed that Trinidad was being used as a transit point for Chinese seeking to enter the United States.[117]

AND NOW THEY COME AS SPANIARDS.

N. Y. Customs Officer: What! You are a Spaniard!
Don John: Paper say so, so be.
N. Y. Customs Officer: That's so; pass in.

Similarly, in 1919 the bureau in Los Angeles received confidential information that "Chinese coolies" were being brought from Cuba to Mexico by a "notorious smuggler" who would then transport them to U.S. Gulf ports by boat.[118] Smugglers were not simply moving Chinese from point A in China to point B in the Americas, they were shuttling Chinese through various countries before landing at their final destination, most often the United States.

In 1922, in the wake of quota restrictions, the commissioner of immigration commented that smuggling of aliens, including Chinese, Europeans, and "Hindus" into the United States was increasing because of the more stringent quota, passport, and visa requirements. As the Immigration Bureau focused its attention on the Mexican border, and obtained some cooperation from the Mexican government, Chinese clandestine entries shifted to Cuba. "The number of Chinamen who have been successful in gaining entrance to the United States from Cuba is, of course, unknown," stated one inspector in Jacksonville in 1922, "but there is no use in denying the fact that a considerable number have succeeded in eluding our officers." The commissioner painted an alarming picture, noting that 30,000 young Chinese were waiting in Cuba for a chance to make their way to the "inaccessible and unguarded points on the Florida coast." He concluded that large numbers of Chinese kept arriving in Cuba not to find work there but to use the island as a jumping-off point to come to the United States illegally.[119]

In May 1920 a Cuban fishing boat, the *Reemplazo*, was found by immigration inspectors off the coast of Tarpon Springs, Florida, with seventeen Chinese aboard along with $50,000 in liquor. The *Tampa Sunday* exclaimed, "Gigantic Plot to Smuggle Chinese into US Believed Uncovered Here."[120] While the *Reemplazo* was anchored off Anclote Light, several Greek boats approached it trying to buy liquor, but they were thwarted when the immigration officers arrived and seized the boat. The crew testified that they had no knowledge of the Chinese aboard until they had already set sail from Havana. The captain, Emilio Estévez Infantil, however, admitted that the vessel's Cuban owner had been paid $1,700 to transport the Chinese to the United States. He also admitted that they were intending to sell the liquor in the United States, which had recently enacted Prohibition.[121]

The testimony of the Chinese passengers implicated the whole crew in the smuggling by revealing that the crew was all present when they boarded the boat in Havana. The Chinese also provided information about the person who had recruited them for the journey, a man they referred to as a Chinese Mexican. This Chinese Mexican, who spoke a few words of Chinese, apparently frequented Havana's Chinatown and offered to bring Chinese to the United States for $700 a head. Ong Ying put it this way, "I made arrangements with this half-breed Mexican. I understand that his father was a Chinese, and his mother a native of Cuba, so they called him 'Chinese Mexican.'" All of the captured Chinese testified that they had landed in either San Francisco or Vancouver before traveling through the United States to Havana, where they worked for a period of time before attempting to return to the United States. One of the Chinese, Eng Bow, even admitted to having entered the United States clandestinely twenty years before, also through Cuba. He had managed to live and work in New York for ten years without being detected. The men said they worked in various jobs in Cuba, including in Chinese restaurants and stores, laundries, and farms. All of them decided to go to the United States because they believed they could make more money there. None of the men had documents or visas, except for Eng Bow, who bought a false Cuban passport from a Chinese merchant in Hong Kong.[122] The investigation also revealed that Hgai Yick Ben, a Chinese Mexican active in the Mexican Mercantile Exchange, was involved in the smuggling ring and had sponsored one of the seventeen who were apprehended.[123]

This rare glimpse into a smuggling network showed that a well-traveled route between the United States, Canada, and Cuba brought Chinese legally in transit in one direction, and then clandestinely in the opposite direction. Furthermore, the fact that a Chinese Cuban (aka "Chinese Mexican") acted as a recruiting agent in Havana and that a member of the Mexican Mercantile Exchange sponsored one of the Chinese migrants implies that Chinese Mexicans and Chinese Cubans were also part of this transnational network. Multiethnic and multilingual Chinese were the key intermediaries who developed smuggling networks across national borders.

In addition to learning detailed information about how these seventeen arrived in Florida, immigration authorities seized letters from the Chinese passengers that revealed that other Chinese had already successfully entered the United States from Cuba through Florida. The immigration inspector in Tampa recommended that all seventeen Chinese found on the *Reemplazo* be excluded, but he suggested deportation to China for three of them who had admitted either illegally entering the United States on multiple occasions or using false documents; the other fourteen were returned to Cuba.[124]

Identifying the leaders of smuggling in Havana was only the first step. Breaking up the smuggling rings required the help of government officials in Cuba. Since the U.S. military issued a decree in 1902, Cuba had adopted U.S.-style Chinese exclusion. In 1917 Francisco Menocal, the Cuban commissioner of immigration, asked U.S. immigration officers to send lists of Chinese passing through the United States who claimed to be merchants. Menocal suspected that the alleged Chinese merchants were coming to work on the sugar plantations as laborers, and he hoped that the entry documents for the United States would prove his suspicions and allow him to exclude the Chinese. Apparently the Chinese minister had sufficient influence to enable Chinese to enter Cuba as alleged merchants against the wishes of Cuba's commissioner of labor. U.S. authorities agreed to cooperate because they worried that many of the Chinese landing in Cuba would use the island as a springboard for illegal entry into the United States.[125] Three years later, in 1920, in the wake of the *Reemplazo* incident, Daniel Trasivik, immigration inspector at Galveston, wrote to his Cuban friend Menocal to enlist his support in squelching smuggling to the United States. Menocal acknowledged that there was a large smuggling ring in Havana, and he ordered his detectives to investigate.[126] While it is not clear how effective the Cuban authorities were in clamping down on the smuggling, both the Cuban and U.S. governments shared a desire to control immigration and to restrict the Chinese in particular.

Go-Between Interpreters

The discovery of the seventeen Chinese aboard the *Reemplazo* in 1920 off the coast of Florida was no accident. Immigration inspectors had been tipped off by a Chinese undercover agent in Havana, Chin Yuk, that a shipment of Chinese was on its way. Chin had been sent to Havana to find out information about smugglers, but when World War I broke out in 1914, the absence of ships reduced smuggling opportunities, and his usefulness was diminished. After ten of the Chinese caught in Tampa were deported back to Cuba, Chin wrote in Chinese to Inspector Richard Taylor in Los Angeles and asked why they did not make the effort to question the Chinese to find out more about the leaders of the smuggling ring. Chin claimed that there were another 2,000–3,000 Chinese waiting in Havana to be brought to the United States. Exasperated, he wrote, "If it is the intention of the government of the United States to allow people to enter the country, you will not need me here to investigate anything and spend the government's money." He also complained that his salary was barely enough for his own expenses, and he argued that he deserved a raise so that he could take care of his family.[127]

The interpreters for the Immigration Bureau, who played a key role in undermining smuggling, were also cultural and linguistic brokers. As Mae Ngai wrote in her history of the Tapes, a Chinese American family whose members served as both interpreters for the bureau and as defenders of Chinese American rights, they "were in-between and go-betweens, individuals who found in their bilingualism and biculturalism opportunities for economic and social advancement."[128] Without the interpreters and translators, bureau officers would have been unable to question immigrants, understand what Chinese newspapers and letters said, or prosecute Chinese in the courts. Given the clandestine nature of smuggling, the best information came from Chinese informants like Chin Yuk, who was on the government's payroll. After Chinese were detained, inspectors counted on interpreters to get confessions from the suspects. The interpreters were motivated by the promise of a stable job and the recognition that came from working with the U.S. government in an official capacity.

Given their distrust of Chinese immigrants who claimed U.S. citizenship armed with their own lawyers and interpreters, immigration officers hired thirty-five of their own Chinese interpreters between 1900 and 1907, along with half a dozen white interpreters. Most interpreters were paid four dollars per day. The seven Chinese interpreters, who earned an annual salary of $1,200, made almost as much as a junior-grade inspector, but since they had not taken the civil service exam, they were not eligible for pensions. Nonetheless, the month vacation and status as government employees made this a coveted position for any Chinese who spoke even a little English.[129]

In the midst of this hiring frenzy Fung Ming became an official interpreter for the Immigration Bureau in 1906; in 1932, he was still working for them.[130] Fung was sent around the U.S. South to interpret at hearings and to interrogate Chinese detainees. He routinely went beyond his duty during hearings to try to convince Chinese defendants to tell the truth. In the middle of the *Reemplazo* hearing, for example, he stopped the proceedings to tell the court that he believed the Chinese witness Jew Hing was lying. Fung then had an extended conversation in Chinese with Jew Hing. Although the fact of this conversation was recorded in a parenthetical note in the hearing transcript, the details were not. When the hearing resumed, Jew began by stating, "The truth of the matter was," and he proceeded to reveal the name of his friend in Cuba who had arranged his trip.[131] In a report to the commissioner of immigration in New Orleans, Fung was quite brutal in his assessment of the seventeen Chinese who were captured: "I found most of them were very stupid, and [they] put up the most unreasonable stories[;] however, there were four of them quite willing to tell the truth."[132] Fung's duties also included translating letters being sent from the Chinese in jail in Tampa. In one plaintive letter, Yee Yun wrote to his uncles that he would probably be deported to China. Yee ended the letter wistfully: "The unluckiness of my life is not worth mention, so will not go into detail at this time."[133]

In spite of the key roles Chinese interpreters played, immigration inspectors did not always trust them either, and inspectors often suspected that the translators were in cahoots with the immigrants. Among the possessions found on the seventeen Chinese who were on the *Reemplazo*, inspectors found the business card of Yong Kay, an Immigration Bureau interpreter in San Francisco. One of the captured letters translated from Chinese indicated that Yong Kay would look after them once they arrived in the United States, suggesting that Yong may have been aiding illegal immigration.[134] The inability of inspectors to speak or understand Chinese gave interpreters ample opportunity to collude with Chinese migrants.

Periodically, Chinese interpreters would be fired from the Immigration

Bureau for helping smuggle Chinese. However, the need was so great that often the very same interpreters would be rehired at a later time. In 1919 the immigration commissioner in New Orleans, William Christy, argued that the Chinese interpreter Fung Ming, who left the bureau under a cloud of suspicion, should be brought back to help disrupt the smuggling operations from Mexico, Cuba, and Central America.[135] Although Fung found no evidence of major smuggling through New Orleans, he discovered that regular shipments of Chinese were being brought from Cuba to Tampa and Key West, Florida, and then transferred by rail to cities along eastern seaboard.[136] Fung, more than just an interpreter, was now acting as an undercover agent for the Immigration Bureau.

Fung's investigation yielded important information, like the fact that Havana was one of the main points for smuggling Chinese, and that the Chinese also transported opium and liquor. When an inspector in Pascagula, Mississippi, discovered that a Chinese man and a "colored man" were smuggling "chow mixed with opium" from Mobile, Alabama, to New Orleans, and that these two traffickers were in league with a Chinese "leader" in Havana in "steering" contraband Chinese from Cuba, it was Fung Ming who was sent to investigate further.[137] Fung went to Pascagula immediately to interview a Chinese laundryman who confirmed that lots of opium was being brought into the United States from Cuba.[138]

Given his zeal, Fung Ming was assigned as an interpreter for many of the major court cases against Chinese who had been smuggled into the U.S. South, from Florida to Alabama. By befriending the jailed Chinese, Fung was able to ask them informally about conditions in Cuba and the identities of people involved in the smuggling. For example, he discovered that most Chinese coming from Cuba would be sent to New York or Philadelphia. Furthermore, it was not usually the average manual laborer who made the journey but rather someone who had acquired some money to start a business. Given the $600 cost of smuggling to the United States, the poorest of the Chinese in Cuba or Mexico would be unable to pay the cost of such a journey. As Fung was told, "Chinese in Cuba those who have capital are good, for laborers are bad, too many of them."[139]

Chinese were heading not only to the United States but also to Cuba. According to Fung's informants, approximately 10,000 Chinese had landed in Cuba in 1918–19, mostly coming through Canada and New York, but some also arriving from San Francisco, New Orleans, Tampa, and Key West. In 1917 the Cuban government temporarily lifted the ban on Chinese laborers to supply the booming sugar industry. The average salary for a farm worker in

Cuba was three to four dollars per day, the same as the Immigration Bureau paid its Chinese interpreters, and store helpers earned fifty to seventy-five dollars a month. The informants reported that "the Chinese in Cuba [were] having great success in all kinds of business," noting, in what must have been an exaggeration, that 60 percent of retail businesses were owned by the Chinese.[140] The sugar boom was propelled by skyrocketing prices, which reached twenty-three cents per pound in May 1920, only to fall to four cents per pound by December.[141] The decimation of the sugar economy had an immediate impact on the Chinese. In 1922 the U.S. commissioner general of immigration reported that there were almost no jobs for Chinese in Cuba, and that 30,000 of them had the goal of "making their way to near-by inaccessible and unguarded points on the Florida coast and entering surreptitiously."[142] The direction and force of Chinese clandestine migration was highly sensitive to the vagaries of the international market.

Even though Chinese interpreters played key roles in enforcing anti-Chinese restrictions in the United States and Canada, they also defended the rights of Chinese in North America and sometimes even helped migrants fraudulently gain entry. In *Brokering Belonging*, Lisa Mar describes the complex role played by Yip On, a Chinese merchant and immigration interpreter in Vancouver. Yip led the boycott on U.S. and Japanese goods to protest discrimination against the Chinese and helped found the Baohuanghui (Chinese Empire Reform Association, or CERA). He managed CERA's business investments, including a newspaper in Shanghai and a streetcar line in Torreón, Mexico. At the same time as he worked for the Canadian immigration service as an interpreter, he also struck a secret deal with the Liberal Party. Yip's family emigration business facilitated entry for illegal Chinese migrants into Canada in exchange for bribes that would be passed along to the Liberal Party. What Mar demonstrates so well is that Chinese brokers, often acting as interpreters for the immigration bureaucracies designed to keep Chinese out, helped defend Chinese interests in the Americas and also helped migrants evade restriction laws. They also made themselves rich in the process.[143] There were dyed-in-the-wool anti-Chinese restrictionists on one side and Chinese who might never be willing to collaborate with the immigration bureaucracy that caused them so much trouble on the other. Between these poles were many Chinese and non-Chinese who were willing to play both sides against the middle and to serve their own interests by doing so. Chinese brokers, merchants, and interpreters—along with corrupt immigration officers and a whole industry of people dedicated to providing safe houses, jobs, and false papers—made possible a transnational smuggling network that outsmarted the most earnest efforts of governments throughout Greater North America.

Conclusion

Chinese migrants kept coming to the United States in spite of the increasingly restrictive immigration legislation and stricter enforcement at the borderline. Laws did matter, but not always in the same way that was intended by the politicians who established them. The Chinese exclusion acts pushed Chinese to seek clandestine entry through the long stretches of unguarded land and sea borders, in addition to their efforts to seek fraudulent entry through the official ports of entry by using forged papers or creating paper families. Immigration inspectors faced the impossible task of guarding thousands of miles of land borders and coastline, as well as examining tens of thousands of railroad cars and ships that crossed into U.S. territory each year. The efforts to stop clandestine smuggling of Chinese and other migrants gave birth to the border patrol as well as justifying the dramatic expansion of the entire immigration bureaucracy. It is not an exaggeration to say that the immigration bureaucracy in the United States owes its existence to the clandestine Chinese migrant.

As this chapter has shown, Chinese took advantage of every conceivable point of entry into the United States. Chinese came from the north from British Columbia, Montreal, and Ontario. They came from the south, from Mexico, Cuba, and other points in the Caribbean. They also continued to arrive from the east to San Francisco, and from the west to ports along the East Coast. Many who arrived on the Pacific or Atlantic coasts passed through the United States en route to Canada, Mexico, or the Caribbean and then made their way back into the United States secretly. I argue that during the exclusion era clandestine and illegal entry from the north and the south became much more important than legal entries. In short, more Chinese entered clandestinely than came through legal ports. Even Chinese who could enter the United States through legal ports often chose the illegal routes to save money and the humiliation of being poked and prodded by U.S. inspection officers. At the center of this vast transnational smuggling operation were Chinese brokers and merchants who helped recruit laborers in China, arranged transportation, snuck them across borders in the Americas, and provided jobs for them once they reached their destinations. These clandestine entries gave rise to the notion of the "illegal alien" and led to the criminalization of the act of crossing the border without inspection. The powerful idea that President Theodore Roosevelt expressed in 1903, that there are good and deserving immigrants and bad and undeserving ones, continues to reverberate today. The "illegal alien" is by definition the "wrong kind" of immigrant—one who is vulnerable to the violence of state authorities and common citizens alike.

PART 3

Competing Revolutionary Nationalisms, 1900–1940

CHAPTER 6

Revolutionary Nationalism
and Xenophobia

The situation is of life or death. If we continue indifferently to the
depressing action of the foreign races, soon we will have lost our nationality
and for this catastrophe we will have only ourselves to blame.
—José Angel Espinoza, *El ejemplo de Sonora* (1932)

Nationalism and xenophobia swept the Americas in the first three decades of
the twentieth century, leading to tighter immigration restrictions in general
and discriminatory legislation against the Chinese in particular. Although
the coolie period had officially ended by the twentieth century and all new
Chinese arrivals came to the Americas as free migrants, they were seen as unwanted aliens. The 1910 Mexican Revolution overthrew a decrepit oligarchic
regime and brought new urban working classes and peasants to the political stage. Although the Revolution called for land distribution, labor rights,
and other populist measures, it also fostered xenophobic nationalism, leading to the worst outburst of violence against the Chinese in North America.
The racial ideology of *mestizaje* on which the new revolutionary state built
its legitimacy was ultimately just as racist and anti-Chinese as any white
supremacist settler society. Whereas Cuba, Canada, and the United States
developed legislation and an immigration bureaucracy that disciplined and
controlled the Chinese population in the 1910s and 1920s, and thereby diminished vigilante anti-Chinese violence, the weakness of the Mexican state
allowed for popular anti-Chinese movements to flourish. Within a few short
years, Mexico went from being the most welcoming country for Chinese to
becoming the most virulently Sinophobic in the Americas.

This chapter focuses on Mexico as the culmination and apex of the anti-
Chinese movement in the Americas, but it is worth situating that national
study in a regional a global context. The Cuban wars of independence (1868–
98), followed by the founding of the republic in 1902, also sparked intense
national pride, but Chinese in Cuba were not the targets of pogroms like they
were in Mexico, the United States, or Canada. The active participation of the

Chinese in the wars of independence and the ideology of racial equality propounded by José Martí helped the Chinese be accepted as patriotic citizens of a new Cuba. Although Chinese along the Pacific coast of the United States and Canada experienced the same kinds of pogroms and harassment as they would in Mexico, by the 1920s immigration enforcement in Anglo America had largely replaced populist violence.

While the story of the Chinese in Cuba is one of slavery to freedom, the narrative for Mexico runs in the opposite direction. In the late nineteenth century, the Mexican government of dictator Porfirio Díaz defended the absolute right of Chinese to migrate to Mexico, based on the liberal constitution of 1857. By the beginning of the twentieth century, Porfirians began to study the issue of migration and considered regulating and limiting Chinese entry. However, it was not until the Mexican Revolution swept away Díaz in 1911 that a more robust and modern state could implement stricter controls on migration. With the new revolutionary 1917 constitution, the government was empowered to create legislation designed to restrict immigration by Chinese and control their activities once in the country. In the first sentence of Article 11, the new constitution reiterated the former document's guarantee of the right of free entry and movement, but it altered the next sentence in a way that rendered the first moot. It added a clause that restricted the right of migration to "the limits imposed by laws on emigration, immigration, and health safety laws in the Republic, or over foreigners residing in our country."[1] Although Mexico never implemented a U.S.-style Chinese exclusion law, state authorities created hygiene, labor, and health laws designed to harass the Chinese in the country, keep new ones from entering, and ultimately to force Chinese out entirely. A Mexican newspaper reported in 1919 that the Mexican Congress was reforming the immigration law "to protect the nationals against the Chinese invasion." Senator Benito Reynoso of Querétaro, who warned about the dangers posed by the "atavistic diseases" of the "Asian races," recommended regulating or restricting Chinese immigration to Mexico.[2] Federal legislative action was slow in coming, however, and it was less evenly enforced than the sustained anti-Chinese violence carried out by activists and local authorities. In early 1920 the Chinese government complained about the "systematic plundering, killings, humiliations, threats of expulsion, [and] prohibitions on immigration" that Chinese suffered in the northern states of Sonora and Sinaloa.[3] The anti-Chinese drumbeat continued in Mexico throughout the 1920s, culminating in 1931 with the expulsion from the northwestern states of Mexico of almost all Chinese residents.

Much had changed for Chinese since the Revolution. Porfirian *científicos* (technocrats) had pushed for Chinese immigration, seeing in them a source of cheap labor needed to build railroads and exploit mines and plantations. The Chinese were an essential element in their modernization plan. From the onset of Chinese migration, however, Mexican newspapers criticized the Chinese for being physically inferior, diseased, and unwilling to assimilate. According to them, Chinese depressed wages, took jobs from women, and competed unfairly with Mexican workers. These racist sentiments crystallized in sporadic anti-Chinese violence, including riots in Mazatlán in 1886 and Monterrey in 1894, as well as a wildcat strike in 1891 after a Nogales lumber mill hired Chinese workers.[4] Nonetheless, Porfirian elites not only defended the right of Chinese to migrate to Mexico but were willing to pay subsidies to steamship lines that brought Chinese laborers directly to Mexico's shores. According to anti-Chinese activist José Angel Espinoza, Chinese tongs based in California recruited workers in Shanghai and Hong Kong and paid Mexican government officials for every migrant imported.[5] Whether the Porfirians received kickbacks or not, they had an economic interest in providing cheap labor to work on their vast haciendas. As historian Moisés González Navarro wrote, "The positivists had no preference when it came to peons. They were interested not in the origin but in the efficacy of the labor."[6]

1903 Raigosa Commission

In spite of their desire and need for cheap labor, Porfirians were forced to respond to complaints about the Chinese as their presence grew. In 1903, the Consolidated Commercial Steamship Company established the first direct line from Hong Kong and Yokohama to Mexico, leading to a new wave of Chinese migration. One Chihuahua newspaper greeted the first shipment of Chinese to Manzanillo by declaring, "We join those who demand that, were it not possible to stop the inrush of the people of the queue, let's at least have the greatest precautions and procure the greatest isolation of the yellow flesh." When the bubonic plague broke out four months later, the Chinese were temporarily banned from entry by the secretary of the interior.[7] In this context, the Interior Ministry established a commission led by Genaro Raigosa to study the impact of Asian immigration. The commission concluded that Chinese were racially incompatible with Mexicans and suggested restricting further immigration. In 1904 the commission met with Interior Minister Ramón Corral and recommended a ban on permanent Asian immigration, preference for Japanese over Chinese for temporary economic migrants, and stricter regulations of contract labor, including requiring steamship companies to repatriate Chinese at the end of their contracts. Historian Grace Delgado summed up well the commissioners' conclusions: "Regulation of Chinese immigration was a necessity, but restricting free immigration was not."[8] The fact that the commission was disbanded, apparently without having submitted a formal report, and that the government did not act on its recommendations, indicates the extent to which the Porfirian regime maintained a laissez-faire approach to Chinese immigration.[9] Ramón Corral and other high-ranking *porfiristas* had profited handsomely by bringing in Chinese laborers, so it was unlikely that they would lead the suppression of Chinese immigration.[10] Nonetheless, anti-Chinese sentiment continued to fester among the populace, particularly in the north and in the southern state of Oaxaca, where most Chinese landed.

Increasing Chinese migration to Mexico had a direct impact on U.S. efforts to control Chinese entry, and U.S. inspectors repeatedly tried to get permission to enter Mexican territory to prevent Chinese from crossing the border. In 1890 the governor of Baja California, Luis E. Torres, granted U.S. customs officers permission to enter Mexico, but only as private citizens and with no power as U.S. officials.[11] Even after the Raigosa Commission issued its findings, the Mexican government refused to restrict the immigration of Chinese or prevent their crossing the border to the United States. Without any authorization, U.S. immigration agents inspected vehicles on the Mexican side of the border. In one case in November 1904, a U.S. Chinese inspector stopped a mail carriage in Tijuana, seeking to inspect the vehicle to see if the carrier was transporting Chinese. The mail carrier, Mauricio Castro, refused the inspection and said that the next time the inspector tried to do so "he would be shot."[12] U.S. inspectors in San Diego petitioned the Mexican consul to allow them to cross into Mexico to stop the flow of Chinese from Ensenada. The Mexican consul refused, fearing that Mexicans crossing the border would also be stopped.[13] In response, the *San Francisco Chronicle* published an article titled "Mexico Not Likely to Lend Her Aid," predicting that any request from the United States for restricting Chinese immigration "will not receive favorable consideration owing to the fact that Mexico welcomes Chinese immigrants." The article continued, "Neither can [Mexico be] expected to detain them in case they desire to leave the country. Where they go is not her concern."[14] The next day the *Chronicle* ran another story complaining about "Mexico's Chinese Policy" in which it accused the Chinese of "abusing the privilege of landing on Mexican soil by using it as a base to invade our own territory from which they are excluded by law."[15]

While U.S. newspapers saw Chinese migration from Mexico as an "invasion," Mexican newspapers saw the U.S. attempt to impose restrictions on Mexico as unwarranted interference in their country's affairs. The *Mexican Herald* responded to the *Chronicle*'s characterization of Mexico's pro-Chinese policy by denying that the government encouraged Chinese immigration; instead, it was Mexico's constitution that "prevent[ed] federal authorities from denying admittance to the national territory to any honest man never mind what may be his race or color."[16] The *Herald* noted that U.S. immigration agent Marcus Braun had come to Mexico in 1904 as a representative of the U.S. government to ask for cooperation in stopping Chinese migration, and the Mexican government had declined all of his proposals. The newspaper supported this position by arguing that Mexico was in a stage of its development when it needed "able-bodied immigrants."[17]

In response to increasing domestic and foreign pressure to restrict Chinese migration, Mexico passed an immigration law in 1908 that created the Migration Service. The Inspection Service started a year later to prevent entry of those with "obvious moral and medical incapacity," but determining the moral fitness of prospective immigrants was a tricky business. The Migration Service also began collecting data on all entries and exits from the country, but it was not until 1926 that identity cards were issued to immigrants.[18] The weakness of the Porfirian state and the chaos of the revolutionary period that began in 1910 rendered the new immigration laws and the nascent bureaucracy ineffectual. In the absence of state controls on Chinese, popular vigilantes and revolutionary soldiers stepped in to assume the government's disciplining function.

Anti-Chinese Violence during the Mexican Revolution

Although there were occasional riots and acts of violence against Chinese during the Porfirian era, it was not until the Mexican Revolution erupted in 1911 that the most egregious attacks on Chinese occurred. The Revolution unleashed class and race antagonisms that had been simmering below the surface during the Porfiriato and kept from boiling over by a strong central state. Once the lid was removed, armed insurgents took revenge on the storeowners and merchants they viewed as most alien: the Chinese. The worst massacre during the Revolution and the deadliest one-day attack on Chinese in North America occurred in Torreón on 15 May 1911. The stage was set a week earlier when Jesús C. Flores, a stonemason and supporter of the revolutionary leader Francisco Madero, gave a fiery speech at a Cinco de Mayo celebration in the neighboring city of Gómez Palacio, Durango. Flores complained that the Chinese had monopolized women's work, depriving them of their livelihood, and declared that "it was a necessary . . . even a patriotic duty, to finish with them."[19]

When the rebel army under the leadership of Francisco Madero finally made its way into Torreón, the soldiers, along with mobs from nearby villages, set about pillaging businesses and private homes, particularly targeting Chinese homes and stores. Chinese found in the city were brutally murdered by the revolutionary army, resulting in 303 deaths, nearly half of the city's Chinese population. The brutality with which the Chinese were massacred was shocking. The report prepared by lawyers for the Chinese government described the events in gory detail:

> In one instance the head of a Chinaman was severed from his body and thrown from the window into the street. In another instance a soldier took a little boy by the heels and battered his brains out against a lamp post. In many instances ropes were tied to the bodies of the Chinamen and they were dragged through the streets by men on horseback. In another instance a Chinaman was pulled to pieces in the street by horses hitched to his arms and legs. When the massacre ended the bodies of the dead were robbed and mutilated. Most of the bodies were entirely stripped of their clothes and left naked. . . . No language can adequately depict the revolting scenes which attended the carnival of human slaughter. . . . The mind recoils in horror from the contemplation of such an atrocity.[20]

After the killings ended, the humiliation of Chinese continued. Mexicans buried their dead in the cemetery, but they refused to allow the Chinese to be buried along with them. Instead, naked Chinese corpses were thrown into an open trench.[21] Not everyone was so horrified by this massacre. In 1932 the anti-Chinese activist José Angel Espinoza justified the Torreón killings in his book *El ejemplo de Sonora*, arguing that once the Chinese took up arms to defend the dictatorship they had broken with their obligation as foreigners to remain neutral.[22] Unlike the Chinese in Cuba, who were praised for their revolutionary credentials, Chinese in Mexico were seen as antirevolutionary and unpatriotic.

In the wake of the massacre, representatives from the Chinese and Mexican governments investigated. The Chinese issued a legal brief outlining the breach of treaty stipulations and other international laws, and Mexico agreed to pay $3.1 million in compensation for the loss of life. In the 1920s, after the Chinese government complained that it had still not been paid, the Mexicans offered to pay a reduced amount between $300,000 and $500,000. In 1934, twenty-three years after the Torreón massacre, the Mexican government told the Chinese that it would not pay the indemnity until the economy of the country recovered.[23] It appears that the debt to the Chinese was never paid.

The Torreón massacre was the largest and most deadly attack on Chinese in Mexico, but it was hardly unique. It was simply the most dramatic expression of regular harassment and violence against Chinese that began even before the Revolution. During one of the key events in the lead-up to the Revolution, a strike in the Cananea mines in 1906, several Chinese stores were sacked and pillaged. Two of the Chinese owners demanded indemnity for their considerable losses, but the governor refused to take responsibility.[24] Throughout the Mexican Revolution, soldiers and civilian mobs ransacked and stole property from Chinese stores and homes. On two days in July 1915, for example, looters pillaged forty-four Chinese stores in Cananea, taking over half a million dollars in cash and merchandise. In the first year of the Mexican Revolution alone, Chinese in Mexico filed 608 claims, for property losses totaling more than $1 million. According to a U.S. consular agent, Mexican soldiers' "favorite past-time" was robbing Chinese merchants, stripping them, and tying them to a tree in a desolate area until someone came by to release them.[25]

In March 1916 representatives of the Chinese community in Cocorit, Sonora, wrote to the governor to complain that municipal authorities had ordered their removal to the outskirts of town within two months. This removal order was part of a more general call to establish special ghettoes for Chinese to contain their supposed diseases, prevent social and sexual mixing with Mexicans, and make it easier for police to watch over them. The Chinese in Cocorit had already suffered losses during the Revolution, being sacked by both Yaqui Indians and Villistas, and they argued that they would be unable to earn a living if they were removed from town. They made their plea to the Sonoran governor as law-abiding foreigners who always paid their taxes and never harmed anyone. The Chinese also petitioned the U.S. consul for assistance in this matter, demonstrating the power exerted by U.S. representatives in northern Mexico, the lack of Chinese diplomatic representation, and the desperate situation of Chinese migrants.[26]

Although most of the attacks and robberies of Chinese occurred in the northwestern states because that is where Chinese were most prevalent, mobs threatened Chinese throughout the country. In early June 1911, just six months after the Torreón massacre, the president of the Chinese colony of 500 in Tapachula, Chiapas, in Mexico's southwestern tip, requested asylum from the U.S. consulate. The president of the Chinese colony, a U.S. citizen, feared that the lower classes there would massacre the Chinese like they had in Torreón. The attacks were never consummated, but the reaction of the Chinese in Tapachula demonstrates the terror in which Chinese lived. The U.S. ambassador, Henry Lane Wilson, wrote to the Mexican government informing them of the reports of an imminent massacre and requesting protection of U.S. lives and property. After the tensions died down, Wilson made it clear that he was only concerned with protecting U.S. citizens. "Naturally," Wilson wrote, "the Embassy had no intention of asking for protection for Chinese citizens."[27] Another example of the kind of attacks that Chinese suffered happened at the end of July, when shots were fired and a dynamite bomb exploded at Kwong Say Tay's store in Salina Cruz, Oaxaca. The Chinese legation complained to the Mexican government and asked for protection of its citizens, but little could be done.[28] Pillaging of Chinese stores, mob violence, and terrorist bomb attacks persisted in spite of the federal government's claims to protect Chinese lives and property. Given the central government's instability and weakness throughout the first phase of the Mexican Revolution (1910–15), its ability and willingness to quell the violence was limited, especially when local authorities and revolutionary soldiers were often the instigators.

Patriotic Chino Cubanos

Unlike in Mexico, where the Chinese quickly became enemies of the Revolution, in Cuba, Chinese were protagonists in the wars of independence. In the Ten Years War (1868–78), the first stage in the movement for Cuban independence, between 2,000 and 5,000 Chinese joined the rebel forces, accounting for at least 30 percent of the revolutionary army. They included not only foot soldiers but also several celebrated Chinese officers. In the last phase of the independence war (1895–98), only about 300 to 350 joined the rebellion, but by that time Chinese were no longer trying to escape their coolie contracts and there were also far fewer Chinese in Cuba.[29] Declarations from Cuban independence hero Máximo Gómez, and praise from other prominent Cubans like diplomat Gonzalo de Quesada, solidified this image of the Chinese as patriotic Cubans. Gómez famously proclaimed: "There has never been a Chinese traitor or deserter."[30] Antonio Chuffat, an Afro-Chinese Cuban who published a history of the Chinese in Cuba in 1927, glossed José Martí's view that the experience of fighting together in the wars of independence united races and classes in Cuba. "Democracy, equality, the union of the Cuban man, began in the field of battle, where the black slave hobnobbed with his master, and the Chinese contract laborer with his boss. . . . . Cuba is the only land where hate does not exist; there is only love between brothers, in which the Chinese also participated."[31] While this idyllic picture was more a hope than a reality, the ideology of racial equality mitigated to some extent the most overt forms of racism and discriminatory legislation.[32]

In spite of this ideology of racial equality, however, the new Cuban republic in 1902 reaffirmed the exclusion of Chinese laborers that had been mandated by U.S. General Leonard Wood just five days before the end of U.S. occupation. The Chinese already in Cuba may have been patriotic heroes, but that did not stop the government from wanting to exclude new Chinese laborers from entering the country. When a group of forty-three Chinese arrived on the ship *Monterrey* shortly after the declaration of Military Order 155, they were not allowed to land and were forced on to Mexico, where they remained jobless eighteen months later. Intellectuals and politicians drew on eugenicist ideas to argue that Asian and African migration would hurt the new nation. In 1906 the president of the Academy of Sciences, Juan Santos Fernández, argued against the further immigration of Asians and Africans, saying that it had caused the "purer" races to mutate and reappear "as they do in animals; from there comes the regressive type, the cruel, thieving, hypocritical atavist." During congressional debates over an immigration bill in February 1906, one proposal that made it to the floor explicitly welcomed the Caucasian race and excluded "individuals and families of the race of color, be they black, Malaysians, Mongoloid, or the Oceanic races as well as the copper-toned and all mestizos, and the gypsies also known as *zingaros*."[33] Although the 1906 Law of Immigration and Colonization did not end up explicitly prohibiting the entry of Asians or blacks, it reserved funding for Canary Islanders and Northern Europeans, thus making it clear that the desired immigrants were white and not black or Asian. In 1909 the interim Chinese chargé d'affaires petitioned the Cuban Congress to revoke Order 155. The Cuban commissioner of immigration, F. E. Menocal, rejected the Chinese request for four basic reasons: "economic or social, ethnic or racial, sanitary, and diplomatic." Menocal referred to the Chinese as coolies to invoke the image of enslaved laborers and gave the example of violent conflict in the United States over the Chinese as a warning of what Cuba should avoid. Menocal not only recommended denying the Chinese petition but also insisted that the current law should be enforced more rigorously. The Cuban Congress rejected the Chinese petition and the exclusion law remained in place.[34]

In spite of this official policy of Chinese labor exclusion, the Cuban government allowed the Chinese legation in Havana to determine which Chinese were merchants, students, or travelers and thus exempt from the prohibition. In October 1911 the newspaper *El Día* criticized the "secret door through which so many are introduced." A couple of years later the Department of Sanitation announced that it would enforce Chinese exclusion more strictly because it was "convinced that many Chinese are obtaining admission into Cuba by falsely representing themselves to be students or tourists."[35] Newspapers on the island criticized the Cuban government's willingness to cede the power to control Chinese immigration to Chinese diplomats, arguing, as *El Mundo* did in 1915, that this would result in an "invasion of students and merchants." In spite of these protestations, the Chinese legation maintained control over Chinese immigration to Cuba until 1926.[36]

El Mundo's fear of an invasion may have been overblown, but Chinese migration to Cuba in the early twentieth century grew dramatically, especially after 1917, when the ban on Chinese labor was temporarily lifted. The statistics for Chinese entries to Cuba are unreliable in part because the government did not directly control it. Official Cuban sources, including the census, count between 300 and 530 Chinese entering between 1902 and 1916, while other sources indicate that in just two years, 1907–8, almost 8,000 Chinese entered, mostly from the United States and Mexico. The Chinese consulate in Havana, responsible for managing entries, enumerated 6,258 Chinese arrivals between 1903 and 1916. Whatever the exact number, the restrictions on Chinese slowed migration from what it had been during the coolie period (1847–74). With the sugar planters desperate for cheap labor, however, Cuba temporarily suspended the exclusion of Chinese in 1917 and threw the gates open. From 1917 to 1924, another wave of more than 17,000 Chinese entered Cuba.[37] The Chinese consulate counted 16,005 entries between 1917 and 1924, but these just included students and merchants. The shipping pages of the *Havana Post* in 1920 noted that more than 2,000 Chinese entered in just ten days.[38] As in the previous period, the number of Chinese who entered illegally and were not counted probably far outstripped those who were registered by the Chinese legation. Contemporary writers and journalists estimated that 30,000–35,000 Chinese entered Cuba in the first three decades of the twentieth century. With Cuba becoming an important launching pad for Chinese entering the United States, such a figure seems reasonable. In spite of the fact that more Chinese passed through Cuba than ended up staying there, the Cuban census documented a rapid increase in the Chinese population on the island, from 10,300 in 1919 to 24,647 in 1931.[39] Chen Kwong

Min, a Chinese scholar, estimates that the Chinese population in Cuba in the mid-1920s reached as high as 70,000.[40] In the wake of the sugar market crash in 1923 there were vociferous calls to end further Chinese migration and to expel criminal Chinese from Cuba. Although Chinese in Cuba were subject to harassment and discrimination, especially in the 1920s, official and unofficial anti-Chinese acts were mitigated by the ideals of racial equality and the notion of patriotic Chinese Cubans.

Mexico: 1920s Restrictions and Expulsions

With Venustiano Carranza assuming the Mexican presidency in 1915 and writing a new constitution in 1917, the chaos of the Revolution began to subside; state governments in the north turned their attention to the Chinese. Anti-Chinese efforts crystalized in 1919, when the Sonoran legislature passed a law to mandate that 80 percent of laborers in any foreign-owned business be Mexican. Enforcement of these provisions varied from town to town, but towns near the border with large Chinese populations, such as Cananea and Magdalena, enforced the law strictly. In 1919 two Chinese merchants in Cananea, José Hum Fook and José Chang, represented scores of other Chinese merchants when they fought expulsion orders in court. It is likely that José Chang is the same man who Marcus Braun followed and who acted as a "padrone" for Chinese arriving in Salina Cruz, Oaxaca, in 1907. The courts ended up siding with the Chinese and suspending the Cananea expulsions, and President Carranza ordered Governor Adolfo de la Huerta, who would briefly serve as interim president in 1920, to not only prevent the expulsions but also protect the Chinese.[41] This first effort to expel Chinese from Mexico ended with the central government and courts acting as protectors of the Chinese, but the anti-Chinese movement pushed ahead. Chinese mutual aid societies and the Chinese legation protested the discriminatory legislation and appealed to state governors and the president by invoking Mexican constitutional protections.

The expiration of the 1899 treaty between Mexico and China in November 1921 provided an opportunity to tighten immigration restrictions on the Chinese. Senator A. Magallón wrote to the foreign minister in Mexico to propose new draconian restrictions, including the absolute prohibition of Chinese immigration; using identity cards and censuses for Chinese residents to prevent and detect clandestine entry; deportation of those who entered illegally, had contagious or hereditary diseases, smoked opium, or gambled; and establishment of Chinese ghettoes. This proposal was the most extreme reversal of the generally open immigration policy up until that point. President Alvaro Obregón favored a more modest restriction plan modeled on the U.S. policy. It would prohibit Chinese workers but allow small groups of merchants, intellectuals, and diplomats, and it would permit Chinese residents in Mexico to leave and return if they obtained a passport with a photograph.[42] In an exchange of diplomatic notes on 26 September 1921, Mexico and China agreed to prevent laborers from either country from entering the other one. Explicitly exempted from this prohibition were students, diplomats, merchants, and any Chinese already within Mexico. Similar to the Gentleman's Agreement between the United States and Japan in 1907, this diplomatic exchange gave the impression of mutuality and prevented an overt exclusion of Chinese laborers.[43] Nonetheless, this agreement, together with stricter enforcement against the Chinese of general immigration laws, had effect of stopping Chinese migration by the late 1920s. While the federal anti-Chinese campaign was weak compared to the United States, state and local campaigns to harass and expel the Chinese from northern Mexico were harsher than anything experienced in the United States, at least in the twentieth century.

Chinese Mexicans actively claimed their rights as naturalized Mexican citizens, both to be able to travel to the United States and to protect their civil rights in Mexico. In the 1920s and 1930s, facing increasingly harsh laws that sought to expel Chinese from northern Mexico, Chinese Mexicans petitioned the federal government and invoked the constitution for protection. In October 1924, six naturalized Chinese Mexicans were arrested in Cananea and threatened with deportation. One of those arrested, Manuel Jean Sop, sent an urgent telegram to President Alvaro Obregón. "In my name and the others, we ask for guarantees granted to us as nationals by the General Constitution." In this case, the petition worked. One month later, Obregón issued orders to release the Chinese Mexican nationals and only deport those who were "directors of mafias."[44] In 1932–33, when the anti-Chinese movement reached its height in northern Mexico, scores of naturalized Chinese Mexicans wrote to the president to ask that their rights as Mexicans be defended. One of the petitioners was José Hum Fook, who had resided in Cananea, Sonora, since 1904 and who had become a naturalized citizen. This was the same Hum Fook who persuaded a Sonoran court to stop the Cananea expulsions in 1916. By the time he wrote to President Abelardo Rodríguez in 1932, he had been living in Mexico for twenty-eight years. Hum complained about harassment and said he had been forced from his home and property in Cananea by the anti-Chinese movement. His letter to the president asking for protection emphasized that he had been a hardworking and honorable citizen.[45] There is no indication in the archives of how or if the president responded to their protests; given the tenor of the anti-Chinese movement, it is likely that they were forced to leave Mexico. While the national government and courts had served to impede local anti-Chinese harassment in the early 1920s, by the end of the decade the central government began to bow to pressures from anti-Chinese activists. In July 1927 President Plutarco Elías Calles finally abrogated the Treaty of Amity, Commerce, and Navigation with China.[46] Although the treaty had not adequately protected the Chinese, they had frequently invoked it when demanding fair treatment in Mexico. By the 1930s almost all the central government's impediments to anti-Chinese activists had been swept aside.

Remote Control

At the beginning of the twentieth century, governments throughout the world began to recognize that the best way to control immigration was before the migrants left a foreign port. Given the legal difficulties and expense of deporting foreigners who arrived in a new country, the visa system was created to determine in advance whether a prospective migrant would be eligible to enter. During this period an international system of visas and passports that had existed in piecemeal fashion in the nineteenth century began to be standardized and recognized globally. In the 1920s, with anti-Chinese sentiment gathering force in Mexico and with the United States pressuring Mexico to seal its border, the Mexican government used "remote control" by tightening visa requirements for Chinese wishing to travel to Mexico.[47] The consulate in Yokohama, Japan, served as the central Mexican outpost for Chinese wishing to migrate and therefore had great latitude in determining which Chinese would be granted visas. In November 1925 the Mexican consul at Yokohama, Angel Cano del Castillo, refused to grant seventeen Chinese visas to travel to Mexico, suspecting that they intended to cross into the United States. Cano del Castillo went undercover on the steamer *President Wilson*, mixing with the passengers, playing mah jong, and engaging them in conversation to learn about their intentions. He discovered that many of the passengers who had visas for Mexico or South American countries intended to land in Mexico but then travel clandestinely to the United States.[48] Refusing to issue visas to Chinese before they left Asia was one way to limit migration, but there were multiple ways for Chinese to enter Mexico.

In 1923 the Mexican Inspection Service proposed reforms to the ineffective 1908 migration law and began tightening enforcement of Chinese immigration.[49] Enforcement, however, was made more difficult because major government officials were themselves recruiting Chinese laborers. Although all migrants were required to have passports, immigration officers in Mexicali discovered that most of the Chinese and Japanese working there in 1927 had no passports because they had been brought in illegally by Governor Esteban Cantú between 1916 and 1920, often in groups of up to 100.[50] Reforms and additional enforcement mechanisms were largely ineffective when state authorities flouted the law. A memorandum that circulated in the Mexican Foreign Ministry in 1929 noted that although Chinese became subject to the same rules as other immigrants on 1 December 1928, this did not do enough to restrict or "avoid [Chinese] immigration which is harmful for others, nor that of other individuals from other races, like the Lebanese, Syrians, Arabs, Palestinians, Blacks, etc."[51] The memorandum suggested a series of measures to prevent the fraudulent entry of Chinese by creating special identity cards with portraits of the holder, along with signatures and fingerprints. This proposal allowed Chinese in Mexico to travel to China as long as they returned within six months. The new identity cards would be stamped once they reached Hong Kong and then a visa issued when they wanted to return to Mexico. Chinese who had capital invested in Mexico would be given a two-year period in which to return. Consular officials suspected, however, that Chinese who claimed they had lost their passports in China were simply passing along their old passports to other Chinese who wanted to enter Mexico.

In addition to creating a more effective system for controlling and identifying individual Chinese as they exited and entered the country, the memorandum pushed for an agreement with China to prevent the entry of more laborers. Citing competition with Mexican workers, officials also pointed to the "dangers that are brought by mixing our indigenous race with that of the Mongolian, whose descendants—everyone knows—bring with them highly harmful defects."[52] The new regulations were tested a few months later in December 1929, when twenty Chinese arrived at the border in Naco, Arizona, and were denied entry into Mexico because they lacked proper papers.[53] Centralization of control over immigration was the key to successful implementation of restrictions. In July 1930, Andrés Landa y Piña, the author of the lengthy report on Chinese immigration and head of the Department of Migration, warned the Foreign Ministry that 1,000 Chinese would be arriving on Mexican coasts and told the ministry to deny them entry unless they had specific authorization from his department.[54]

Up until the 1920s it was relatively easy for Chinese to travel to Mexico. In the 1920s Chinese continued to enter Mexico in spite of the agreement with China to prohibit the entry of Chinese laborers. After 1930, however, it became increasingly difficult to enter Mexico, as the government required visas and approval directly from the Interior Ministry. Following the 1931 decree banning all foreign laborers, Chinese workers who could not prove they had been in Mexico in the past six months were barred from entry. The new restrictions required the establishment of a more sophisticated immigration bureaucracy, along with identity documents and records of all entries and exits.

Taking over from Cano, the new consul in Yokohama, Manuel Tello, was at the frontline of this strategy, checking to see if prospective Chinese immigrants to Mexico had the paperwork required for travel. Tello tried to enlist the cooperation of the *Dollar* steamship line, but he discovered that that the steamship company lied when he asked it for a list of Chinese traveling to Mexico.[55] On another occasion, Tello went aboard a steamer heading to San Francisco and forced the steamship captain to disembark passengers who said they intended to go to Mexico but lacked the proper papers for entry. Tello also checked the passports of passengers with Mexican-sounding names who were listed as traveling to San Francisco. Presuming that they too intended to travel to Mexico without proper documentation, he also had them removed from the ship. Some of the passengers who listed San Francisco as their destination simply refused to present themselves when called by the interpreter, thus frustrating the consul's efforts.[56] In 1930 Consul Tello began sending lists to the Foreign Ministry of all the people to whom he had granted visas for Mexico so that immigration officers could check to see if the arriving passengers matched his list.[57] In an effort to stem the movement of Chinese, the Mexican immigration bureaucracy had to engage in "remote control," a process by which Mexico extended its enforcement of immigration restrictions around the globe to Hong Kong, Yokohama, and San Francisco.[58]

State versus Central Government Authority

Although the anti-Chinese movement was strong throughout northern Mexico, state governments varied in their degree of collaboration with anti-Chinese activists. In Sonora, the state government was tightly aligned with anti-Chinese activists, whereas in Baja California the governor of the northern district, Esteban Cantú (1911–20), was one of the principal importers of

Chinese. The census shows an increase of Chinese in Baja California from 851 in 1910 to 2,873 in 1920, but these official numbers certainly undercounted the Chinese population. A more accurate estimate of Chinese day laborers in the Mexicali Valley put the number at between 7,000 and 8,000 in 1919. Governor Cantú was suspected of receiving 10 million pesos each year from taxes on land and opium, in addition to charging 270–340 pesos per person for granting labor contractors the right to import Chinese. In July 1920 a prominent businessman in the region, Rafael Conrado Silver, wrote to President Adolfo de la Huerta complaining about Cantú's involvement in importing Chinese.

> For each Chinese that arrives, Cantú pockets 150 dollars, giving the concessionaire 25 dollars. All of these Chinese dedicate themselves to all the vices, especially smoking opium and gambling, and Cantú receives for each one of them a personal tax that reaches 50,000 dollars monthly (10 dollars for each one every trimester). These Asiatic hordes are also leaving out in the cold the Mexicans who are forced to emigrate to the United States because it is impossible for them to compete with the coolies.[59]

Even though Cantú claimed to have suspended all further importations of Chinese to the district, Conrado Silver asserted that 281 Chinese had recently arrived on two boats and that the governor "was enriching himself more with this traffic, just as the Spanish slave traffickers had in the colonial era."[60] The Mexican consul in New York provided the government with copies of contracts that had been signed between Cantú's political partners and various banks in San Francisco; the documents indicated that Mexican officials were paid 100 dollars for every Chinese brought to Baja California.[61]

Faced with Cantú's blatantly illegal acts, President de la Huerta eventually sent an expedition, led by General Abelardo L. Rodríguez, to force Governor Cantú to relinquish control of the state. Cantú began to prepare militarily to defend himself and demanded a 1 million-peso loan from the Chinese immigrants under threat of death. The Chinese were in a difficult situation. If they gave the money to Cantú, they could be accused of intervening in internal politics and subject to deportation. Furthermore, the Sino-Mexican treaty had a clause in it that prohibited Chinese immigrants from making any kind of political contributions. The Chinese legation in Calexico advised the Chinese not to give the loan to the governor. Meanwhile, Cantú demanded that Chinese volunteer to join his military force given all that he done to allow them into Baja California. More than 700 Chinese immigrants petitioned the

U.S. government through the Fraternal Union China Association to permit them into California to avoid being drafted into the impending armed conflict. In the meantime, Chinese began to swim across the Colorado River to escape to the United States. In the end, Cantú was forced to give up power to Rodríguez and the Chinese were able to stay out of the conflict.[62] This power struggle between a state governor who profited from Chinese migration and a central government that was trying to manage and limit that migration signaled a shift. The central government was trying to act as a mediator between those who advocated Chinese migration and those who vehemently condemned it. Although the central government was not at this point willing to give the *anti-chinistas* everything they wanted, it was also unwilling to allow governors, local officials, and corrupt immigration officers to flout restrictions passed by Congress.

The 1926 revision of the ineffective 1908 immigration law was part of this effort by the central government to gain control over migration. The new law barred the entry of a long list of undesirables, including old and infirm people who may become public charges, women under twenty-five, children not under the care of an older family member, illiterate men, fugitives from justice, drug addicts, anarchists, and foreign laborers without a one-year contract. Chinese were not specifically mentioned as an excluded class.[63] The new law also established a registry for nationals and foreigners entering and exiting the country, created standardized identity cards for both immigrants and emigrants, and gave the Servicio de Salubridad (Public Health Service) and special sanitation agents the power to admit or reject immigrants.[64] The requirement that foreign laborers have contracts was the exact opposite of U.S. law, which specifically prohibited contract laborers from entry. The registry for all immigrants was part of the government's broader attempt to centralize control and gain a handle on the kind of illegal crossings that occurred frequently in the border region. Stricter enforcement of immigration restrictions occurred throughout the Greater North American region in the mid-1920s. The United States passed its quota restrictions during this period, Canada imposed Chinese exclusion in 1923, and in 1926 Cuba took away the Chinese legation's power to issue certificates.

In Mexico, however, the registry did not effectively keep track of the growing Chinese population. From 1926 to 1950 the registry only counted 14,000 Chinese in Mexico, a number far below the population enumerated in the census, which itself undercounted the Chinese.[65] For example, in the entire period from 1877 to 1949, only 132 Chinese day laborers and 590 Chinese farmers were registered as living in the Mexicali Valley. According to the 1921 census, 1,300 Chinese worked in the Mexicali Valley. Other sources estimated that 7,000 to 8,000 Chinese day laborers worked there in 1919 alone and that 80 percent of the Colorado River Land Company's 325 million hectares of cotton was being worked by Chinese day laborers.[66] The registry's failure to keep track of Chinese indicates that while the federal government was pushing for immigration restrictions in the mid-1920s and passing more restrictive legislation, it lacked an effective bureaucracy to enforce its rules.

Even at the height of the anti-Chinese movement in northern Mexico, the weak state could not prevent Chinese from crossing illegally into Mexico. In 1929 the Mexican consul in Nogales reported that immigration officers at the border smuggled Chinese into Mexico for $300 per person. On one occasion Chinese were stopped from coming into Mexico by a Mexican general and then turned over to immigration officers. These same Chinese arrived in Nogales later that day escorted by the interpreter for the Chinese consulate and two armed immigration agents. The federal government and the military were thus impotent to stop Chinese entries because local officials were facilitating the trade. The consul also noted that the corrupt immigration officers lived in "insolent luxury," spending large sums of money in cabarets and brothels that they would not have been able to afford on their small salaries.[67] Given the corruption of the very officials charged with enforcing immigration laws, not to mention the complicity of highly placed politicians, it is not surprising that so many Chinese continued to enter Mexico clandestinely.

In the 1920s labor unions, political parties, and anti-Chinese activists in Baja California argued against further Chinese immigration and pushed the government to adopt discriminatory legislation. A new law required Chinese to carry identification as proof of their legal status in the country. In 1924 the Partido Radical Agrarista complained to the president that the Chinese worked all the lands in the Mexicali Valley. Ricardo Covarubias, a deputy from the northern district, took up the cause and demanded that the president modify the immigration law "to prevent the entry into the district of Chinese workers, who cause a serious problem." The lack of effective border control led Mexicans to take matters into their own hands. On one occasion, people simply refused to allow 200 Chinese to disembark from a ship landing on the coast.[68] Although the local government gave in to pressure to adopt anti-Chinese measures, Baja California never adopted the harsh laws of Sonora.

By the 1930s the central government increasingly acceded to pressure by anti-Chinese activists in northern Mexico and began to flex its muscles in favor of restriction. Historian Grace Delgado attributes that responsiveness to the Revolutionary National Party's attempt to consolidate its control over the country's distant provinces.[69] On 14 July 1931, in the midst of economic crisis, anti-Chinese hysteria, and expulsions of Chinese from Sonora, the federal government issued a decree barring all immigrant laborers. Only immigrants who had more than 10,000 pesos to invest in Mexico and cover their living expenses would be allowed into the country. There were exemptions for professionals, travel agents, landlords, students, and immigrants from countries with which Mexico had convened special treaties. One week after the decree barring foreign laborers was issued, the Mexican Congress passed legislation that required employers to hire at least 90 percent native Mexican workers, a law that echoed the 80 percent native labor requirement in Sonora.[70] In 1929 in Baja California, various farmer, worker, and business associations passed resolutions calling for 80 percent of workers to be native Mexicans, but these were never enforced by the local authorities. Although these laws and resolutions were ostensibly directed at all foreign laborers, enforcement targeted Chinese, Jews, and other migrants considered undesirable. The synchronicity of anti-Chinese state and federal legislation suggests that the two were coordinated or at least working toward a common purpose for the first time.[71]

A general wave of antiforeign xenophobia swept through the Americas in the 1930s. In Mexico, Jews, Arabs, Poles, Lebanese, Chinese, and even African Americans were targets of the restrictionist fervor. The Unión de Comerciantes Mexicanos de Fresnillo in Zacatecas distributed a pamphlet that proclaimed "Jew Means War, Hunger, and Prostitution; Chinese Means Syphilis, Trachoma, Degeneration, and Tuberculosis."[72] In the late 1920s, Mexican border agents even refused entry to Harry Willis, an African American boxer scheduled to fight in the country. Although there was no official ban on African Americans, border agents felt empowered to keep out "undesirable" races in light of the state-sanctioned racism of the day.[73] A similar phenomenon in the United States led to an estimated 100,000 Mexicans and Mexican Americans being "repatriated" from the United States between 1920 and 1923, and during the Great Depression another 400,000 were sent south of the border.[74] All told, between 1929 and 1939, 1.6 million Mexicans and Mexican Americans returned to Mexico.[75] The synchronicity of the anti-immigrant measures throughout Greater North America indicates the extent to which these policies were responding to a regional and global economic crisis, and were part of a transnational xenophobic movement directed against particular ethnic groups, including Asians, Arabs, Jews, southern and eastern Europeans, Mexicans, and blacks.

The Anti-Chinese Movement in Cuba

Although the anti-Chinese movement in Cuba never achieved the status or reach of the one in Mexico, similar discriminatory legislation was adopted in Cuba. Like in Mexico, the fighting among the tongs in Havana led to calls for a crackdown on crime and sanitation in the Chinese community. In September 1926 health inspectors raided Havana's Chinatown, issuing fines for overcrowding, and police stepped up their enforcement of drug laws. By the 1930s public anti-Chinese pronouncements began to appear, including one poster signed by an anonymous group calling itself "the shadows" that warned people not to trade or do business with Chinese: "There is a danger in trading with the Chinese! Do not conduct any transactions with any yellow person: Do not sell to the Chinese, do not rent to the Chinese. Do not install electric or telephone service. Nobody is exempt from the power of the shadows. Everyone who deals with the Chinese will equally be considered traitors to Cuba. The shadows are watching you. Do not forget. Everything for Cuba!"[76] The poster portrayed all Chinese as dangerous foreigners, even those who were Cuban citizens, and made it a patriotic duty to boycott them. Failure to comply, the poster menacingly suggested, would be punished as treason.

In the 1930s sentiments such as those expressed by "the shadows" began to appear in newspapers throughout the island, highlighting labor competition with Chinese. At the end of 1931, the magazine *Alma Hispanoamericana* from Cienfuegos published a warning to its readers, imploring them to wake up: "Our economic liberty is being threatened by death, 75 percent of the citizens of the Pearl of the Antilles are displaced from our businesses. The *yellow octopus*, with its new tentacles, threatens to take over everything, . . . signs with Chinese names and other languages, represent the abolition of our rich languages."[77] The idea of the Chinese as a "yellow octopus" taking over commerce and public spaces in Cuba was far from the notion of Chinese as the quintessential patriotic citizens. In 1933 *El Comercio*, a Havana newspaper, ran an article that criticized the Chinese for not assimilating into Cuban society. "The Chinese is the worst kind of foreigner who does not make a home in Cuba," it argued. *Vindicación*, the newspaper of the Union of Dependents of Small Food Retailers, linked Chinese to disease and asserted that they would not assimilate: "The yellow race is accommodating, almost parasitic, and does not need to create to live. . . . The yellow ones are not interested in our problems, the majority don't understand the spirit of progress."[78] Between 1930 and 1933 at least twenty Chinese were victims of targeted assassinations in Cuba, part of a broader xenophobic wave that included more than 5,000 bombs in places and monuments linked to Spain, the United States, and Jews in 1931.[79] The monument to Chinese who fought in Cuban independence wars was scheduled to be inaugurated on 10 October 1931, the twentieth anniversary of Sun Yat-sen's revolution in China, but it was postponed after Japan's invasion of northeastern China in September of that year.[80] With so much antiforeign and specifically anti-Chinese mobilization, the early 1930s was not a propitious moment for erecting a monument to *chinos mambises* (Chinese who fought in independence wars).

In 1933 the collapse of the Machado regime and the rise of the fiercely nationalistic Ramón Grau San Martín government led to even more anti-immigrant policies. At the center was the Nationalization of Work law, which mandated that 50 percent of all workers in a company be native Cubans. Follow-up legislation raised the proportion of native workers to 80 percent, echoing the earlier Mexican law.[81] Ostensibly this law affected all foreigners, but it was written in such a way that the native-born children of Spanish parentage who maintained their Spanish citizenship remained unaffected. A Venezuelan journalist who wrote about the impact of the 50 percent labor law explained: "This law mostly affected the Chinese, the West Indian blacks, and the Jewish Poles who had invaded small commerce in the last few years."[82] As in Mexico, a labor law that ostensibly affected all foreigners was implemented in such a way as to target the Chinese and other unwanted immigrants. Although the ideal of racial equality remained the dominant ideology in Cuba, this did not prevent politicians and ethnologists from trying to construct a unified "Cuban race" from which certain foreign elements would be excluded.[83]

Popular anti-Chinese campaigns also picked up in the 1920s in British Columbia and elsewhere in Canada. These campaigns appealed to the importance of keeping Canada a white nation and preventing economic competition by Asians. A 1922 report by Rev. N. Lascelles Ward began by asserting that "Orientals are human beings, not animals; that they have bodies, souls and spirits just as we have." He continued by pointing out all of the reasons why "Orientals" should be prevented from entering Canada. Chief among these reasons was biological incompatibility. As he put it, the important question to ask was, "Would you like your sister to marry a Chinaman or a Japanese?"[84] That same year, the Sons of England Lodge in Regina issued a resolution that highlighted the dangers of intermarriage and called on the government to close its doors to "further Asiatic immigration."[85] One pamphlet distributed in Vancouver in early 1923, titled "Community Shoppers

Guide," warned consumers to patronize "white merchants only." Arguing that people should not rely on government action, the pamphlet declared: "YOU can stop the Oriental invasion if you act NOW."[86] In 1927, four years after Canada banned Chinese labor immigration, anti-Asian organizations like the Maple Leaf Association were calling for an "absolute Oriental exclusion," prohibition on alien land ownership, racially segregated schools, and a special census for Asians.[87] That same year, Vancouver's branch of the Ku Klux Klan sent a resolution to the Canadian government asking not only that it "completely prohibit Asiatic immigration" but that all property of Asians be seized and that domiciled Asians be repatriated.[88] From Cuba to Canada, xenophobic nationalists called for boycotts of Asians and pushed for their total exclusion. It was only in Mexico, however, that such racist fantasies became a reality.

Organizing the Anti-Chinese Movement in Northern Mexico

Ideologies that promoted *mestizaje* did not promote all kinds of race mixing. In Mexico, the *mestizaje* ideal included the Indian and the Spaniard, while in Cuba the focus was on the blending of the African and Spanish elements. In both countries, the Chinese were either ignored as a historical legacy or explicitly rejected as unassimilable. The anti-Chinese violence during the Mexican Revolution can be linked to the rise of a revolutionary nationalism undergirded by a racial ideology that excluded Chinese. During the Porfirian era, Mexico's national identity began to be linked with a positive vision of *mestizaje*. The Indian could not be pushed aside onto reservations and disappeared through extermination campaigns as had happened in the United States and Argentina, so *indigenistas* sought to incorporate and whiten the indigenous element in the country through a process of racial mixing. As historian Gerardo Renique has shown, the mestizo ideal was heavily tilted toward the *blanco-crillo* (white-creole) racial prototype, especially in the north, where wars against Indian groups like the Apaches and Yaquis lasted into the late nineteenth and early twentieth centuries. Chinese and blacks were decidedly excluded from this mestizo ideal. In 1900 the newspaper *El Tráfico*, representing the vision of Sonora's commercial elite, argued against the sexual mixing of Chinese men and Mexican women, who together, they claimed, produced offspring "of a new racial type still more degenerated than [Mexico's] naturally abject indigenous castes." According to this eugenic calculus, the children of these unions would inherit the worst "vices and degeneration" of both races, and the "product of these filthy unions"

La Mestización

mestizo indolatino de
12 años.

Producto de la mezcla chino-
mexicana de 14 años.

"Twelve-year-old Indo-Latino mestizo. Fourteen-year-old product of Chinese-Mexican mixture." From José Angel Espinoza, *El ejemplo de Sonora* (Mexico City: n.p., 1932).

would ultimately destroy Mexican patriotism.[89] The anti-Chinese "crusade" organized by *El Trafíco* found little support among the populace or the state government in the Porfirian era. Although the Chinese merchants competed with lower-middle-class Mexican businesses, their low prices and easy credit helped consumers, and their commercial trade added to the state's coffers.[90] By the 1930s, however, with the economic crisis and repatriation of hundreds of thousands of Mexicans from the United States, anti-Chinese hysteria gained traction throughout the country. A cartoon titled "Mestización" from José Angel Espinoza's 1932 anti-Chinese book, portrays the stark contrast between a strong, healthy, and tall "Indo-Latino" hybrid boy of twelve and a scrawny and sickly looking Chinese Mexican boy of fourteen.

Mestizaje ideology tinged with anti-Chinese ideas provided the justification for a range of violent acts during the revolutionary era. Sporadic outbursts crystallized into a more coordinated and institutionalized movement as the revolutionary state emerged in Mexico. Historian Robert Chao Romero traces the consolidation of these dispersed anti-Chinese acts into a movement to a meeting of small businessmen in Magdalena, Sonora, on 5 February 1916, where they founded the Junta Commercial y de Hombres de Negocios (Council of Commerce and Businessmen). José Maria Arana, who became the "first ranking member" of the junta, would become the mastermind for a large network of anti-Asian societies over the next fifteen years. The junta promoted Mexican businessmen and pushed to eliminate Asian merchants in Mexico. It condemned the Chinese for fraud, evading taxes, and for posing a public health threat to society. Unlike some of the other xenophobic movements in Mexico, the junta welcomed all other foreign businessmen except Asians.[91] Although businessmen spearheaded this organization, it mobilized a multiclass coalition whose adherents all saw the Chinese as the source of their economic woes. A few months later, in June 1916, several Chinese in Agaponeta, a town in the northern state of Nayarit, complained to the foreign minister that the local government had ordered them to leave the country within forty-eight hours.[92] The *anti-chinistas* expulsion campaign had begun.

The anti-Chinese movement was centered in Sonora, but eventually anti-Asian clubs like the Junta Nacionalista (Nationalist Group), the Liga Nacional Pro-Raza (Pro-People National League), and El Club del Pueblo (Club of the People) spread throughout Mexico's northern states, and into Nayarit, Durango, Veracruz, and Chiapas in the south. By 1932 there were 215 anti-Chinese clubs in Mexico boasting a membership of almost 2 million people. These clubs spread their message through periodicals such as *Pro-Patria, La Palabra, El Malcriado, Nuevos Horizontes,* and *El Nacionalista,* whose descriptive tagline was "Organo del Antichinismo Nacional" ("Organ of National Anti-Chineseness"). These clubs organized protests and boycotts of Chinese stores. One editorial in *El Nacionalista* cast the boycott in decidedly racial and nationalist terms: "Onward children of the race, let us go triumphant. . . . Nothing else matters when what you fight for is the life or death of our nationality. . . . I WHO AM A MEXICAN BOY, SWEAR, BY THE BONES OF MY ANCESTORS THAT FROM TODAY ON I WILL NOT SPEND EVEN ONE CENT AT THE CHINESE STORES."[93] Anti-Chinese societies also demanded that the government use Article 33 of the Mexican constitution to expel Chinese who had been caught gambling or smoking opium.[94] Photographs from José Angel Espinoza's anti-Chinese book *El ejemplo de Sonora* glorified popular protests that called on the government to expel Chinese from the country for their involvement in politics.

In addition to leading the popular protests and media campaign, anti-Chinese clubs worked to pass state laws that would give legal sanction to

Arriba: Manifestantes antichinistas de Guasave, pidiendo el 33 para los infames mercaderes de Asia.—Abajo: Manifestación de vecinos de Guasave y Verdura que agitan el emblema de la República condenando a los exóticos explotadores de los mexicanos.

"Top: Anti-Chinese demonstrators of Guasave, asking for the 33 for the infamous merchants from Asia. Below: Demonstration of neighbors from Guasave and Verdura waving the emblem of the Republic to condemn the exotic exploiters of the Mexicans." From José Angel Espinoza, *El ejemplo de Sonora* (Mexico City: n.p., 1932).

their efforts. In March 1919 Sonora passed Laws 60 and 61 ordering municipalities to create "special neighborhoods" for Chinese homes and businesses to protect the hygiene of their communities. In a report to the Foreign Ministry, the governor of Sonora laid out his reasons for establishing Chinese ghettoes. To demonstrate how the state had been overwhelmed, he pointed to the rapid increase of Chinese in the state, from only 859 in 1900, to 4,486 in 1910, to between 10,000 and 15,000 by 1919. While it is true that Sonora had the highest proportion of Chinese in the country, the idea of being overrun by a group of 15,000 immigrants was paranoid. According to the census, which counted far fewer Chinese than the governor reported, Sonora had a total foreign-born population of less than 2 percent in 1921 and 1930. Although the Chinese were the largest foreign group, with 3,639 in 1921 and 3,571 in 1930, they still only comprised 1 percent of the state's population.[95] Even if the 15,000 figure the governor gave was accurate, it still only represented 5 percent of the total state population.

In spite of these miniscule numbers, the governor criticized the ability of the Chinese to live on very little as evidence of their avarice and unfair competition with Mexican businesses. Furthermore, he asserted that the Chinese adulterated their sausages with dog meat robbed from their customers, carried contagious diseases, and were drug addicts.

> In society, the Chinese is repulsive, inadmissible, not only because he is feared as a vehicle of contagious diseases but because his personal abandonment, his degenerate vices and depraved customs, always in conflict with every social sphere, make him unable to be admitted to even the most humble spheres of society. It is enough to simply pass in the vicinity of a house of Chinese to perceive the disagreeable smell and the disastrous anti-hygienic state in which they live. . . . In Sonora, the Chinese is perfectly identified as an opium, marijuana, and gambling addict.[96]

As if this litany of ills were not enough, the governor also fixated on the "stunted, sick" offspring of interracial sexual relations, who end up being abandoned, he asserted, by both the Chinese and the Mexican communities. He ended his lengthy screed against the Chinese by noting that because the Mexican constitution did not allow for discrimination based on race, as did the United States and other "advanced countries of the world," the state legislatures were obligated to do what they could to stop the spread of the Chinese.[97] The Chinese representative of business interests in Mexico complained to the Foreign Ministry, but the Sonoran authorities stood by their

"One of the most modern sausage factories." From José Angel Espinoza, *El ejemplo de Sonora* (Mexico City: n.p., 1932).

Una choricería de las más modernas.

decision, arguing that Chinese immigration had caused the state and the country grave damage.[98] Throughout the spring and summer of 1919, Chinese faced harassment in Sonora and Sinaloa, including the arrest of several young women accused of prostitution, the shuttering of restaurants, the imposition of high taxes on Chinese businesses, and the jailing of twenty shopowners for violating labor laws.[99]

Newspapers in northern Mexico fanned the flames of racism against the Chinese by linking them to disease and presenting them as a public health threat. *El Eco de Yaqui*, published in Cocorit, Sonora, applauded the state legislation's idea of setting up ghettos for Chinese to protect hygiene and public health. *El Eco* also pushed for municipal inspections of Chinese stores, where, it asserted, Chinese lived "crammed" together with their produce thus creating a particularly unhealthy environment. Chinese merchants, the paper argued, "although presenting disgusting syphilitic sores on their hands, quietly do business and handle with their filthy hands the food of a poor family." Other Chinese "carry hidden ulcers in other parts of their body, and for this reason they are the most dangerous; and they even say that various semilepers work selling vegetables."[100] Espinoza's book had a cartoon that showed smiling Chinese secretly adding cats to their sausages. Even when

Chinese appeared healthy, they carried "hidden ulcers" that would transmit disease to unsuspecting Mexicans who bought food from them. The message was simple: Chinese were vectors of disease.

Chineras, Racial Degeneration, and the Raza Cósmica

Anti-Chinese protests and racist broadsheets were prevalent throughout northern Mexico in this period (1919–20s). The general theme was that Chinese were diseased and that sexual mixing with them would lead to racial degeneration of the Mexican population. One such poster, published in Culiácan, Sinaloa, on 30 March 1919, had a blaring headline in large bold typeface: "Todo por la Raza" ("Everything for the Race/People"). The poster warned that Mexican women who mix with Chinese men led to the "degeneration of the race," and it recommended isolation of the Chinese as a way to prevent "contagion." For the Junta Nacionalista, the issue was one of patriotism: "The country demands the purity of castes and it falls to our legislators to make laws that prohibit the Chinese from marrying Mexicans, punishing severely the woman who disobeys the provisions that are ordered."[101] José Angel Espinoza's El ejemplo de Sonora included several drawings depicting the dangers that result from sexual mixing between Chinese men and Mexican women. In one image, a Mexican woman is left destitute and decrepit with her grotesque children when her Chinese husband leaves her. In another drawing, Mexican women are warned that they will be enslaved and treated like animals if they return to China with their Chinese husbands. The caption under the drawing reads: "If craziness or ignorance makes you a wife or mistress of a Chinese man and he wants to bring you to his country, before you decide to follow him, take a dose of venom or stab yourself in the heart."[102]

In spite of the racist propaganda against intermarriage, Robert Chao Romero finds that Chinese men married Mexican women at "relatively high rates" compared to their counterparts in the United States, where strict state antimiscegenation laws prevented marriages to whites. Although there is no global study of intermarriage rates in Mexico for Chinese, Romero discovered that in 1930 there was a 35 percent intermarriage rate in Chihuahua and 12 percent in Hermosillo.[103] In addition to officially recorded marriages, many Chinese men had free unions with Mexican women or had extramarital relations with them and fathered children. Interracial marriages, and especially the offspring of interracial unions, were upsetting to Mexican eugenicists, leading to demands for antimiscegenation laws in northern Mexico.

La noche de bodas.....

y cinco años despúes

"The wedding night . . . and five years later." This drawing depicts the dangers of sexual relations between Chinese men and Mexican women. From José Angel Espinoza, *El ejemplo de Sonora* (Mexico City: n.p., 1932).

The Sonoran legislature responded by passing Law 31 on 13 December 1923, which prohibited marriage of Mexican women to Chinese men, even if the men were naturalized Mexican citizens. Furthermore, the law punished free unions between Chinese men and Mexican women with stiff fines of between 100 and 500 pesos.[104] In 1930, Luis Chong Ruiz, a naturalized Mexican citizen of Chinese descent living with his Mexican wife in Navajoa, Sonora, was arrested on charges of violating the antimiscegenation law and fined ten pesos by local authorities. In spite of his protest to the federal government, local and state authorities prevailed, arguing that Chong Ruiz had violated the law.[105] Romero concludes, however, that this draconian antimiscegenation law "was not widely or consistently enforced by Sonoran state and local officials." In most cases, Chinese hired savvy lawyers to evade the law or simply bribed judges, but the courts upheld Law 31 in at least one case in 1930. Francisco Hing was a naturalized Mexican of Chinese descent whose marriage to a Mexican woman was deemed invalid by Sonoran officials. Hing appealed his case all the way to Mexico's Supreme Court, but the court ruled

MUJER MEXICANA:—Si la locura o la ignorancia te hace esposa o manceba de un chino y éste te quiere llevar a su patria, antes que resolverte a seguirlo apura una dósis de veneno o clávate un puñal en el corazón......

"Mexican Woman: If craziness or ignorance makes you a wife or mistress of a Chinese man and he wants to bring you to his country, before you decide to follow him, take a dose of venom or stab yourself in the heart." From José Angel Espinoza, *El ejemplo de Sonora* (Mexico City: n.p., 1932).

against him and affirmed the constitutionality of the law by an overwhelming majority. Although an anomaly, this case shows just how dominant anti-Chinese racism was, not just in Sonora but at all levels of society throughout Mexico.[106]

Anti-Chinese activists highlighted Mexican women's vulnerability to Chinese men and ignored Mexican men's potential sexual mixing with Chinese women. Sonora's antimiscegenation law did not, for example, prevent Mexican men from marrying or having free unions with Chinese women. The lack of restrictions for Chinese women may have resulted from the relatively small number of Chinese women in Mexico. Until 1910 there were fewer than 100 Chinese women living in Mexico, and even though that number grew by 1930 to 2,711, Chinese men still outnumbered women six to one.[107] Another reason the miscegenation law focused on Chinese men was because Mexican men feared the contamination of what they saw as the vessels of Mexican nationhood, namely, Mexican women.

Although the antimiscegenation law was erratically enforced, anti-

Chinese newspapers regularly published the names and photographs of Mexican women who maintained intimate relationships with Chinese men, seeking to shame them and push the state to enforce the law. Law 31 also justified violent raids on homes and assaults against Chinese. Some Sonoran women wrote public letters to newspapers in which they invoked their right to freely enter into relationships with anyone they chose, including Chinese men.[108] The fact that so many Mexican women and Chinese men continued to have romantic and sexual relationships and form families in spite of the law is a sign of their resistance to state intervention in their private lives.

The fear of Mexican women's relationships with Chinese men may have also resulted from Mexican men's anxieties about the changing role of women in society during the Mexican Revolution. Although by no means completely liberated, Mexican women were taking on increasingly public roles as *soldaderas* (women soldiers), workers outside the home, and activists in political campaigns. In his anti-Chinese tract "Contact between Chinese Men and Mexican Women Is Dangerous," Ramón García told a story of a Chinese man and a Mexican woman who worked in his cigar factory. García was horrified by the "familiarity" between "yellow-skinned" men and Mexican women workers. He was particularly upset about the "illicit friendship" of a Mexican woman with one of the "Mongols": "If we continue to tolerate the perilous daily contact between Mexican women and the hateful Asian microbe," he warned, "our race will take rapid, giant steps toward ruin and degeneration"; before too long, he predicted, "children with slanted eyes and sickly constructions [will] emerge from the factory."[109] García's morality tale warned that diseased Asians would lead to the racial, biological, and economic downfall of the nation. His picture of "sickly constructions" emerging from the factory linked economic production to biological reproduction. For Mexican nationalists, biological health and economic health were inextricably connected.

García's story also reflected Mexican men's anxieties about competition from wealthier Chinese men for the affections of Mexican women. The economic and sexual competition formed part of the same struggle to assert patriarchal control over the Mexican nation through domination of women and commerce. One article in the Sinaloa newspaper El Toro de Once condemned the Chinese extension of their "tentacles," like an "octopus," to take over Mexican commerce. The article focused its attack, however, on the way Chinese merchants took advantage of poor Mexican widows by making them work day and night sewing clothes for them. "We have watched with horror as the high society of Culiacán has organized sumptuous festivals in honor of

"Oh wretched woman! ... You thought you would enjoy a cheap life by giving yourself to a Chinese man, and instead you are a slave and the fruit of your mistake is a freak of nature." This drawing shows an enslaved Mexican wife and a rat-like mixed-race Chinese Mexican offspring. From José Angel Espinoza, *El ejemplo de Sonora* (Mexico City: n.p., 1932).

¡Ah infeliz!. . . . Crefste disfrutar de una vida barata al entregarte a un chino y eres una esclava y el fruto de tu error es un escupitajo de la naturaleza . . . .

the sons of Confucius, where the most popular young Culiacán women, the ones of proverbial beauty, have swayed voluptuously to the beat of a waltz or a dance, in the yellowing and emaciated arms of a disgusting and degenerate Mongol."[110] The sexualized image of a young beautiful Mexican woman in the hands of a weak Chinese man was a frequent trope used by anti-Chinese crusaders. The caricature published in Espinoza's book depicts the life of a Mexican women married to a Chinese man as one of slavery and abjection. The mixed-race child in the image is portrayed as a tiny, almost rat-like creature who tugs at the woman's dress. The caption reads: "Oh wretched woman! . . . .You thought you would enjoy a cheap life by giving yourself to a Chinese man, and instead you are a slave and the fruit of your mistake is a freak of nature."[111]

The desire to keep Mexican women from Chinese men stemmed from the relatively high rates of interracial sexual mixing and the public visibility of these relationships. *El Toro de Once* referred to women who had relationships with Chinese men as "chineras," complaining that they paraded around the streets in a "shameless ostentatious display of luxury in which they cover their damaged bodies with Chinese money." The danger was not only for these women who had "given themselves to the Chinese" but for other women who might be persuaded to follow their examples by such displays of wealth. The newspaper ended by calling for "radical measures" to protect the "health and the moral safety of the Mexican race."[112] In addition to corrupting Mexican women who lived in "shameless concubinage with the men of backward eyes," Chinese men kept Mexican women locked up as prostitutes for their fellow countrymen, *El Toro de Once* asserted.[113]

Mexican women were depicted as either unwitting victims of "wily" Chinese men or their all-too-willing sexual partners, but women also led an important branch of the anti-Chinese movement. In a 1917 speech, Professor María de Jesús Valdez told people in Magdalena, Sonora, that the "sacrosanct call of patriotism also burns in women's hearts." She ended her speech by leading the audience in the chant: "Down with the Chinese!" Historian Julia Maria Schiavone Camacho shows how in the 1920s anti-Chinese organizations set up women's subcommittees that leveraged women's moral power to pressure other women not to have relationships with Chinese men. In 1932 the Cooperativa Mexicana de Lavandería Antiasiática (Anti-Asian Mexican Laundry Cooperative) in Sonora pleaded with Mexicans to boycott Chinese laundries and to bring them their clothes to wash instead. The Mexican laundrywomen blamed competition with Chinese laundries for undermining their ability to work and thereby making their children suffer.[114] Mexican women were thus both the targets of the anti-Chinese movement and some of its fiercest proponents.

The fear of sexual mixing was only one way the Chinese were seen as a biological threat. The other main biological critique against the Chinese was that they were vectors for disease and illness. One typical flyer posted in the streets of Santiago Ixcuintla, Nayarit, in 1921 declared Chinese to be a threat to the economy, public health, and the nation:

PEOPLE:

Each Asian who arrives in Mexico comes to take away the bread and honor of your children. Combat them with reason.

THE CHINESE:

Are the vilest measure of our race and the greatest danger for our dear country.

THE CHINESE:

Are the most terrible threat to our health because of their natural infections: Bubonic Plague, Yellow Fever, Black Vomit, Syphilis, Trachoma, etc., etc.

THE CHINESE:

Stay strong against them before our race is further mixed, because later it will be difficult when we see the markets set up by their own chil-

Arriba: Simpático grupo de valerosas damas que recorren las calles de Estación Naranjo, patentizando su aversión efectiva contra el sucio explotador ama-
rillo.—Abajo: Multitud de manifestantes en Culiacán. Un orador
que combate la cobarde inactividad de las clases pu-
dientes de la capital sinaloense.

"Top: Nice group of valiant women who walked the streets of the Naranjo station, showing
their effective aversion against the yellow exploiter. Below: Multitude of demonstrators
in Culiácan. An orator who combats the cowardly inactivity of the wealthy classes in the
Sinaloa capital." From José Angel Espinoza, *El ejemplo de Sonora* (Mexico City: n.p., 1932).

Los terribles males del Oriente, de fácil contagio, que los chinos encubren con ropajes limpísimos cuando desempeñan trabajos de mozos de café, lavanderos o dependientes.

"The terrible easily contagious maladies of the Orient, which the Chinese cover
with very clean clothes when they work as waiters at a café, at a laundry, or as a clerk."
From José Angel Espinoza, *El ejemplo de Sonora* (Mexico City: n.p., 1932).

dren: thus we will avoid for our compatriots the worst shame of having
children with Chinese physiques.[115]

The emphasis on the dangers posed by sexual mixing between Chinese and
Mexicans, as well as the diseases that Chinese were thought to carry, cast Chinese as not simply an economic threat, but a menace to the biological survival of the nation. The very presence of Chinese bodies was seen as a danger
that could only be handled by isolating Chinese in ghettos and ultimately
removing them altogether from Mexico. This image, also from Espinoza's
book, depicted Chinese with gaping and puss-leaking wounds. The caption
suggested that Chinese service workers in restaurants, laundries, and stores
wore clean clothes to hide their contagious sores.[116] Espinoza also caricatured
the Chinese ambassador as a horrifying, diseased man with open sores who
brought "agony and suffering" to Christ-like "young America."[117]

Government officials in northern Mexico also worried about the dangers Chinese posed to the nation's biological health. In July 1924 Walter
Pesqueira, the municipal president of Nogales, Sonora, issued a circular
in which he outlined an argument for the establishment of special Chinese

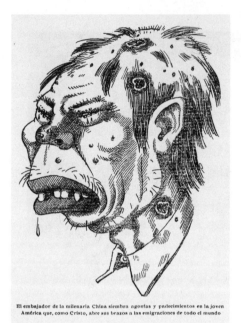

"The ambassador of the millennial Chinese sows agony and suffering in young America, which like Christ opens its arms to the migrations of the entire world." From José Angel Espinoza, *El ejemplo de Sonora* (Mexico City: n.p., 1932).

El embajador de la milenaria China siembra agonías y padecimientos en la joven América que, como Cristo, abre sus brazos a las emigraciones de todo el mundo

ghettoes and called for the stricter enforcement of the antimiscegenation laws. Pesqueira wanted medical and blood tests for all Chinese so that the sick ones could be isolated. He also pushed Congress to pass a law to prohibit Mexican women from marrying Chinese, prevent naturalization of Chinese, and deport those found living with Mexican women. The link between defending the nation and protecting Mexican women from Chinese men was made explicit in a passage in which Pesqueira described war widows forced to watch their daughters be corrupted by the Chinese: "The poor mother, after crying over being a widow, has to put up with the heartbreaking spectacle of the dishonoring and prostitution of her daughters!"[118] Pesqueira became a federal congressman for Sonora and served as the vice president of the anti-Chinese campaign based in Mexico City. In a speech to Congress, Pesqueira noted with horror that a 1925 census counted almost 9,000 Chinese men in Sonora and only 14 Chinese women. The gender imbalance suggested that Chinese men must be having sex with Mexican women, leading to "racial degeneration."[119]

José Vasconcelos, rector of Mexico's national university, minister of education, and promoter of *mestizaje* in the early 1920s, also argued in favor of restricting Chinese migration to Mexico for economic as well as biological reasons. Although his 1925 book *La raza cósmica* (*The Cosmic Race*) advocated racial mixing to create a supreme master race, the Chinese were not part of his utopian vision: "We recognize that it is not fair that people like the Chinese, who under the saintly guidance of Confucian morality multiply like mice, should come to degrade the human condition precisely at the moment when we begin to understand that intelligence serves to refrain and regulate the lower zoological instincts, which are contrary to a truly religious conception of life." Vasconcelos's fear of the supposed unrestrained "zoological instincts" of Chinese was strange given the lack of Chinese women and the relatively few Chinese-Mexican intermarriages. Nonetheless, in Vasconcelos's calculus of aesthetic eugenics, the Chinese would be rejected because their high birthrates undermined equality. As he put it, "If we reject the Chinese, it is because man, as he progresses, multiplies less, and feels the horror of numbers, for the same reason that he has begun to value equality." Vasconcelos condemned Anglo-Saxons for refusing to mix with blacks and Chinese and lauded the greater frequency of racial mixing in Latin America where, he declared, "a thousand bridges are available for the sincere and cordial fusion of all races." In typically contradictory fashion, Vasconcelos thus both rejected the Chinese as a biological threat and argued that all races must mix to forge what he called the "definitive race, the synthetical race, the integral race."[120]

Chinese Resistance

The Chinese in Mexico were not passive victims of these attacks. The Chinese legation in the country and Chinese migrants persistently demanded that the Mexican government protect them based on treaty stipulations, international law, and Mexican law. In 1926 a group of Chinese businessmen in the state of Veracruz wrote to President Plutarco Elías Calles complaining about the anti-Chinese activities of the Liga Nacional Pro-Raza and defending themselves as law-abiding and honorable merchants.[121] When they could not seek satisfaction by direct appeals to the Mexican government, they petitioned the Chinese legation to intercede on their behalf. The president of the Fraternal Union China Association, based in Mexico City, put pressure on the government to squash the anti-Chinese campaign in Nayarit, and forced it to remove one of the key anti-Chinese leaders from the town of Tuxpan. In spite of this success, the president of the association noted that harassment was beginning again, and he offered proof by sending a copy of the flyer from Santiago Ixcuintla discussed in the previous section.[122]

Diplomatic protests by the Chinese legation had some effect, at least on the position of the federal government. In September 1925 President Elías

Calles, whose brother would later become the governor in Sonora responsible for the expulsion of the Chinese, sent a memorandum to all governors blaming the anti-Chinese associations for creating "a serious danger for the tranquility of the interior of the country." The president worried that these conflicts could cause an international incident and ruin Mexico's good name in the international community.[123]

The situation became so alarming by 1919 that the Foreign Ministry in China got involved. In April 1919 the Chinese vice minister of foreign relations, Tcheng Loh, met with the Mexican ambassador in Peking to complain about the harassment of Chinese in Sonora and Sinaloa, which included killings, overtaxation, closing businesses, and forcing Chinese to leave the state.[124] In addition to these overt forms of discrimination, the Chinese government was also attentive to the negative portrayals of Chinese in the mass media. In the same month as the meeting in Peking, a representative in the Chinese legation in Mexico complained about a film being exhibited in the Victoria cinema in Mexico City. The Chinese diplomat described the film, *La flor del destino* (*The Flower of Doom*), as anti-Chinese propaganda, depicting "Chinese customs that are untrue" and disseminating images of Chinese as people dedicated to "vice, robbery and assassination."[125] The film, shot in New York City's Chinatown and directed by the well-known silent cinema director Rex Ingram, depicted a kidnapping in the world of Chinese criminal gangs.[126] The Mexican government investigated the matter and provided a detailed description of the film to the Chinese government, but it argued that the film had been shown throughout the United States without any protest and that there was no evidence to link the film to the recent spate of violence against Chinese in northern Mexico.[127] Notwithstanding the Mexican government's analysis of the film, the Chinese were right to worry about how Chinese were depicted in the mass media, through newspapers, cartoons, and films. Ultimately, these images helped demonize Chinese, popularizing negative stereotypes of them and creating a hostile environment that enabled anti-Chinese legislation as well as vigilante violence.

Sonora Governors Francisco S. Elías and Rodolfo Elías Calles, the 80 Percent Labor Law, and the Anti-Chinese Movement

Anti-Chinese propaganda in the mass media, the formation of anti-Chinese clubs, and the passage of discriminatory legislation all served to create the conditions for the final solution to the Chinese problem: the expulsion of Chinese from the country. Ever since 1916, there were local efforts to push

Chinese out of specific towns. At the end of 1919 the Fraternal Union China Association in Cananea wrote to the Chinese legation in Mexico asking for protection given the municipal authorities' recent decision to close down all Chinese businesses by the end of the year and kick the Chinese out of town.[128] Sonora's governor, Adolfo de la Huerta, responded that the municipal government had not ordered the Chinese to leave but only told them that their licenses would be revoked and their stores closed if they did not comply with the 80 percent labor law. The governor did, however, suggest that the Chinese leave Cananea temporarily to avoid any potential conflict.[129]

By 1930 the anti-Chinese Unión Nacionalista was pressuring the government to stop naturalizing Chinese.[130] The group had powerful allies in this campaign, including the governor of Sonora, Francisco S. Elías (1929–31), a close relative of Plutarco Elías Calles, who argued that the Chinese were only trying to become Mexican citizens to protect themselves from the anti-Chinese campaigns. Elías railed against the "disastrous consequences, in both the ethnoracial order as well as in the economic one," and begged the government not to give the Chinese more "arms" and tools to compete against Mexicans.[131] The 1930 Sonora census indicated that only 233 Chinese had become naturalized Mexican citizens, demonstrating that Elías's claim was pure hyperbole.[132] Nonetheless, the governor's propaganda was appreciated by activists like José Angel Espinoza, who credited Elías with enforcing anti-Chinese laws that had been passed. Until Elías became governor in 1929, Espinoza declared, "there was not a judge who would dare to condemn a slanty-eyed delinquent; there was not an inspector who had the pants to stop the astute trafficker in stupefying drugs, or inspector of public health capable of ordering the destruction of the enormous poppy plantations."[133]

As governor, Elías issued a series of circulars about public health, marriage, and labor that strengthened the existing anti-Chinese laws and established strict mechanisms for their enforcement. Despite the existence of anti-miscegenation laws since the early 1920s, many Chinese men and Mexican women lived together and had children. Circulars 277 and 278 were designed to punish these interracial relationships by enforcing fines even when the couples were not formally married and fining Mexican mothers who registered births of children to Chinese fathers.[134] The most far-reaching measure was passed on 13 May 1931, when Sonora's legislature reformed Article 106 of the state labor law to require all commercial businesses to employ at least 80 percent Mexican workers in their establishments. Naturalized Mexican citizens would be treated as foreigners by this law, and all foreign managers and owners would be considered employees. The state government also ordered all foreigners to register themselves at a cost of ten pesos per person.[135] By June municipalities throughout Sonora and Sinaloa began to inspect Chinese businesses to monitor their compliance with the new labor law. When Chinese merchants responded to the law by shutting their stores, thus leading to a scarcity of basic goods, Governor Elías ordered them to reopen their stores to sell off inventory or vacate the premises so Mexicans could take their places.[136] In Ciudad Obregón, even when Chinese business-men tried to comply with the law by hiring Mexican laborers, the Comité Nacionalista Antichino (Nationalist Anti-Chinese Committee) insisted that the owners be counted as employees and that at least four Mexicans be hired in every Chinese establishment. On 24 July all Chinese businessmen were called to the town hall and forced to sign an agreement with the Comité Na-cionalista. The agreement allowed Chinese businesses to open, but only to liquidate their stock, deposit the money in the Sonoran bank, and vacate the premises. Only Mexicans who were members of the Comité Nacionalista were supposed to be hired, and no Chinese other than the owners could live or eat at the stores.[137]

The story of harassment of the Chinese Mexican owner of a small cloth-ing and dry goods store, Alejandro Llanes, demonstrates how the 80 percent law was used to bankrupt and expel Chinese. We have Llanes's story because he wrote to the Chinese ambassador in Mexico City to describe his ordeal and to beg for help. His narrative is especially interesting because it is a well-documented first-person account that has not been mediated by diplomats. Llanes lived in the small town of Los Angeles in the municipality of Ures in central Sonora. According to Llanes's story, a group of men from the Comité Nacionalista arrived at his store on 12 July 1931, at around 6:00 P.M., de-manding that he hire four Mexicans to work in his store as required by the 80 percent labor law. The men handed him a summons signed by the local police commissioner that gave him ten days to comply with their orders. Meanwhile the Comité placed two guards outside the door of his store, pre-vented customers from entering, and directed them to another store owned by the police commissioner. In addition to suffering the humiliation and harassment of having guards outside his store, he was forced to pay each of them for their work. Llanes even provided the receipts signed by the presi-dent and secretary of the Comité and the local police commissioner. The receipts totaling sixty pesos said that Llanes gave the money "voluntarily." After ten days, Llanes received another summons, this one signed by the Comité's president, giving him eight hours to comply with the law. Llanes tried to explain to the men that given the small size of his business it would

......y el celo de "Las Guardias Verdes" era la prueba más evidente de que el pueblo respaldaba los actos del gobierno.

"...And the vigilance of the 'green guards' was the best evidence that the people supported the government's actions." The sign held by the guards reads, "80% law or no more sales." From José Angel Espinoza, *El ejemplo de Sonora* (Mexico City: n.p., 1932).

be impossible for him to hire four employees, but they would not listen. The next day the store was forcibly closed. Llanes wrote plaintively to the Chinese ambassador: "I, for my part, have attempted by all possible means to reach an agreement with the authorities but materially it has been impossible to arrange anything."[138]

In a well-coordinated effort, anti-Chinese clubs throughout Sonora and Sinaloa impeded customers from going into Chinese stores and prevented the Chinese owners from going onto the streets.[139] By the end of July it was clear that the anti-Chinese activists would not stop until they had purged Sonora and Sinaloa of every last Chinese person. Chinese consul Yau Hsiang Peng in Nogales, Sonora, tried repeatedly to set up meetings with the new state governor, Rodolfo Elías Calles (son of former Sonora governor and Mexican president Plutarco Elías Calles and nephew of former governor Francisco S. Elías), but the latter ignored all such requests. The Chinese consul complained that even after the Chinese stores were closed, their owners were still being fined for not employing Mexicans and their land was being taken before they could harvest the crops.[140]

The Chinese minister in Mexico City, Samuel Sung Young, wrote urgently to the Mexican government in July, detailing the anti-Chinese laws, protests, violence, and boycotts. Young complained that there was a coordinated campaign by anti-Chinese societies and the state government in Sonora "to expel Chinese from the state using force and unjust means," and he warned that the movement was spreading to Sinaloa.[141] Finally, on 12 August, the Chinese minister met with President Porfirio Díaz in Chapultepec Castle and laid out the litany of complaints. Díaz told Young that the Chinese should not obey the orders of the Comité Nacionalista and should only listen to legitimate local and state authorities.[142] While such a distinction may have made sense in Mexico City, in Sonora and Sinaloa, state and municipal authorities and the Comité worked hand in glove to harass Chinese. When the federal government asked the governor of Sonora, Rodolfo Elías Calles, for an explanation, he insisted that he was protecting the rights of the Chinese. He also blamed the Chinese, however, for not obeying the 80 percent labor law and evading taxes. It was this, the governor asserted, that had caused "hatred toward the Chinese" and the recent spontaneous explosions of protest against them.[143]

Eugene Chen, minister of foreign affairs of the Chinese national government in Canton, issued a strongly worded official protest. Chen denounced the expulsions as an act of "barbarism" and compared it to pogroms against the Jews and the "dark deeds of Abdul Hamid" against the oppressed races of the Ottoman Empire. In what amounted to a veiled threat, Chen argued that Mexico's "coldblooded expulsion of thousands of Chinese" would give the United States added cause to annex their country.[144] The Mexican consul in Yokohama, Manuel Tellez, told the press that "he was exerting his utmost efforts" to try to stop the expulsions.[145] Whether or not Tellez was sincere, there was little the federal government or Mexico's diplomatic corps could do to rein in the fiercely anti-Chinese northern states.

El Machete *and the Communist Call for Class Solidarity*

The views of radical liberals, anarchists, and communists in Mexico regarding Chinese evolved over time from one of antipathy in the early twentieth century to solidarity by the 1920s and 1930s.[146] However, the path to solidarity was not simple. As late as 1922 the president of the Mexican Communist Party petitioned the governor of Sonora to expel the Chinese.[147] Nonetheless, communists and anarchists stand out in Mexico as among the few groups to eventually embrace Chinese laborers as fellow workers in an international struggle against capitalism. The evolving position of the radical Left in Mexico is surprising, especially given the almost universal antipathy among socialists toward Asian immigration in the United States. In 1907 the national executive committee of the Socialist Party in the United States unanimously opposed Asian immigration. The general sentiment was expressed succinctly by the writer Jack London, who said, "I am first of all a white man and only then a Socialist."[148] The Industrial Workers of the World (IWW) has generally been seen as welcoming Asian workers into its ranks, but locals often adopted anti-Asian positions or simply refused to recruit Asian workers.[149]

The first program of the radical Mexican Liberal Party (PLM), issued in July 1906, articulated the popular xenophobic attitude toward Chinese in Mexico and called for the prohibition of Chinese immigration. The PLM argued that Chinese were unfair competition for Mexican workers and that "Chinese immigration does not benefit Mexico in the least bit."[150] This anti-Chinese sentiment came on the heels of the violent strike, organized by the PLM, at Cananea in June that left twenty-three people dead and several Chinese stores ransacked by miners.[151] Striking miners blamed Chinese merchants for high prices that were actually due to the peso's devaluation in 1905.[152] Right before the strike and the PLM manifesto, the Chinese issue was debated in the pages of the PLM newspaper *Regeneración*. One PLM supporter argued against the prohibition of Chinese immigration, stating that it was "antihumanitarian and opposed to the liberal spirit." The anonymous author went on to state, "It is manifest that the spirit of freedom should be cosmopolitan and that, furthermore, it should not fear Asian immigration."[153] By 1911 the PLM had veered radically to the left, articulating anarchist principles and supporting class solidarity over racial division. In that year, *Regeneración* called on its readers to realize that all ethnicities and nationalities faced the same enemy, namely, poverty and hunger: "Wake up, people, wake up; stop admiring the riches of the executioners, the link in the strong chain that enslaves us equally, Mexicans and Americans, French and Spanish, Japanese or Chinese, all of humanity. Therefore, our chain is your chain; the Problem of Hunger is universal."[154] Although labor unions in Mexico and the United States continued to blame the Chinese for low wages and economic competition, the most radical elements in both countries tried to unite workers across racial lines. The early 1920s was one of the most anti-Chinese periods in Mexico, one during which tong wars broke out and mass public protests in northern Mexico called for Chinese to be expelled. In this context, Ricardo Flores Magón, a founder of the PLM, wrote a letter from his jail cell in Fort Leavenworth, Kansas, expressing his cosmopolitan vision of a united working class, "the common aspiration for those who carry the chains in whatever latitude, under whatever sky, in whatever corner or area of this Earth: the hope of the Asian coolie, and the Egyptian fellah, the Russian serf and the Mexican peon."[155]

The PLM was not the only leftist party to defend the Chinese in the wake of popular racism in revolutionary Mexico. The most vigorous defense of Chinese workers came from the Communist Party newspaper *El Machete* in the early 1930s. At the height of the anti-Chinese movement in northern Mexico, *El Machete* ran a series of articles condemning the movement's xenophobia as distracting Mexican workers from their true class interests. The newspaper chided a group of workers in Tijuana who petitioned General Plutarco Elías Calles to expel low-wage Chinese workers because it lowered their own wages. It was "infantile," they explained, to petition Calles, who was a "bourgeois revolutionary" who owned large-scale enterprises in Baja California that earned large profits by exploiting Chinese and other workers. The government and other capitalists, they argued, just wanted to distract Mexican workers from their own exploitation by making them think that the Chinese "degenerate the race," "pervert our customs," and "take work from Mexican laborers." They compared the situation of Chinese workers in Mexico to that of Mexican workers in the United States and called for unity among all workers: "What needs to be done is to organize the Chinese comrades, who precisely because of their condition of slavery in which they work and live must be good and self-abnegating fighters. We must incorporate them into our revolutionary organizations and lead them to struggle against all exploiters—Chinese, Mexicans, and Yankees—who are also our exploiters."[156]

El Machete also decried the nationalist campaigns against Jews, Syrian-Lebanese, and other foreigners. The communists believed that large business owners, the government, and even wealthy Jews were behind the attacks because they focused on small businesses. In Russia, *El Machete* argued, the czar, facing potential revolution, used the police to provoke massacres of Jews to "redirect the anger of the masses."[157] The Mexican government, the communists believed, was using the same tactics. *El Machete*'s position was very clear: "We are resolutely against this infamous campaign." The paper's internationalist communist principles trumped its nationalism and led it to side with Chinese workers even when portions of the Mexican working class blamed the Chinese for their economic woes. In a context of heightened revolutionary nationalism and xenophobia, *El Machete*'s principled anti-racist position in favor of the Chinese was striking.

> The revolutionary movement of workers is fundamentally international. For us, there should be no nationals and foreigners, only exploiters and the exploited. The struggle of Mexicans against foreigners should be substituted by the struggle of all workers against all capitalists, without distinction of nationalities or races. The situation and the fortune of the Chinese bosses, who also exploit their fellow countrymen does not interest us: they are as much bandits as the Mexican, Spanish and Yankee capitalists, etc., but we have an obligation to defend the Chinese workers to remove them from the influence of their rich countrymen, to incorporate them into the revolutionary movement of the country and lead them to the struggle together with all the exploited against the exploiters.[158]

El Machete's attempt to unite all workers in Mexico along class lines failed. In 1930s Mexico, revolutionary and often xenophobic nationalism had much more popular appeal than internationalist communist ideals.

Exodus

By the end of August news about Chinese expulsions from Mexico had circled the globe. An article in the *Japan Advertiser* with the headline "Anti-Chinese Move in Mexican States Growing" predicted that no Chinese would be left in Sonora by the end of the month. The newspaper reported on a demonstration in Tampico, Tamaulipas, in which the crowd chanted, "Death to the Chinese!" According to the *Japan Advertiser*, the Liga Nacional was also anti-Semitic and had proposed suspending the licenses for stores operated by Asians and Jews in the capital, as well as prohibiting marriages of Mexican women with men from these groups.[159] Newspapers in Shanghai covered the anti-Chinese movement in Mexico, including stories of riots and dramatic photographs of demonstrations and blockades of Chinese stores. By the end of September, Chinese who had been expelled from Mexico were beginning to arrive back in China. Shanghai newspapers ran sympathetic stories about them while city officials provided them with food, clothing, and other basic necessities.[160]

As the stories of harassment of Chinese in Mexico began to filter back to China, Chinese businessmen responded and the Chinese government launched an official investigation. The Mexican honorary consul in Shanghai, Mauricio Fresco, attempted to discredit the stories of anti-Chinese pogroms by claiming that the Mexican government had always protected Chinese, insisting there was no boycott of Chinese businesses in Mexico, and arguing that Chinese who left the country did so only because they did not want to follow the laws of the country.[161] The Chinese government investigations, published by Reuters news agency, described the forcible expulsion of 20,000 Chinese and the wholesale theft of Chinese property, directly contradicting the Mexican consul's claims.[162] In 1933 the Overseas Chinese Federation sent a telegram to the Chinese government urging it to issue a strong protest against the deportations. Prominent merchants in Shanghai's French Concession and the Canton-Chaochow Fellow Provincials Association contributed money to help support their returning countrymen.[163] Merchants were key actors in recruiting workers and promoting migration to the Americas. They were also often leaders of the movement to defend Chinese migrants from xenophobic attacks.

The anti-Chinese campaign was linked to a broader xenophobic movement in Mexico that targeted Jews as well as eastern Europeans and Arabs.[164] One pamphlet calling for a boycott in Mexico demanded that citizens "not spend one penny on the Chinese, Russians, Poles, Czechoslovacs, Lithuanians, Greeks, Jews, Sirio-Lebanese, etc."[165] Another poster distributed in Mexico City called for the "boycott, sabotage, and expulsion from the country of all foreigners in general, considered as pernicious and undesirable." The poster warned that the Chinese being expelled from Sonora and Sinaloa were moving to Mexico City; it proposed tripling rents for Chinese and enlisted Mexican women in particular to boycott Chinese men: "WHATEVER IT COSTS, MEXICAN WOMAN! Do not fall asleep, help your racial brothers boycott the undesirable foreigners, who steal the bread from our children."[166] The foreign press also noted the link between anti-Chinese and anti-Semitic movements in Mexico, with one article asserting that there was a simultaneous effort to expel Mexico's 20,000 Jews.[167]

U.S. xenophobia also had a direct impact on Chinese in Mexico as hundreds of thousands of Mexicans in the United States were "repatriated." In March 1933 the *St. Louis Daily Globe Democrat* argued that the "repercussion of the repatriation of so many Mexicans in the United States is seen in the way in which citizens of the Mexican state of Sinaloa are driving out the Chinese." The newspaper estimated that 150,000 Mexicans were forced out of the United States in 1932 and contended that the Mexicans expelled Chinese to make room for them. The *Globe Democrat* contrasted the two expulsions, however: "We naturally condemn this heartless treatment and compare it with our sympathetic and helpful repatriation of our excess Mexicans." Nonetheless, the newspaper asked its readers to "not forget that at one time Chinese were almost as badly treated in this country."[168] Beyond the heartlessness of the anti-Chinese movement, the expulsions caused economic dislocation in northern Mexico, where the Chinese had played a vital role. In 1933 the Mexican Chamber of Commerce in Barcelona wrote to the Mexican Foreign Ministry asking from which states the Chinese had been expelled because they would have to suspend shipments of products consumed specifically by the Chinese. Expelling Chinese from Sonora may have helped Mexican workers and local merchants, but it did not necessarily help Mexican merchants who supplied Chinese with provisions.[169]

In September 1931 the Comité Nacionalista Antichino in Sonora called for a major state convention to be held in Hermosillo. The goal of this convention was to give the governor executive authority to deport, without judicial review, any foreigner he deemed unwanted. As Martín Mier, a delegate for the Comité de la Costa Occidental (Committee of the Western Coast), said, "With this rapid fire cannon, not one pernicious foreigner would remain in Sonora." The goal was to convene a national convention together with the Unión Nacionalista Mexicana in Mexico City to push forward a national anti-Chinese campaign. The proposals included stopping Chinese immigration for ten years, revoking naturalization for Chinese who had become Mexican citizens, general deportation for all Chinese for violating Mexican laws, and breaking off diplomatic relations with China.[170]

José Angel Espinoza, president of the Comité Directivo Nacionalista de la Costa Occidental (Nationalist Steering Committee of the Western Coast), responded publicly in the pages of *El Nacional* to the efforts of Minister Sung Young to protect the Chinese in Mexico. He claimed that the Chinese were not being expelled from Sonora at all but that they had transferred their businesses on paper to other people so that they could leave the state and abandon their debts. Espinoza also found it surprising that the Chinese would ask their government for protection when they were treated so badly in China and had benefited so much in Mexico: "If the Mexican hospitality does not inspire gratitude on the part of those who have benefited from it, the benefited ones do not have the right to involve us in international difficulties or to denigrate us in front of the civilized world, which, confronting an anguishing crisis, only tries to look for a little relief for the many people without work."[171] Espinoza cast the Chinese as ungrateful and greedy.

In late August 1931 Sonora governor Francisco S. Elías wrote to the congressman Walterio Pesqueira to explain the success of his state's anti-Chinese laws in the previous three months. Elías noted with glee that the Chinese had closed their businesses and that Mexicans were taking over; Chinese farmers were also leaving. "I assure you," he wrote, "that by next September first, there will not be one Chinese business left in the state."[172] As the Chinese were forced out of Sonora, many of them moved to the neighboring states of Sinaloa and Chihuahua. A small number of wealthy Chinese returned to China through San Francisco. The few Chinese who remained in Sonora, having been deprived of their ability to work, began to beg for money and food. Rodolfo Elías Calles, who took over as governor of Sonora in the fall of 1931, declared victory over the "Chinese problem," but he also remarked on a new issue: "The Chinese problem has been completely finished in Sonora; what bothers us now over there is a new problem: that of vagrant Chinese."[173] Of course, the Sonoran government had created the new problem it was complaining about by preventing Chinese from earning a living in their state.

The international press reported the expulsions, generally siding with the Chinese and presenting the Chinese legation's version of events. One example of this coverage was the *United Press* story on 2 September 1931, which described "persecution in [Sonora and Sinaloa] in which 2,000 Chinese have been stripped of all of their legal rights to dedicate themselves to commercial enterprises, having been thrown out of their houses and in which three Chinese were assassinated in cold blood."[174] José Angel Espinoza argued that if the United States could deport Chinese immigrants, Mexico should have the same right. The expulsion of the Chinese from Sonora was part of a larger nationalist campaign that promoted the purchase of only Mexican-made products and pushed for immigration restrictions, antimiscegenation laws, anti–foreign labor laws, and strict enforcement of public health measures. "The situation is of life or death," Espinoza proclaimed. "If we continue indifferently to the depressing action of the foreign races, soon we will have lost our nationality and for this catastrophe we will have only ourselves to blame."[175]

Given the anti-Chinese movement in Mexico, it is surprising that Chinese would have wanted to go there, but even at the end of the 1920s Chinese continued to arrive at the U.S.-Mexico border as transit passengers. It is likely that many of these Chinese intended to return to the United States clandestinely. In 1929 an open letter to the authorities published in the Nogales, Arizona, newspaper *El Imparcial* complained about Chinese transit passengers who arrived at the border and simply walked across the bridge into Mexico. "These Chinese do not speak Spanish nor have they ever been to Mexico. They are 'new' Chinese, or to say it in popular slang, they are 'rough' Chinese to whom the federal government had not conceded permission to enter Mexico according to the current laws."[176] An immigration officer in Mexico told *El Imparcial* to stop reporting on illegal Chinese crossings into Mexico and threatened to stop distribution of the newspaper in Mexico if it did not comply. It is not clear if the officer wanted to stop the publicity to prevent more Chinese from taking advantage of the route or if he was in cahoots with the illegal trafficking. In either case, the newspaper stuck by its story, arguing that it was doing its patriotic duty in raising the issue.[177] In 1930, perhaps in response to this criticism, the Mexican Foreign Ministry hired someone to board ships in San Francisco to check the papers of Chinese sailing for Mexico. If they had fraudulent papers, or lacked the correct visas, they were to be deported immediately to China.[178]

The expulsions of Chinese from Sonora led to tragicomic scenes at the border echoing events on the U.S.-Canadian border in the late 1880s. This time Mexican and U.S. officials literally shoved the Chinese back and forth across the border, each trying to keep them out of their countries. On 15 March 1932, three Chinese men were marched in the middle of the night to the border in Nogales and ordered to crawl through a hole in the fence. Mexican officers fired shots to scare the Chinese into crossing the border, but a U.S. Border Patrol officer "jumped from behind the bushes and shoved the Chinese back through the hole." That night, Border Patrol officers apprehended or turned back more than twenty Chinese, including the three who had been shoved through the hole.[179] In March 1932, 217 Chinese from various parts of Sonora and Sinaloa waited in jail to be brought by train to San Francisco and deported to China. For the next year, reports streamed in from all along the California and Arizona border of hundreds of Chinese caught illegally entering the United States.[180] The bodies of Chinese being pushed back and forth across the border suggests the liminal position of Chinese as aliens in the Americas. The issue was not whether to deport the Chinese but who would be responsible for paying the cost of deporting them back to China.

In April 1932 four Chinese in a Douglas, Arizona, city jail became a test case as the district court decided whether the Chinese could be forced back across the border to make Mexico pay for their deportation to China.[181] In March 1933 the Mexican president agreed to pay deportation expenses to the United States for 297 Chinese who were picked up in Nogales after being deported from Sonora. The Mexican government, however, worried that this would create a precedent and make it responsible for paying the expenses for all Chinese leaving Mexico who were deported to China. It also feared the consequences of the British government's demand for indemnification for South Asian Indians expelled from Mexico.[182] In June 1933, in the midst of this deportation debate, a Chinese businessman on his way to China by way of Nogales and San Francisco was forced off the train by Mexican soldiers. The governor of Sonora explained that he had to prevent Chinese without the proper papers from traveling to the United States. Ostensibly the businessman had the right to transit through the United States en route to China, and as a merchant he would have been exempt from U.S. exclusion laws.[183] The borderlands that had served as a middle ground where the Chinese could find a home in the late nineteenth and early twentieth centuries had by the 1930s been reduced to a thin fence line demarcating two nations, neither of which wanted the Chinese. One day Mexicans were forcing Chinese through the border fence to the United States and the next Mexican soldiers were preventing Chinese from trying to get back to China by way of the United States. It was a confusing time for Chinese living in the borderlands.

Conclusion

The Sonora and Sinaloa expulsions in 1931–33 pushed almost all Chinese out of these states, either across the border to the United States, to other Mexican states, or back to China. The anti-Chinese crusade in northern Mexico continued throughout the 1930s. On 23 May 1933, three Chinese men suspected of having killed a young Mexican girl were lynched in Aldama, a small town in Sonora. The next day, the anti-Chinese society in Chihuahua together with the local police prevented Chinese from leaving their homes or opening their businesses.[184] Two years later, the man accused of lynching the Chinese was found innocent and released.[185] Anti-Chinese violence continued sporadically throughout the 1930s, and the perpetrators of such violence generally acted with impunity. The anti-Chinese movement that had been centered in Sonora began to spread in the 1930s after the mass expulsions. In 1933 the Partido Nacionalista Pro-Raza (Pro-People Nationalist Party) was founded in Baja California. In the following years it pushed for the creation of Chinese ghettoes, harassed Chinese businesses, tried to prevent mixed-race marriages, held demonstrations, and burned Chinese ranches. In 1934 the National Chamber of Commerce and the National Party in Ensenada called Chinese merchants to a meeting and gave them ninety days to leave the city. Lack of support from the local government, however, impeded the success of Chinese expulsions from Baja California. Nonetheless, in the 1940 census, only 618 Chinese were recorded as living in the state, a fifth of the number listed in the 1930 census.[186] Meanwhile, by 1940 Chihuahua's Chinese community was reduced to 520, Sinaloa's to just 283, Coahuila's to 256, and Sonora's to 92. By the mid-1930s, only 1,000 Chinese were left in northern Mexico, more than 20,000 having been chased out during this era of expulsions.[187]

In spite of this constant terrorism, Chinese continued to live and work throughout Mexico in the 1930s. In 1936 the Mexican government passed a new General Law of Population establishing quotas for immigration based on "racial and cultural assimilability." The Chinese legation argued that Chinese should be treated as citizens of a most-favored nation because they were hard workers and because ethnologists believed there was no incompatibility between Chinese and Mexicans.[188] The fact that the Chinese government was forced to make its case based on questionable ethnographic theories of racial compatibility shows the extent to which the terms of debate had been set by the eugenics movement of the day. In the late 1930s there was a campaign in the southern state of Chiapas against Chinese, Turks, and Jews, all seen as economic competitors who had unfairly monopolized commerce.[189] The Chinese expulsions in Sonora were only the most extreme expression of a generalized revolutionary nationalist xenophobia that permeated Mexico in the 1930s.

Although this chapter has focused on Mexico, Cuba and Canada passed similar anti-Chinese legislation in the 1920s and 1930s. The United States developed its anti-Chinese legislation earlier than other countries, and by the 1920s it began to extend these policies to other immigrant groups. By the 1930s, although U.S. immigration authorities devoted many resources to keeping the Chinese out, they began to increasingly focus their energies on Mexicans, southern and eastern Europeans, and Jews. At the very time when Chinese were being expelled from Mexico, Mexicans were being expelled from the United States. The passage of anti-immigrant legislation and development of more robust deportation mechanisms signaled the strengthening of nation-states throughout Greater North America. However, in spite of tightening immigration restrictions and draconian legislation to isolate, intimidate, and harass aliens, Chinese managed to survive by relying on transnational organizations and networks that linked their communities throughout the Americas. The next chapter turns to these diasporic networks that allowed Chinese to survive as their movements were increasingly regulated and their space for maneuver narrowed.

CHAPTER 7

Chinese Diasporic Networks

I am broke now and have no way to get the money. I hope that my nephew
will send me some money to save me. I have suffered the trouble of cold.
If you won't send me the money for board, I will some day be starved.
—Louie Fat Quon, Veracruz, Mexico, to Tang Horn, Montreal, 19 August 1914

To the immigration bureaucrats, politicians, and anti-Chinese activists, Chinese migrants were illegal aliens. The alien label, however, does nothing to describe the communities and lived experience of Chinese who migrated through the Americas. They may have been strangers, sojourners, and aliens to outsiders, but they were enmeshed in transnational diasporic communities with deep bonds of solidarity. These networks remained largely invisible to state authorities because the networks' survival depended on their invisibility. Smugglers did not produce and preserve large archives to document their activities. Their goal was to remain undetected. Nonetheless, traces of these networks can be found in the archives of state agencies that tracked migration and arrested illegal migrants. So far, in this book, I have described these diasporic communities in terms of the interdiction efforts of immigration officials and anti-Chinese activists. This chapter will focus on Chinese merchants, political leaders, labor recruiters, brokers, and smugglers who forged the political and social webs that allowed Chinese to find employment, communicate across vast distances, settle in new towns, and sneak clandestinely across borders.

Transpacific migratory and trading networks developed in tandem, extending from China to the Americas and splaying out in a thick web through the hemisphere. Hong Kong merchants in particular played a central role in moving goods and people from China to the Americas and elsewhere in the world.[1] In addition to merchant connections, family or surname associations based loosely on kinship and lineage also helped organize the movement of people to and fro across the oceans. Unlike in China, where clan and lineage associations requiring blood connections were dominant, in the Americas, surname associations created kinship ties among distant relatives.

Typically an uncle or a cousin from a family association would meet new arrivals and help them find lodging, employment, and get settled. There were also several district associations or *huigan* depending on the region or the dialect that was spoken. In the United States, representatives from various *huigan* formed the Chinese Six Companies (Chinese Consolidated Benevolent Association). The Six Companies resolved disputes in the community, fought anti-Chinese legislation, insured that debts were paid, helped return the bones of the dead to China, and represented the Chinese community in broader political campaigns for civil rights. Similar umbrella organizations existed in other countries. The secret Triad societies, known as "tongs" to outsiders, were associated with political rebellion in China and were linked to gambling, opium, prostitution, and human smuggling in the Americas. Tongs were linked to particular political organizations. At the beginning of the twentieth century, Chinese in the Americas formed hundreds of chapters of the Baohuanghui (literally, the "Protect the Emperor Society"), better known as the Chinese Empire Reform Association. After the Chinese Nationalist Party (Kuomintang or KMT) was founded in 1912, Chinese began to join its affiliates as well. Although these associations and parties were crucial in defending the rights of Chinese in the Americas, they also competed with each other for political and economic power, and occasionally their conflicts broke out in violence.[2] Although merchants, hometown associations, Triad societies, and political leaders may have had different goals and interests, all of these groups helped move people in and out of China and the Americas, often clandestinely and illegally.

In Cuba, tongs, family associations, and political parties represented the Chinese community, as in the United States, Mexico, and Canada, but the dominant umbrella association there was the Casino Chung Wah.[3] The Casino, established in 1893, was controlled by the Chinese legation in Havana, which managed the traffic of Chinese laborers, maintaining a registry of all Chinese who arrived and issuing certificates that permitted them to reside in the country legally. After 1926 the Casino lost its monopoly when the government took away its power to regulate migration. Other organizations competed with the Casino for control over the Chinese, and they grew in prominence in the 1920s as the Casino lost ground. Between 1900 and 1929, thirty-five different family or surname Chinese associations were registered with the Cuban government, twenty-six of them between 1921 and 1929. In 1913 importers formed the Chamber of Chinese Commerce of Cuba to represent the interests of Chinese merchants. The Chamber pushed unsuccessfully for broad reforms, like the elimination of Order 155 that restricted Chinese immigration to the island, but its membership dwindled in the mid-1920s after the sugar bust, and by 1930 it had only forty members.[4]

The Chinese political parties in Cuba had ties not only to China but also to affiliates throughout the Americas. The two parties, the nationalist KMT and the republican Chee Kung Tang (CKT, or Patriotic Rising Society), both advocated a republican form of government and the overthrow of the Qing dynasty. At the beginning of the twentieth century, these groups came together in Havana, California, New York, Texas, and London to form a political association, Republican Circle or Young China, to support the nationalist revolution in China. In 1909 Young China held a meeting in Texas of delegates from the Chinese diaspora, including one from Havana.[5] Chinese political parties thus became an informal means to form transnational organizations that could also advocate for local change and provide fraternity and protection to overseas Chinese. After Sun Yat-sen came to power, the CKT felt sidelined by the KMT, and by the 1920s hostilities broke out between these two groups.

It is important to remember that these were transnational organizations linking family members, political comrades, and people from the same regions across national boundaries. Although scholars studying Chinese migration to the Americas often focus on the virulent anti-Chinese movements that saw all Chinese as a threat, and thereby lumped all Chinese together, Chinese spoke different dialects, came from different hometowns, and had different class backgrounds and political sympathies. In short, there was no reason to expect all Chinese to act and think alike. To the extent that racism and discrimination in the Americas affected all Chinese, they could unify to fight for their rights, but as we have seen, some Chinese claimed U.S. or Mexican citizenship and others invoked their exempt status as merchants and students. The Chinese community in the Americas was shot through with conflicting class interests and political goals and had different local, regional, and familial affinities. Exploring both the cooperation among Chinese that is evident in their letters and the conflict among Chinese that can be seen in the so-called tong wars reveals a more complex picture of the Chinese transborder migrant community.

Kang Yu Wei, Wong Foon Chuck, and the Baohuanghui

Chinese political leaders looking for support took advantage of the transnational networks in the Americas that had been well developed by the early twentieth century. Chinese merchants in Hong Kong and other ports rose to prominence as trade and migration increased. By 1939 more than 6.3 million Chinese emigrants had embarked at Hong Kong for a foreign destination, and 7.7 million returned to China through Hong Kong. In the 1870s the British governor in Hong Kong enlisted the Chinese merchant directors of the Tung Wah hospital to inspect emigrants and curb the abuses in the coolie trade. Merchants therefore insinuated themselves into every part of the migratory process from inspections before they departed, helping migrants gain entry, legal or illegal, to various countries, making sure they repaid debts, and overseeing the return of their bones when they died.[6]

Kang Yu Wei took advantage of these well-developed networks in the first decade of the twentieth century to form the Baohuanghui, or Chinese Empire Reform Association. The political organizing of Baohuanghui chapters and the business ventures of a Chinese businessman in Mexico, Wong Foon Chuck, intersected in 1906, revealing the fluid collaborations between businessmen and political leaders. Kang Yu Wei, a former tutor to the emperor, led a constitutional monarchy reform movement in China in the late nineteenth century. After being exiled from China in 1898, he established hundreds of chapters of his association throughout the Americas. Kang piggybacked on the merchants' trading and migratory networks to form a political organization focused on change in China. The first Baohuanghui in the Americas was founded on 20 July 1899 in Victoria, British Columbia. From 1899 through 1911, the Baohuanghui expanded rapidly throughout the Americas, especially along the Pacific coast; by 1911, there were thirteen chapters in Canada, close to eighty in the United States, nine in Mexico, five in Central America, one in Cuba, and three in South America.[7] By the early part of the twentieth century, the Baohuanghui became the most extensive transnational Chinese organization in the Americas.[8]

A more common path than Kang's was that of a young Chinese boy, Wong Foon Chuck from Guandong province, who moved to San Francisco in the mid-1870s at age twelve. Wong attended a mission school and learned English. Over the years, Wong would return to China several times to visit his parents, but each time he came back to the Americas. In the early 1880s he worked building the Southern Pacific Railway line from Los Angeles to San Antonio, and eventually he settled in the Texas-Mexico border town of Eagle Pass in the mid-1880s. There he became a successful businessman, taking advantage of railroad construction and a mining boom in the Mexican state of Coahuila. He bought the Hotel Central and started an adjacent restaurant and laundry. When the International Railroad Company line was being constructed from Eagle Pass to Torreón, Wong sold Japanese and Chinese goods at various stores along the route. In 1890 he returned to Eagle Pass and began working as a labor contractor for the Coahuila Coal Mining company. Within a couple of years Wong had 400 Chinese laborers under his supervision. By 1901 Wong owned six hotels along the International Railroad Line, including the Hotel del Ferrocarril in Torreón.[9] Wong's multiple occupations as a railroad worker, hotel owner, merchant, and labor contractor complicates the notion of Chinese as either destitute manual laborers or wealthy merchants. The same person could occupy various social and class positions throughout his or her life.

In addition to his entrepreneurial activities, Wong developed close ties to Mexican politicians and integrated himself into Mexican border society by marrying a Mexican woman from Tampico, Cristina Vega Domínguez, in 1895. Wong eventually had ten children with her. After the birth of their first daughter, Wong moved his family across the river from Eagle Pass to Piedras Negras, which would serve as the base for his business enterprises. Wong's success in Mexico partly resulted from his ingratiating himself with powerful figures in the borderlands, like Miguel Cárdenas, who would become Coahuila's long-standing governor (1894–1909).[10] By the early 1890s Wong had become a naturalized Mexican citizen, had a Mexican wife, Mexican children, spoke Spanish, lived in Mexico, and had a thriving business there. His arrest in 1892 in San Antonio, and his forcible deportation from the United States for being Chinese, may have helped convince Wong that his future was brighter in Mexico. Although most Chinese headed north to the United States from Mexico, some Chinese, facing legal restrictions and discrimination in the United States, headed south to Mexico. For enterprising Chinese, northern Mexico offered opportunities to make money and start businesses in the rapidly developing mining towns and along the newly constructed railroad lines.

As Wong was developing his business in Mexico, Kang was seeking support from the diasporic Chinese communities in the Americas. In the first decade of the twentieth century, Kang traveled up and down the Pacific coast organizing chapters of the Baohuanghui. Pressed for financing for his movement to establish a constitutional monarchy in China, Kang formed the Commercial Corporation in Victoria, British Columbia, in 1902. In 1906 Kang visited Mexico City, staying at the home of Wong Foon Chuck, and then headed to Torreón, which was in the midst of an agricultural and industrial boom. Kang invested in land in an undeveloped part of the city, earning huge profits by selling the land back to Chinese and other foreigners.[11] One of the Chinese who bought this land was Wong Foon Chuck. The value of land in the Lagunera region, adjacent to Torreón, was skyrocketing, but so much of it had been taken over by cotton that food was scarce. Wong acquired fourteen hectares of well-irrigated land in Torreón, renting parcels to other Chinese, who produced food and grew cotton. Wong's land was adjacent to the Metallurgic Company of Torreón, owned by the Madero family.[12] Francisco Madero would end up leading the 1910 Mexican Revolution and became the first revolutionary president of Mexico. The two nationalist movements, one in China advocating a constitutional monarchy and the other in Mexico to overthrow Porfirio Díaz, existed side-by-side but unconnected on the outskirts of Torreón.

Even though Kang was a noted political figure and Wong a wealthy businessmen, both of them encountered difficulties crossing the border into the United States. In 1906 Kang sought to return to New York by way of Eagle Pass because it was a more direct route than going by boat through Veracruz. Wong sent a telegram to President Theodore Roosevelt asking that Kang be allowed to enter at Eagle Pass, which was not one of the five designated ports of entry for Chinese. The Chinese legation informed the Immigration Bureau that Kang was not a representative of the Chinese government and that they wanted nothing to do with him. Kang made overtures to the bureau's New Orleans office, armed with a letter from the city's mayor, but he was denied entry there as well. Wong had himself been denied entry through Eagle Pass in 1905. Kang eventually secured a letter from the U.S. consul in Tampico to facilitate his entry into New York. When Kang arrived in New York, immigration officers discovered that he had been issued an entry visa in Vancouver by U.S. officials in 1904, but the papers were never forwarded to the bureau. Kang was finally allowed to enter the United States. The circuitous route he traveled and the obstacles he encountered along the way demonstrate the kinds of difficulties that even prominent Chinese had entering the United States.[13] In 1906 Kang wrote to President Roosevelt, lauding him for his intervention on behalf of Chinese merchants, diplomats, and students during the 1905 boycott of U.S. goods but also criticizing the harsh enforcement of the exclusion act. As Kang put it, "The future historian will marvel why the enlightened American, who permits the free dumping of the riff-raff and the off-scouring of Europe, who welcomes the assisted emigration of European paupers and criminals—should single out the Chinese for exclusion."[14] Kang pointedly condemned the United States not for excluding poor people and criminals but for lumping all Chinese together as an undesirable class.

Given the discrimination Chinese faced in the United States, Kang turned to Mexico for business opportunities. Kang had so much success in Torreón that in 1906 he established a bank there, the Compañía Bancaria Chino y México, and in 1907 formed a company to build a tramway in the city. He appointed Wong Foon Chuck as director of the bank and brought Lee Fook Kee from Vancouver as director of the Commercial Corporation to oversee operations in Torreón. Although building of the tram stalled after just seven miles had been constructed and land values began to fall precipitously, by 1908 the bank had amassed close to $1 million in assets. The financial collapse of the Commercial Corporation resulted from an economic crisis in 1907 and Wong's refusal to release funds for the completion of the tramline.[15] However, in addition to internecine fighting among Chinese, the local Mexican elite feared a rising Chinese business class. Not only were the Madero family and Wong in the same vicinity, but the Chinese bank was a direct competitor of the Banco Mercantil de Monterrey in Torreón, in which the Madero family held a majority stake. The emerging Chinese business elite in Torreón posed a threat to Mexican capitalists like the Madero family. That antipathy, together with the populist racism against Chinese in Mexico, combined as a powerful force once the Mexican Revolution erupted in 1911.

In the 1911 massacre of Chinese in Torreón at the hands of Maderista forces, Wong lost forty-five men, four in his laundry, nine in his railroad hotel, and thirty-two on his hacienda.[16] One of Kang's relatives was also among the 303 Chinese killed that day.[17] Most of the remaining Chinese left the city fearing for their lives. Historian Leo M. Dambourges Jacques argues that the prosperity of the Chinese community in Torreón, combined with the latent anti-Chinese racism, created an explosive mix: "Mexicans resented the presence of the prosperous alien colony in their midst, and this helped set the stage for violence."[18] Even after the massacre, Wong Foon Chuck continued to do business in Mexico and evidently used his hotels, restaurants, laundries, and dry goods stores as safe houses for Chinese being smuggled northward to the United States, but the Chinese community in Mexico would increasingly face hostility during the revolutionary period. For his part, Kang continued to organize the reformist movement in North America until 1909, when he returned to Asia for good. The importance of Kang's reformist movement diminished as Sun Yat-sen's nationalist revolution gained steam and finally succeeded in 1912.

Kang's reformist party and Sun Yat-sen's nationalist party vied to control the Chinese community in the Americas by tapping into preexisting organizations and networks. By 191, Sun Yat-sen managed to unite the Hung League and the CKT for the purpose of overthrowing the Qing government.[19] Tongs served as key sources of both political and material support for revolutionary movements in China. Sun Yat-sen received close to $100,000 from tongs throughout North America in the lead-up to his nationalist revolution.[20] By the 1920s, however, dissension among tongs grew as Sun Yat-sen's KMT marginalized the CKT. Although secret societies in China had their origins in military and political organizations that opposed imperial authority, these groups became mutual-aid societies and criminal syndicates in the Americas. Rival tongs frequently fought each other, and occasionally these conflicts erupted into pitched battles.

In spite of the differences, however, tongs provided spaces for migrant Chinese men, who may have been cut off from their biological families, to reconstitute alternative family structures. In his article "Performing Exclusion and Resistance," Floyd Cheung analyzes the initiation ceremony of the CKT in Tucson, Arizona, in the 1860s and 1870s to show how Chinese used this martial ritual to reinforce their sense of manhood in the face of attacks by whites in the United States. The CKT was a nativist Chinese group that formed in 1647 to oppose foreign encroachers, to overthrow the Manchu rulers, and to return the deposed Ming dynasty. The secret ceremony, Cheung argues, allowed tong members to "both speak softly and carry a sharp, if concealed or imaginary sword." The tongs provided protection, but they also served as spaces for political organizing and psychological resistance as well as fraternity for emigrants who felt isolated and persecuted.[21] The importance of this kind of psychological support and brotherhood should not be underestimated in a community of mostly men who had been separated from their families and thrust into a foreign and often hostile environment. While Chinese may not have held public rallies to protest discrimination, the CKT performed elaborate initiation rituals in the interior halls of their association in which members reenacted the history of the organization's founders and transformed their marginal spaces into the center of the world for the descendants of the Middle Kingdom. Chinese emigrants were brothers, not aliens, inside the tongs.

Although the tongs and political parties provided psychic spaces for solidarity, they also created and reflected competition within the Chinese community. The violence that broke out in the Chinese Mexican community in the 1920s revealed transnational political conflicts. The Chinese in Mexico were more or less united prior to the nationalist revolution of Sun Yat-sen in China in 1911. After that point supporters of the Nationalist Party (Kuomintang, or KMT) opposed those of the CKT. In the spring of 1922 gun battles and assassinations in northern Mexico broke out between supporters of the KMT and their secret society, Lung Sing Tong, and supporters of the CKT.[22] According to the anti-Chinese activist José Angel Espinoza, the conflict between the two was over not merely politics but also control of opium trafficking and Chinese laborers. Sonoran authorities rounded up 250 to 300 Chinese, put them in jail in Hermosillo without trial and began deportation proceedings; 60 to 70 percent of those detained were members of the CKT, and only 10 percent were in the KMT. Gun battles continued into the summer of 1922, with assassins from the CKT killing twelve nationalists. By the time it was over twenty-five Chinese had been killed.[23]

Before the deportations could be carried out, however, President Alvaro Obregón intervened and halted them. Juan Lin Fu, interim president of the CKT, wrote to Obregón to complain that basic rights to a defense had not been granted to the incarcerated Chinese. He also blamed the seventeen members of the KMT who remained free for instigating the violence. Obregón condemned the violence and told Lin Fu that he planned to deport all of the Chinese in jail. Wealthy Chinese merchants from Sonora and Sinaloa appealed to Obregón to launch an investigation to find out who were the guilty parties. In the end Plutarco Elías Calles, then secretary of the interior, concluded that the KMT was largely responsible for the violence and that most of the jailed Chinese were innocent.[24] In July 1922 Francisco L. Yuen of the KMT wrote Obregón to thank him for rescinding the deportation order against him. The deportation order stemmed, he explained, from false charges made against him by his opponents in the CKT. This secret society referred to itself as a masonic lodge, but Yuen explained that they were "conservatives, traditionalists, monarchists, and rejected Western civilization and the harmony of human progress."[25]

The CKT had been founded two centuries earlier to overthrow the Manchu government, but by the mid-nineteenth century, it was a global organization with branches from Singapore to San Francisco.[26] The CKT had formed in Arizona as early as the 1860s, and it had affiliates throughout North America in cities like Vancouver and San Francisco. The first branch in Mexico was founded in Cananea, Sonora, in 1903 by Wong Lan Sing, who came from San Francisco. Although the CKT had supported the nationalist revolution, its members felt betrayed by Sun Yat-sen and later broke with the Nationalist Party. A report by the Nationalist Chinese League in Mexico accused the CKT of involvement in smuggling Chinese across the border to the United States and in various assassination attempts on its members. Echoing anti-Chinese stereotypes, Yuen claimed that the CKT "had done nothing other than commit crimes, flout the law, and establish opium dens." In contrast, Yuen portrayed the Nationalist League as an organization comprised of "sane elements, of serious culture, of real honorability and above all respectful of the laws of this country." Yuen pleaded with the governor to deport members of the secret society using Article 33 of the Mexican Constitution, which allowed for the expulsion of undesirable foreigners.[27]

In June 1922 massive protests broke out throughout Sonora demanding the expulsion of Chinese as pernicious foreigners. Telegrams flooded into the governor's and president's offices demanding that judges who prevented expulsion be removed, including one signed by the president of the Communist Party.[28] By December the immediate crisis ended with most Chinese being released from prison and Obregón ordering the deportation of forty-three tong members, mostly from the KMT.[29] The Mexican anti-Chinese movement thus coincided with conflict among the Chinese themselves, with each side calling for the others to be expelled from the country. Although many Chinese were expelled from Mexico, especially in the early 1930s, a relatively small number were expelled using Article 33. Article 33 of the Mexican constitution provided for the expulsion of foreigners who interfered in domestic politics. According to a 1935 report by Gilberto Loyo of the National Revolutionary Party, no Chinese were expelled using Article 33 before 1927. In the period between 1921 and 1934, the report found that of a total of 850 expulsions, there were 256 Guatemalans, 140 U.S. citizens, 124 Spaniards, and only 106 Chinese. Almost half of these expulsions were for violations of the migration law rather than for political or criminal activities.[30] These figures suggest that although there was popular pressure to expel Chinese using Article 33, most Chinese were deported for other violations.

Although bloodshed between tongs stopped in September 1922, the conflict continued in the pages of Chinese-language newspapers published in the United States and Mexico, particularly *Chung Sai Yat Po*, a CKT paper in San Francisco, and *Sam Wa*, a KMT paper in Nogales, Sonora. Violence erupted once again in 1924 during a Cinco de Mayo celebration in Mexicali, when agents of the CKT assassinated a member of the nationalist Lung Sing Tong. This killing rekindled a cycle of assassinations and reprisals. The CKT sent out a notice to its members on 22 June 1924, saying that its patience in dealing with the KMT peacefully had come to an end and that it was preparing for war. "If these people try to abuse us and the moment arrives when we can't stand it any longer, then surely there will be a terrible and dreadful war."[31] Finally, on 28 September 1924, Francisco Yuen, a prominent merchant of the Lung Sing Tong, was killed by a CKT assassin in a train station in Naco, Sonora, in front of crowds of people. In the wake of Yuen's assassination and the international scandal it provoked, the governor of Baja California, Abelardo L. Rodríguez, convinced the president to expel fifty Chinese leaders of the CKT in 1924.[32] Local authorities sympathetic to the CKT obstructed Obregón's orders, however, and released many of the leaders, thus preventing their deportation. The federal government's efforts to bring an end to the tong wars were thwarted by its limited power to impose its will in the north.[33] In 1929 the nationalist Lung Sing Tong was still active in Coahuila and apparently using its influence with the government to have its Chinese enemies expelled from the country.[34]

The violence caused by the tongs and their ability to fight deportation further enraged *anti-chinistas* in Mexico's north. José Angel Espinoza excoriated the tongs in his *El ejemplo de Sonora*, reproducing a series of Chinese letters (translated into Spanish) that supposedly demonstrated the corruption of the Chinese in Mexico. One letter from Juan A. Wong in Magdalena to his older brother José Wong in Guaymas stated that he had been jailed by the "diabolical party" (presumably the KMT) and was only released when his brother's wife brought his naturalization card to the district judge. He recommended doing the same in Guaymas, where a number of men had been similarly jailed. Espinoza saw the use of naturalization papers to get released from jail as an opportunistic and strategic claim to rights as Mexican citizens when, in fact, they continued to "belong to Tongs, [and] continued their clan-like activities with their compatriots."[35] The letter, however, gave no indication that the author was using naturalization as a way to evade the law. Rather he was using his rights as a Mexican citizen to avoid being jailed and possibly deported as a foreigner. As Espinoza put it, "Each naturalization letter that our government extends to a Chinese citizen is a rattlesnake deposited in the breast of nation."[36] At the height of the anti-Chinese pogroms in northern Mexico, the critique of Chinese naturalization became more than simply a question of opportunism, it was an issue of protecting the Mexican nation from racial degeneration. In 1930 General Norberto Rochin, president of the Unión Nacionalista Mexicana (Pro-Raza y Salud Pública) (Mexican Nationalist Union [Pro Race and Public Health]) wrote to the minister of foreign relations, asking him in the name of the Anti-Asian Nationalist League of Tijuana to reconsider the naturalization of Chinese "who are invading the Republic, displacing our compatriots from all of their activities and degenerating our race, with grave prejudice to our nationality."[37]

Although anti-Chinese activists saw the tongs and other Chinese defense groups as dangerous for the nation, the central government was not keen to follow through on the chorus of calls to deport the tong leaders. Tongs had the ability and the political connections to fight such deportations, and they were important political and economic forces in their localities. Deporting the leaders would have political costs too high for the central government.

Tong Fights in Cuba

In Cuba, competition between the KMT (Nationalists) and the CKT (Republicans) broke into violent conflict in the 1920s, around the same time as it did in Mexico. In 1923 the KMT was reorganized and began to cooperate with the Communist Party of China, while the CKT remained more open and democratic. The influx of new Chinese immigrants to Cuba in the 1920s unsettled the balance of power in the Chinese community, leading to sometimes violent disputes, increasing crime rates, public scandals, and a struggle to represent the new migrants. Meanwhile in the midst of an economic crisis (1924–26), the Casino and the Chinese legation lost their power to control Chinese migration as corrupt Cuban immigration officials began to allow thousands of illegal Chinese to enter the country. The government blamed the Chinese community for drug trafficking, gambling, and corruption. Criminal convictions for Chinese also skyrocketed from 99 in 1919 to 940 in 1925. In 1919 Chinese represented only 2 percent of all criminal convictions, but by 1925 this portion had grown to 20 percent. The increase in criminal convictions seems to have resulted from increased targeting of Chinese communities by the police, leading the Chinese minister in Cuba to write to the secretary of state lamenting the "true state of alarm that exists among the colony of Chinese residents in Cuba."[38]

The Cuban government responded to these internal conflicts much as the Mexican government had, by deporting the guilty parties. However, the infighting among the Chinese also led to a broader harassment campaign by the Cuban government that would affect the entire Chinese community, including wealthy merchants. The interior minister proposed a series of measures designed to root out the supposed vice and criminality in the Chinese community in Havana, including closing all Chinese political parties and the Casino Chung Wah, posting more police in Chinatown, shutting down all Chinese-language newspapers, expelling Chinese with criminal records, and reinforcing immigration laws. In September 1926 public health officials issued fines to twenty-five overcrowded houses in Chinatown, and in that same year the police discovered 145 opium dens. Police action focused on enforcing public health codes and cracking down on drug use and trafficking in Chinese neighborhoods.[39]

In Cuba and Mexico, conflicts between tongs gave the central government an excuse to exert executive authority through deportations, policing, and stricter enforcement of immigration laws. The Cuban central government was more successful in gaining the upper hand in managing Chinese migration, probably because it had greater influence in Havana, the center of the Chinese community, and because Cuba was an island where entry could more easily be controlled. The Mexican central government used deportation as a means to rid the country of the Chinese held responsible for tong violence, but the local and state authorities in the north were able to impede the government's deportation orders in some cases and to harass Chinese in others. In comparison to Cuba, the relative weakness of Mexico's central government rendered it ineffective in controlling Chinese migration and the violent anti-Chinese movements in the north.

Tongs as Conduits for Smugglers

American governments viewed tongs and other Chinese associations as troublesome criminal syndicates, but for the Chinese community they were vital institutions that facilitated entry and adaptation to a new country. Although labor recruiters were vilified in the press and government reports as unscrupulous exploiters, they were often revered and respected by the Chinese, who relied on them for survival. Businessmen like Wong Foon Chuck used their networks of connections in the borderlands to establish an underground railroad for Chinese seeking clandestine entry into the United States. Like Wong, other transnational smugglers were go-betweens and cultural brokers, men who had in many cases managed to integrate into the local culture by marrying native women and learning the local language. They used secret societies, political parties, business dealings, and family ties to help them establish transnational networks.

Some of the most successful smugglers of Chinese from Mexico worked for the Chinese Six Companies and often worked with corrupt U.S. officials. Yung Ham, who lived in Nogales, Sonora, had reportedly smuggled 3,000 Chinese from Mexico to the United States. In 1899 Harry K. Chenoweth, the head of customs at Nogales, was found to be colluding with Yung to traffic Chinese girls through Nogales dressed as Mexicans. The girls would then be sold to gambling and opium den operators for $2,900 each. The Indiana man chosen to replace Chenoweth, William M. Hoey, became involved in his own Chinese smuggling operation within a year, in collaboration with Frank Ho, a Chinese resident of Nogales, Sonora, and Quong Wing of the Chinese Six Companies. In the course of their investigation, two U.S. customs agents, after being unable to gain Mexican cooperation to extradite two Chinese suspects, crossed the border illegally and seized the two Chinese to bring them back to the United States to testify against Hoey.[40] Controlling Chinese smuggling operations on the border was an uphill battle given corrupt U.S. officers and a lack of official Mexican cooperation. Under these circumstances, U.S. agents felt justified in transgressing Mexico's national sovereignty to secure U.S. borders against illegal entry by the Chinese.

As soon as the authorities began to investigate, smugglers from one region adeptly moved to another region or country. One such smuggler, Jim Bennett, moved his operations from British Columbia to the Arizona-Sonora border in 1901. He received migrants in the Sonoran port city of Guaymas and brought them up through Hermosillo, Cananea, Magdalena, and Naco. Two forgers, Louis Greenwaldt and B. C. Springstein, the first of whom had done time in San Quentin for Chinese smuggling, provided the Chinese with fake certificates of residency. Lee Quong and Frank How, who had been involved with Hoey in Nogales, helped load the Chinese in boxcars heading to northern Sonora. They had their Chinese clients "cut off their queues and dress . . . as Mexicans" so they could cross the border. After the ring was discovered Greenwaldt escaped to Vancouver and Bennett to Mexico, where he lived in a princely fashion and continued to smuggle Chinese.[41] When smugglers ran into trouble with the law, they simply crossed the border to continue their operations in another country.

Cuba was another central node in the Chinese smuggling network run through the Chinese National League. One of the ringleaders in both the labor and opium smuggling operations was a long-time resident of Havana named Lou Yat Sun who spoke Spanish fluently, had married a Cuban woman, and was reported to be a gambler and involved in other shady activities.[42] Sun, president of the Chinese National League of Havana, tried to establish a new smuggling route to the United States through Gulfport, Mississippi. He sent a young emissary to meet with the president of the Chinese National League in New Orleans, Shou Min, known by locals as an opium dealer and Chinese smuggler.[43] It appears as if Shou Min was being groomed to be Sun's agent in New Orleans to oversee the smuggling operations from there. These efforts were frustrated, however, when immigration authorities arrested the young emissary and deported him to Cuba.[44]

In addition to specific names of smugglers, the investigation revealed the important link between the Chinese National League operations in Havana and New Orleans. The Chinese National League emerged in China in 1912 as a political party and quickly established affiliates throughout the world wherever there was a sizable Chinese community. The fact that the National League branches in both Havana and New Orleans were involved in smuggling Chinese shows that this was not a marginal activity by lower-class criminals but an enterprise orchestrated by some of the most prominent and wealthy business and political leaders in the Chinese community.

In December 1920 John Williams, another key Havana smuggler, was identified by a ship captain, who was able to provide the smuggler's name and address in Havana. Williams had approached the captain in Havana to try to get him to transport Chinese to the United States.[45] Immigration authorities had been keeping an eye out for Williams ever since he was named as a smuggler by a Jamaican stowaway on a United Fruit Company ship, the SS *Tipton*. The Jamaican stowaway, Leonard Spence, said he had boarded a ship in Havana along with two Chinese brought there by John Williams. According to Spence, Williams was born in China but was a Jamaican. He spoke English, Spanish, and Chinese. The transnational connections and identities of men like Williams and Lou Yat Sun equipped them for success in human smuggling.[46]

Immigration service records are full of reports about Chinese being smuggled into the United States, but there are very few detailed descriptions of the experience of the journey itself. Inspectors were more interested in learning about who organized the smuggling than about the migrants' deprivations. However, Leonard Spence, the Jamaican stowaway, offered one such account, describing his ten-day journey to Tela, Honduras, and then to Mobile, Alabama. His story helps us appreciate the conditions on the treacherous journeys that so many Chinese took as they sought illegal entry into the United States. Spence was locked in a small carpenter's storeroom with the two Chinese. When they arrived in Honduras and the ship was inspected by a customs agent, the Chinese were hidden in a small compartment for the steering apparatus. During the journey, they were fed bread, potatoes, and sometimes meat, and they were forced to defecate on paper in the same room where they slept. One of the Chinese men spoke a little Spanish and was able to communicate with Spence, but for the most part, they spent days below decks, lying down in silence, awaiting their arrival in the United States. When they landed in Mobile, the three men were brought to the railway depot, where they were eventually arrested waiting for a train to New York. Although the smugglers were supposed to pay for transport to New York, Spence explained that he and the two Chinese were just dumped in Mobile. At his hearing, Spence was asked if he was an anarchist or member of the IWW, neither of which brands of politics he seemed to know anything about. He was deported back to Cuba for illegally entering the United States without undergoing inspection.[47]

The two Chinese men with Spence were able to identify two of the seamen who had been involved in the smuggling. The boatswain, a native of Finland, admitted to having been paid by the Chinese men, but he claimed that he was only paid to keep quiet about their presence on the boat. The carpenter, also Finnish, claimed to have only seen the Chinese onboard once they had landed in Mobile.[48] Imagine for a moment the polyglot storeroom on the United Fruit Company ship where a Jamaican, two Chinese migrants, and two Finnish sailors met and exchanged money and perhaps a few words in broken English or Spanish while the vessel sailed the Gulf from Cuba to Honduras to the United States. At least for the time they spent in the Gulf, they remained in a zone beyond the control of any nation. Once they landed in Mobile, however, they all quickly became enmeshed in the web of U.S. immigration law.

When the two Chinese men were interrogated, one of them concocted an elaborate story about having lived in New York and come to Mobile to buy a laundry. The fact that he still had with him a Cuban registry document indicating that he had arrived in Cuba in 1918 made his story suspect. Inspector Vincent suspended his interrogation and began to question the other Chinese migrant. Law Ngou had a certificate of residence issued in Brooklyn in 1894. When the inspector pressed him, saying that the picture on the residency certificate did not look like him at all, the interpreter Fung Ming broke in and began to speak with Ngou in Chinese. "You are a countryman of mine," Fung explained to the "alien." "I do not want you to commit a crime you do not know anything about; it means very serious trouble for you; it might lead you to imprisonment; it would be better for you to discard that paper and tell the truth, though it is hard luck. I realize that, but once you are caught, you simply have to be a good fellow, and be brave and face the music." After that pep talk, the suspect Law Ngou admitted that the residency certificate was not his, and he identified the smuggler in Havana as Sen Kow of 107 Merced Street. The Jamaican stowaway had given the exact same address but indicated that the smuggler's name was John Williams. It is likely that the smuggler used the name John Williams with a U.S. ship captain and the Jamaican stowaway, and a Chinese name with the Chinese migrants. The use of various names, Chinese and Western, was common for Chinese migrants attempting either to fit in or to develop a second identity to elude detection by authorities. After Law Ngou admitted to having been smuggled in from Cuba, the first man also confessed. Inspector Vincent recommended that the Chinese be deported back to Cuba.[49]

The smugglers were a polyglot multilingual and multiethnic group including Chinese, Mexican, Cuban, Jamaican, Italian, Greek, and North Americans who relied on familial, business, and political networks to facilitate their trade. While some smugglers merely helped Chinese cross the border, other operations offered transportation to interior cities like New York or Chicago, job placement, and fraudulent papers. Much like the Italian, Greek, and Mexican padrones Gunther Peck described in *Reinventing Free Labor*, Chinese recruiters and smugglers were simultaneously paternalistic and exploitative.[50]

Many smuggling rings seemed to be run as family enterprises like Mafia organizations. William Riley and his brother Jack led one particularly successful family ring in Buffalo. Riley, who had been an Immigration Bureau agent, was able to use his knowledge of the bureau's inner workings to help him set up his smuggling operation and evade capture.[51] Riley's sister-in-law, Mrs. Carrick, lodged the Chinese in her barn in Fort Erie, just across the border from Buffalo, until they could be moved across the river. Then, Mr. Carrick, pretending he was a fisherman, brought the Chinese across the river, and Riley would transport them all the way to New York City.[52] In 1908 Riley was caught after several loads of Chinese were intercepted and arrested by authorities in Buffalo. Within a couple of months, however, Riley was out of jail and back in business. Along with several other members of his ring, Riley moved to Canada, but he returned to the United States in March 1909 and gave himself up for arrest. This time the judge sentenced Riley to the maximum one year and one day in jail. When he got out, Riley returned to smuggling.[53] This family smuggling operation extended to the southern border with Mexico as well. In 1915 one inspector in Los Angeles noted that a Fred Carrick, possibly the same Mr. Carrick from Fort Erie, displayed at a café a wad of $215 in cash "which he claim[ed] he made hauling chinks."[54] Although there were several high profile arrests of smugglers in the Niagara area in 1914, the Riley brothers continued their operations, and were even heard bragging that "they were too smooth" for the agents to catch them.[55]

Merchants who had business in multiple countries were in a perfect position to orchestrate transnational smuggling. They had the contacts and could easily disguise their movements as part of their regular business operations. Since at least 1909 immigration agents had identified the New Orleans–based merchant Chin Bing as a business partner of one of the main smugglers in Havana, Chaw Lin Hong.[56] In May 1919 a New Orleans inspector reported that Chin Bing was a key smuggler in the area and that he had recently moved his family across Lake Pontchartrain to be close to rail lines on which he could distribute Chinese to Jackson and Memphis. The inspector had information that 10,000 Chinese "coolies" had been contracted in Cuba to work on sugar plantations; just the previous Sunday, 250 Chinese heading to Cuba had passed through New Orleans.[57] So when Chin Bing applied for a return certificate from the U.S. Immigration Bureau in 1919 to visit Tampico, Mexico, and Havana, Cuba, ostensibly to sell dried shrimp, he was denied permission because the bureau believed Bing's purpose on the trip was to orchestrate smuggling from the Gulf. The immigration commissioner in New Orleans suspected that Bing might leave and return surreptitiously anyway, so he gave instructions to watch for him.[58] In addition to the Chinese, Cuban, Mexican, Jamaican, Italian, and North American traffickers, at least one Japanese man in Havana reportedly tried to smuggle Chinese into the United States.[59]

Smuggling was big business, and not just for the labor brokers. There was plenty of money to be made by people lower down the food chain who took their cut, including sailors. When the Norwegian ship SS *Nils* arrived in Progreso, Mexico, local Chinese residents lavished the crew with free beer and dinner and told them that they could earn $300 a trip smuggling Chinese to the United States.[60] Another U.S. ship captain admitted to inspectors in New Orleans that members of his crew had arranged for four Chinese to sneak onto his ship in Cuba for $500 each.[61] Opium and liquor was often brought in with the Chinese, thus increasing potential profits exponentially. With incentives like this it was no wonder that sailors and others became accomplices in the smuggling trade.

Although there were many freelance Chinese smugglers, some of the most effective brokers were actually employed by the immigration bureaucracy. In her book *Brokering Belonging*, historian Lisa Mar describes the key roles that interpreters in the Immigration Branch of the Canadian Department of the Interior played in helping Chinese evade restriction legislation in Canada. Mar highlights the complicated role that such brokers played, helping enforce anti-Chinese restrictions, on the one hand, and enabling Chinese migrants to evade those same restrictions, on the other, all for a fee. Yip On, a merchant and immigration interpreter in Vancouver who helped found the Baohuanghui and manage its business holdings, including the Torreón tramway and a Shanghai newspaper, was exemplary of this dual role as immigration enforcer and sometime smuggler. Yip acted as a powerful broker in Vancouver in the first decade of the twentieth century, extorting large bribes from Chinese migrants in exchange for allowing their entry; he also had a secret deal to provide Canada's Liberal Party with a portion of the bribes. In 1910 another Chinese interpreter, David Lew, attempted to unseat Yip by exposing his corruption. The Royal Commission that investigated found Yip guilty, but it also questioned Lew's motives for exposing Yip. The commission recommended a series of reforms, including using fingerprints to avoid falsified documents, but this recommendation was never implemented. Photographs, however, began to be used in 1910 on exit certificates and in 1913 on entry documents to limit fraudulent entry. In spite of these measures, Mar argues that Canada's Immigration Branch largely ignored illegal entry until the Great Depression of the 1930s.[62] With so much money to be made in the smuggling business, many powerful people made sure the migrants kept coming.

Tracing Clandestine Networks through the Mail

Clandestine migrants, like smugglers, have little interest in preserving documents that might incriminate them in illegal activities. However, they wrote letters to their relatives in various countries in the Americas to arrange border crossings, ask for money, and secure employment. These letters were occasionally intercepted by immigration officials, translated, and placed in state archives. They provide a rare window into the family networks throughout the Americas that facilitated Chinese cross-border migration. On one occasion naval intelligence reported on a letter sent from Fun Nam Wu of Cincinnati to Hung Man Lew in Havana. "If you know of anybody who wants to go to New York," Fun wrote, "please let me know." Fun invited Hung to come and work with him in Cincinnati or to contact a friend in New York City if he wanted to go there. Unaware that his own letters were being intercepted, Fun warned Hung to be "careful what you write in your letters. . . . Everything must be kept secret, otherwise it will be a complete failure."[63] Whether through friendship or clan networks, Chinese in the United States and Cuba helped each other secure jobs and gain entry into the United States. One letter sent from Detroit to Havana in 1919 indicated that Mei

Chung Tsing was going to try to come to the United States because of the lack of work in Havana. The letter writer, however, told his cousin that the smuggling operation from South America "has been practically dissolved, owing to the vigilance of the Customs house."[64]

Chinese correspondence demonstrates intricate familial and business networks that extended throughout the Americas. One example of the extent of these networks is revealed in the letters that Louis Lit and Louie Fong had with them when they were arrested in 1914 in Philadelphia. These letters, translated by the Immigration Bureau, were all in an envelope addressed to George Yee in Philadelphia, bearing postmarks from Montreal or Ontario and a business stamp for Pong Wah Lee in Ontario. The letters demonstrate that Chinese corresponded regularly between Canada, Mexico, and the United States, telling their friends and relatives about job opportunities, communicating about debts, giving medical advice, and generally keeping each other up-to-date about their lives. One letter from Montreal by Shey Loud complained about the large number of Chinese arriving every month and the lack of job opportunities, noting "everything is Canada is dull." According to Shey Loud, five or six ships arrived there every month, each one overstuffed with hundreds of Chinese. Even when they did find work, as he and ten of his cousins had in a "western man's building," "the wages [were] small, just enough for living."[65] The difficulties finding work in both Canada and Mexico help explain why so many Chinese chose to enter the United States clandestinely. One letter from Quock to his uncle Tang Horn thanked him for sending him five dollars, explaining that he was living in Veracruz but found no work. The costs associated with travel to the Americas and clandestine entry into the United States directly impacted Chinese families. Yee Fong sent his uncle Tang Horn money to distribute to his family, but at the same time he complained, "Now I have no money for Ah Foo's marriage, if mother desires to have his ceremony performed she can mortgage the farm."[66] Although most migrants were men, the ripple effects of migration directly impacted women who remained behind in China.

In some of the letters, the pleas for money were desperate. Louie Fat Quon wrote to his nephew Tang Horn letting him know that he had left from Hong Kong and arrived safely in Mexico but that he had no friends or cousins there. He explained that it was very hard to borrow money and living expenses were high, seventy-five cents a day: "I am broke now and have no way to get the money. I hope that my nephew will send me some money to save me. I have suffered the trouble of cold. If you won't send me the money for board, I will some day be starved."[67] In another letter Quon told his nephew that it was hard to find a job in Mexico because of the Revolution and that there were several thousand Chinese in Mexico City who were unemployed.[68] Although the correspondence suggests a tight transnational network of Chinese, the threads in that network could at times be broken. In January 1914 Louie Quong Kee wrote to ask about one of his sons who had gone to Havana and had not been heard of for five months.[69]

In addition to painting a picture of the difficulties faced by Chinese migrants, the letters also help us understand how the transnational smuggling rings worked. A family or friend would pay a portion of the fee to have a Chinese person smuggled into the United States and the rest would be paid on arrival. One letter addressed to three people, including Tang Horn, informed them that Louie Kim and Louie Jin were leaving from Canada and would arrive in the United States that weekend. Shu Gee wrote, "Get ready the money to pay the guide. If the two persons are arrived safely, please let me know immediately."[70] Apparently there was some negotiation over the cost of smuggling a person to the United States, and when Louie Tang Horn balked at the price, Pong Shu Gee wrote to him explaining that $260 was the price if they did not send a guide along, but it would be more because he will have a guide. Shu Gee insisted, "Please do not suspect and I will order him attend the matter earnestly and carefully."[71] Pong Shu Gee was at the nexus of a complex transcontinental smuggling scheme that brought Chinese into Vancouver, transferred them across Canada to Hamilton, Ontario, a border town near Buffalo, New York, and from there arranged for the migrants to cross clandestinely into the United States. One letter from Yee Tung enumerated various expenses for the transfer of Ah You and Ah Bing, including fifty-three dollars each for passage, eight dollars for board, and four dollars for rent.[72] Ah You wrote six days later to his uncle Tang Horn explaining how he had spent the $160 that had been sent and requesting more money to pay from the passage to the United States: "Also send us money to buy Western dresses. Answer soon."[73]

The commissioner of immigration at the Philadelphia station, E. E. Greenwalt, was extremely frustrated by the trial of Louie Lit and Louie Fong. In spite of all the letters that implicated the men in smuggling activities and an inspector from Buffalo who testified that he saw these two Chinese men on a train in Canada, he worried that "six or seven apparently respectable and reliable white witnesses have offset this valuable testimony as a matter of legal evidence by swearing that the Chinamen were in Philadelphia for years before the date the inspector saw them in Canada."[74] So either the inspector who testified in court lied or the Chinese smugglers were collaborating with prominent white people in Philadelphia who were willing to perjure themselves to protect the smuggling activities. Smuggling operations were profitable businesses that involved corrupt immigration officials, Chinese businessmen, political leaders, forgers, and prominent white men. The more the immigration authorities cracked down on illegal immigration, the more it cost to cross clandestinely, and therefore the more profitable the business became. Enforcement of immigration laws was like pumping oxygen into a smoldering fire. Rather than extinguishing the fire, enforcement fueled it.

Conclusion

Chinese communities in the Americas all suffered from discrimination, but different classes suffered differently. Elites like merchants, students, and travelers were sometimes subject to the same kind of humiliating treatment and Bertillon measurements at the U.S. border as Chinese laborers, but the law made important distinctions. Exempt classes were not supposed to be sent to Angel Island for rigorous exams and interrogations. Conditions in communities were also affected by political differences, as Chinese in the Americas began to participate actively in Chinese politics in the early twentieth century, joining the revolutionary movement and the Nationalist and Republican parties. Class tensions, political rivalries, and competition to control gambling, opium, and illegal Chinese smuggling all led to violence among the Chinese in the 1920s. Divisions over political questions in China illustrated the extent to which this diasporic community still maintained psychic and material links to its homeland. These well-publicized fights gave anti-Chinese activists more ammunition to push for tighter police surveillance of the Chinese community and stricter enforcement of immigration laws.

The networks and organizations that tied Chinese together across the Americas also provided them with the tools to survive in a new land and allowed them to come together to fight discriminatory legislation. Chinese businessmen, along with political, tong, and hometown association leaders, played key roles in facilitating clandestine entry in the Americas. The captured letters of Chinese show how relatives helped prospective migrants with money, jobs, and information about how to cross borders clandestinely. There was a highly developed underground railroad and transportation network that not only moved Chinese across borders but helped them get settled when they reached their destinations. These associations run by merchants provided material support in the form of health benefits, burial expenses, legal resources, an alternative family structure, and, most important, a psychic space in which individuals thousands of miles from home could reproduce their social lives. No matter how much politicians and anti-Chinese activists tried to render Chinese socially dead by casting them as "perpetual aliens," their ability to refashion family structures and bonds of solidarity allowed them to survive and forge new communities. Some made claims as Mexican, Cuban, Canadian, or U.S. citizens and some, often the same ones, became involved in nationalist politics in China, but it was their transnational diasporic networks that formed the foundation on which those communities were built.

If the present drift be not changed, we whites are all doomed.
—Lothrop Stoddard, *The Rising Tide of Color against White World Supremacy*, 1922

The idea of the alien or stranger has a very long and sordid history, but it was not until the late nineteenth century that the concept of alien became a formal bureaucratic status linked to increasingly complex immigration restrictions around the globe. African slaves and Indians were certainly seen as Others and excluded from political life in the Americas. As outsiders, they were necessary not only as laborers but as the excluded against whom to define the rights-bearing citizen. In the nineteenth century, as slavery was being abolished around the world and indigenous people were gaining citizenship, a new Other emerged: the illegal alien. For the first time, centralized government bureaucracies established rigorous procedures to distinguish citizens from aliens and legal from illegal immigrants. Governments developed passports, visas, and residency certificates to track and control the movement of people across borders and within national territory. Entering a country without authorization or inspection became a crime punishable by incarceration and possibly deportation. The Chinese in the Americas were the first ethnic group explicitly subject to these regulations, and modern immigration bureaucracies developed largely in response to them. Since the 1930s immigration restrictions have been expanded and applied to a host of other unwanted people.

In 1933, at the height of this era of immigration restriction, the U.S. writer Alexander Laing wrote a novel titled *The Sea Witch* that looked back to the mid-nineteenth-century coolie trade to explore the intimate and symbiotic relationship between good and evil. Laing's novel was partially based on the true story of a U.S. clipper that ran into a reef off the coast of Cuba in 1856, killing 500 coolies onboard, along with the entire crew.[1] Laing altered the facts in his fictional account of the *Sea Witch*, making Peru the destination and a coolie mutiny the cause of the ship's demise. Nonetheless, the novel borrows heavily from actual accounts of coolie mutinies, like that aboard the *Norway* and others described in this book. Although the nineteenth-century coolie trade in Latin America may seem quite distinct from Depression-era concerns over immigrants in the United States, the two are related by the long history of the alien.

Laing's novel focuses on the intimate connection between profit and exploitation, or, as he put it, the symbiotic relationship of god and the devil. The wanderer, a "madman" and "former whaler" in the novel gives voice to this central contradiction:

Think of the wretches below—coolies, you called them. There's nothing but darkness and despair for them—yet they're agencies of hope. They're to dig manure, and die in the dust of it, to make the wheatlands golden, and quell a million hungers somewhere. How can you set that evil apart from that good, and save either? No one will dig on those islands, unless you kidnap him and take him there. There's no hope of having good apart from evil, Chips. That's why I say, set yourself up with the devil for a whist partner, and learn his system of play. Think of a gold vein in the black rock, spread spidery-thin amongst the rock crystals. How will you refine the good from the evil? How will you know which is evil, even,—the rock or the gold?[2]

Laing saw through the contradiction of the coolie trade and modern capitalism. The goods are the product of brutal exploitation; you cannot have the gold without the black rock. Coercion was always necessary to get people to mine the guano in Peru that would fertilize fields in Europe, to cut the cane in Cuba that would sweeten drinks in New York City, and to build the railroads that would link Atlantic and Pacific coasts in North America. Forced labor was inherent in the development of capitalism. But the kinds of coercion used to extract labor changed over the course of the nineteenth century. Slavery slowly gave way to a new form of coercion under the paradoxical title of free labor.

There have always been insiders and outsiders determined by religion, family and kin, place, gender, sexuality, race, or class. What changed in the modern era during the rise of nationalism in the nineteenth century is that the imagined community became more democratic and encompassed all adults. Women, indigenous people, and blacks were initially excluded from this community, but eventually they too became part of the "horizontal comradeship" that Benedict Anderson described so well in *Imagined Communities*.[3] In 1908 sociologist Georg Simmel wrote about the "stranger" who was "near and far *at the same time*," part of the human family but of a qualitatively different group. In 1928, in the midst of hysteria about the United States being flooded with racially degenerate people, sociologist Robert Park warned about the difficulty of assimilating the bicultural immigrant, whom he called the "marginal man."[4] From the end of the nineteenth century through the 1920s, as the community of citizens expanded, immigration restrictions were enacted across the Americas and the rest of the globe. As citizenship was extended more broadly, the idea of the illegal alien, the outsider on the inside, emerged. Exclusion and criminalization of aliens became the corollary to the democratization of citizenship, the black rock in which the gold vein was embedded.

Citizenship is supposed to create equality for insiders, and although that has never been the case, the myth of equality is sustained on the basis of a more fundamental exclusion of aliens. In the Americas, white and mestizo elites erected racially skewed barriers to immigration, naturalization, and citizenship to maintain racist hierarchies. Eugenicists argued that nonwhite immigrants threatened the health of the nation and the purity of the national racial stock. In Latin America, certain already existing nonwhite elements were accepted as long as they were thoroughly transculturated or blended into the national norm. In Mexico, this took the form of mestizophilia or the hybrid cosmic race advocated by José Vasconcelos.[5] In Cuba, Fernando Ortiz wrote about the creation of a unique national type through mixing of Africans and Spaniards in *Cuban Counterpoint*.[6] The Chinese were never seen as part of this grand mestizo hybridization, and even the most antiracist intellectuals like José Martí depicted Chinese in crudely racist terms. Opting for purity over mixture, eugenicists in the United States and Canada contended that continued migration of nonwhites would swamp "white civilization." The U.S. eugenicist Lothrop Stoddard captured the zeitgeist of the era in his 1922 book *The Rising Tide of Color against White World Supremacy*. Stoddard argued that since modern transportation had eliminated the "natural barriers" to mixing, white supremacy would be undermined by nonwhite migrants. "Unless man erects and maintains artificial barriers," he declared, "the various races will increasingly mingle, and the inevitable result will be the supplanting or absorption of the higher by the lower types." The artificial barriers Stoddard referred to were the immigration restrictions that would be adopted in the United States a couple of years later. "If the present drift be not changed," Stoddard exclaimed, "we whites are all ultimately doomed."[7]

Eighty years after Stoddard predicted doom for the whites, Harvard political science professor Samuel Huntington sounded the alarm again to defend white Anglo-Saxon Protestant America from what he called the "Hispanic challenge."[8] While the immigration restrictions of the 1920s provided a brief respite for white supremacy, after the 1960s whites in Anglo North

America would once again face what they perceived as a rising tide of color. From the nineteenth century until today, the specter of the nonwhite alien has haunted the Americas.

Chinese in the Americas, 1960s to the Present

Chinese migrations to Anglo North America and Latin America have two distinct trajectories when we look at the long period from the mid-nineteenth through the early twenty-first century, with roughly equal numbers going to each place through the coolie era (1847–74) but many more going to Anglo North America afterward. Immigration restrictions throughout the Americas put a damper on Chinese migration, but tight controls on emigration and return after the 1949 Revolution in China also contributed to the interruption of the migratory circuits between China and the Americas.[9] Although there has been an increase in Chinese migration to Latin America since the 1980s, the large Chinese communities in Cuba, Peru, and Mexico from the nineteenth through early twentieth centuries never regained their former size or importance.

In Cuba, after the Revolution in 1959, the Chinese community almost disappeared. In 1980 a census by the Casino Chung Wah counted only 4,302 Chinese remaining on the island.[10] By 2010 there were no more than 200 elderly "chinos naturales" (foreign-born Chinese) on the island. Nevertheless, thousands of mixed race descendants who have recently rediscovered their Chinese heritage form part of a revitalizing Chinese Cuban community today.[11] A new crop of Chinese visitors can be seen on the streets of Havana these days, including tourists, investors, and students. In just six years of the first decade of the twenty-first century, 3,500 Chinese students graduated from Cuban universities as part of a cultural program to improve bilateral relations.[12] The population of foreign-born Chinese in the rest of Latin America also dwindled from the 1920s through the 1980s to a few thousand in each country. There has been a resurgence of new Chinese migration to Latin America since the 1980s, including tens of thousands of Chinese migrants who use Panama, Honduras, and Peru as springboards for entering the United States.[13] These new migrations are happening in the context of expanded Chinese government investments in Latin America.

The declension story of Chinese in Latin America contrasts with Anglo North America, where the Chinese population has reached unprecedented levels. Although U.S. exclusion dampened Chinese migration in the first part of the twentieth century, the Chinese population grew dramatically after the

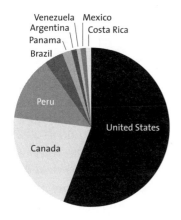

Venezuela Mexico
Argentina Costa Rica
Panama
Brazil

Peru

Canada

United States

FIGURE 4.

Overseas Chinese Population Distribution in the Americas, 2012. Based on statistics by Overseas Community Affairs Council Republic of China (Taiwan), http://www.ocac.gov.tw/.

1980s. By 2010 there were 1.8 million foreign-born Chinese (including from Hong Kong) in the United States, representing 4.5 percent of the approximately 40 million immigrants.[14] Canada followed roughly the same trajectory as the United States, with about half a million foreign-born Chinese in Canada in 2006, representing 8 percent of the total population. It is projected that by 2031 there will be almost 3 million foreign-born Chinese in Canada.[15] Looking back over more than a century and half of Chinese migration to Anglo North America, the exclusion era was just a long pause in an ever-growing population of Chinese, not to mention growing populations of other Asian groups as well. The migratory patterns established before exclusion continued during exclusion and then accelerated after Deng Xiaoping's economic reforms in China in the late 1970s. Chinese migration policies must be considered in conjunction with those in the Americas in order to fully understand the shifting migratory patterns. Over more than a century and a half, almost all Chinese migrants to the Americas have come from just two southeastern coastal provinces, Fujian and Guangdong.[16] Although migration of Chinese to the Americas has ebbed and flowed since the mid-nineteenth century, the sending communities have remained remarkably consistent.

The Chinese population imbalance between Anglo and Latin America can also be seen when one also considers the total population of overseas Chinese, including people of Chinese heritage or mixed-race Chinese living in the Americas. Who counts as a mixed-race Chinese person varies according to country and whether an individual identifies as such. Nonetheless, based on government data, one can begin to paint a picture of the overseas Chinese community in the Americas. In 2012 there were an estimated 7.7

million ethnic Chinese in the Americas, 55 percent of them in the United States and another 20 percent in Canada (see figure 4). The remaining quarter are spread through Latin America with Peru (990,000), Brazil (280,000), and Panama (140,000) representing the top three countries. It is striking that Cuba, which had the largest population of Chinese in Latin America in the nineteenth century and was in many ways the most welcoming of Chinese, today has one of the smallest communities in the hemisphere. In contrast, the United States, which imposed the harshest and longest lasting restrictions on the Chinese, has by far the largest population. Based on this long-term view, restrictive immigration legislation and racist discrimination appears to have had much less impact on Chinese migration than global economic conditions. Globally, three-quarters of overseas Chinese live in other parts of Asia, and less than one-fifth live in the Americas.[17]

Making Aliens Illegal in the Postwar Era

After World War II, U.S. immigration laws slowly began to shed their racist logic and adhere to an "internal security" rationale. In the wake of the Holocaust in Europe and in the context of the Cold War with the Soviet Union, the United States tried to project an image of race neutrality and liberal immigration policies. The culmination of those efforts was the 1965 Immigration Act, which was hailed as the end of a race-based quota system but which also tightened immigration restrictions in other ways. As Mae Ngai points out, "The postwar immigration debate was never over whether to restrict, but by how much and according to what criteria."[18]

Mexico also revised its exclusionary policies toward the Chinese in the new geopolitical context. The government began to repatriate Chinese Mexicans who had been expelled from Sonora in the early 1930s. Mexican women who had married Chinese men in Mexico and lost their Mexican nationality (a law in place until 1930) were in a particularly vulnerable quasi-stateless position when they arrived in China, especially if their husbands abandoned them.[19] Repatriations from Macao began under the left-leaning president Lázaro Cárdenas in the late 1930s, but Mexican law only permitted Mexican women and their Chinese Mexican children to return, thus splitting families. In 1960 President Adolfo López Mateos restarted the program and repatriated 250–350 Chinese Mexicans and their families.[20]

Although postwar U.S. immigration acts appeared to open up more avenues for migration, they also resulted in increasing deportations and stricter enforcement. The 1952 McCarran-Walter Act maintained tight restrictions on the numbers of new immigrants at 155,000 per year, but it also continued the Western Hemisphere exemption, meaning that Mexicans could continue to migrate without quota restrictions. The act also eliminated the racial bar to citizenship that put the final stake in Asian exclusion policies. However, the Asia-Pacific quota of 100 per country applied to people of Asian descent no matter where they resided in the world, thus severely restricting Asian migration by other means. At the same time as the McCarran-Walter Act seemed to create a fairer immigration system, it also increased the government's exclusion and expulsion powers, raising the number of excludable classes from six to thirty-one. The administrative procedures for deportation were reformed, allowing aliens some rights to due process while streamlining the procedures to allow for speedier deportations. Perhaps most significantly, the act affirmed the preference for skilled workers, shifting the criteria for admission from racial preferences to education, occupation, and family ties.[21] A modicum of fairness and slight opening to previously excluded groups thus came at the expense of the solidification of the immigration restriction and deportation regime.

Although the Western Hemisphere was exempted from the McCarran-Walter Act, politicians and activists began complaining about Mexicans crossing into the United States without authorization in the 1950s. Even the liberal senator from New York Herbert Lehman criticized the act for allowing "'undesirable aliens' by the thousands to stream across the Mexican and Canadian border without any surveillance whatever."[22] As Julius Edelstein, Lehman's executive assistant, put it in a speech to social workers, "We stand triple guard, at the front door, bayonets at the ready, to repel legal immigration, while illegal immigration swarms in at the back door and through the windows."[23] The same concerns about clandestine entry through Mexico and Canada that had been the focus of Chinese restrictionists from the late nineteenth century through the 1920s were now directed at the Mexican "wetback," who became the prototypical illegal alien.

In 1942 the U.S. government, facing a wartime shortage of workers, recruited Mexican farm laborers in what became known as the Bracero program. The recruitment and employment of Mexicans by the federal government reversed long-standing nineteenth-century legislation against contract labor from the 1862 Anti-Coolie Bill to the 1885 Foran Act. When this program ended in 1964, Mexicans did not stop coming to the United States. They continued to follow the same paths and kinship networks that had been established but now they came as "illegals." The 1965 Immigration Act finally ended race-based quotas, but it also included the Western Hemisphere for the first time in its restrictions. A total annual limit was fixed at 290,000 immigrants; 170,000 were reserved for the Eastern Hemisphere and 120,000 for the Western Hemisphere. In 1976 country quotas for the Western Hemisphere were introduced, with Mexico allotted only 20,000 slots. Given that there were upward of 235,000 legal Mexican migrants annually in the early 1960s, the new quotas represented a slamming shut of the door on Mexicans in the same way that the exclusion acts had tried to keep Chinese out. And just as with the Chinese, the restrictions did not keep migrants out, but they did help criminalize them and strengthen the policing and deportation regime.

This deportation regime has ebbed and flowed over the course of the century, picking up in the 1930s, when half a million Mexicans were "repatriated," spiking in 1954 with more than 1 million apprehensions in the first year of "Operation Wetback," and then exploding since the 1980s. Ever since 1927 the United States distinguished between "forced removal" through the regular deportation process and "voluntary departure," which meant that migrants caught near the border could be returned to Mexico and bypass a formal hearing and a criminal record. By the end of the 1940s, voluntary removal far outpaced formal deportations, and by 1985 "voluntary" removal of Mexicans reached more than 1 million annually.[24] Total removals of aliens, including voluntary and forced, reached a record of over 1.8 million in 2000. Since that time, the total number of removals has shrunk to less than 1 million annually, but under the Obama administration the proportion of forced removals has increased, reaching a record of almost 400,000 annually.[25] However, even as deportations rose and the legal channels for migration tightened, immigrants used the loopholes that allowed family members of U.S. citizens to immigrate outside of the quotas.[26] The combination of quota and nonquota immigrants and continued illegal entries changed the shape and color of the U.S. population in the half a century since the 1965 Immigration Act. By 2012 more than half of the foreign-born people in the United States were from Latin America, mostly from Mexico, and a quarter from Asia. The U.S. Census Bureau estimates that by 2042, the majority of people in the United States will be nonwhite.[27] Lothrop Stoddard must be turning in his grave.

In the 1990s the pace of illegal migration to the United States, mostly from Mexico but also from China, grew so quickly that President Bill Clinton in 1993 declared human smuggling a "threat to national security."[28] By 2005 there were an estimated 11 million illegal aliens in the United States, accounting for 28 percent of the immigrant population.[29] Although estimates vary widely, the numbers of illegal Chinese entries to the United States in the 1990s far outstripped those in the late nineteenth and early twentieth centuries. One government agency estimated that 50,000 Chinese were smuggled into the United States illegally each year in the 1990s; in 1994, CIA director R. James Woolsey put the number at 100,000. Sociologist Ko-Lin Chin interviewed 300 illegal Chinese migrants in the late 1990s and found that they were tied into transnational networks organized by Triad societies and deeply enmeshed in Chinese communities throughout the Americas that would harbor and protect them.[30] Since the 1990s smuggling of Chinese migrants, mainly to the United States and Canada through third countries in Central America, South America, and Mexico, has boomed.

There is a striking resemblance between today's Chinese smuggling networks and those of a century ago. In the spring of 1995 U.S. officials noticed a pattern of groups of Chinese men arriving in Belize from Cuba on airplanes. They arrived without luggage, boarded vans, and quickly crossed the border to Guatemala; several of them were later arrested in Los Angeles. The investigation revealed that the men had traveled from China to Southeast Asia, Amsterdam, and Cuba before flying to Belize.[31] Since the early twentieth century, transportation has improved and some of the routes have shifted to take advantage of easier airplane travel. Ko-Lin Chin's study found that the average Chinese illegal migrant visited two or more sites before arriving in the United States and spent more than three months in transit. Half of these migrants arrived in the United States by airplane, often with fraudulent documents, 40 percent came across the U.S.-Mexican or U.S.-Canadian land borders, and only 12 percent arrived by boat. Migrants who arrived by boat suffered some of the worst conditions and harshest treatment, echoing the horrifying stories from the coolie ships. Many migrants who came by boat were held up to two weeks until their families could pay the smuggling fee, endured fights over food, robberies, and rape. On one ship, a Chinese woman migrant was gang raped by the captain and crew of the ship. She jumped overboard to commit suicide. On another ship a sixteen-year-old boy was forced to masturbate publicly, and two men were coerced into performing anal sex in public. Some of the passengers on this ship were so traumatized by the harassment that they attempted to commit suicide. A mutiny erupted on another ship that was being prevented from entering U.S. waters near Honolulu. The Chinese migrants seized the captain and crew, ignoring the captain's threats to blow up the ship, and sailed the vessel into U.S. waters, where they were arrested.[32]

Smuggling of so many humans across vast distances and multiple national borders could not take place without the complicity of many officials and the migrants themselves. Corrupt government officials facilitate the smuggling by selling false documents and taking bribes. The migrants themselves, however, are the ones who propel the movement. As during the coolie trade, migrants even sign contracts with the smugglers. The contracts stipulate that smugglers will hold migrants until their families deliver full payment. Why do migrants take the risk, given the expense and dangers of trying to cross illegally into the United States? Although some migrants interviewed by Chin expressed regret at their decision to migrate, most were willing to make the sacrifice to provide money to their families in China and to gain respect in their hometowns and villages. As one migrant put his reasons for migrating, "A slave turn [sic] around completely and become [sic] a master."[33] The possibility of this metamorphosis still inspires hundreds of thousands of migrants to make the dangerous journey. While Chinese migrant lifestyles in the Americas may not look like success to outsiders, they are experienced as a substantial improvement by the migrants.

As a broader global pattern, coolie labor has returned with a vengeance in the Gulf States under the *kafala* or sponsorship system. Millions of foreign workers from all over the world, principally South Asia, have been recruited since the 1970s to perform menial labor and construction work in Persian Gulf countries. The migrants often work longer hours and receive lower wages than they were promised; live in squalid, overcrowded, and segregated housing; and their sponsors hold their passports, limiting their mobility and ability to assert their basic rights.[34] The sheer size and proportion of this labor migration to the Gulf States dwarfs the coolie trade. In 2000 the foreign labor population in the Gulf States ranged from 25 percent to 75 percent of the total workforce.[35] In Qatar, the $100 billion building spree in preparation for the 2022 World Cup has led to the importation of millions of foreign workers, who now comprise an astonishing 94 percent of the workforce. According to Amnesty International and an investigation by the *Guardian*, Nepalese construction workers are dying at a rate of one a day, many suffering from heart attacks after not being allowed to eat or drink and being overworked in 120-degree heat. As one worker said, "We'd like to leave, but the company won't let us. If we run away, we become illegal and that makes it hard to find another job."[36] The coolie trade continues.

Model Minorities and Aliens

Since the mid-1960s there are two competing narratives of Chinese migrants in the Americas. The long-standing image of the poor, indebted Chinese worker as unassimilable alien remains side-by-side with that of the "model minority" who excels in school, professions, and business, and who assimilates into the nation. Nowhere is the model minority more evident than in U.S. education. Asian Americans now comprise over 70 percent of the student body at the highly competitive Stuyvesant Public High School in New York City, which bases admission solely on a standardized test. Achievement on standardized tests has been so astounding for Asian Americans that highly selective colleges have begun to require higher scores of them. Sociologist Thomas Espenshade calculated that Asian American students must score 140 points higher on the SAT than white students to have the same chance of admission.[37] At the same time, Chinese Americans are also gaining prominence in U.S. politics in states that were centers for anti-Chinese violence just a century before. Gary Locke, the former governor of Washington State (1997–2005), and David Wu, Oregon representative in the U.S. House (2004–11), were the first Chinese Americans to ever reach such high offices. The global hysteria, dubbed "Linsanity" by the media, over the 2012 exploits of Taiwanese American point guard Jeremy Shu-How Lin in the National Basketball Association illustrates new popular recognition for certain Asian Americans.

The success of Chinese Americans, however, like the rising economic strength of China, is often cast as a threat to mainstream America. Just as in the nineteenth century, seemingly positive traits like hard work and thrift can easily be cast through twisted racist logic as dangerous to other Americans. The success of Chinese Americans on tests in U.S. schools is often depicted as the product of robotic-like preparation.[38] The model minority is therefore the flip side of the poor marginalized Chinese migrant, remaining equally alien to modern liberal society.

In Cuba, Chinese became "model minorities" *avant la lettre* because of their participation in the late nineteenth-century independence wars. In 1931 work began on a memorial to commemorate Chinese *mambises* who fought during the independence wars. It was not until 1946 that the doric-style black marble column was finally inaugurated in Havana. A plaque on the pedestal quotes Gonzalo de Quesada's paraphrase of Máximo Gómez's dictum: "There was not a single Chinese Cuban deserter, there was not a single Chinese Cuban traitor."[39] Today it stands in a lonely small traffic island in

Vedado, an upscale neighborhood in Havana that has no historical connection to the Chinese community. In the 1920s and 1930s, however, the heroic Chinese *mambí* was counterposed in the popular press to more recent Chinese immigrants, who were seen as clannish, diseased, and economic competitors to Cubans. As historian Kathleen López shows, these two opposing discourses, one lauding the patriotic and pure coolies and the other criticizing the corrupt and dangerous Chinese immigrants existed side by side in the twentieth century.[40] Like the *indigenista* discourse in Latin America that glorifies an ossified indigenous past at the expense of present-day Indians, the image of the patriotic coolie serves to undermine today's Chinese who do not fit that mold.

Since the early 1990s, the Cuban government has promoted Havana's *barrio chino* in an effort to boost tourism, part of its response to the severe economic crisis that followed the collapse of the Soviet Union. A ceremonial archway has been constructed on a small street lined with a half dozen Chinese restaurants in the heart of what used to be a thriving Chinese community. One Chinese Cuban compared the 1993 visit of China's President Jiang Zemin to Havana's Chinatown to the Cuba Commission that reported on conditions of coolies in 1874.[41] In addition to creating a touristic venue, the Cuban government has an economic incentive to promote historical ties with the Chinese, given that China is now Cuba's second-largest trading partner, with annual trade that reached $1.8 billion by 2010.[42] In November 2008, on the occasion of signing trade deals with China, Cuba's president, Raúl Castro, stunned his Chinese guests by singing an ode to Mao Zedong in Chinese.[43]

In Peru, the Chinese community followed the same path as in Cuba, its population dwindling to just over 1,714 people by 1981. However, a new wave of migration began in the 1980s, reviving the same migratory networks that had existed in the nineteenth century. Poor migrants borrowed upward of $45,000 to make the journey to Peru and often worked two to four years in restaurants or shops in Lima's Chinatown to pay off their debts. By 1993 the census counted 3,728 Chinese in Peru, but this figure drastically undercounted many more undocumented Chinese. Historian Isabelle Lausent-Herrera argues that many Chinese immigrants were being channeled through Peru by Chinese criminal organizations like Dragón Rojo (Red Dragon) and then transferred either to the United States or Canada. The same kinds of smuggling networks that shuttled Chinese migrants through the Americas in the late nineteenth and early twentieth centuries still function today. As migration grew, trade between China and Peru boomed in the 1990s, going from an annual volume of $231 million in 1993 to $7.8 billion by 2008. During this same period (1993–2003) Lausent-Herrera discovered that an unprecedented 18,604 Chinese became naturalized Peruvians. Given that only 3,000 to 4,000 Chinese were registered as being in the country during this period, how could so many Chinese who were not in Peru become naturalized citizens? This high number of naturalized Peruvians could partly result from President Alberto Fujimori's policy of selling Peruvian citizenship to Chinese in the 1990s.[44] It is likely that Chinese purchased Peruvian passports so they could travel more easily to Latin America and then make their way to the United States.

The renewal of Chinatowns across Latin America, from Havana to Lima to Mexicali, since the 1990s symbolizes a redefinition of the Chinese community. No longer are these Chinatowns the sole or even the central quarters of Chinese residents; today they provide an important symbolic space for the community to gather, do business, celebrate holidays, and open restaurants and stores for tourists. Although the numbers of foreign-born Chinese in Latin America never recovered, there are signs of strengthening of Chinese identity among children born in the Americas of mixed Chinese and non-Chinese parentage. An example of this rebirth of identity can be seen in the Min Chi Tang association in Cuba, which was founded in 1887 and was finally recognized by the Cuban socialist government in 1976. By 2012 it had almost 200 members, but only twenty-four of them were foreign-born Chinese. Some of its members have discovered their Chinese ancestry recently and have developed an interest in the Chinese language and culture.[45] A similar effort to revitalize the seedy Chinatown of Mexicali, Mexico, in the late 1980s never fully succeeded, but by 1995 the population of Chinese in the city, including those of mixed-race background, was estimated to be 10,000.[46] The foreign-born Chinese immigrant community in Mexico has certainly "never recovered" as Robert Romero Chao and others argue, but a renewal of Chinese American identity can be seen across the Americas. In Peru, the children of Chinese parents or from a mixed-race background are referred to as *tusan* (tusheng). Originally designating only first- and second-generation immigrants, the term is now used more loosely to include the third generation as well.[47] The willingness of the Chinese to recognize a wider swath of mixed-race children of Chinese descent as *tusan* suggests that Chinese American identity is being reinvented, opening the possibility for a revitalization of the community by means of more inclusive identification rather than through continual arrival of new immigrants.

Returning Home: Bones and Spirits

The custom of sending bones of dead relatives back to China for their final burial suggests that Chinese migrants thought of their journey to the Americas and elsewhere as a temporary sojourn. Even if they were unable to ever return to China for a visit or to retire, they wanted their bones to rest in posterity in their home country. The ritual of bone return began in 1855 when a shipment was sent from San Francisco to Hong Kong, the first in thousands of such deliveries from overseas Chinese communities throughout the world. Burial at home was an almost universal desire for Chinese migrants, but it was not until the nineteenth century and the relative cheap transportation costs of steamships that ordinary workers could afford the two-dollar cost of shipping bones across the sea.[48] According to Elizabeth Sinn, every Panyu native had to make a "donation" of ten dollars to the Chow How Tong to guarantee a proper burial, exhumation, and reburial of bones in China. By 1913, 10,000 boxes of bones were being sent back annually. In cases where bodies could not be recovered, "spirit boxes" were returned to China. Destitute Chinese who died overseas would also have their bones returned, paid for by wealthy donors. The return of bones continued through at least 1931, when 889 boxes were returned from Vietnam and 9 from Victoria, British Columbia. Correspondence from the Tung Wah hospital in Hong Kong illustrates the vast transnational network that it had established with Vietnam, Thailand, and Myanmar, as well as Australia, Peru, Panama, the East Coast of the United States, and California. With the U.S. embargo on communist China after the 1949 Revolution, boxes of bones piled up unable to make the journey to China. With return blocked, Chinese turned their temporary cemetery outside of San Francisco into a final resting place. The choice of some Chinese who died in Hong Kong and Macao to have their remains buried in this California cemetery suggests a new sense of home in the Americas.[49]

Connections between Chinese in Cuba and their families in China were also interrupted by both the Chinese Revolution in 1949 and the Cuban Revolution in 1959.[50] When I visited Havana's Chinese cemetery in 2010, scores of metal boxes were piled precariously to the ceiling of a crypt, bones jutting out of the ones without lids. The return of the bones seemed to have stopped, leaving the migratory Chinese once again in limbo. In the postwar era some Chinese continue to be buried in the Chinese cemetery in Havana, while others with particularly strong revolutionary credentials are buried among the family graves of prominent communist leaders. When Federico

Bones in boxes in a Chinese cemetery in Havana, 2010. One of the boxes is dated from 1963, suggesting a disruption in the return of Chinese bones after the Revolution in 1959. Photograph by author.

Chi Casio died in China in 1964 on a visit from Cuba, half his ashes were left in China and the other half were returned to Cuba.[51] Like his life, his death was marked by transnational connections.

The Golden Venture

The 286 Chinese migrants who jumped into the chilly waters when the rickety *Golden Venture* tramp freighter ran aground off the Rockaway coast in Queens, New York, in 1993 are symbols of the continuing alien status of Chinese migrants. The story splashed across front pages around the world depicted poor, emaciated Chinese migrants, mutinous "snakeheads," and wealthy smugglers. The way U.S. newspapers reported the event echoed moralistic arguments against the coolie trade from the nineteenth century. One *New York Times* editorial after the incident demanded that something be done to stop illegal trafficking of Chinese. "The alternative is not just tolerating more *Golden Ventures*," the newspaper exclaimed. "It's tolerating slavery, in New York, in 1993." The migrants on the freighter were generally cast as innocent and vulnerable victims of "Asian gangs and freelance criminals [who] profited from this human traffic [and] grow increasingly rich, brazen and violent." However, it was not just the smugglers brutality that exercised the *Times*. The editorial warned that beyond the nearly 300 Chinese on the *Golden Venture* were another 100,000 just like them who succeeded in coming illegally to the United States each year.[52]

In 2006 the courts sentenced Chen Chui Ping to thirty-five years in federal prison for human trafficking and money laundering in the *Golden Venture* voyage. For her part, Sister Ping, as she was known by her Chinese migrant devotees, blamed the Triad societies that she claimed forced her to conduct the illegal trade. The way the U.S. government handled the tragedy, in which ten Chinese died while trying to swim ashore, speaks to the continuities between the harsh immigration restrictions of the late nineteenth century and our present moment. Rather than granting the Chinese asylum, the government deported 110 of them, many of whom first languished for years in prison. One of the men deported was named Dong. His request for asylum based on China's one-child policy was denied, and when he returned to China he was beaten, fined, and forcibly sterilized.[53]

The deportations, however, have not stopped the *Golden Venture* migrants. Of the 110 who were deported, half of them have returned illegally, including Dong. In 1999 Dong paid $50,000 for a false passport and returned to the United States via Los Angeles and once again sought asylum through the courts. In 2006 he was working seventy-two hours a week as a cook in a Chinese restaurant in Arkansas. The courts kept denying his appeals, arguing that his asylum had already been denied in 1993. In spite of his trials, Dong told a *New York Times* reporter, "I still hope one day to live freely in this country." Dong's daughter followed in her father's footsteps and tried to enter the United States illegally, but she was caught trying to cross the Mexican border and imprisoned. The thirty-one *Golden Venture* migrants who did not win asylum live constantly under threat of deportation. In the meantime, they opened businesses and had children who speak English and are U.S. citizens.[54]

The *Golden Venture* tragedy, and many less-publicized cases of Chinese migrants' clandestine voyages to the Americas, demonstrates that routes taken by Chinese in the nineteenth century are still functioning. In 1984 Weng Yu Hui agreed to pay $18,000 to Sister Ping to be smuggled to New

York from his village in Fujian. Sister Ping arranged for a letter to be written to Weng from fictitious relatives in Guatemala asking him to visit. With that letter, he was able to travel to Guatemala, where he met Sister Ping, and after a month there, he was transported by land to Tijuana. Ten Chinese migrants were squeezed into a false bottom in a van and driven across the border to Los Angeles. Sister Ping met Weng in Los Angeles and flew with him and the other migrants to Newark. Once in New York City, she set up Weng in an apartment in Chinatown and helped him find work in a Chinese takeout restaurant in the Bronx.[55] Newspapers and prosecutors tended to portray Sister Ping as a heartless and greedy criminal, but the Chinese who used her services revered her as a saint. After all, Sister Ping did not write the laws that made it so hard for people to migrate legally. She merely helped them evade those laws and profited in doing so. On 24 April 2014, Sister Ping died in prison. It is easy to blame the Chinese smugglers for the dangerous conditions endured by thousands of migrants, but the politicians who created the immigration restrictions bear the main responsibility for tragedies like that of the *Golden Venture*.

The immigration bureaucracies designed to track, control, and incarcerate illegal aliens are stronger than ever, and exploitative contract labor is on the rise. The dream of migration, however, still spurs thousands of Chinese and others to cross borders, legally and illegally. Faced with exclusion and discrimination in an era of globalization, migrants throughout the world have claimed rights beyond the confines of national citizenship, what scholars have begun to call "transnational citizenship."[56] Of the 286 *Golden Venture* migrants, six managed to escape in the chaos and fog of that early morning in June 1993.[57] Those six Chinese and the countless others who escape the grasp of the nation remain unnamed and hidden to journalists, politicians, and scholars. Although they exist between and betwixt nation-states, they are not lost, isolated, or deviant. They are part of a diasporic transnational world whose outlines we can only barely make out. Although that world appears on the horizon like a mirage, the aliens of the past may very well become the transnational citizens of the twenty-first century.

Notes

Abbreviations

AGN   Archivo General de la Nación, Mexico City, Mexico

AHN   Archivo Histórico de la Nación, Madrid, Spain

ANC   Archivo Nacional de Cuba, Havana, Cuba

AREM Archivo Histórico de la Secretaría de Relaciones Exteriores,
       Mexico City, Mexico

NARA National Archives and Records Administration, Washington, D.C.,
       and Seattle, Washington

Introduction

1. Marcus Braun, Immigrant Inspector, New York, to Frank P. Sargent, Commissioner General, Department of Commerce and Labor, Bureau of Immigration and Naturalization, 12 February 1907, NARA, RG 85, entry 9, 52271/74A.

2. Michel de Certeau makes a similar argument about the legibility of people walking in the city. Certeau, *Practice of Everyday Life*, 91–93.

3. For a more in-depth discussion of the promise of regions as a way to see beyond nations, see Young, "Regions."

4. Gilroy, *Black Atlantic*, 4. For an interesting critique of national history, and a proposal for writing the history of the Pacific region in a nonlinear manner, see Duara, *Rescuing History from the Nation*.

5. Marcus Braun, Immigrant Inspector, New York, to Frank P. Sargent, Commissioner General, Department of Commerce and Labor, Bureau of Immigration and Naturalization, 12 February 1907, NARA, RG 85, entry 9, 52271/74A, pp. 30–32.

6. Brandenburg, "Stranger within the Gate," 1114–15.

7. Marcus Braun, Immigrant Inspector, New York, to Frank P. Sargent, Commissioner General, Department of Commerce and Labor, Bureau of Immigration and Naturalization, 12 February 1907, NARA, RG 85, entry 9, 52271/74A.

8. Ngai, *Impossible Subjects*, 5; Lee, *At America's Gates*.

9. Simmel, *Sociology of Georg Simmel*, 402.

10. Siu, "Sojourner," 34; Siu, *Chinese Laundryman*.

11. McKeown, "Conceptualizing Chinese Diasporas."

12. Using Thailand as a counterexample to the United States, Yuen-fong Woon argues that, in addition to racism, there were internal Chinese reasons for Chinese migrants to remain sojourners. Woon, "Voluntary Sojourner among the Overseas Chinese." Mae Ngai makes a similar argument that historians emphasize Japanese internees' U.S. patriotism and overlook their dual or conflicted national identities. Ngai, *Impossible Subjects*, 199–200.

13. Lisa Lowe makes a similar point about Asian American culture in *Immigrant Acts*, 28–29.

14. Ralph, "Chinese Leak," 522. Erika Lee analyzes this image in *At America's Gates*, 167–68.

15. In Brazil, for example, despite repeated plans to recruit Chinese at the end of the nineteenth century, domestic opposition and Chinese government opposition to restarting the coolie trade after 1874 kept these efforts from getting off the ground. Lesser, *Negotiating National Identity*, chap. 2.

16. López, *Chinese Cubans*, 208.

17. Books focusing on the coolie period in Latin America include Pérez de la Riva, *Los culíes chinos en Cuba*; Yun, *Coolie Speaks*; Meagher, *Coolie Trade*; and Stewart, *Chinese Bondage in Peru*. Books and dissertations focusing on the postcoolie period include López, "Migrants between Empires and Nations"; Romero, *Chinese in Mexico*; Schiavone Camacho, *Chinese Mexicans*; and Herrera Jérez and Castillo Santana, *De la memoria a la vida pública*.

18. Some broader histories of Asians in the United States cover the preexclusion, exclusion, and postexclusion eras. See, for example, Daniels, *Asian America*. Mae Ngai breaks out of the exclusion era periodization by focusing on 1924–65 in *Impossible Subjects*. Kathleen López also traverses the historiographical divide in *Chinese Cubans*.

19. "Alien."

20. Parker, "State, Citizenship, and Territory," 637.

21. Seeman, "On the Meaning of Alienation"; Dean, "Alienation."

22. Ko-Lin Chin's interviews of 300 Chinese migrants to the United States in the 1990s reveal a variety of different views, from extreme alienation to belief that the United States was great to willingness to sacrifice for family. Chin, *Smuggled Chinese*, 128–31.

23. Marcus Braun, Immigrant Inspector, New York, to Frank P. Sargent, Commissioner General, Department of Commerce and Labor, Bureau of Immigration and Naturalization, 12 February 1907, NARA, RG 85, entry 9, 52271/74A, p. 32.

24. Ibid., 41–42.

25. Cohen, *Chinese in the Post–Civil War South*, 156; Romero, *Chinese in Mexico*, 71; Schiavone Camacho, *Chinese Mexicans*, 31–34.

26. M. A. Beach, representative of Vancouver Trades and Labor Council, at annual convention of Washington Federation of Labor, Tacoma, 1907, quoted in Chang, *Pacific Connections*, 96. For an excellent analysis of transnational anti-Chinese ideologies in white settler societies, see Lake and Reynolds, *Drawing the Global Colour Line*.

27. Stoddard, *Rising Tide of Color against White World Supremacy*, 281, 268, 301.

28. Cohen, *Chinese in the Post–Civil War South*, 167–68.

29. Knight, "Racism, Revolution and *Indigenismo*," 86–87; Bonfil Batalla, *México Profundo*, 115–18.

30. For a good discussion of racial democracy in Cuba, see Fuente, *Nation for All*; and Helg, *Our Rightful Share*.

31. Mariátegui, *Seven Interpretive Essays on Peruvian Reality*, 279.

32. Shah, *Stranger Intimacy*, 6, 7, 67.

33. In her study of Chinese in Panama, Lok Siu found that her informants engaged in similar circuitous open-ended journeys, crossing multiple national boundaries over an extended period in what she refers to as "serial migration." Siu, "Serial Migration," 144–45.

34. Ong, *Flexible Citizenship*, 6.

35. Mae Ngai's book about the Chinese American Tape family is just one story of gaining social acceptance through upward mobility. Ngai, *Lucky Ones*. For more on Chinese brokers, also see Mar, *Brokering Belonging*; Chang, *Pacific Connections*; and Cohen, *Chinese in the Post–Civil War South*.

Chapter 1

1. Holden, "Chapter in the Coolie Trade." Newspaper accounts provided a different death toll than the one Holden gave. His *Harper's* article also includes a typo suggesting that the *Norway* mutiny occurred in 1857 rather than 1859. "Terrible Mutiny: Revolt of Coolies on Board a New York Ship—Thirty Killed and Ninety Wounded," *New York Times*, 26 March 1860.

2. Holden, "Chapter in the Coolie Trade."

3. Ibid., 3–4.

4. Ibid., 4–5.

5. William Reed, U.S. Legation to China, to Lewis Cass, U.S. Secretary of State, 13 January 1858, United States Senate, *Executive Documents*, 59–62.

6. Irick, *Ch'ing Policy toward the Coolie Trade*, 16–20.

7. Nicasio Cariete y Moral, Consul General of Spain, to S. B. Rawle, U.S. Consul, Macao, 8 January 1858, United States Senate, *Executive Documents*, 76–77.

8. William Reed, U.S. Legation to China, to Lewis Cass, U.S. Secretary of State, 13 January 1858, United States Senate, *Executive Documents*, 62.

9. Meagher, *Coolie Trade*, 190.

10. Ibid., 174–79. According to one report by the British governor in Hong Kong, mutinies and disaster struck the coolie ships thirty-four times between 1845 and 1872. Of these cases, twenty-six involved violent revolts by the coolies. "Memorandum of the Coolie Ships on Board of Which Mutinies Have Occurred, or in Which the Vessels or Passengers Have Met with Disaster, from the Year 1845 up to the Year 1872," in *British Parliamentary Papers*, 4:386–87.

11. Lubbock, *Coolie Ships and Oil Sailors*, 49.

12. Meagher, *Coolie Trade*, 179.

13. For discussions of Chinese coolie mutinies, see Hu-Dehart, "La Trata Amarilla." Also see Meagher, *Coolie Trade*, chap. 5; Lubbock, *Coolie Ships and Oil Sailors*; and Narvaez, "Chinese Coolies in Cuba and Peru," 107–28. For an analysis of literature describing coolie mutinies, see Yun, "Under the Hatches."

14. Klein et al., "Transoceanic Mortality," table VI (a), p. 4.

15. Northrup, *Indentured Labor in the Age of Imperialism*, 89–90, 108–10, 156, 163; Meagher, *Coolie Trade*, 172.

16. Klein et al. provide a lower number of Chinese mortality for passages to the Americas (9.9%), but Meagher's and Northrup's data are more complete for the Chinese. Klein et al., "Transoceanic Mortality," table III.

17. Rediker, *Slave Ship*, 5; Klein et al., "Transoceanic Mortality." Klein et al. estimate a mortality rate for Chinese indentured labor to the Americas (1847–74) of only 9.9 percent, but Meagher's estimates seem more accurate and detailed. Meagher, *Coolie Trade*, 169–73.

18. Pérez de la Riva, *Los culíes chinos en Cuba*, 93.

19. California Department of Insurance, "Slavery Era Insurance Registry."

20. Lawrence, *Visitation and Search*, 157.

21. *The Friend of China*, 5 January 1861, quoted in Meagher, *Coolie Trade*, 166.

22. "Instructions Which Should Be Put in Practice on Board Vessels Carrying Asiatic Passengers from the Port of Macao," *British Parliamentary Papers*, 4:401–3.

23. "Reglamento para la introducción y régimen de los colonos españoles chinos o yucatecos en la isla de Cuba, Real Decreto de 22 de marzo de 1854," in Jiménez Pastrana, *Los chinos en la historia de Cuba*, 161–74.

24. Meagher, *Coolie Trade*, 169.

25. During the coolie era, 750,000 Chinese emigrated from Hong Kong and Macao, but statistics from other ports along the coast are unavailable; at least as many and probably more emigrated to Southeast Asia from these ports. Ibid., 61.

26. These figures are for immigrant arrivals, meaning that one individual may have entered and therefore be represented more than once in the data. The data for the United States and Canada are much more reliable than for Latin America in the postcoolie period. The data for Latin America include estimates for the British West Indies during the period of indenture (1830–1917) but do not include free migrants. The other data are culled from sources on Cuba, Peru, and Mexico, which were the main but not the only receiving countries for Chinese migrants. The Latin American estimates are the very lowest figures because important periods are missing data. Nonetheless, these estimates give a sense of the scale of migration to the Americas and the relative size of that migration to the United States and Latin America.

27. Kuhn, *Chinese among Others*, 107–12.

28. Ibid., 13–16, 27, 110.

29. Meagher, *Coolie Trade*, 66–71.

30. Pérez de la Riva, *Los culíes chinos en Cuba*, 16; Stewart, *Chinese Bondage in Peru*, 17. For discussion of the various estimates for Chinese migration to Cuba and estimate of Chinese to British Guiana, see Meagher, *Coolie Trade*, 206–8, 250.

31. McKeown, *Melancholy Order*, 48–49.

32. Kuhn, *Chinese among Others*, 186–92.

33. Irick, *Ch'ing Policy toward the Coolie Trade, 1847–1878*, 11–12; Kuhn, *Chinese among Others*, 87.

34. "Imperial Edict against Unauthorized Migration, 1728," quoted in Kuhn, *Chinese among Others*, 19–20.

35. Laú, the governor general of the Two Kwangs, made a further declaration, 2 January 1860, United States House, "Chinese Coolie Trade," 15.

36. Harry Parkes would become British consul and be appointed to the Allied Commission following the Arrow War of 1857, in which the British and French attacked and occupied Canton. Harry Parkes, "General Remarks on Chinese Emigration," in *British Parliamentary Papers*, 3:39.

37. "American Ships and the Coolie Trade," *New York Times*, 4 August 1860.

38. John E. Ward, American Legation, Macao, to Lewis Cass, Secretary of State, 24 January 1860, United States House, "Chinese Coolie Trade," 2.

39. Yen, *Coolies and Mandarins*, 93.

40. Macao was a Portuguese territory even though it was not officially recognized as such by the Chinese government; in 1849 Portugal stopped paying the lease it had convened with China almost 300 years earlier. Ibid., 53.

41. Kuhn, *Chinese among Others*, 135–38.

42. Yen, *Coolies and Mandarins*, 90–100.

43. Ibid., 94, 101–15, 155–57.

44. Irick, *Ch'ing Policy toward the Coolie Trade*, 14.

45. John Bowring to Earl of Malmesbury, 17 May 1852, in *British Parliamentary Papers*, 3:12.

46. John Bowring, Hong Kong, to Earl of Malmesbury, 3 August 1852, in *British Parliamentary Papers*, 3:4.

47. Adam W. Elmslie, Consul, Canton, to Bowring, 25 August 1852, in *British Parliamentary Papers*, 3:17.

48. Francis Darby Syme, "Minutes of Evidence Taken at the Court of Inquiry Held at Amoy to Investigate the Causes of the Late Riots, and into the Manner in Which Coolie Emigration Has Been Lately Carried on at That Port," 13 December 1852, in Campbell, *Chinese Coolie Emigration to Countries within the British Empire*, 97. For a description of the Amoy riot, see also *British Parliamentary Papers*, 3:59–62.

49. Yen, *Coolies and Mandarins*, 48–52.

50. Yun, *Coolie Speaks*.

51. "Proclamation Issued by the Scholars and Merchants of Amoy," in *British Parliamentary Papers*, 3:83–84.

52. Ibid., 3:84.

53. "Petition of Chin Sha," December 1852, in *British Parliamentary Papers*, 3:108.

54. Frederick Harvey to John Bowring, Hong Kong, 22 December 1852, in *British Parliamentary Papers*, 3:52–53.

55. Ibid., 3:53.

56. Minutes of Consular Court at Amoy, 18 December 1852, in *British Parliamentary Papers*, 3:49–51.

57. Petitions of Lae Chinse, Kwo Chin She, Le, Hien, and Chin Sha, December 1852, in *British Parliamentary Papers*, 3:106–8.

58. Paper Read in Court by Vice Consul Blackhouse to Mr. Connolly, in *British Parliamentary Papers*, 3:93.

59. Ibid., 93–95.

60. Wang, Subprefect of Amoy, "Proclamation," 25 November 1852, and "Further Proclamation," 27 November 1852, in *British Parliamentary Papers*, 3:94–95.

61. John Bowring, Hong Kong, to Earl of Malmesbury, 7 February 1853, in *British Parliamentary Papers*, 3:112–13.

62. "China: Kidnapping Coolies—Excitement at Shanghai," *New York Times*, 21 October 1859.

63. Yen, *Coolies and Mandarins*, 81–82.

64. Meagher, *Coolie Trade*, 75.

65. Kuhn, *Chinese among Others*, 127. Benjamin Narvaez makes a similar point, emphasizing coercion of the labor recruiters, in "Chinese Coolies in Cuba and Peru," 101–3.

66. Gideon Nye Jr., Vice Consul of the United States for Macao, to John E. Ward, Envoy Extraordinary and Plenipotentiary of the United States, 25 November 1859, United States House, "Chinese Coolie Trade," 27–28.

67. Antonio Sergio de Souza to Minister of Marine and Colonies, 10 November 1871, in *British Parliamentary Papers*, 4:260.

68. McKeown, *Melancholy Order*, 44.

69. For an excellent analysis of the testimonies in the Cuba Commission Report, see Yun, *Coolie Speaks*.

70. Helly, *Cuba Commission Report*, 36–37.

71. Ibid., 69.

72. These statistics are derived from the 962 coolies who left from Macao and gave testimony to the Cuba Commission. Ibid., 37.

73. Kuhn, *Chinese among Others*, 113–14.

74. Statement of Albert Herker before the Magistracy, Hong Kong, 19 May 1871, in *British Parliamentary Papers*, 4:274.

75. Acting Governor Whitfield to Earl of Kimberley, 24 May 1871, in ibid., 267–68.

76. "Six-Hundred and Fifty Packed into a Ship—Six Hundred Perish in the Flames," *New York Times*, 22 June 1871.

77. Statement of Wong Ahfhat before the Magistracy, Hong Kong, 16 May 1871, in *British Parliamentary Papers*, 4:268–69.

78. Statements of Wong Ahfhat, Lum Apak, So Ayung, and Chan-a-Sin before the Magistracy, Hong Kong, 16–17 May 1871, in *British Parliamentary Papers*, 4:268–73.

79. Helly, *Cuba Commission Report*, 38–42.

80. Ethnographies of contract laborers in the Gulf States today echo coolie accounts of being coerced, misinformed, and unable to defend their basic rights. Gardner, "Why Do They Keep Coming?"

81. Cohen, *Chinese in the Post–Civil War South*, 49–76; Jung, *Coolies and Cane*, 4. Roger Daniels notes that in the nineteenth century "informed commentators" differentiated between involuntary migration to plantations in the Pacific, the Indian Ocean, and Latin America and the voluntary migration to North America. Daniels, *Asian America*, 14. Arnold Meagher's *Coolie Trade* only discusses Latin America.

82. Meagher, *Coolie Trade*, 136–39.

83. "Arrival of Coolies at San Francisco," *New York Times*, 30 June 1882.

84. Stevens, "Brokers between Worlds," 111.

85. *El Comercio*, 10 June 1868, quoted in Stewart, *Chinese Bondage in Peru*, 148.

86. William Stafford Jerningham, Lima, to Earl of Clarendon, 9 March 1869; "Extract from the Lima 'Comercio' of February 27, 1869"; Mendes Leal, Lisbon, to Charles A. Murray, 8 January 1870, in *British Parliamentary Papers*, 4:247–53; Stewart, *Chinese Bondage in Peru*, 149.

87. John Bowring, Hong Kong, to the Earl of Malmesbury, 3 August 1852, in *British Parliamentary Papers*, 3:14.

88. Jose Tavares Mondo, Acting Director General, Department of Marine and Colonies, Lisbon, 29 August 1871, in *British Parliamentary Papers*, 4:286.

89. Ibid., 4:283–85.

90. Ibid., 286.

91. Richard Graves MacDonnell to the Earl of Kimberley, Hong Kong, 8 January 1872, in *British Parliamentary Papers*, 4:287–89. Statistics about dead Chinese in Macao in *Daily Advertiser*, 8 January 1872, in *British Parliamentary Papers*, 4:291.

92. T. W. C. Murdoch to Herbert, 2 November 1871, in *British Parliamentary Papers*, 4:291–93.

93. Benjamin D. Manton, Master of American Ship Messenger, to John E. Ward, Envoy Extraordinary and Minister Plenipotentiary to China, United States House, "Chinese Coolie Trade," 4–5.

94. The rest of the ships flew under the flags of a host of European nations, as well as those of Peru, El Salvador, and Chile. Meagher, *Coolie Trade*, table 11, p. 149.

95. Ibid., 184; Stewart, *Chinese Bondage in Peru*, 152–98.

96. Dana, *To Cuba and Back*, 195–96.

97. Ibid., 196.

98. Trefoil, *South Pacific Times*, 27 May, 7 August 1873, quoted in Stewart, *Chinese Bondage in Peru*, 81.

99. Quoted in Zegarra, *La condición jurídica de los extranjeros en el Perú*, 128.

100. Helly, *Cuba Commission Report*, 47–48.

101. Patterson, *Slavery and Social Death*, 54–55.

102. Trefoil, *South Pacific Times*, 27 May 1873, quoted in Stewart, *Chinese Bondage in Peru*, 92–93.

103. Ibid., 93; Rippy, "Henry Meiggs," 112.

104. Abbott, *South and North*, 50–51.

105. "The Coolie Trade," *New York Times*, 19 July 1873.

106. Townshend, *Wild Life in Florida*, 197.

107. Ibid., 199–200.

108. Stewart, *Chinese Bondage in Peru*, 5, 13–14.

109. Ibid., 118–19, 126–27.

110. Patterson, *Slavery and Social Death*, 33–34.

111. Meagher, *Coolie Trade*, 184–85.

112. Pär Kristoffer Cassel argues that extraterritoriality was not just a Western imposition but also part of an older Chinese practice to incorporate foreigners into the Chinese orbit. Cassel, *Grounds of Judgment*.

113. Kuhn, *Chinese among Others*, 110–11, 137.

114. "Piracy and Murder," *New York Times*, 6 December 1868.

Chapter 2

1. Whitelaw, *After the War*, 417, quoted in Jung, *Coolies and Cane*, 79.

2. Jung, *Coolies and Cane*, 4.

3. "Coolies and Hoodlums," *New York Times*, 15 August 1874.

4. "Labor at the South: The Introduction of Coolies," *New York Times*, 7 April 1867.

5. "The Cooly Importation," *Harper's Weekly*, 31 August 1867, 546–47.

6. Lesser, *Negotiating National Identity*, 18–19.

7. Simon-Nicolas-Henri Linguet, *Théories des lois civiles, etc.* (London, 1767), 472, quoted in Marx, *Theories of Surplus Value*, 349.

8. "British Philanthropy: The Coolies at the Chincha Islands," *New York Times*, 24 January 1854.

9. Davis, *Inhuman Bondage*, 30–31; Patterson, *Slavery and Social Death*, 13.

10. Patterson, *Slavery and Social Death*, 6.

11. Brown, "Social Death and Political Life in the Study of Slavery," 1236.

12. Coolies were equivalent to what Achille Mbembe refers to as the "living dead." Mbembe, "Necropolitics," 11, 40.

13. Stewart, *Chinese Bondage in Peru*, 19; "Reglamento para la introducción y régimen de los colonos españoles, chinos y yucatecos en la isla de Cuba, Real Decreto, 22 de marzo de 1854," in Jiménez Pastrana, *Los chinos en la historia de Cuba*, 161–67.

14. "Chie Lom Contract," in Trefoil, *South Pacific Times*, 19 June 1873, quoted in Stewart, *Chinese Bondage in Peru*, 42.

15. Stewart, *Chinese Bondage in Peru*, 26–27.

16. "Chie Lom Contract," in Trefoil, *South Pacific Times*, 19 June 1873, quoted in Stewart, *Chinese Bondage in Peru*, 43.

17. "Editorial," *La Patria*, 17 March 1874; "Some Friends of Justice," *El Comercio*, 15 September 1870, quoted in Stewart, *Chinese Bondage in Peru*, 44–45.

18. "Reglamento para la introducción de trabajadores chinos en la isla de Cuba, 6 de julio de 1860," in Jiménez Pastrana, *Los chinos en la historia de Cuba*, 183.

19. "Virginia Slave Code 1705" and "Code Noir (1685) in Louisiana," in Drescher and Engerman, *Slavery*, 121, 117.

20. "Cuban Slave Code 1842," in Drescher and Engerman, *Slavery*, 136–37.

21. Patterson, *Slavery and Social Death*, 22.

22. Sumner, *What the Social Classes Owe to Each Other*, 26.

23. "Commerce in Coolies," *New York Times*, 12 April 1856.

24. Appendix K, "Form of an Agreement," *British Parliamentary Papers*, 3:89.

25. "Chie Lom Contract," in Trefoil, *South Pacific Times*, 19 June 1873, quoted in Stewart, *Chinese Bondage in Peru*, 43.

26. Fraginals, "Plantations in the Caribbean," 18.

27. "Chinese Laborer's Contract for Indenture for Cuba," in Meagher, *Coolie Trade*, 358–60.

28. Stewart, *Chinese Bondage in Peru*, 19.

29. Meagher, *Coolie Trade*, 360. "Reglamento para la introducción y régimen de los colonos españoles en la Isla de Cuba, Real Decreto de 22 de marzo de 1854," in Jiménez Pastrana, *Los chinos en la historia de Cuba*, 162.

30. Pérez de la Riva, *Los culíes chinos en Cuba*, 38.

31. Arona, *La inmigración en el Perú*, 43.

32. Cohen, *Chinese in the Post-Civil War South*, 117.

33. T. Chisolm Anstey, Attorney-General, Hong Kong, 26 March 1858, in *British Parliamentary Papers*, 4:98.

34. Ibid.

35. "Reglamento para la introducción y régimen de los colonos españoles, chinos o yucatecos en la Isla de Cuba, Real Decreto de 22 de marzo de 1854," Articles 5 and 7, in Jiménez Pastrana, *Los chinos en la historia de Cuba*, 161–62.

36. Consul of Spain, Amoy, to Consul General of Spain in China, 22 July 1859, in AHN, Ultramar, Fomento, leg. 85-6.

37. Translation into Spanish of article in *Hong Kong Daily Mail*, 4 December 1857, included in Gov. of Philippines to Min. of State, 14 January 1858, AHN, Ultramar, leg. 85-5.

38. Quoted in Helly, *Cuba Commission Report*, 38–39.

39. Benjamin, "Critique of Violence," 243.

40. "Reglamento del Gobierno para el manejo y trato de los colonos asiáticos e indios," 10 April 1849, in Jiménez Pastrana, *Los chinos en la historia de Cuba*, 153–54.

41. Stewart, *Chinese Bondage in Peru*, 21–23.

42. *El Peruano*, March 1856, quoted in Arona, *La inmigración en el Perú*, 45–46.

43. Stewart, *Chinese Bondage in Peru*, 25–27.

44. Ibid., 116–17.

45. "Reglamento del Gobierno para el manejo y trato de los colonos asiáticos e indios," 10 April 1849, in Jiménez Pastrana, *Los chinos en la historia de Cuba*, 154–55; Pérez de la Riva, *Los culíes chinos en Cuba*, 208.

46. "Reglamento del Gobierno para el manejo y trato de los colonos asiáticos e indios," 10 April 1849, in Jiménez Pastrana, *Los chinos en la historia de Cuba*, 156.

47. Consejo de Administración, ANC, leg 8/605, quoted in Pérez de la Riva, *Los culíes chinos en Cuba*, 224–25.

48. Peloso, "Racial Conflict and Identity Crisis in Wartime Peru," 471.

49. Arona, *La inmigración en el Perú*, 43.

50. Ibid., 50–53.

51. Peloso, "Racial Conflict and Identity Crisis in Wartime Peru," 474–83.

52. Arona, *La inmigración en el Perú*, 51.

53. Peloso, "Racial Conflict and Identity Crisis in Wartime Peru," 473.

54. Arona, *La inmigración en el Perú*, 51.

55. Ibid.

56. Ibid., 50–52.

57. Ibid., 52–53.

58. *La Verdad* (New York), 15 October 1850, no. 70, quoted in Pérez de la Riva, *Los culíes chinos en Cuba*, 206.

59. Ampère, *Promenade en Amérique*, quoted in Pérez de la Riva, *Los culíes chinos en Cuba*, 206–7.

60. Dana, *To Cuba and Back*, 88.

61. Townshend, *Wild Life in Florida*, 200.

62. Pérez de la Riva, *Los culíes chinos en Cuba*, 208.

63. "Reglamento para la introducción y régimen de los colonos españoles en la Isla de Cuba, Real Decreto de 22 de marzo de 1854," in Meagher, *Coolie Trade*, table 13, p. 169.

64. Stanley, *From Bondage to Contract*, 18, 29.

65. *Reglamento para la introducción de los trabajadores chinos en la isla de Cuba*, quoted in Jiménez Pastrana, *Los chinos en la historia de Cuba*, 183.

66. Dorsey, "Identity, Rebellion, and Social Justice," 22.

67. Helly, *Cuba Commission Report*, 115.

68. "The Coolie Trade," *New York Times*, 19 July 1873.

69. "Reglamento para la introducción y régimen de los colonos españoles en la isla de Cuba, Real Decreto de 22 de marzo de 1854," quoted in Jiménez Pastrana, *Los chinos en la historia de Cuba*, 172.

70. Ibid., 170.

71. Pérez de la Riva, *Los culíes chinos en Cuba*, 215–17.

72. Helly, *Cuba Commission Report*, 42–47, 50, 99–109.

73. Pérez de la Riva, *Los culíes chinos en Cuba*, 186–89.

74. Howe, *Trip to Cuba*, 219.

75. José Antonio Saco, "La estadística criminal en Cuba," *La América* (Madrid), 12 February 1864, quoted in Pérez de la Riva, *Los culíes chinos en Cuba*, 188.

76. Pérez, *To Die in Cuba*, 23.

77. "Discurso del Sr. Regente de la Real Audiencia Pretorial de la Apertura de Tribunales y Juzgados en el año que empieza de 1858," *Revista de Jurisprudencia* 3 (1858): 55, quoted in Pérez, *To Die in Cuba*, 55.

78. Huc, *Chinese Empire*, quoted in Pérez, *To Die in Cuba*, 63.

79. Ibid., 61–63.

80. "British Philanthropy: The Coolies at the Chincha Islands," *New York Times*, 24 January 1854.

81. "Reglamento para la introducción y régimen de los colonos españoles en la Isla de Cuba, Real Decreto de 22 de marzo de 1854," quoted in Jiménez Pastrana, *Los chinos en la historia de Cuba*, 166.

82. Pérez de la Riva, *Los culíes chinos en Cuba*, 188.

83. Fernando Ortiz, *Hampa afrocubana*, 322.

84. Quoted in Dorsey, "Identity, Rebellion, and Social Justice," 21.

85. "Reglamento para la introducción de trabajadores chinos en la isla de Cuba," in Pérez de la Riva, *Los culíes chinos en Cuba*, 215–17.

86. "Decreto del Gobierno Superior acerca de las contratas de chinos, antes y después de febrero de 1861," 14 September 1872, in Jiménez Pastrana, *Los chinos en la historia de Cuba*, 166.

87. "Legislación sobre asiáticos," *Boletín de Colonización*, 15 May 1873.

88. Scott, *Seeing Like a State*, esp. chap. 1.

89. Jiménez Pastrana, *Los chinos en la historia de Cuba*, 178, 180.

90. "Reglamento para la introducción y régimen de los colonos españoles en la Isla de Cuba, Real Decreto de 22 de marzo de 1854," in Jiménez Pastrana, *Los chinos en la historia de Cuba*, 161–76.

91. "Testimoniado sobre introducir en la isla de seis a ocho mil colonos asiáticos con destino a la agricultura," 31 January 1852, AHN, Ultramar, 85-1; Ultramar to Min. de Estado, 5 May 1866, AHN, Ultramar, 85-9.

92. Jiménez Pastrana, *Los chinos en la historia de Cuba*, 167, 173. Joseph Dorsey argues that because the coolies were not expected to form families and become part of Cuban society, homosexuality among the Chinese was tolerated if not accepted. Dorsey, "Identity, Rebellion, and Social Justice," 24, 42.

93. Miguel de los Santos to Min. de Estado, 8 June 1854, AHN, Ultramar 85-3.

94. Report of commission named to examine issue of Asian immigration to Cuba, 3 September 1852, in AHN, Ultramar, 85-1.

95. "Memorandum Concerning Legislation of Spanish and Colonial Governments Regarding Chinese Immigrants," in Helly, *Cuba Commission Report*, 125.

96. Ibid., 126.

97. Helly, *Cuba Commission Report*, 75–76.

98. "Memorandum Concerning Legislation of Spanish and Colonial Governments Regarding Chinese Immigrants," in Helly, *Cuba Commission Report*, 126.

99. Dorsey, "Identity, Rebellion, and Social Justice," 41.

100. Jiménez Pastrana, *Los chinos en la historia de Cuba*, 163–64.

101. Stewart, *Chinese Bondage in Peru*, 134–35.

102. Peru, *Memoria que presenta al congreso ordinario de 1876 el ministro de gobierno, policía y obras públicas*, xxvi.

103. Ibid., xxvi–xxvii.

104. "Coolies for the South," *New York Times*, 26 July 1867.

105. Jung, *Coolies and Cane*, 52.

106. Ibid., 67. For more on the convention, see Cohen, *Chinese in the Post-Civil War South*, 65–81.

107. Jung, *Coolies and Cane*, 99–104.

108. Ibid., 110–17.

109. "Coolies in New Jersey," *New York Times*, 22 September 1870. Koopmanschap also

went to China in 1875 as a representative of a company from Rio de Janeiro that wanted to import 10,000 coolies. "Coolies for Brazil," *New York Times*, 27 February 1875.

110. Cohen, *Chinese in the Post–Civil War South*, 106–7.

111. Letter from Salina Cruz, Mexico, to Immigration Bureau, 20 July 1909, NARA, RG 85, entry 9, 52229/1E.

112. Quoted in Jung, *Coolies and Cane*, 120–22.

Chapter 3

1. Arendt, *Origins of Totalitarianism*, 293–96.

2. Kuhn, *Chinese among Others*, 135–38, 240–43.

3. McKenzie, *Oriental Exclusion*, 9.

4. Chang, "Chinese in Latin America," 23; Jiménez Pastrana, *Los chinos en la historia de Cuba*, 133–34.

5. McKeown, *Chinese Migrant Networks and Cultural Change*, 135–36.

6. Hsu, *Dreaming of Gold, Dreaming of Home*; Lee, *At America's Gates*; Delgado, *Making the Chinese Mexican*; Schiavone Camacho, *Chinese Mexicans*; Romero, *Chinese in Mexico*. Recent dissertations on the subject include Mandujano López, "Transpacific Mexico"; and Chang, "Outer Crossings." See also Yun, *Coolie Speaks*; and López, *Chinese Cubans*. For an insightful analysis of Chinese coolies in Cuba and Peru, see Narvaez, "Chinese Coolies in Cuba and Peru."

7. Lee, "Orientalisms in the Americas"; Hawk, "Going Mad in Gold Country." Marilyn Lake and Henry Reynolds use a global framework to examine race in white settler societies. Lake and Reynolds, *Drawing the Global Colour Line*.

8. Adam McKeown's work provides both hemispheric and global perspectives on Chinese migration. McKeown, *Chinese Migrant Networks*, 3–5; McKeown, *Melancholy Order*. Erika Lee's current project to narrate the history of Asians in the Americas from the sixteenth century to the present is an example of the move toward transnational histories of Asians in the Americas. For an overview of this idea, see Lee, "Orientalisms in the Americas."

9. Quoted in "Chinese Coming from Mexico," *New York Herald*, 11 November 1888, AREM, 15-2-69, p. 83. The newspaper mistakenly indicated that this was Article 2 of the constitution instead of Article 11. For the original text of the constitution, see *Constitución Federal 1857*, Archivo General de la Nación, www.agn.gob.mx/constitucion1857/constitucion1857.html (accessed 1 December 2011).

10. Y. L. Vallarta to Ignacio Mariscal, Minister of SRE, 20 January 1891, AREM, 7-11-28, p. 9.

11. Ibid., 10.

12. Ibid.

13. Anghie, *Imperialism, Sovereignty and the Making of International Law*, 17–21.

14. Samuel Pufendorf, *The Law of Nature and Nations* (1688), quoted in McKeown, *Melancholy Order*, 24–25.

15. Emmerich de Vattel, *The Law of Nations* (1758), quoted in McKeown, *Melancholy Order*, 25–26.

16. "Act Providing for the Relief and Support, Employment and Removal of the Poor," 488–93.

17. Parker, "State, Citizenship, and Territory," 623–25.

18. Zolberg, *Nation by Design*, 4–5, 75, 111.

19. United States House and Senate, *Act to Prohibit the "Coolie Trade,"* 340–41.

20. Jung, *Coolies and Cane*, 37–38.

21. Salyer, "'Laws Harsh as Tigers,'" 3–5; Salyer, *Laws Harsh as Tigers*.

22. Hirota, "Moment of Transition."

23. Salyer, *Laws Harsh as Tigers*, 12–13.

24. Ibid., 15.

25. *Report of the Royal Commission on Chinese Immigration*, xi.

26. Anderson, *Vancouver's Chinatown*, 37, 50.

27. *Report of the Royal Commission on Chinese Immigration*, cxxvi.

28. "The Honorable Commissioner Gray's Report Respecting Chinese Immigration in British Columbia," in ibid., v.

29. Anderson, *Vancouver's Chinatown*, 50–51, 57–58.

30. *Report of the Royal Commission on Chinese Immigration*, cxxxiii–cxxxiv.

31. Anderson, *Vancouver's Chinatown*, 53, 61–62.

32. Canadian Human Rights Commission, "Human Rights in Canada."

33. Origins of the Population, Census of Canada, www.statcan.gc.ca (accessed 12 June 2012).

34. Chinese Head Tax Searchable Database, University of British Columbia, chrp.library.ubc.ca/headtax_search/ (accessed 12 June 2012).

35. In 1916, there were an estimated 16,000 Chinese in British Columbia compared to a white population of 129,000. Anderson, *Vancouver's Chinatown*, 53, 61–62.

36. "Asiatic Influx Fast Becoming Grave Menace," *Vancouver World*, 17 July 1917, in Public Archives Canada, Immigration Branch, RG 76, vol. 474, file 799921, pt. 1.

37. Ibid., 140–41.

38. Compañía de Colonización Asiática, "Estatutos."

39. Cott, "Mexican Diplomacy and the Chinese Issue," 65–66; Romero, *Chinese in Mexico*, 25–26.

40. *Ontario Times*, 27 October 1888, clipping in AREM, 15-2-69.

41. For an excellent study of the importance of steamship lines between Asia and Mexico in the forging of transpacific ties, see Mandujano López, "Transpacific Mexico."

42. "Contrato, Compañía Mexicana de Navegación del Pacífico," Carlos Pacheco, L. Larraza, E. E. Guillermo Vogel, and Salvador Malo, 10 March 1884, AREM, 44-6-35.

43. Telegram, Fernández, special Mexican envoy, London, to SRE, 6 October 1884, AREM, 44-6-35.

44. Ignacio Mariscal, London, to SRE, 15 November 1884, AREM, 44-6-35, p. 29.

45. Spenser St. John, British special envoy, Mexico City, to SRE, 22 December 1884;

Edward Winfield, London, to Theodor Schneider, representative for Mexican Pacific Navigation Company, 19 February 1885; Lionel Carden, British Legation in Mexico, to Ignacio Mariscal, 1 May 1885, AREM, 44-6-35.

46. Mandujano López, "Transpacific Mexico," 100–101.

47. Cott, "Mexican Diplomacy and the Chinese Issue," 69.

48. Harrison Gray Otis, Los Angeles, to A. P. Wilder, U.S. Consul, Hong Kong, 21 December 1908, NARA, RG 85, entry 9, 52271/70.

49. F. H. Larned to Inspector in Charge, San Diego, 18 June 1909; "Translation of Contract for Laborers Working for the Land Investment and Cattle Rearing Company of the United States," NARA, RG 85, entry 9, 52271/70.

50. Oscar S. Straus, Secretary of Commerce and Labor, to Elihu Root, Secretary of State, 12 January 1909, NARA, RG 85, entry 9, 52271/70.

51. Mandujano López, "Transpacific Mexico," 146–47.

52. Romero cites a statistic that the Chinese population reached 24,218 by 1926, and Kenneth Cott, who argues that the census undercounted Chinese, cites the figure of 19,000 by 1930. Romero, *Chinese in Mexico*, 55–56; Cott, "Mexican Diplomacy and the Chinese Issue," 70.

53. In Cuba in 1950 there were 4.4 Chinese per 1,000, while in the United States there were only 0.7 per 1,000. Chang, "Chinese in Latin America," 3.

54. "Translation of Petition," 27 March 1899, AREM, 17-21-55, pp. 5–6.

55. "Translation of Letter from Certain Chinese of Tampico," 13 June 1899, AREM, 17-21-55, p. 4.

56. Representative of Ferrocarril Central de México to SRE, 31 August 1899, in Oficial Mayor to SRE, 2 September 1899, AREM, 17-21-55, p. 15.

57. H. R. Nickerson, General Manager of Ferrocarril Central de México, to Han Sing, 6 July 1898, translation into Spanish, AREM, 17-21-55, pp. 16–17.

58. Manuel de Aspiroz, Ambassador to the United States, Washington, D.C., to Wu Ting-Fang, Chinese Minister Plenipotentiary, 19 September 1899, AREM, 17-21-55, p. 21.

59. Colección Porfirio Díaz (CPD), leg. 24, docs. 7174–76, quoted in Cott, "Mexican Diplomacy and the Chinese Issue," 71.

60. "Los chinos en México," *El Tráfico*, 8 February 1899, no. 501, p. 2, in Monteón González and Trueba Lara, *Chinos y antichinos en México*, 37.

61. "A propósito de los chinos," *El Tráfico*, 11 February 1899, no. 508, p. 2, in ibid., 38–39.

62. "Contra los chinos," *El Tráfico*, 11 March 1899, no. 530, p. 1, in ibid., 45.

63. "Sobre los chinos," *El Tráfico*, 2 March 1899, no. 525, p. 1; "Los chinos en México," *El Tráfico*, 8 February 1899, no. 501, p. 2, in ibid., 42, 37–38.

64. "Los chinos," *El Tráfico*, 6 June 1899, no. 601, p. 1, in ibid., 52.

65. "Pro bono público," *El Tráfico*, 7 March 1899, no. 526, p. 1, in ibid., 42.

66. "Cuidado con los chinos," *El Tráfico*, 11 March 1899, no. 530, p. 1, in ibid., 44.

67. "La lepra," *El Tráfico*, 13 March 1899, no. 531, p. 1, in ibid.

68. "Los chinos," *El Tráfico*, 2 March 1899, no. 522, p. 2, in ibid., 40.

69. "La higiene de los chinos: Que dice la comisión?," *El Tráfico*, 29 March 1899, no. 545, p. 1, in ibid., 51.

70. "Los chinos," *El Tráfico*, 6 June 1899, no. 601, p. 1, in ibid., 53.

71. Lake and Reynolds, *Drawing the Global Colour Line*, 181–89.

72. "Gray's Report," in *Report of the Royal Commission on Chinese Immigration*, xxvi, cxxvi.

73. Salyer, *Laws Harsh as Tigers*, 13, 18.

74. Anderson, *Vancouver's Chinatown*, 128, 142.

75. Matías Romero to SRE, 17 March 1892, AREM, 15-2-69, pp. 190–91.

76. S. F. Maillefert, Consul in Eagle Pass, to SRE, 23 April 1892, AREM, 18-27-31, pp. 4–5.

77. Jefe Político, Ciudad Juárez, to SRE, 31 August 1904, AREM, VII (N) 15-37, p. 1.

78. Cott, "Mexican Diplomacy and the Chinese Issue," 79–80.

79. "Arrest of Chinese Mexican," *New York Tribune*, 17 May 1892, AREM, 18-27-31, p. 2a.

80. Martínez Sánchez, *Monclova en la revolución*, 163 (n. 159).

81. S. F. Maillefert, Consul in Eagle Pass, to SRE, 16 May 1892, AREM, 18-27-31, pp. 6–8.

82. "Los Estados Unidos contra Foon Chuck," Eagle Pass, 14 May 1892, translation into Spanish, AREM, 18-27-31, pp. 9–10.

83. "Mexico and the Chinese," *Washington Post*, 18 May 1892, AREM, 18-27-31, p. 2a.

84. *New York Post*, 17 May 1892, clipping in AREM, 18-27-31, p. 2a.

85. "Chinese Mexicans," unknown newspaper clipping in AREM, 15-2-69, p. 191a.

86. Ibid.

87. Ignacio Mariscal to U.S. Minister, AREM, 7-11-28, 16 July 1892, p. 31.

88. "Lista de chinos naturalizados mexicanos desde el 16 de julio de 1892 hasta el 29 de marzo de 1899," AREM, 15-7-94, p. 4.

89. "John's Latest Scheme," *San Diego Union*, 24 September 1892, AREM, 15-5-1.

90. Coolidge, *Chinese Immigration*, 296.

91. Ibid., 295.

92. William H. Taft, "Rules Governing the Granting and Issuing of Passports in the United States," 28 May 1909, NARA, RG 85, entry 9, 52088/64, box 419.

93. Department of Commerce and Labor to State Department, 23 October 1905, NARA, RG 85, entry 9, 52088/64, box 419.

94. Acting Commissioner General, "Memorandum: Issuance of Passports to Chinese Persons Claiming to Be American Citizens by Birth," 10 October 1905, NARA, RG 85, entry 9, 52088/64, box 419.

95. Department of Labor and Commerce, 26 September 1910, NARA, RG 85, entry 9, 52088/64A box 419.

96. George E. Anderson, American Consul General, Hong Kong, 5 October 1911, NARA, RG 85, entry 9, 52088/64A, box 419.

97. Matías Romero to SRE, 13 April 1896; A. Lomeli, Consul of San Diego to SRE, 3 April 1896; Anthony Godbe, U.S. Consul in Ensenada, 28 March 1896, AREM, T 440, pp. 123–31.

98. Matías Romero to SRE, 26 April 1896, AREM, T 440, p. 322.

99. Pedro A. Magana to SRE, 27 March 1899, AREM, 15-7-94, p. 11.

100. Powell Clayton, U.S. Ambassador, Mexico City, to Ignacio Mariscal, Foreign Minister, 22 June 1899, AREM, 15-7-94, p. 14.

101. U.S. Secretary of Treasury to U.S. Secretary of State, 10 June 1899, AREM, 15-7-94, p. 15.

102. McKeown, *Melancholy Order*, 42.

103. "The Honorable Commissioner Gray's Report Respecting Chinese Immigration in British Columbia," in *Report of the Royal Commission on Chinese Immigration*, v.

104. Herrera Jérez and Castillo Santana, *De la memoria a la vida pública*, 23, 28.

105. Matías Romero to SRE, 17 April 1886, AREM, T 354, pp. 1071–72.

106. *The World* (Philadelphia), 13 April 1886; "Chinese Emigration to Mexico," *New York Herald*, 13 April 1886; *Philadelphia Press*, 13 April 1886, AREM, 15-2-69, pp. 48–49.

107. Matías Romero to George Childs, 9 May 1886, AREM, 15-2-69, p. 57.

108. "Extracts from Report of Consul Richardson, U.S. Consul at Matamoros, May 13, 1891," in *Laws of the American Republics Relating to Immigration and Sale of Public Lands*, Bureau of the American Republics, 52nd Congress, 1st session, Senate, exec. doc. 149, part 4, p. 110; Romero, *Chinese in Mexico*, 59.

109. "Anti-Chinese Feeling in Mexico," *San Francisco Call*, 7 April 1886, AREM, 15-2-69, p. 50.

110. Ibid.

111. "To Colonize Chinamen: A Movement to Settle All Celestials in This Country in Mexico," *New York Recorder*, 17 May 1892, clipping in AREM, 18-27-31, p. 2a.

112. "Is John Chinaman to Go?," *New York Times*, clipping in AREM, 44-12-59.

113. Jacoby, "Between North and South."

114. "Chinese Colonists in Mexico," *Washington Post*, 17 May 1892, clipping in AREM, 44-12-59.

115. McKeown, *Chinese Migrant Networks*, 44–45.

Chapter 4

1. Pfaelzer, *Driven Out*; Daniels, *Asian America*, 59–66.

2. Lee, *At America's Gates*, 49–52.

3. In 1907, the immigrant fund also began to receive extra money from "fines and rentals." Bureau of Immigration, *Annual Report of the Commissioner General of Immigration to the Secretary of Commerce and Labor (1913)*, 31.

4. Lytle Hernández, *Migra!*, 26–27. The 1917 Immigration Act applied a head tax to Mexicans, for the first time, but within three months farm growers pressured the government to exempt Mexican laborers from the head tax, literacy test, and contract labor clauses. Ettinger, *Imaginary Lines*, 142–43.

5. Bureau of Immigration, *Annual Report of the Commissioner General of Immigration (1913)*, 32.

6. Bureau of Immigration, *Annual Report of the Commissioner General of Immigration to the Secretary of Commerce and Labor (1911)*, 11, 166–67.

7. Bureau of Immigration, *Annual Report of the Commissioner General of Immigration to the Secretary of Labor (1904)*, 163–64.

8. Ettinger, *Imaginary Lines*, 96, 129, 141.

9. Bureau of Immigration, *Annual Report of the Commissioner General of Immigration (1911)*, 170; Bureau of Immigration, *Annual Report of the Commissioner General of Immigration to the Secretary of Labor (1930)*, 32–34.

10. Bureau of Immigration, *Annual Report of the Commissioner General of Immigration to the Secretary of Labor (1904)*, 94.

11. Bureau of Immigration, *Annual Report of the Commissioner General of Immigration (1911)*, 170.

12. Bureau of Immigration, *Annual Report of the Commissioner General of Immigration to the Secretary of Labor (1916)*, xxiv.

13. Bureau of Immigration, *Annual Report of the Commissioner General of Immigration to the Secretary of Labor (1921)*, 13.

14. Bureau of Immigration, *Annual Report of the Commissioner General of Immigration to the Secretary of Labor (1922)*, 3, 9.

15. Bureau of Immigration, *Annual Report of the Commissioner General of Immigration to the Secretary of Labor (1924)*, 30–31.

16. Bureau of Immigration, *Annual Report of the Commissioner General of Immigration to the Secretary of Labor (1925)*, 14; Bureau of Immigration, *Annual Report of the Commissioner General of Immigration (1930)*, 33, 43.

17. Data culled from financial reports in Bureau of Immigration, *Annual Report of the Commissioner General of Immigration to the Secretary of Labor (1920–1930)*.

18. Lytle Hernández, *Migra!*, 33.

19. Bureau of Immigration, *Annual Report of the Commissioner General of Immigration (1930)*, 39.

20. Bureau of Immigration, *Annual Report of the Commissioner General of Immigration (1911)*, 168; Salyer, "'Laws Harsh as Tigers,'" 58–61.

21. Salyer, *Laws Harsh as Tigers*, 80–82; *United States v. Sing Tuck*, 194 US 161 (1904).

22. Salyer, *Laws Harsh as Tigers*, 108–11.

23. Bureau of Immigration, *Annual Report of the Commissioner General of Immigration to the Secretary of Labor (1904)*, 139.

24. Judge John R. Hazel, "In Matter of Applications of Ho Jung, Ley, Jeung Bow, Lee Tuck, and Lee Moy for Writs of Habeas Corpus, U.S. District Court, Western District of New York," 14 August 1914, NARA, RG 85, E135, box 3, folder 309/11.

25. Salyer, "'Laws Harsh as Tigers,'" 79–80, 84.

26. Ibid., 82.

27. Dillingham, *Immigration Situation in Canada*, 42–43, 58–59, 44.

28. Ibid., 43.

29. Bureau of Immigration, *Annual Report of the Commissioner General of Immigration (1911)*, 142–43.

30. Salyer, *Laws Harsh as Tigers*, 115.

31. Based on statistics culled from ibid., 89–90; Bureau of Immigration, *Annual Report of the Commissioner General of Immigration (1913)*, table 7, p. 147.

32. Bureau of Immigration, *Annual Report of the Commissioner General of Immigration (1930)*, 22.

33. Bureau of Immigration, *Annual Report of the Commissioner General of Immigration (1913)*, 254.

34. Bureau of Immigration, *Annual Report of the Commissioner General of Immigration to the Secretary of Labor (1904)*, 163–64.

35. Bureau of Immigration, *Annual Report of the Commissioner General of Immigration (1911)*, table 7, p. 117.

36. Dillingham, *Immigration Situation in Canada*, 52–55.

37. Williams, "Chinese Must Go," 372–73, 378; Coolidge, *Chinese Immigration*, 210.

38. Daniel Keefe, "Operation of Present Immigration Law," in Dillingham, *Immigration Situation in Canada*, 52–55.

39. "Report of Hearing, Department of Labor, Conducted by Shirley D. Smith, Immigrant Inspector of Lum Sing (aka Chew Chee, aka Chew Quan Ng An), through Interpreter T. W. G. Wallace," 22 September 1914, NARA, RG 85, E 135, box 1.

40. "Adjourned Hearing in the Case of Alien Lee Foo, alias Lee Fook, Plattsburgh, New York," 10 December 1919, NARA, RG 85, E 135, box 4, folder 309/26.

41. "Report of Record of Hearing in the Case of Alien Charley Sun, alias Ching Hoy Soon," 21 August 1914, NARA, RG 85, E135, box 2, Chinese Smuggling File, 8–9.

42. Ibid., 2.

43. John H. Jenkins, Immigrant Inspector, Corpus Christi, to Inspector in Charge, San Antonio, 27 August 1914, in U.S. Department of Labor to Samuel Backus, Commissioner of Immigration, Angel Island Station, 2 September 1914, NARA, RG 85, E135, box 2, Chinese Smuggling File.

44. F H. Larned, Acting Commissioner General, to Inspector in Charge, Galveston, 25 August 1914, NARA, RG 85, E135, box 2, Chinese Smuggling File.

45. A. E. Leston, 25 August 1914, Matamoros, in U.S. Department of Labor to Samuel Backus, Commissioner of Immigration, Angel Island Station, 2 September 1914, NARA, RG 85, E135, box 2, Chinese Smuggling File.

46. G. R. Ohlin, Inspector, Buffalo, to Inspector in Charge, 30 January 1915, NARA, RG 85, E 135, box 1.

47. Thomas Thomas, Immigrant Inspector, Cincinnati, to Inspector in Charge, Cleveland, 17 March 1920, NARA, RG 85, E135, box 3, folder 309/6, Chinese Smuggling File.

48. Lee, *At America's Gates*, 190–91.

49. Mar, *Brokering Belonging*, 27–29.

50. Chin Chung, alias, Chin Taing, Department of Commerce and Labor Emigration Service, 8 October, 1912; "Application for Alleged American-Born Chinese for Preinvestigation Status," 12 July 1911; United States Commissioner's Court, Northern District of New York, 28 October 1902, NARA-Seattle, RG 85, Port of Vancouver, British Columbia, 1905–25, box 1, Van 12.

51. John F. Dunton, Chinese Immigrant Inspector, Vancouver, B.C., 29 April 1914, NARA Seattle, RG 85, Port of Vancouver, British Columbia, 1905–25, box 1, Van 30.

52. Translated letters, Chinese Inspector, New York City, 6 January 1916, NARA, RG 85, entry 9, 53990/162.

53. "In the Matter of Dea Kay Sing," Globe, Ariz., 15 September 1919, NARA, RG 85, E 135, box 4, folder 309/14.

54. "Memorandum reservado: Inmigración clandestina de chinos," 7 July 1930, AREM, IV-397-3.

55. Interim Commerce Representative, Chinese Legation, to Aaron Saenz, Subsecretary of SRE, 14 November 1923, AREM 38-9-65.

56. Mar, Brokering Belonging, 27.

57. Testimony of Chinamen Onboard the Remplaza, 21 May 1920, NARA, RG 85, E135, box 3, folder 309/10, esp. pp. 32, 36.

58. Anderson, Vancouver's Chinatown, 58.

59. Lee, At America's Gates, 190–91.

60. Lau, Paper Families, 25; Pfaelzer, Driven Out, 297–331.

61. Lee, At America's Gates, 84–85, 125; Coolidge, Chinese Immigration, 471.

62. Wang, In Search of Justice, 194.

63. Cowley's Report on Canadian Border, 9 December 1905, in "Compilation from the Records of the Bureau of Immigration of Facts Concerning the Enforcement of the Chinese Exclusion Laws," NARA RG 85, entry 9, 52600/48, part 2, pp. 220–22.

64. Coolidge, Chinese Immigration, 482–83.

65. President Theodore Roosevelt, 16 May 1905, quoted in Daniel Keefe, "Memorandum for Assistant Secretary, 'Re: Circumstances Which Led to the Discontinuance of Making of Arrests of Chinese Unlawfully in the Interior Districts of the US,'" 8 June 1909, NARA, RG 85, entry 9, 52516/10.

66. Daniel Keefe, "Memorandum for Assistant Secretary, 'Re: Circumstances Which Led to the Discontinuance of Making of Arrests of Chinese Unlawfully in the Interior Districts of the US,'" 8 June 1909, NARA, RG 85, entry 9, 52516/10.

67. V. H. Metcalf, Secretary, Department of Commerce and Labor, "Circular No. 91," 24 June 1905, NARA, RG 85, entry 9, 52516/10.

68. Assistant Commissioner General, "Memorandum for the Commissioner General," 27 October 1913, NARA, RG 85, entry 9, 52516/10.

69. Ettinger, Imaginary Lines, 76–96.

Chapter 5

1. Dick Hoerder argues that back door was a racialized term used only for entry from Mexico, but it was also used frequently for entry from Canada. Hoerder, "Migration, People's Lives, Shifting and Permeable Borders," 31.

2. Bureau of Immigration, Annual Report of the Commissioner General of Immigration to the Secretary of Labor (1930), 1.

3. "The Chinese Bill in the Senate," *New York Times*, 17 February 1879; Salyer, *Laws Harsh as Tigers*, 14.

4. Gibson and Jung, "Historical Census Statistics on the Foreign-Born Population of the US," 1.

5. U.S. Census Bureau, quoted in Daniels, *Asian America*, table 3.1.

6. Bureau of Immigration, *Annual Report of the Commissioner General of Immigration (1930)*, table 86, pp. 212–14, table 287, p. 216.

7. The growth in the Chinese U.S. citizen population must be due to natural growth rates as well as entry of Chinese with fraudulent U.S. citizenship papers. In 1900 women made up less than 1 percent of Chinese entries, but the proportion of women steadily increased to 25 percent by 1930. Lee, *At America's Gates*, 116; Liu, "Comparative Demographic Study," 55.

8. *Secretary of Treasury in Response to Senate Resolution of March 28, 1890*, 51st Congress, 1st session, exec. doc. 97, in AREM, 15-2-69, pp. 99–102.

9. In his ethnographic study, Paul Siu similarly found that the exclusion laws kept Chinese migrants from returning to China for fear that they would be unable to reenter the United States. Siu, *Chinese Laundryman*, 202.

10. Lee, *At America's Gates*, 12. Statistic on entries during exclusion era also cited in Lee, "Defying Exclusion," 1.

11. Liu, "Comparative Demographic Study," 51.

12. Daniels, *Asian America*, 67–68, 96.

13. William Windom, Sec. of Treasury, to President of Senate, 19 April 1890, "Letter from Secretary of Treasury," 51st Congress, 1st session, exec. doc. 106, AREM, 15-2-69, p. 119.

14. For an excellent discussion of the transit privilege for Japanese migrants through North America, see Geiger, "Caught in the Gap."

15. Moore, *Digest of International Law*, 232–33. Also see Geiger, "Caught in the Gap," 201.

16. Coolidge, *Chinese Immigration*, 288.

17. Bureau of Immigration, *Annual Report of the Commissioner General of Immigration to the Secretary of Labor (1904)*, 148.

18. Dillingham, *Immigration Situation in Canada*, 64.

19. Bureau of Immigration, *Annual Report of the Commissioner General of Immigration to the Secretary of Commerce and Labor (1913)*, 25.

20. Siu, *Chinese Laundryman*, 203.

21. Averages derived from tables 1 and 72 of AR-CGI (1920–29); Bureau of Immigration, *Annual Report of the Commissioner General of Immigration to the Secretary of Labor (1904–30)*.

22. Information culled from AR-CGI (1904–30); for data on 1918, see Bureau of Immigration, *Annual Report of the Commissioner General of Immigration to the Secretary of Labor (1922)*, table 1, p. 150.

23. According to Helen Chen, 193,795 Chinese transited through the United States be-

tween 1894 and 1940. Chen, "Chinese Immigration into the United States," tables 15 and 17.

24. In the fiscal year ending June 30, 1913, 9,136 seamen deserted. Bureau of Immigration, *Annual Report of the Commissioner General of Immigration (1913)*, 26; Bureau of Immigration, *Annual Report of the Commissioner General of Immigration to the Secretary of Labor (1925)*, 21–22.

25. Bureau of Immigration, *Annual Report of the Commissioner General of Immigration to the Secretary of Labor (1921)*, 8.

26. Coolidge, *Chinese Immigration*, 290.

27. Lee, *At America's Gates*, 151.

28. Lau, *Paper Families*, 33.

29. Fry started with the population of Chinese in 1910 and added to that all the registered entries, plus the estimated the number of possible births. Then he subtracted the registered departures and deaths in that decade to arrive at a maximum population. The difference between the maximum population he derived from the registered entries and exits, and the census figure for 1920 equaled the number of illegal entries. Fry calculated that as many as 50,000 but probably 27,000 Chinese and Japanese entered between 1910 and 1920. Fry, "Illegal Entry of Orientals into the United States between 1910 and 1920," 174–76.

30. Calculations based on 1920 and 1930 U.S. Census; and Bureau of Immigration, *Annual Report of the Commissioner General of Immigration (1930)*, tables 86 and 87, pp. 212–16.

31. Cott, "Mexican Diplomacy and the Chinese Issue," 72.

32. Bureau of Immigration, *Annual Report of the Commissioner General of Immigration to the Secretary of Commerce and Labor (1911)*, 168.

33. Memorandum, in "Re: Measures Which Are Adopted by Chinese Persons to Secure Admission to and Residence within the United States, in Defiance of the Chinese Exclusion Treaty and Laws," NARA, RG 85, entry 9, 52600/48

34. Interview with Mr. F. W. Berkshire, Supervising Inspector, Immigration Service, stationed at San Antonio, in "Re: Chinese Smuggling in El Paso District," C. R. Hillyer, 20 June 1908, NARA, RG 85, entry 9, 52541/45.

35. Several stories of Chinese clandestine migrants dying in the process of being smuggled into the United States are recounted in Siu, *Chinese Laundryman*, 201.

36. Marcus Braun, Immigrant Inspector, New York, to Frank P. Sargent, Commissioner General, Department of Commerce and Labor, Bureau of Immigration and Naturalization, 12 February 1907, NARA, RG 85, entry 9, 52271/74A.

37. Ibid.

38. Ibid.

39. Ibid.

40. Ralph, "Chinese Leak," 515–20.

41. Ibid., 525.

42. Ibid., 520.

43. "Portland a Headquarters for Smugglers of Chinese Coolies," *Portland (Oregon) Telegram*, 16 November 1899, in NARA, RG 85, entry 9, 52730/84 #9.

44. Bureau of Immigration, *Annual Report of the Commissioner General of Immigration to the Secretary of Labor (1904)*, 138.

45. Boston Chamber of Commerce, "Resolution Adopted by the Board of Directors," 11 November 1909, NARA, RG 85, entry 9, 52516/22A.

46. John H. Clark, Commissioner, Montreal, to Commissioner General, 28 October 1909, NARA, RG 85, entry 9, 52165/22A.

47. From 1896 to 1906, 836,597 immigrants were admitted, and from 1906 to 1915, there were 2,278,396 admitted. "Ethnic Origin of Immigrants Admitted to Canada, 1896–1961," Department of Citizenship and Immigration, *Immigration Statistics*.

48. Charles L. Babcock, Immigrant Inspector, Buffalo, to Commissioner General, 3 August 1908, NARA, RG 85, entry 9, 52165/1.

49. John. H. Clark, Commissioner, Montreal, to Commissioner General, 28 October 1909, NARA, RG 85, entry 9, 52165/22A.

50. Samuel D. Dodds, Chinese Inspector, Niagara Falls, to Richard H. Taylor, Immigrant Inspector, Washington, D.C., 21 September 1914, NARA, RG 85, E 135, box 1.

51. Siener, "Through the Back Door," 53.

52. Commissioner of Immigration, Montreal, quoted in Bureau of Immigration, *Annual Report of the Commissioner General of Immigration (1922)*, 13.

53. G. Oliver Frick, Inspector in Charge, to Inspector in Charge, Cleveland, 19 September 1914, NARA, RG 85, E 135, box 1.

54. John Smith, Rock Island, Illinois, to Customs House, Buffalo, 12 March 1917, NARA, RG 85, E 135, box 3, folder 309/7.

55. James, Inspector in Charge, St. Louis, to Richard Taylor, Buffalo, 23 March 1917, NARA, RG 85, E 135, box 3, folder 309/7.

56. Sterling P. Helmick, Inspector, Buffalo, to H. R. Landis, Inspector in Charge, Buffalo, 18 November 1914, NARA, RG 85, E135, box 3, Chinese Smuggling File.

57. Samuel D. Dodds, Inspector, Buffalo, to Richard H. Taylor, Washington, D.C., 20 December 1914, NARA, RG 85, E 135, box 1.

58. William R. Baldwin, Inspector in Charge, Niagara Falls, to John H. Clark, Commissioner of Immigration, Montreal, 5 December 1914, NARA, RG 85, E 135, box 1.

59. D. A. Ansell, Consul General, Montreal, to SRE, 21 May 1907, AREM, 27-3-110.

60. "Report of the Chief Controller of Chinese Immigration, W. D. Scott," Public Archives Canada, Immigration Branch, RG 76, vol. 474, file 799921, pt. 1.

61. S. J. Buford, Office of Inspector in Charge, Victoria B.C., U.S. Dept. of Labor, to Commissioner of Immigration, Montreal, 2 December 1914, NARA, RG 85, E 135, box 1.

62. King, "Report of the Royal Commission," 70–71.

63. Ettinger, *Imaginary Lines*, 90–92.

64. Cott, "Mexican Diplomacy and the Chinese Issue," 72.

65. Interview with Mr. F. W. Berkshire, Supervising Inspector, Immigration Service, stationed at San Antonio, in "Re: Chinese Smuggling in El Paso District, C. R. Hillyer," 20 June 1908, NARA, RG 85, entry 9, 52541/45.

66. "Chinamen Coming in from Mexico," *New York Times*, 14 November 1892, clipping in AREM, 15-5-57, p. 2.

67. "The Mexican Leak," *San Francisco Examiner*, 11 April 1890, AREM, 15-2-69, p. 85.

68. John R. Berry, Collector of Customs, San Diego, to Secretary of Treasury, 7 April 1890, in "Letter from Secretary of Treasury," 51st Congress, 1st session, exec. doc. 97, part 2, AREM, 15-2-69, p. 103.

69. John R. Booth, Collector of Customs, San Diego, to Secretary of Treasury, 9 April 1890, in "Letter from Secretary of Treasury," 51st Congress, 1st session, exec. doc. 97, part 2, AREM, 15-2-69, p. 103.

70. "'John' Gets Fare Paid," *Washington Post*, 29 July 1910, AREM, Leg 352, exp. 2 (July–August 1910).

71. Ibid.

72. "Smuggling Chinese from Mexico," *New York Evening Star*, 29 April 1890, AREM, 15-2-69, p. 115.

73. Matías Romero, Mexican Ambassador, to SRE, 17 April 1890, AREM, 15-2-69, pp. 106–8.

74. Collector T. G. Phelps to Sec. of Treasury, 12 April 1890, "Letter from Secretary of Treasury," 51st Congress, 1st session, exec. doc. 97, part 4, AREM, 15-2-69, p. 118.

75. "Stopping the Chinese," *New York Sun*, 16 April 1890, AREM, 15-2-69, p. 109.

76. "Coming by Way of Mexico," *New York Herald*, 30 April 1890, AREM, 15-2-69, p. 115.

77. Matías Romero to SRE, 17 April 1890, AREM, T 391, pp. 614–15.

78. "A Peculiar Compact," *San Diego Union*, 24 November 1892, AREM, 15-5-57.

79. Ibid.; "Kidnapped the Chinaman," *Washington Post*, 25 November 1892, AREM, 15-5-57.

80. "As You Like It," *San Diego Union*, 27 November 1892, and "His Side of It," *San Diego Union*, 28 November 1892, AREM, 15-5-57.

81. "The Fuentes Gang," *Los Angeles Times*, 31 May 1894.

82. Ibid.; Luis G. Bolsero to SRE, 6 December 1893, AREM 15-5-57.

83. "Copia de la sentencia pronunciada en la causa instruida contra Ildefonso C. Fuentes y socios por plagio," 16 April 1897, AREM, 15-5-57.

84. *Los Angeles Herald*, 9 January 1893, AREM, 15-5-57.

85. Lau, *Paper Families*, 2–4.

86. Richard Taylor to Commissioner General, 5 October 1909, NARA, RG 85, entry 9, 52229/1E.

87. Ibid.

88. Office of Inspector in Charge, Seattle, to Commissioner General, 28 October 1910; F. R. Larned, Acting Commissioner General, to Commissioner of Immigration, Philadelphia, 13 October 1909, NARA, RG 85, entry 9, 52229/1E.

89. Letter from Salina Cruz, Mexico, to Immigration Bureau, 20 July 1909, NARA, RG 85, entry 9, 52229/1E.

90. Ibid.

91. Annual Report of Inspector in Charge, El Paso, 30 June 1905, NARA, RG 85, entry 9, 52600/48, part 2.

92. Ettinger, *Imaginary Lines*, 137–39.

93. Clarence A. Miller, U.S. Consul, Matamoros, "Possibilities of Present Conditions Favorable for Smuggling Chinese and Other Immigrants to the US," Confidential Report to Secretary of State, 28 April 1909, NARA, RG 85, entry 9, 52265/6.

94. Johnson, *Revolution in Texas*.

95. Ettinger, *Imaginary Lines*, 136–37.

96. Supervising Inspector of the Mexican border district, quoted in Bureau of Immigration, *Annual Report of the Commissioner General of Immigration (1922)*, 14.

97. F. P. Sargent, Commissioner General, to I. C. Slater, P & O Steamship Co., 21 October 1904, NARA, RG 85, entry 9, 52085/, Part 7, box 419; F. P. Sargent, Commissioner General, to James Twohey, 20 February 1908, NARA, RG 85, entry 9, 51831/28; Rick K. Campbell, Special Immigrant Inspector, Memo, 21 October 1904, NARA, RG 85, entry 9, 51831/28.

98. Daniel J. Keefe, Commissioner General, to James Twohey, Attorney, Peninsular & Occidental SS Co., Washington, D.C., 30 January 1909, NARA, RG 85, entry 9, 51831/28.

99. Office of Solicitor, Department of Commerce and Labor, 19 January 1909, NARA, RG 85, entry 9, 51831/28.

100. James Twohey to Daniel J. Keefe, Commissioner General, 7 January 1909, NARA, RG 85, entry 9, 51831/28.

101. Herrera Jérez and Castillo Santana, *De la memoria a la vida pública*, 23, 28.

102. "Chinese Smuggling Trade Unearthed on Gulf Coast," *New Orleans Daily Picayune*, 5 January 1909, NARA, RG 85, entry 9, 52229/1A.

103. A. P. Schell, Immigrant Inspector, to Commissioner General, 29 May 1909, NARA, RG 85, entry 9, 52229/1D.

104. "Los Estados Unidos contra Foon Chuck," Eagle Pass, 14 May 1892, translation into Spanish, AREM, 18-27-31, pp. 9–10.

105. Richard Taylor to Commissioner General, 5 October 1909, NARA, RG 85, entry 9, 52229/1E.

106. Ibid.

107. R. A. Haynes, Immigration Inspector, to Office of Inspector in Charge, Laredo, Texas, 27 December 1908, NARA, RG 85, entry 9, 52229/1D.

108. Acting Commissioner General to Inspector in Charge, New Orleans, 2 December 1908, NARA, RG 85, entry 9, 52229/1.

109. Alfred Hampton, Inspector, Galveston, to Richard H. Taylor, Inspector, Washington, D.C., 9 April 1914, NARA, RG 85, E135, box 2, Chinese Smuggling File.

110. Richard H. Taylor, Inspector, Buffalo, to A. W. Brough, New Orleans, 25 April 1914, NARA, RG 85, E135, box 2, Chinese Smuggling File.

111. "Statement Taken on Board SS 'Minnesota,'" 5 October 1914, NARA, RG 85, E135, box 3, Chinese Smuggling File.

112. Ibid.

113. J. E. Williams, Inspector, Norfolk, Virginia, to Richard H. Taylor, Inspector, Washington, D.C., 6 February 1920, NARA, RG 85, E135, box 3, Chinese Smuggling File.

114. Ibid.

115. J. Hughes, Gloucester, to Taylor, Confidential, 23 May 1919, NARA, RG 85, E135, box 3; Greenwalt to Taylor, 23 December 1919, NARA, RG 85, E135, box 3; Albert B. Wiley, Inspector, New York and New Jersey, to Taylor, Los Angeles, 1 July 1920, NARA, RG 85, E135, box 3, folder 309/10.

116. W. O. Downey, Richmond, Virginia, to U.S. Dept. of Labor, 14 February 1920, NARA, RG 85, E135, box 3, Chinese Smuggling File.

117. Taylor to Inspector in Charge, Norfolk, Virginia, 11 August 1916, NARA, RG 85, E135, box 3, Chinese Smuggling File.

118. Inspector, Los Angeles, to Inspector in Charge, Galveston, 13 February 1919, NARA, RG 85, E135, box 3, folder 309/9.

119. Inspector in Charge, Jacksonville, Florida, quoted in Bureau of Immigration, *Annual Report of the Commissioner General of Immigration (1922)*, 13–15.

120. "Gigantic Plot to Smuggle Chinese into US Believed Uncovered Here," *Tampa Sunday*, 23 May 1920, NARA, RG 85, E135, box 3, folder 309/10.

121. "Investigation in Connection with the Seizure of the Cuban Fishing Smack 'Reemplazo,' off Anclote Light, Florida, May 14, 1920," p. 42, NARA, RG 85, E135, box 3, folder 309/10.

122. Testimony of Chinamen onboard the *Remplaza*, 21 May 1920, NARA, RG 85, E135, box 3, folder 309/10, esp. pp. 32, 36.

123. Taylor, Los Angeles, to Inspector, Calexico, 10 June 1920, NARA, RG 85, E135, box 3, folder 309/10.

124. William A. Whalen, Inspector in Charge, Tampa, to Inspector in Charge, Jacksonville, 28 May 1920, NARA, RG 85, E135, box 3, folder 309/10.

125. Inspector, Buffalo, to Commissioner General of Immigration, Washington, D.C., 14 March 1917, NARA, RG 85, E135, box 3, folder 309/10.

126. Francisco E. Menocal, Immigration Commissioner, Havana, to Daniel Trasivuk, Immigration Service, Galveston, 17 March 1920, NARA, RG 85, E135, box 3, folder 309/10.

127. Chin Yuk, Havana, to Taylor, Los Angeles, translated from the Chinese, 31 May 1920, NARA, RG 85, E135, box 3, folder 309/10.

128. Ngai, *Lucky Ones*, ix.

129. Ibid., 120–21.

130. Fung Ming testified about the custom of Chinese marriage names in an exclusion case. Hom Lay Jong v. Nagle, no. 6639, Circuit Court of Appeals Ninth Circuit, 4 April 1932.

131. "Testimony of Jew Hing," 21 May 1920, p. 29, NARA, RG 85, E135, box 3, folder 309/10.

132. Fung Ming, Interpreter, to Commissioner of Immigration, New Orleans, 26 May 1920, NARA, RG 85, E135, box 3, folder 309/10.

133. Translated letter from Yee Yun, Tampa Jail, to Dew Fong and Seung Fong, 22 May 1920, NARA, RG 85, E135, box 3, folder 309/10.

134. Confidential, Inspector in Charge, Los Angeles, to Inspector, San Francisco, 10 June 1920, NARA, RG 85, E135, box 3, folder 309/10.

135. William T. Christy, Commissioner, New Orleans, to Commissioner General of Immigration, Washington, D.C., 6 February 1919, NARA, RG 85, E 135, box 3, folder 309/9.

136. William T. Christy, Commissioner, New Orleans, to R. H. Taylor, Los Angeles, 23 May 1919, NARA, RG 85, E 135, box 3, folder 309/9.

137. Martin Turnbull, Inspector, Pascagoula, Mississippi, to Commissioner, New Orleans, 17 March 1920, NARA, RG 85, E135, box 3, folder 309/9.

138. Fung Ming, Interpreter, to Commissioner, 22 March 1920, NARA, RG 85, E135, box 3, folder 309/9.

139. Fung Ming, Interpreter, to W. T. Christy, Commissioner of Immigration, New Orleans, 26 November 1919, NARA, RG 85, E135, box 3, folder 309/10.

140. Copy of Fung Ming, Interpreter, report, sent by William Christy, New Orleans, to Taylor, 21 August 1919, NARA, RG 85, E135, box 3, folder 309/9.

141. Pérez, *Cuba: Between Reform and Revolution*, 225.

142. Inspector in Charge, Jacksonville, Florida, quoted in Bureau of Immigration, *Annual Report of the Commissioner General of Immigration (1922)*, 15.

143. Mar, *Brokering Belonging*, 6–7.

Chapter 6

1. "Constitución política de los Estados Unidos Mexicanos," *Diario Oficial de la Federación*, 5 February 1917.

2. "Será reformada la ley de inmigración contra los chinos," *Demócrata*, 14 June 1919, AREM, 16-29-42.

3. Telegram, Commerce Secretary, Peking, to SRE, 4 January 1920, in AREM, 16-29-42.

4. Monteón González and Trueba Lara, *Chinos y antichinos en México*, 117–18.

5. Espinoza, *El ejemplo de Sonora*, 16–18.

6. Moisés González Navarro, *El Porfiriato: La vida social* (Mexico City: Hermés, 1957), quoted in Cott, "Mexican Diplomacy and the Chinese Issue," 81–82.

7. Mandujano López, "Transpacific Mexico," 146–52.

8. Delgado, *Making the Chinese Mexican*, 102.

9. Cott, "Mexican Diplomacy and the Chinese Issue," 82.

10. Espinoza, *El ejemplo de Sonora*, 16.

11. Delgado, *Making the Chinese Mexican*, 84.

12. District Judge, Ensenada, to SRE, 9 July 1906, in AREM, 15-15-2.

13. Marín, "La migración china el en norte de Baja California," 209.

14. "Mexico Not Likely to Lend Her Aid," *San Francisco Chronicle*, 29 May 1905, in AREM, 15-15-2.

15. "Mexico's Chinese Policy," *San Francisco Chronicle*, 30 May 1905, in AREM, 15-15-2.

16. "The Immigration Question," *Mexican Herald* (Mexico City), 14 June 1905, in AREM, 15-15-2.

17. "Mexico's Attitude to Immigration," *Mexican Herald* (Mexico City), 29 May 1905, in AREM, 15-15-2.

18. Landa y Piña, *El servicio de migración en México*, 9, 11, 16.

19. King and Bassett, *Report*, 10.

20. Wilfley and Bassett, *Memorandum*, 6.

21. Dambourges Jacques, "Chinese Massacre in Torreon (Coahuila) in 1911," 240.

22. Espinoza, *El ejemplo de Sonora*, 31.

23. Nota Verbal de Hacienda y Crédito Público to SRE, 26 September 1927; SRE to Yuen Su Wong, Minister of China, 3 January 1934, AREM, III-124-20.

24. Quong San Lung and Fong Fo Qui to Governor of Sonora, 27 June 1906; Respuesta del Gobierno de Sonora to Quong San Lung and Fong Fo Qui, 29 June 1906, AGN, Fondo González Ramírez, caja 2, vol. 23, in Monteón González and Trueba Lara, *Chinos y antichinos en México*, 57–58.

25. Romero, *Chinese in Mexico*, 152.

26. Letter from Chinese Colony to Governor of Sonora and Municipal President of Cocorit, 15 March 1916; Message from J. R. Chon, representative of Chinese Colony of Cocorit, to Louis Hostetter, U.S. Consul, 25 March 1916, AGN, Fondo González Ramírez, caja 8, vol. 100, in Monteón González and Trueba Lara, *Chinos y antichinos en México*, 59–60.

27. Henry Lane Wilson, U.S. Ambassador, to Salado Alvarez, SRE, 2 June 1911, AREM, 16-4-34, p. 1; Telegram, Tuxtla Gutiérrez, to Mexico City, 7 June 1911, AREM, 16-4-34, p. 13; Henry Lane Wilson, U.S. Ambassador, to Salado Alvarez, SRE, 19 June 1911, AREM, 16-4-34, pp. 22–23.

28. Kwong Say Tay, Salina Cruz, to Chang You Tang, Chinese Minister, Mexico City, 31 July 1911, AREM 16-4-33; Chang You Tang, Chinese Minister, to Foreign Minister, SRE, 29 September 1911, AREM, 16-4-33.

29. García Triana and Eng Herrera, *Chinese in Cuba*, 23–24.

30. Pérez de la Riva, *Los culíes chinos en Cuba*, 271. Pérez de la Riva attributes the quote to Máximo Gómez. Gonzalo de Quesada, the Cuban ambassador in Germany, quotes this phrase in his book about Chinese participation in the independence wars, and it is often attributed to him. This quote is engraved on a monument in Havana to the Chinese who fought in the independence wars in Cuba. Quesada, *Mi primera ofrenda*, 136.

31. Chuffat Latour, *Apunte histórico de los chinos en Cuba*, 51.

32. For a good discussion of the "myth of racial democracy" in Cuba, see Helg, *Our Rightful Share*. For an argument that the myth of racial equality has benefits, see Fuente, *Nation for All*.

33. Guerra, "From Evolution to Involution in the Early Cuban Republic," 153–54.

34. "Expediente referente a la inmigración china," Havana, 1 September 1909–21 June 1914, esp. 83, leg. 121, Secretaría de la Presidencia, ANC, quoted in López, *Chinese Cubans*, 146, 148–49, 151–55.

35. Ibid., 154.

36. Herrera Jérez and Castillo Santana, *De la memoria a la vida pública*, 22.

37. Ibid., 19–37.

38. López, *Chinese Cubans*, 156.

39. Herrera Jérez and Castillo Santana, *De la memoria a la vida pública*, 19–37.

40. Chen Kwong Min, *Meizhou huaqiao tongjian* (The Chinese in the Americas) (New York: Overseas Chinese Publishing Co., 1950), 673–74, quoted in López, *Chinese Cubans*, 185.

41. Delgado, *Making the Chinese Mexican*, 118–21.

42. Senator A. Magallón to Alberto J. Pani, Secretary of Foreign Relations, 10 November 1921, AGN, Fondo Obregón-Calles, 104-ch-1; Agreement of President Alváro Obregón to SRE, 1921, AGN, Fondo Obregón-Calles, 104- ch-16, in Monteón González and Trueba Lara, *Chinos y antichinos en México*, 60–63.

43. League of Nations, "China and the United States of Mexico," 204–10.

44. Telegram from Manuel Jean Sop to President Obregón, 23 October 1924, AGN, Fondo Obregón-Calles, 104-ch-1; and Tel. from Obregón to N. C. Yillén, 11 November 1924, AGN, Fondo Obregón-Calles, 104-ch-16, in Monteón González and Trueba Lara, *Chinos y antichinos en México*, 53.

45. Extracto de la Oficialía Mayor de la Presidencia a una carta de Ramon Wong Gil (Nuevas Casas Grandes, Chih.) to President Abelardo Rodríguez; Extracto de la Oficialía Mayor de la Presidencia a una carta de José Hum Fook (Nogales, Sonora) to President Abelardo Rodríguez, 24 October 1932, AGN, Ramo Abelardo L. Rodríguez, 525.3 (51)/26; Tel. from Nicolás Chantee to President Abelardo Rodríguez, 28 February 1933, AGN, Ramo Abelardo L. Rodríguez, 519.3/1, in ibid., 86.

46. Delgado, *Making the Chinese Mexican*, 179.

47. Aristide Zolberg uses this term "remote control" to talk about the U.S. extension of its power beyond its borders to implement immigration control. Zolberg, *Nation by Design*, 9.

48. G. Landers de Negri, Consul, Yokohama, to SRE, 9 November 1925; Angel Cano del Castillo, Consul, Yokohama, to SRE, 4 November 1925, AREM, AUR-3-47.

49. Romero, *Chinese in Mexico*, 185–86.

50. Office of Delegate of Migration, Mexicali, to Secretario de Industria, Comercio y Trabajo, 2 July 1927, in Monteón González and Trueba Lara, *Chinos y antichinos en México*, 93.

51. "Memorandum: Sugestiones para restringir la inmigración de chinos," 19 March 1929, AREM, IV-135-15.

52. Ibid.

53. Telegram, Gobernación to SRE, 11 December 1929; Fernando D. Chacon, Consul, Naco, to SRE, 13 January 1930, AREM, IV-396-6.

54. Andrés Landa y Piña to SRE, 7 July 1930, AREM, IV-396-17.

55. Manuel Tello, Mexican Consul, Yokohama, to SRE, 1 September 1930, AREM, IV-396-20.

56. Manuel Tello, Mexican Consul, Yokohama, to Consul General in San Francisco, 31 December 1930, AREM, IV-397-16.

57. Lists of visas issued in Yokohama, Japan, AREM IV-397-16.

58. Zolberg, *Nation by Design*, 264–65.

59. Marín, "La migración china el en norte de Baja California, 1877–1949," 217.

60. Ibid.

61. Mexican Consul, New York, 12 November 1919, AREM, 16-26-87.

62. Marín, "La migración china el en norte de Baja California," 215–19.

63. Secretaría de Gobernación, *Ley de migración de los Estados Unidos Mexicanos*, 9–10.

64. Cott, "Mexican Diplomacy and the Chinese Issue," 82–84.

65. Mishima, *Destino México*, 12, 14.

66. Marín, "La migración china el en norte de Baja California," 219–25.

67. José A. Valenzuela, Consul, Nogales, to SRE, 30 October 1929, AREM, IV-397-4.

68. Marín, "La migración china el en norte de Baja California," 231.

69. Delgado, *Making the Chinese Mexican*, 188.

70. Romero, *Chinese in Mexico*, 186.

71. Marín, "La migración china el en norte de Baja California," 246.

72. "Cámara Israelita de Industria y Comercio, queja contra Unión de Comerciantes Mexicanos de Fresnillo," 1936, 2/360 (28) 17737, esp. 54, caja 8, serie Israel, DGG, AGN, quoted in Mays, "Transplanting Cosmopolitans," 192.

73. Weise, "Mexican Nationalisms, Southern Racisms," 762.

74. Ngai, *Impossible Subjects*, 72.

75. Lytle Hernández, *Migra!*, 81.

76. Herrera Jérez and Castillo Santana, *De la memoria a la vida pública*, 107.

77. *Alma Hispanoamericana*, no. 2 (1931), quoted in ibid., 108.

78. *El Comercio*, April 1933; "Tuberculosis e inmigración," *Vindicación*, October 1933, quoted in Herrera Jérez and Castillo Santana, *De la memoria a la vida pública*.

79. Herrera Jérez and Castillo Santana, *De la memoria a la vida pública*, 109.

80. García Triana and Eng Herrera, *Chinese in Cuba*, 26.

81. López, *Chinese Cubans*, 201; Herrera Jérez and Castillo Santana, *De la memoria a la vida pública*, 110–11.

82. Herrera Jérez and Castillo Santana, *De la memoria a la vida pública*, 111.

83. Dr. Angel C. de Arce, "La raza cubana: Etnología y sociología experimental," conference paper, 19 October 1934, quoted in ibid., 111–12.

84. Rev. N. Lascelles Ward, "The Oriental Problem, Submitted to the General Ministerial Association," 9 January 1922, Vancouver, B.C., in Public Archives Canada, Immigration Branch, RG 76, vol. 474, file 799921, pt. 1, pp. 11–12.

85. Sons of England, Regina Lodge no. 317, "Resolution," 22 May 1922, Public Archives Canada, Immigration Branch, RG 76, vol. 474, file 799921, pt. 1.

86. "Community Shoppers Guide," 8 February 1923, Public Archives Canada, Immigration Branch, RG 76, vol. 474, file 799921, pt. 1.

87. "Maple Leaf Association, Victoria Branch No. 1," Public Archives Canada, Immigration Branch, RG 76, vol. 474, file 799921, pt. 1.

88. "To the Right Honourable W. L. Mackenzie King, M. P., Premiere of Canada, and Honourable Members of the Cabinet and Members of the House of Commons," 8 February 1927, Public Archives Canada, Immigration Branch, RG 76, vol. 474, file 799921, pt. 1.

89. "Los chinos y sus matrimonios con las mexicanas," *El Tráfico*, 18 January 1900, and "La inmigración asiática, la cuestión racial y nuestras relaciones con China," *El Tráfico*, 5 March 1900, quoted in Romero, *Chinese in Mexico*, 147–48.

90. Rénique, "Race, Region and Nation," 217.

91. Ibid., 217–18.

92. Telegram, Juan L. Carillo et al. to SRE, 6 June 1916, AREM, 16-16-159.

93. "Carísimos niños, amigos nuestros," 3, Arana manuscripts, quoted in Romero, *Chinese in Mexico*, 157–65 (Romero's translation altered to mine).

94. Telegram from Comité Anti-chino, Torreón, Coahuila, to Secretaría de Gobernación, 14 July 1929, AGN, Gobernación, 2/362.2 (3)16, caja 2, exp. 17.

95. Secretaría de la Economía Nacional, *Quinto censo de población 1930 del Estado de Sonora*, cuadro 22, p. 108.

96. Governor of Sonora to SRE, 2 April 1919, AREM, 18-7-162, pp. 6–7.

97. Ibid.

98. T. K. Fong, Representative of Business Interests for China, to SRE, 21 March 1919, AREM, 18-7-162, p. 629.

99. "Extracto de las representaciones hechas por la Legación China con motivo de la campaña anti-china en el Estado de Sonora en 1919," AREM, 18-7-162, pp. 268–70.

100. "La ley ante el peligro chino," *El Eco del Yaqui*, 29 March 1919, clipping in AREM, 18-7-162, p. 33.

101. José Gándara, President of Junta Nacionalista, and Tomás N. Millen, Secretary, "Todo por la Raza," AREM, 18-7-162, 30 March 1919, p. 33.

102. Espinoza, *El ejemplo de Sonora*, 77.

103. Romero, *Chinese in Mexico*, 71.

104. Espinoza, *El ejemplo de Sonora*, 35.

105. Luis Chong Ruiz to Secretaría de Gobernación, 3 November 1930, AGN, Gobernación, 2/367(22)4, caja 3, exp. 28.

106. Romero, *Chinese in Mexico*, 94; Espinoza, *El ejemplo de Sonora*, 58.

107. Romero, *Chinese in Mexico*, 93–94.

108. Schiavone Camacho, *Chinese Mexicans*, 60–61.

109. Ramón García, "Contact between Chinese Men and Mexican Women Is Dangerous," in Papers of José María Arana, Special Collections, University of Arizona, Tucson, Miscellaneous Material Folder, quoted in ibid., 50–51.

110. "Ante el peligro asiático," *El Toro de Once*, 30 March 1919, clipping in AREM, 18-7-162, p. 35.

111. Romero, *Chinese in Mexico*, 79.

112. "Las chineras," *El Toro de Once*, 30 March 1919, clipping in AREM, 18-7-162, p. 35.

113. Ibid., p. 32.

114. Schiavone Camacho, *Chinese Mexicans*, 52–53.

115. "Pueblo" pamphlet, Santiago Ixcuintla, AREM, 18-7-162, p. 308.

116. Espinoza, *El ejemplo de Sonora*, 95.

117. Ibid., 102.

118. Circular from Walter Pesqueira, Municipal President of Nogales, Sonora, to President of the Republic, 17 July 1924, AGN, Fondo Obregón-Calles, 104-ch-1, in Monteón González and Trueba Lara, *Chinos y antichinos en México*, 84–85.

119. Espinoza, *El ejemplo de Sonora*, 59–60.

120. Vasconcelos, *Cosmic Race*, 17–18.

121. Antonio Chon Ying et al., Pánuco, Veracruz, to President Elías Calles, 14 October 1925, AGN, Gobernación, 2/362.1 (6-1)1, caja 14, exp. 1.

122. Wn. Yes Kan, President, Unión Fraternal Asociación China, to Carlos Si, Sec. General of Chinese Legation, 4 June 1921, AREM, 18-7-162, p. 309.

123. Office of President to Governors, 23 September 1925, AGN, Fondo Obregón-Calles, 104-ch-1, leg. 2; in Monteón González and Trueba Lara, *Chinos y antichinos en México*, 92–93.

124. Mexican Legation in China to SRE, 13 April 1919, AREM, 18-7-162, p. 38.

125. T. K. Fong, Chinese Legation in Mexico, to SRE, 23 April 1919, AREM, 18-7-162, p. 48.

126. Description of *The Flower of Doom* can be found at www.siskelfilmcenter.org /flower-of-doom (accessed 12 June 2012).

127. Mexican Legation in China to SRE, AREM, 18-7-162, pp. 54–56.

128. Tick Chong, Jim Quong Chong, et al., Unión Fraternal Asociación China, to Julián González, Municipal President, 11 December 1919, AREM, 18-7-162.

129. Telegram, Adolfo de la Huerta, Governor of Sonora, to SRE, 28 December 1919, AREM, 18-7-162, p. 232.

130. General Norberto Rochin, President of Unión Nacionalista Mexicana, 22 September 1930, AREM, VII (N) 60-54.

131. Francisco S. Elías, Governor of Sonora, to SRE, 28 November 1930, AREM, VII (N) 60-54.

132. Secretaría de Economía Nacional, *Quinto censo de población 1930 del Estado de Sonora*, cuadro 23, p. 111.

133. Espinoza, *El ejemplo de Sonora*, 47.

134. Ibid., 52–57.

135. Samuel Sung Yung, Chinese Minister, to SRE, 8 July 1931, AREM, III-297-26 (I). Ibid., 74.

136. Circular no. 194, 25 August 1931, in ibid., 119.

137. "Condiciones en Ciudad Obregón, Sonora," AREM, III-297-26 (I).

138. Alejandro H. Llanes to Chinese Ambassador to Mexico, July 1931, AREM, III-297-26 (I).

139. "Condiciones en Cananea, Nogales, Huatambo, Etchojoa, Esperanza, Cocorit, Nacozari, y Agua Prieta, y Ahome y Guasave, Sinaloa," AREM, III-297-26 (I).

140. Samuel Sung Young, Chinese Minister, to SRE, 30 November 1931, AREM, III-297-26 (I); "Resumen del oficio girado por el señor Cónsul Yao-Hsiang Peng en Nogales, Sonora, al Gobernador del Estado," 21 September 1931, AREM, III-297-26 (I).

141. Samuel Sung Young, Chinese Minister, to SRE, 8 July 1931 and 18 July 1931, AREM, III-297-26 (I).

142. "Memorandum," 13 August 1931, AREM, III-297-26 (I).

143. Telegram, Elías Calles, Governor of Sonora, to SRE, 2 September 1931, AREM, III-297-26 (I).

144. Telegram, Eugene Chen, Minister of Foreign Affairs, Canton, to SRE, 5 September 1931, AREM, III-297-26 (I).

145. Mauricio Fresco, Honorary Consul of Mexico, Shanghai, to SRE, 29 August 1932, AREM, III-297-26 (I).

146. Bassols, "Ricardo Flores Magón."

147. Tel. F. S. Elías, Governor of Sonora, to President of the Republic, 23 June 1922, AGN, Fondo Obregón-Calles, 104-ch-1, in Monteón González and Trueba Lara, *Chinos y antichinos en México*, 64.

148. Quoted in Daniels, *Asian America*, 118–19.

149. Mellinger, "How the IWW Lost Its Western Heartland," 308.

150. "Programa del Partido Liberal y manifiesto a la nación," *Regeneración*, 2a. epoca, no. 15, 1 July 1906, in Bassols, "Ricardo Flores Magón," 433.

151. Quong San Lung and Fong Fo Qui to Governor of Sonora, 27 June 1906, AGN, Fondo González Ramírez, caja 2, vol. 23, in Monteón González and Trueba Lara, *Chinos y antichinos en México*, 58.

152. Hart, *Revolutionary Mexico*, 64.

153. "Junta Organizadora del Partido Liberal Mexicano," *Regeneración*, no. 12, 1 June 1906, in Bassols, "Ricardo Flores Magón," 437.

154. "Al pueblo americano," *Regeneración*, no. 25, 18 February 1911, in Bassols, "Ricardo Flores Magón," 443.

155. Ricardo Flores Magón, Fort Leavenworth, to Ellen White, New York, 14 March 1922, in ibid., 447.

156. *El Machete* (Mexico City), 1 February 1931, in Monteón González and Trueba Lara, *Chinos y antichinos en México*, 100.

157. "El fondo de la 'Campaña Nacionalista," *El Machete* (Mexico City), 1 March 1931, in ibid., 101.

158. "Campaña nacionalista ofensiva contra los chinos," *El Machete* (Mexico City), 30 September 1931, in ibid., 109–10.

159. "Anti-Chinese Move in Mexican States Steadily Growing," *Japan Advertiser*, 31 August 1931, AREM, VII (EX) 3-12.

160. "Mexican Riots Break out Again," *China Press*, 5 October 1931; "Chinese Settlers Back from Mexico," *Evening Post & Mercury*, 31 September 1931, clippings in AREM, VII (EX) 3-12.

161. Mauricio Fresco, Honorary Consul, Shanghai, to SRE, 10 May 1933, AREM, III-297-26 (II).

162. "Canton Investigator Returns from Mexico, *Reuter's Agency*, Canton, 15 June 1933, AREM, III-297-26 (II).

163. "Deportations of Chinese," *North China Daily News*, 10 May 1933, AREM, III-297-26 (II).

164. For an excellent dissertation about Jews in Mexico in this period, see Mays, "Transplanting Cosmopolitans."

165. "Boycot en toda la República," 28 September 1931, AREM, VII (EX) 3-12.

166. Amador E. Velez, "Alerta mexicanos!," 28 September 1931, AREM, VII (EX) 3-12.

167. H. G. W. Woodhead, "One Man's Comment for Today: Mexico and China, the Recent Expulsions," clipping in AREM, VII (EX) 3-12.

168. "There Is a Difference," *St. Louis Globe Democrat*, 8 March 1933, AREM, 111-297-26 (II).

169. Mexican Chamber of Commerce, Barcelona, to SRE, 27 May 1933, AREM, III-121-53.

170. "Martín Mier, Authorized Delegate of Comité Nacionalista Anti-Chino de la Costa Occidental," Nogales, Sonora, September 1931, AREM, VII (EX) 3-12.

171. José Angel Espinoza, President, Comité Directivo Nacionalista de la Costa Occidental, "El problema chino y las causas que lo originaron," *El Nacional* (New York), 8 September 1931, clipping in AREM, III-297-26 (I).

172. Tel. Francisco S. Elías to Walterio Pesqueira, 19 August 1931, in Espinoza, *El ejemplo de Sonora*, 131–32.

173. Ibid., 138–40.

174. *United Press*, 2 September 1931, in ibid., 157.

175. Ibid., 186.

176. "Continúan pasando los chinos," *El Imparcial* (Mexico City), 2 December 1929, AREM, IV-397-4.

177. "El asunto de los chinos," *El Imparcial* (Mexico City), 10 December 1929, AREM, IV-396-7.

178. Departamento Consular, SRE, to Consul, Los Angeles, 19 June 1930, AREM IV-397-2.

179. Lytle Hernández, *Migra!*, 78–79.

180. C. Palacios Roji, Consul, Nogales, to SRE, 10 March 1932; Memorandum, 19 April 1932, AREM, III-297-26 (I); Leopoldo Díaz, Vice Consul, Nogales, to SRE, 7 March 1933, AREM, IV-397-13.

181. "Chinese Problem Will Be Settled by a Test Case," *Douglas (Ariz.) Daily Dispatch*, 14 April 1932, AREM, IV-397-10.

182. J. M. Puig Cassurano, to Rodolfo Elías Calles, Governor of Sonora, 15 May 1933, AREM, III-297-26 (II).

183. Samuel Sung Young, Chinese Legation, to Manuel Puig Cassurano, SRE, 8 June 1933, AREM, III-297-26 (II); Eduardo Vasconcelos, Secretary, to SRE, 12 July 1933, AREM, III-297-26 (II).

184. Legation of China, 24 May 1933, AREM III-297-25; Memorandum of Minister of China, 13 June 1933, AREM III-297-25.

185. Y. S. Wong to SRE, 11 May 1935, AREM, III-297-25.

186. Marín, "La migración china el en norte de Baja California," 243–48.

187. Delgado, *Making the Chinese Mexican*, 187; Dirección General de Estadística, *Censo general de la República Mexicana, 1940* (Mexico City: Ministerio de Fomento, 1940).

188. Y. S. Wong, Chinese Legation, to SRE, 28 September 1936, AREM, III-162-17.

189. Camara Nacional de Comercio e Industria de Huixtla, Chiapas, to Governor of Chiapas, 10 November 1938; V. Alatorre to Governor of Chiapas, 30 September 1937, AGN, Gobernación, 2/360(5)24732, caja 2, exp. 20.

Chapter 7

1. Sinn, *Pacific Crossing.*

2. Salyer, *Laws Harsh as Tigers*, 40–41; Ma, "Chinatown Organizations and the Anti-Chinese Movement," 148–51.

3. López, *Chinese Cubans*, 177.

4. Herrera Jérez and Castillo Santana, *De la memoria a la vida pública*, 74, 62–66.

5. Ibid., 70–73.

6. Sinn, *Pacific Crossing*, 4, 245, chap. 247.

7. "Mapping the Boahuanghui," docs.google.com/document/pub?id=1DTwav82GT4R mq85iSZVbKZjjM2QRk_dY_zdQp65Vzoc (accessed May 21, 2012).

8. The most extensive treatment of Kang Yu-Wei's time in the Americas can be found in Worden, "Chinese Reformer in Exile."

9. Martínez Sánchez, *Monclova en la revolución*, 163 (n. 159).

10. Ibid.

11. Robert Worden states that the Commercial Corporation was founded in 1904 in Hong Kong. Worden, "Chinese Reformer in Exile," 189–90, 193–94.

12. Dambourges Jacques, "Chinese Massacre in Torreon (Coahuila) in 1911," 234–36; Pérez Jiménez, "Raza, nación y revolución," chap. 5.

13. Worden, "Chinese Reformer in Exile," 194–99.

14. Kang to Roosevelt, 30 January 1906, quoted in ibid., 211.

15. Worden, "Chinese Reformer in Exile," 222–23.

16. Dambourges Jacques, "Chinese Massacre in Torreon (Coahuila) in 1911," 239–40.

17. Worden, "Chinese Reformer in Exile," 224.

18. Dambourges Jacques, "Chinese Massacre in Torreon (Coahuila) in 1911," 234–40, 245–46.

19. Tsai, *China and the Overseas Chinese in the United States*, 125–27, 141.

20. Cheung, "Performing Exclusion and Resistance," 40, 54.

21. Ibid., 40–48, 54.

22. Espinoza, *El ejemplo de Sonora*, 231–43, 267.

23. Delgado, *Making the Chinese Mexican*, 159–60.

24. Ibid., 161.

25. Francisco L. Yuen to President Alvaro Obregón, 20 July 1922, AGN, Fondo Obregón-Calles, 104-ch-1, in Monteón González and Trueba Lara, *Chinos y antichinos en México*, 67–69.

26. Ma, "Chinatown Organizations and the Anti-Chinese Movement," 148–60.

27. Manifesto of Chinese Nationalist Party in which they refute charges by Chee Kung Tong society, October 1922, AGN, Fondo Obregón-Calles, 104-ch-1, in Monteón González and Trueba Lara, *Chinos y antichinos en México*, 70–78.

28. Tel. F. S. Elías, Governor of Sonora, to President of Republic, 23 June 1922, AGN, Fondo Obregón-Calles, 104-ch-1, in ibid., 64–65.

29. Delgado, *Making the Chinese Mexican*, 161.

30. Gilberto Loyo, to Julián Garza Tijerina, President of Instituto de Estudios Sociales, Políticos y Económicos, 7 March 1935, AGN Gobernación, 2.360(29)34, caja 9, exp. 70.

31. Lui Hoj Ping, Chee Kung Tong headquarters, Hermosillo, 22 June 1924, translated from the Chinese into Spanish in Espinoza, *El ejemplo de Sonora*, 273–74.

32. Marín, "La migración china el en norte de Baja California," 243.

33. Espinoza, *El ejemplo de Sonora*, 276–84.

34. Félix Pérez, Gran Logia Benito Juárez, Torreón, Coahuila, to Felipe Canales, Ministerio de Gobernación, 2 July 1929, AGN, Gobernación, 2/363.2 (3)16, caja 2, exp. 17.

35. Juan A. Wong, Magdalena, to José Wong, Guaymas, 24 October 1924, in Espinoza, *El ejemplo de Sonora*, 296–97.

36. Ibid., 327.

37. General Norberto Rochín, President of Unión Nacionalista Mexicana, to Genaro Estrada, Minister of SRE, AREM, VII (N) 60-54.

38. Herrera Jérez and Castillo Santana, *De la memoria a la vida pública*, 87–98.

39. Ibid., 98–101.

40. Delgado, *Making the Chinese Mexican*, 90–93.

41. Ibid., 94–99.

42. Copy of Fung Ming, Interpreter, report, sent by William Christy, New Orleans, to Taylor, 21 August 1919, NARA, RG 85, E135, box 3, folder 309/9.

43. Fung Ming, Interpreter, to William Christy, New Orleans, 14 August 1919, NARA, RG 85, E135, box 3, folder 309/9.

44. Joseph H. Wallis, Commissioner, New Orleans, to Commissioner General of Immigration, Washington, D.C., 14 August 1919, NARA, RG 85, E135, box 3, folder 309/9.

45. H. C. Brownlow, Mobile, to Inspector in Charge, Jacksonville, 5 December 1919, NARA, RG 85, E135, box 3, folder 309/10.

46. Hearing for Arrow Leonard Spence Ethical before Immigrant Inspector Isaac H. Vincent, City Jail, Mobile, Alabama, 1 October 1919, NARA, RG 85, E135, box 3, folder 309/10.

47. Ibid.

48. Statement of Henry V. Kavisto and Charles Elo, to Inspector Isaac H. Vincent, Mobile, Alabama, 24 September 1919, NARA, RG 85, E135, box 3, folder 309/10.

49. Hearing of Lo Lok Agau and Arrow Jung Chou by Inspector Isaac H. Vincent, Mobile, Alabama, 23 September 1919, NARA, RG 85, E135, box 3, folder 309/10.

50. Peck, *Reinventing Free Labor*.

51. J. R. Archibald, Immigrant Inspector, to Charles L. Babcock, Immigrant Inspector, Buffalo, 11 July 1908, NARA, RG 85, entry 9, 52165/1.

52. Justice to Landis, 30 November 1914, NARA, RG 85, E 135, box 1.

53. Siener, "Through the Back Door," 47–54.

54. Chas T. Connell, Inspector, Los Angeles, to Inspector in Charge, San Diego, 11 January 1915, NARA, RG 85, E 135, box 1.

55. Siener, "Through the Back Door," 55.

56. A P. Schell, Immigrant Inspector, to Commissioner General, 29 May 1909, NARA RG 85, entry 9, 52229/1D.

57. William F. Christy, Inspector, New Orleans, to R. H. Taylor, Inspector, Los Angeles, 29 May 1919, NARA, RG 85, E135, box 3, folder 309/10.

58. William F. Christy, Immigration Commissioner, New Orleans, to Taylor, Immigrant Inspector, Los Angeles, 9 May 1919, NARA, RG 85, E 135, box 3, folder 309/9.

59. Randall McDonnel, Jacksonville, to Inspector in Charge, 12 February 1919, NARA, RG 85, E 135, box 3, folder 309/10.

60. Hans A. M. Jacobsen, Junior Watchman, to Commissioner of Immigration, New Orleans, 5 February 1915, NARA, RG 85, E 135, box 2.

61. "Statement of C. F. Klintberg, Master of American SS *Lake Pepin*, Arriving from Caiberian, Cuba, before Inspector W. W. Eyster," 19 November 1919, NARA, RG 85, E 135, box 3, folder 309/6.

62. Mar, *Brokering Belonging*, 6, 44–45.

63. Thomas V. Kiefer, Inspector, Jacksonville, to All Inspectors in Charge of Sub-ports, Immigration District 7, 10 March 1919, NARA, RG 85, E135, box 3, folder 309/10.

64. Thomas V. Kiefer, Inspector, Jacksonville, to Richard Taylor, Los Angeles, 25 February 1919, NARA, RG 85, E135, box 3, folder 309/10.

65. Shey Loud to Shere You, 16 August 1914, NARA, RG 85, E135, box 3, Chinese Smuggling File.

66. Yee Fong to Tang Horn, 18 December 1913, NARA, RG 85, E135, box 3, Chinese Smuggling File, 16-b.

67. Louie Fat Quon to Tang Horn, 19 August 1914, NARA, RG 85, E135, box 3, Chinese Smuggling File.

68. Louie Fat Quon to Tang Horn, 21 August 1914, NARA, RG 85, E135, box 3, Chinese Smuggling File.

69. Louie Quong Kee to son, 6 January 1914, NARA, RG 85, E135, box 3, Chinese Smuggling File. 15-b.

70. Shu Gee to Fat Yip, Fat Chuck, and Tang Horn, 6 November 1914, NARA, RG 85, E135, box 3, Chinese Smuggling File.

71. Pong Shu Gee to Louie Tang Horn, NARA, RG 85, E135, box 3, Chinese Smuggling File, 7-a.

72. Yee Tung to Third Uncle, 18 June 1914, NARA, RG 85, E135, box 3, Chinese Smuggling File, 7-b.

73. Ah You to Tang Horn, 24 June 1914, NARA, RG 85, E135, box 3, Chinese Smuggling File.

74. E. E. Greenwalt, Commissioner of Immigration, Philadelphia Station, to Richard H. Taylor, Bureau of Immigration, Washington, D.C., 23 June 1914, NARA, RG 85, E135, box 3, Chinese Smuggling File.

Epilogue

1. My analysis of Laing's novel is indebted to the insightful article by Lisa Yun, "Under the Hatches." See also Laing, *Sea Witch*.

2. Laing, *Sea Witch*, 471.

3. Anderson, *Imagined Communities*, 6–7.

4. Simmel, *Sociology of Georg Simmel*, 407; Park, "Human Migration and the Marginal Man," 893.

5. Vasconcelos, *Cosmic Race.*

6. Ortiz, *Cuban Counterpoint.*

7. Stoddard, *Rising Tide of Color against White World Supremacy*, 302–4.

8. Huntington, *Who Are We?*

9. Woon, "Voluntary Sojourner among the Overseas Chinese," 679–81.

10. López, *Chinese Cubans*, 229.

11. Ibid., 239.

12. W. T. Whitney Jr., "Cuba Reaffirms Ties with Cuba," *People's World*, 5 March 2012, peoplesworld.org/cuba-reaffirms-ties-with-china/.

13. Douglas Farah, "A Free Trade Zone in the Traffic of Humans: Central America Has Become Conduit for World's Illegal Migrants," *Washington Post*, 23 October 1995; Lausent-Herrera, "Chinatown in Peru," 82–85, 111.

14. McCabe, "Chinese Immigrants in the United States"; Hoeffel et al., "Asian Population."

15. Migration Policy Institute Data Hub, "The Top Sending Countries of Immigrants in the United States, Canada and Australia," www.migrationinformation.org/datahub/migrant_sendingcountries.cfm (accessed 16 July 2012); Statistics Canada, "Study Projections of the Diversity of the Canadian Population," www.statcan.gc.ca/daily-quotidien/100309/dq100309a-eng.htm (accessed 16 July 2012).

16. Chin, *Smuggled Chinese*, 11.

17. Overseas Community Affairs Council Republic of China (Taiwan), "Overseas Chinese Population Distribution 2012," www.ocac.gov.tw/ (accessed 1 February 2014).

18. Ngai, *Impossible Subjects*, 237, 248.

19. Secretaría de Relaciones Exteriores, *Exposición de motivos y proyecto de ley sobre nacionalidad y naturalización de los Estados Unidos Mexicanos*, 9–10.

20. Schiavone Camacho, *Chinese Mexicans*, 106–8, 122, 130, 160–63.

21. Ngai, *Impossible Subjects*, 237–39.

22. Herbert Lehman to Norman R. Sturgis, Jr., 5 March 1954, quoted in ibid., 247.

23. Transcript of Remarks by Julius Edelstein before National Federation of Settlements, 1 March 1954, quoted in ibid.

24. "Table Ad 1072–1075: Deportable Aliens Located, and Aliens Expelled, 1892–1998," in Carter et al., *Historical Statistics of the United States.*

25. "Table 36, Aliens Removed or Returned, Fiscal Years 1892–2010," *Yearbook of Immigration Statistics: 2010*, www.dhs.gov/files/statistics/publications/YrBk10En.shtm (accessed July 18, 2012).

26. Ngai, *Impossible Subjects*, 258–62.

27. The U.S. Census Bureau counts white Hispanics as nonwhite for the purposes of its calculations. Vincent and Velkoff, "Next Four Decades."

28. Chin, *Smuggled Chinese*, 7.

29. Camarota, "Immigrants at Mid-decade," 23.

30. Chin, *Smuggled Chinese*, 6, 98; Douglas Farah, "A Free Trade Zone in the Traffic of Humans: Central America Has Become Conduit for World's Illegal Migrants," *Washington Post*, 23 October 1995.

31. Douglas Farah, "A Free Trade Zone in the Traffic of Humans: Central America Has Become Conduit for World's Illegal Migrants," *Washington Post*, 23 October 1995.

32. Chin, *Smuggled Chinese*, 50, 67–77.

33. Ibid., 10, 37.

34. Gardner, "Why Do They Keep Coming?," 42–43.

35. Naufal and Genc, *Expats and the Labor Force*, 33–34, 55.

36. Amnesty International, *Dark Side of Migration*, 9, 43; "Revealed: Qatar's World Cup 'Slaves,'" *Guardian*, 25 September 2013, www.theguardian.com/world/2013/sep/25/revealed-qatars-world-cup-slaves.

37. Quoted in Wesley Yang, "Paper Tigers," *New York Magazine*, 8 May 2011.

38. Ibid.

39. Quesada, *Los chinos y la independencia de Cuba*, 14.

40. López, *Chinese Cubans*, 190–92.

41. Blas Pelayo, "Breve crónica sobre la visita del presidente de la República Popular de China Jieng Ze Ming a La Habana, del 21/11/93 al 22/11/93, ambos inclusive," quoted in ibid., 251.

42. Chen Weihua, Wu Jiao, and Cheng Guangii, "China, Cuba Sign Host of Cooperation Deals," *China Daily*, 7 June 2011, www.chinadaily.com.cn/cndy/2011-06/07/content_12646298.htm.

43. "Raul Castro Sings in Chinese for His Chinese Guests," www.youtube.com/watch?v=CyZVwENinKI (accessed July 9, 2013).

44. Lausent-Herrera, "Chinatown in Peru and the Changing Peruvian Chinese Community(ies)," 82–85, 111.

45. Espinosa Luis and Luis Quintana, "Hongmen Min Chih Tang de Cuba."

46. Curtis, "Mexicali's Chinatown," 346–47.

47. Lausent-Herrera, "Chinatown in Peru and the Changing Peruvian Chinese Community(ies)," 69.

48. Rouse, "'What We Didn't Understand,'" 37–38; Sinn, *Pacific Crossing*, 59–60, chap. 57.

49. Sinn, *Pacific Crossing*, chap. 7.

50. Kathleen López has been instrumental in bringing together relatives in Cuba and China who have never met. López, *Chinese Cubans*, 249–50.

51. Ibid., 230.

52. "The Golden Venture, Plus 100,000," *New York Times*, 9 June 1993; Philip Shenon, "Suspect in Golden Venture Case Was Leading a Life of Luxury," *New York Times*, 19 November 1995.

53. Nina Bernstein, "Making It Ashore but Still Chasing US Dream," *New York Times*, 9 April 2006.

54. Ibid.

55. Keefe, *Snakehead*, 42–45.

56. Berg and Rodriguez, "Introduction."

57. Nina Bernstein, "Making It Ashore but Still Chasing US Dream," *New York Times*, 9 April 2006.

Bibliography

Archival and Documentary Sources

BRITAIN

British Parliamentary Papers: China, vol. 3, *Correspondence, Dispatches and Other Communications Respecting the Emigration of Chinese Coolies, 1852–58*. Irish University Press Area Studies Series British Parliamentary Papers. Shannon: Irish University Press, 1971.

British Parliamentary Papers: China, vol. 4, *Correspondence, Dispatches and Other Communications Respecting the Emigration of Chinese Coolies, 1858–92*. Irish University Press Area Studies Series. Shannon: Irish University Press, 1971.

CANADA

Department of Citizenship and Immigration. *Immigration Statistics, Year 1896–1961*. Ottawa: Canadian Government Publishing, 1961.

King, W. L. Mackenzie. "Report of the Royal Commission Appointed to Inquire into the Methods by Which Oriental Labourers Have Been Induced to Come to Canada." Ottawa: Government Printing Bureau, 1908.

Public Archives Canada
    Immigration Branch, Record Group 76
Report of the Royal Commission on Chinese Immigration. Ottawa: Order of the Commission, 1885.

CUBA

Archivo Nacional de Cuba, Havana
    Reales, Cédulas y Ordenes
    Secretaría de la Presidencia
Biblioteca Nacional José Martí, Havana
Reglamento para la introducción de los trabajadores chinos en la isla de Cuba. Havana: Imp. del Gobierno y Capitanía General, 1860.

MEXICO

Archivo General de la Nación, Mexico City
    Gobernación
    Fondo Obregón-Calles
Archivo Histórico de la Secretaría de Relaciones Exteriores, Mexico City
Dirección General de Estadísticas. *Censo general de la República Mexicana, 1895*. Mexico City: Ministerio de Fomento, 1895.

———. *Censo general de la República Mexicana, 1910*. Mexico City: Ministerio de Fomento, 1910.

———. *Censo general de la República Mexicana, 1921*. Mexico City: Ministerio de Fomento, 1921.

———. *Censo general de la República Mexicana, 1930*. Mexico City: Ministerio de Fomento, 1930.

———. *Censo general de la República Mexicana, 1940*. Mexico City: Ministerio de Fomento, 1940.

Landa y Piña, Andrés. *El servicio de migración en México*. Mexico City: Secretaría de Gobernación, 1930.

Secretaría de Gobernación. *Ley de migración de los Estados Unidos Mexicanos*. Mexico City: Talleres Gráficos de la Nación, 1926.

Secretaría de la Economía Nacional. *Quinto censo de población 1930 del Estado de Sonora*. Edited by Dirección General de Estadística. Mexico City: Estados Unidos de México, 1930.

Secretaría de Relaciones Exteriores. *Exposición de motivos y proyecto de ley sobre nacionalidad y naturalización de los Estados Unidos Mexicanos*. Mexico City: Imp. de la Secretaría de Relaciones Exteriores, 1930.

PERU

Peru. *Memoria que presenta al congreso ordinario de 1876 el ministro de gobierno, policía y obras públicas*. Lima: El Comercio, 1876.

SPAIN

Archivo Histórico de la Nación, Madrid
  Ultramar, Fomento
Archivo Histórico del Ministerio de Asuntos Exteriores, Madrid
  Ultramar, Fomento
Biblioteca Nacional, Madrid

UNITED STATES

"An Act Providing for the Relief and Support, Employment and Removal of the Poor, and for Repealing All Former Laws Made for Those Purposes (February 26, 1794)." In *Acts and Laws of the Commonwealth of Massachusetts, 1793*, 479–93. Boston: Wright and Potter, 1895.

Bureau of Immigration. *Annual Report of the Commissioner General of Immigration to the Secretary of Labor*. Washington, D.C.: Government Printing Office, 1904–30.

California Department of Insurance. "Slavery Era Insurance Registry: Report to the California Legislature, May 2002." California Legislature. www.insurance.ca.gov /0100-consumers/0300-public-programs/0200-slavery-era-insur/slavery-era -report.cfm.

Dillingham, William P. *The Immigration Situation in Canada*. Washington, D.C.: Government Printing Office, 1910.

Moore, John Bassett. *A Digest of International Law*. Vol. 4. Washington, D.C.: Government Printing Office, 1906.

National Archives and Records Administration, Washington, D.C., and Seattle. Record Group 85, Records of the Immigration and Naturalization Service.

United States House of Representatives. "Chinese Coolie Trade, Executive Document No. 88." Washington, D.C.: Government Printing Bureau, 1860.

United States House of Representatives and Senate. *An Act to Prohibit the "Coolie Trade" by American Citizens in American Vessels.* 37th Congress, 2nd sess. 12 Stat. 340 vols. Washington, D.C.: Government Printing Office, 1862.

United States Senate. *Executive Documents, 1859–60.* 36th Congress, 1st sess. Washington, D.C.: Government Printing Office, 1860.

United States v. Sing Tuck, 194 US 161 (1904).

Newspapers and Periodicals

Alma Hispanoamericana (Cienfuegos, Cuba)
La América (Madrid)
Boletín de Colonización (Havana)
China Press
El Comercio (Lima)
Daily Advertiser
Demócrata (Mexico City)
Douglas (Ariz.) Daily Dispatch
El Eco del Yaqui (Cocorit, Mexico)
Evening Post & Mercury
The Guardian (London)
Harper's New Monthly Magazine (New York)
Harper's Weekly (New York)
El Imparcial (Mexico City)
Japan Advertiser
Los Angeles Times
El Machete (Mexico City)
Mexican Herald (Mexico City)
El Nacional (New York)
New Orleans Daily Picayune
New York Evening Star
New York Herald
New York Magazine
New York Post
New York Sun
New York Times
New York Tribune
North China Daily News (Shanghai)
Ontario Times
La Patria (Lima)
People's World (Beijing)
Philadelphia Press
Portland (Oregon) Telegram
Regeneración (St. Louis and Los Angeles)
St. Louis Globe Democrat
San Diego Union
San Francisco Call
San Francisco Chronicle
San Francisco Examiner
South Pacific Times
Tampa Sunday
El Toro de Once (Culiacán, Mexico)
El Tráfico (Guaymas, Mexico)
United Press
Vancouver World
La Verdad (New York)
Vindicación (Havana)
Washington Post
The World (Philadelphia)

Other Primary Sources

Abbott, John S. C. *South and North, or Impressions Received during a Trip to Cuba and the South.* New York: Abbey & Abbott, 1860.

Amnesty International. *The Dark Side of Migration: Spotlight on Qatar's Construction Sector ahead of the World Cup.* New York: Amnesty International, 2013.

Ampère, Jean-Jacques. *Promenade en Amérique: Etats-Unis–Cuba–Mexique.* Paris: Michel Lévy, 1860.

Arona, Juan de. *La inmigración en el Perú.* Lima: El Universo, 1891.

Basavarajappa, K. G., and Bali Ram. "Origins of the Population, Census Dates, 1871–1971." In Statistics Canada, "Section A: Population and Migration." www.statcan. gc.ca/pub/11-516-x/sectiona/4147436-eng.htm.

Brandenburg, Broughton. "The Stranger within the Gate." *Harper's Weekly*, 5 August 1905, 1114–16, 1133.

Campbell, Persia Crawford. *Chinese Coolie Emigration to Countries within the British Empire.* Preface by W. Pember Reeves. London: P. S. King & Son, 1923.

Carter, Susan B., Scott Sigmund Gartner, Michael R. Haines, Alan L. Olmstead, Richard Sutch, and Gavin Wright. *Historical Statistics of the United States: Millennial Edition Online.* Edited by Robert Barde, Susan B. Carter, and Richard Sutch. New York: Cambridge University Press, 2006.

Chuffat Latour, Antonio. *Apunte histórico de los chinos en Cuba.* Havana: Molina, 1927.

Compañía de Colonización Asiática. "Estatutos de la Compañía de Colonización Asiática." Mexico City: J. M. Lara, 1866.

Coolidge, Mary Roberts. *Chinese Immigration.* New York: Henry Holt, 1909.

Dana, Richard Henry. *To Cuba and Back.* Newport News, Va.: 1500 Books, 2007 [1887].

Espinoza, José Angel. *El ejemplo de Sonora.* Mexico City: n.p., 1932.

Fry, C. Luther. "Illegal Entry of Orientals into the United States between 1910 and 1920." *Journal of the American Statistical Association* 23, no. 162 (1928): 173–77.

Gibson, Campbell, and Kay Jung. "Historical Census Statistics on the Foreign-Born Population of the US, 1850–2000," Population Division, working paper no. 81. Washington, D.C.: Bureau of the Census, 2006.

Helly, Denise, ed. *Cuba Commission Report: A Hidden History of the Chinese in Cuba.* Baltimore: Johns Hopkins University Press, 1993 [1874].

Hoeffel, Elizabeth, Sonya Rastogi, Myoung Ouk Kim, and Hasan Shahid. "The Asian Population: 2010." U.S. Census.

Holden, Edgar. "A Chapter in the Coolie Trade." *Harper's New Monthly Magazine* 29, no. 169 (1864): 1–10.

Howe, Julia Ward. *A Trip to Cuba.* Boston: Ticknor and Fields, 1860.

Huc, M. *The Chinese Empire: A Sequel to Recollections of a Journey through Tartary and Thibet*, rev. ed. London, 1860.

King, Owyang, and Arthur Bassett. *Report of Messrs. Owyang King and Arthur Bassett: Representatives of His Excellency, Minister Chang Yin Tang in an Investigation Made in Conjunction with Licenciado Antonio Ramos Pedrueza, Representative of His*

Excellency, Francisco L. de La Barra, President of Mexico, of the Facts Relating to the Massacre of Chinese Subjects at Torreón on the 15th of May, 1911. Mexico City: American Book & Printing, 1911.

Laing, Alexander. *The Sea Witch: A Narrative of the Experiences of Capt. Roger Murray and Others in an American Clipper Ship during the Years 1846 to 1856.* New York: Farrar & Rinehart, 1933.

Lawrence, William Beach. *Visitation and Search; or, An Historical Sketch of the British Claim to Exercise a Maritime Police over the Vessels of All Nations.* Boston: Little, Brown, 1858.

League of Nations. "China and the United States of Mexico—Exchange of Notes Embodying an Agreement for the Provisional Modification of the Sino-Mexican Treaty, Concluded at Washington, December 14, 1899, Mexico, September 26, 1921." In *League of Nations Treaty Series*, 201–10. Lausanne, Switzerland: League of Nations, 1922.

Lubbock, Basil. *Coolie Ships and Oil Sailors.* Glasgow: Brown, Son & Ferguson, 1981 [1935].

McKenzie, R. D. *Oriental Exclusion: The Effect of American Immigration Laws, Regulations, and Judicial Decisions upon the Chinese and Japanese on the American Pacific Coast.* Chicago: University of Chicago Press, 1928.

Park, Robert. "Human Migration and the Marginal Man." *American Journal of Sociology* 33, no. 60 (1928): 881–93.

Quesada, Gonzalo de. *Los chinos y la independencia de Cuba.* Translated by Adolfo G. Castellanos. Havana: Heraldo Cristiano, n.d.

———. *Mi primera ofrenda.* New York: El Porvenir, 1892.

Ralph, Julian. "The Chinese Leak." *Harper's New Monthly Magazine* 82, no. 490 (1891): 515–25.

Seeman, Melvin. "On the Meaning of Alienation." *American Sociological Review* 24, no. 60 (1959): 783–91.

Simmel, Georg. *The Sociology of Georg Simmel.* Translated by Kurt H. Wolf. Glencoe, Ill.: Free Press, 1950.

Siu, Paul C. P. *The Chinese Laundryman: A Study in Social Isolation.* New York: New York University Press, 1987.

———. "The Sojourner." *American Journal of Sociology* 58, no. 1 (1952): 34–44.

Stoddard, Lothrop. *The Rising Tide of Color against White World Supremacy.* New York: Charles Scribner's Sons, 1922.

Sumner, William Graham. *What the Social Classes Owe to Each Other.* New York: Harper & Brothers, 1911 [1883].

Townshend, Frederick Trench. *Wild Life in Florida, with a Visit to Cuba.* London: Hurst and Blackett, 1875.

Vasconcelos, José. *The Cosmic Race/La raza cósmica.* Translated by Didier T. Jaén. Los Angeles: California State University, 1979 [1925].

Vincent, Grayson K., and Victoria A. Velkoff. "The Next Four Decades: The Older

Population in the United States, 2010 to 2050." In *Population Estimates and Projections*, 1–14. Washington, D.C.: U.S. Census Bureau, 2010.

Whitelaw, Reid. *After the War: A Tour of the Southern States, 1865–66*. Edited by C. Vann Woodward. New York: Harper Row, 1965.

Wilfley and Bassett. *Memorandum on the Law and the Facts in the Matter of the Claim of China against Mexico for Losses of Life and Property Suffered by Chinese Subjects at Torreón on May 13, 14 and 15, 1911*. N.p., 1911.

Zegarra, Félix Cipriano C. *La condición jurídica de los extranjeros en el Perú*. Santiago: Libertad, 1872.

Secondary Sources

"Alien." In *Oxford English Dictionary*. Oxford: Oxford University Press, 2012. www.oed.com/view/Entry/4988.

Anderson, Benedict. *Imagined Communities: Reflections on the Origin and Spread of Nationalism*. London: Verso, 1991.

Anderson, Kay J. *Vancouver's Chinatown: Racial Discourse in Canada, 1875–1980*. Montreal: McGill-Queen's University Press, 1991.

Anghie, Antony. *Imperialism, Sovereignty and the Making of International Law*. Cambridge: Cambridge University Press, 2004.

Arendt, Hannah. *The Origins of Totalitarianism*. Orlando, Fla.: Harcourt, 1973.

Bassols, Jacinto Barrera. "Ricardo Flores Magón, de la xenofobia popular al internacionalismo proletario." In *Xenofobia y xenofilia en la historia de México, siglos XIX y XX*, edited by Delia Salazar Anaya, 433–48. Mexico City: SEGIB/Instituto de Migración/Centro de Estudios Migratorios Instituto Nacional de Antropología e Historia, 2006.

Benjamin, Walter. "Critique of Violence." In *Walter Benjamin: Selected Writings*, vol. 1, *1913–26*, edited by Marcus Bullock and Michael W. Jennings, 236–52. Cambridge: Harvard University Press, 1996.

Berg, Ulla Dalum, and Robyn Magalit Rodriguez. "Introduction: Transnational Citizenship across the Americas." *Identities: Global Studies in Culture and Power* 20, no. 60 (2013): 649–64.

Bonfil Batalla, Guillermo. *México Profundo: Reclaiming a Civilization*. Austin: University of Texas Press, 1996.

Brown, Vincent. "Social Death and Political Life in the Study of Slavery." *American Historical Review* 114, no. 5 (2009): 1231–49.

Camarota, Steven A. *Immigrants at Mid-decade: A Snapshot of America's Foreign-Born Population in 2005*. Washington, D.C.: Center for Immigration Studies, 2005.

Canadian Human Rights Commission. "Human Rights in Canada: A Historical Perspective." www.chrc-ccdp.ca/en/getBriefed/1900/population.asp.

Cassel, Pär Kristoffer. *Grounds of Judgment: Extraterritoriality and Imperial Power in Nineteenth-Century China and Japan*. New York: Oxford University Press, 2013.

Certeau, Michel de. *The Practice of Everyday Life*. Berkeley: University of California Press, 1988.

Chang, Ching Chieh. "The Chinese in Latin America: A Preliminary Geographical Survey with Special Reference to Cuba and Jamaica." Ph.D. diss., University of Maryland, 1956.

Chang, Jason Oliver. "Outer Crossings: History, Culture and Geography of Mexicali's Chinese Community." Ph.D. diss., University of California at Berkeley, 2010.

Chang, Kornel S. *Pacific Connections: The Making of the US-Canadian Borderlands*. Berkeley: University of California Press, 2012.

Chen, Helen. "Chinese Immigration into the United States: An Analysis of Changes in Immigration Policies." PhD diss., Brandeis University, 1980.

Cheung, Floyd. "Performing Exclusion and Resistance: Anti-Chinese and Chee Kung Tong Parades in Territorial Arizona." *TDR* 46, no. 1 (2002): 39–59.

Chin, Ko-Lin. *Smuggled Chinese: Clandestine Immigration to the United States*. Philadelphia: Temple University Press, 1999.

Cohen, Lucy M. *Chinese in the Post–Civil War South*. Baton Rouge: Louisiana State University Press, 1984.

Cott, Kenneth. "Mexican Diplomacy and the Chinese Issue, 1876–1910." *Hispanic American Historical Review* 67, no. 1 (1987): 63–85.

Curtis, James R. "Mexicali's Chinatown." *Geographical Review* 85, no. 3 (1995): 335–48.

Dambourges Jacques, Leo M. "The Chinese Massacre in Torreon (Coahuila) in 1911." *Arizona and the West* 16, no. 3 (1974): 233–46.

Daniels, Roger. *Asian America: Chinese and Japanese in the United States since 1850*. Seattle: University of Washington Press, 1988.

Davis, David Brion. *Inhuman Bondage: The Rise and Fall of Slavery in the New World*. Oxford: Oxford University Press, 2006.

Dean, Dwight G. "Alienation: Its Meaning and Measurement." *American Sociological Review* 26, no. 5 (1961): 753–58.

Delgado, Grace. *Making the Chinese Mexican: Globalism, Localism, and Exclusion in the U.S.-Mexico Borderlands*. Stanford, Calif.: Stanford University Press, 2012.

Dorsey, Joseph. "Identity, Rebellion, and Social Justice among Chinese Contract Workers in Nineteenth-Century Cuba." *Latin America Perspectives* 31, no. 18 (2004): 18–47.

Drescher, Seymour, and Robert Paquette Stanley Engerman, eds. *Slavery*. Oxford Readers. New York: Oxford University Press, 2001.

Duara, Prasenjit. *Rescuing History from the Nation: Questioning Narratives of Modern China*. Chicago: University of Chicago Press, 1995.

Espinosa Luis, Mitzi, and Violeta Luis Quintana. "The Hongmen Min Chih Tang de Cuba (1887–2012): Twenty-Five Years Developing Friendship, Fraternity and Assistance." PowerPoint presentation, Fifth International Conference of Institutes and Libraries for Chinese Overseas Studies, Vancouver, B.C., 16–19 May 2012.

Ettinger, Patrick. *Imaginary Lines: Border Enforcement and the Origins of Undocumented Immigration, 1882–1930*. Austin: University of Texas Press, 2009.

Fraginals, Manuel Moreno. "Plantations in the Caribbean: Cuba, Puerto Rico, and the Dominican Republic in the Late Nineteenth Century." In *Between Slavery and Free Labor: The Spanish-Speaking Caribbean in the Nineteenth Century*, edited by Frank Moya Pons Manuel Moreno Fraginals, and Stanley L Engerman, 3–21. Baltimore: Johns Hopkins University Press, 1985.

Fuente, Alejandro de la. *A Nation for All: Race, Inequality and Politics in Twentieth-Century Cuba*. Chapel Hill: University of North Carolina Press, 2000.

García Triana, Mauro, and Pedro Eng Herrera. *The Chinese in Cuba, 1847–Now*. Translated by Gregor Benton. Lanham, Md.: Lexington, 2009.

Gardner, Andrew. "Why Do They Keep Coming? Labor Migrants in the Gulf States." In *Migrant Labour in the Persian Gulf*, edited by Mehran Kemrava and Zahra Babar, 41–58. London: Hurst, 2011.

Geiger, Andrea. "Caught in the Gap: The Transit Privilege and North America's Ambiguous Borders." In *Bridging National Borders in North America: Transnational and Comparative Histories*, edited by Benjamin H. Johnson and Andrew R. Graybill, 199–222. Durham, N.C.: Duke University Press, 2010.

Gilroy, Paul. *The Black Atlantic: Modernity and Double Consciousness*. Cambridge: Harvard University Press, 1993.

Guerra, Lillian. "From Evolution to Involution in the Early Cuban Republic: Conflicts over Race, Class, and Nation, 1902–1906." In *Race and Nation in Modern Latin America*, edited by Anne S. Macpherson, Nancy P. Applebaum, and Karin Alejandra Rosemblatt, 132–62. Chapel Hill: University of North Carolina Press, 2003.

Hart, John Mason. *Revolutionary Mexico: The Coming and Process of the Mexican Revolution*. Berkeley: University of California Press, 1987.

Hawk, Angela. "Going Mad in Gold Country: Migrant Populations and the Problem of Containment in the Pacific Mining Boom Regions." *Pacific Historical Review* 80, no. 1 (2011): 64–96.

Helg, Aline. *Our Rightful Share: The Afro-Cuban Struggle for Equality, 1886–1912*. Chapel Hill: University of North Carolina Press, 1995.

Herrera Jérez, Miriam, and Mario Castillo Santana. *De la memoria a la vida pública: Identidades, espacios y jerarquías de los chinos en La Habana republicana (1902–1968)*. Havana: Centro de Investigación y Desarollo de la Cultura Cubana Juan Marinello, 2003.

Hirota, Hidetaka. "The Moment of Transition: State Officials, the Federal Government, and the Formation of American Immigration Policy." *Journal of American History* 99, no. 4 (2013): 1092–108.

Hoerder, Dick. "Migration, People's Lives, Shifting and Permeable Borders: The North American and Caribbean Societies in the Atlantic World." In *Migrants and Migration in Modern North America: Cross-Border Lives, Labor Markets, and Politics*, edited by Dick Hoerder and Nora Faires, 1–46. Durham, N.C.: Duke University Press, 2011.

Hsu, Madeline. *Dreaming of Gold, Dreaming of Home: Transnationalism and Migration between the United States and South China, 1882–1943*. Stanford, Calif.: Stanford University Press, 2000.

Hu-Dehart, Evelyn. "La Trata Amarilla: The "Yellow Trade" and the Middle Passage, 1847–1884." In *Many Middle Passages: Forced Migration and the Making of the Modern World*, edited by Emma Christopher, Cassandra Pybus, and Marcus Rediker, 166–83. Berkeley: University of California Press, 2007.

Hung-Hui, Juan. *Chinos en América*. Madrid: Mapfre, 1992.

Huntington, Samuel P. *Who Are We? The Challenges to America's National Identity*. New York: Simon & Schuster, 2004.

Irick, Robert. *Ch'ing Policy toward the Coolie Trade, 1847–1878*. Taipei: Chinese Materials Center, 1982.

Jacoby, Karl. "Between North and South: The Alternative Borderlands of William H. Ellis and the African American Colony of 1895." In *Continental Crossroads: Remapping U.S.-Mexico Borderlands History*, edited by Samuel Truett and Elliott Young, 209–39. Durham, N.C.: Duke University Press, 2004.

Jiménez Pastrana, Juan. *Los chinos en la historia de Cuba: 1847–1930*. Havana: Ciencias Sociales, 1983.

Johnson, Benjamin H. *Revolution in Texas: How a Forgotten Rebellion and Its Bloody Suppression Turned Mexicans into Americans*. New Haven, Conn.: Yale University Press, 2003.

Jung, Moon-Ho. *Coolies and Cane: Race, Labor, and Sugar in the Age of Emancipation*. Baltimore: Johns Hopkins University Press, 2006.

Keefe, Patrick Radden. *The Snakehead*. New York: Doubleday, Doran, 2009.

Klein, Herbert S., Stanley Engerman, Robin Haines, and Ralph Shlomowitz. "Transoceanic Mortality: The Slave Trade in Comparative Perspective." *William & Mary Quarterly* 58, no. 1 (2001): 93–118.

Knight, Alan. "Racism, Revolution, and *Indigenismo*: Mexico, 1910–40." In *The Idea of Race in Latin America*, edited by Richard Graham, 71–113. Austin: University of Texas Press, 1990.

Kuhn, Philip A. *Chinese among Others: Emigration in Modern Times*. Lanham, Md.: Rowman & Littlefield, 2008.

Lake, Marilyn, and Henry Reynolds. *Drawing the Global Colour Line: White Men's Countries and the International Challenge of Racial Inequality*. Cambridge: Cambridge University Press, 2008.

Lau, Estelle T. *Paper Families: Identity, Immigration Administration, and Chinese Exclusion*. Durham, N.C.: Duke University Press, 2006.

Lausent-Herrera, Isabelle. "The Chinatown in Peru and the Changing Peruvian Chinese Community(ies)." *Journal of Chinese Overseas* 7 (2011): 69–113.

Lee, Erika. *At America's Gates: Chinese Immigration during the Exclusion Era, 1882–1943*. Chapel Hill: University of North Carolina Press, 2003.

———. "Defying Exclusion: Chinese Immigrants and Their Strategies during the Exclusion Era." In *Chinese American Transnationalism: The Flow of People, Resources, and Ideas between China and America during the Exclusion Era*, edited by Sucheng Chan, 1–21. Philadelphia: Temple University Press, 2006.

———. "Orientalisms in the Americas: A Hemispheric Approach to Asian American History." *Journal of Asian American Studies* 8, no. 3 (2005): 235–56.

Lesser, Jeffrey. *Negotiating National Identity: Immigrants, Minorities, and the Struggle for Ethnicity in Brazil.* Durham, N.C.: Duke University Press, 1999.

Liu, Fu-ju. "A Comparative Demographic Study of Native-Born and Foreign-Born Chinese Population in the United States." Ph.D diss., University of Michigan, 1953.

López, Kathleen. *Chinese Cubans: A Transnational History.* Chapel Hill: University of North Carolina Press, 2013.

López, Kathleen Maria. "Migrants between Empires and Nations: The Chinese in Cuba, 1874–1959." Ph.D diss.,University of Michigan, 2005.

Lowe, Lisa. *Immigrant Acts: On Asian American Cultural Politics.* Durham, N.C.: Duke University Press, 1996.

Lytle Hernández, Kelly. *Migra! A History of the Border Patrol.* Berkeley: University of California Press, 2010.

Ma, L. Eve Armentrout. "Chinatown Organizations and the Anti-Chinese Movement, 1882–1914." In *Entry Denied: Exclusion and the Chinese Community in America, 1882–1943,* edited by Sucheng Chan, 147–69. Philadelphia: Temple University Press, 1991.

Mandujano López, Ruth. "Transpacific Mexico: Encounters with China and Japan in the Age of Steam (1867–1914)." Ph.D. diss., University of British Columbia, 2012.

Mar, Lisa Rose. *Brokering Belonging: Chinese in Canada's Exclusion Era, 1885–1945.* Oxford: Oxford University Press, 2010.

Mariátegui, José Carlos. *Seven Interpretive Essays on Peruvian Reality.* Austin: University of Texas Press, 1971.

Marín, Rosario Cardiel. "La migración china en el norte de Baja California, 1877–1949." In *Destino México: Un estudio de las migraciones asiáticas a México, siglos XIX y XX,* edited by María Elena Ota Mishima, 189–255. Mexico City: Colegio de México, 1997.

Martínez Sánchez, Lucas. *Monclova en la revolución: Hechos y personajes, 1910–1920.* Monclova: n.p., 2005.

Marx, Karl. *Theories of Surplus Value.* Amherst, N.Y.: Prometheus, 2000 [1883].

Mays, Devi. "Transplanting Cosmopolitans: The Migrations of Sephardic Jews to Mexico, 1900–1934." Ph.D. diss., Indiana University, 2013.

Mbembe, Achille. "Necropolitics." *Public Culture* 15, no. 1 (2003): 11–40.

McCabe, Kristen. "Chinese Immigrants in the United States." Migration Policy Institute. www.migrationinformation.org/feature/print.cfm?ID=876—1.

McKeown, Adam. *Chinese Migrant Networks and Cultural Change: Peru, Chicago, Hawaii, 1900–1936.* Chicago: University of Chicago Press, 2001.

———. "Conceptualizing Chinese Diasporas, 1842–1949." *Journal of Asian Studies* 58, no. 2 (1999): 306–37.

———. *Melancholy Order: Asian Migration and the Globalization of Borders.* New York: Columbia University Press, 2008.

Meagher, Arnold J. *The Coolie Trade: The Traffic in Chinese Laborers to Latin America, 1847–1874.* Bloomington, Ind.: Xlibris, 2008.

Mellinger, Phil. "How the IWW Lost Its Western Heartland: Western Labor History Revisited." *Western Historical Quarterly* 27 (1996): 302–24.

Mishima, María Elena Ota, ed. *Destino México: Un estudio de las migraciones asiáticas a México, siglos XIX y XX.* Mexico City: Colegio de México, 1997.

Monteón González, Humberto, and José Luis Trueba Lara. *Chinos y antichinos en México: Documentos para su estudio.* Guadalajara: Gobierno de Jalisco, 1988.

Narvaez, Benjamin Nicolas. "Chinese Coolies in Cuba and Peru: Race, Labor and Immigration, 1839–1886." Ph.D diss., University of Texas, 2010.

Naufal, George, and Ismail Genc. *Expats and the Labor Force: The Story of the Gulf Cooperation Council Countries.* New York: Palgrave MacMillan, 2012.

Ngai, Mae. *Impossible Subjects: Illegal Aliens and the Making of Modern America.* Princeton, N.J.: Princeton University Press, 2004.

———. *The Lucky Ones: One Family and the Extraordinary Invention of Chinese America.* Boston: Houghton Mifflin Harcourt, 2010.

Northrup, David. *Indentured Labor in the Age of Imperialism, 1834–1922.* New York: Cambridge University Press, 1995.

Ong, Aihwa. *Flexible Citizenship: The Cultural Logics of Transnationality.* Durham, N.C.: Duke University Press, 1999.

Ortiz, Fernando. *Cuban Counterpoint: Tobacco and Sugar.* Translated by Harriet de Onís. Durham, N.C.: Duke University Press, 1995 [1940].

Parker, Kunal M. "State, Citizenship, and Territory: The Legal Construction of Immigrants in Antebellum Massachusetts." *Law and History Review* 19, no. 3 (2001): 583–643.

Patterson, Orlando. *Slavery and Social Death: A Comparative Study.* Cambridge: Harvard University Press, 1982.

Peck, Gunther. *Reinventing Free Labor: Padrones and Immigrant Workers in the North American West, 1880–1930.* New York: Cambridge University Press, 2000.

Peloso, Vincent C. "Racial Conflict and Identity Crisis in Wartime Peru: Revisiting the Cañete Massacre of 1881." *Social Identities* 114, no. 5 (2005): 467–88.

Pérez, Louis A., Jr. *Cuba: Between Reform and Revolution.* Oxford: Oxford University Press, 1995.

———. *To Die in Cuba: Suicide and Society.* Chapel Hill: University of North Carolina Press, 2005.

Pérez de la Riva, Juan. *Los culíes chinos en Cuba, 1847–1880: Contribución al estudio de la inmigración contratada en el Caribe.* Havana: Ciencias Sociales, 2000.

Pérez Jiménez, Marco Antonio. "Raza, nación y revolución: La matanza de chinos en Torreón, Coahuila, mayo de 1911." B.A. thesis, Universidad de las Américas, Puebla, Mexico, 2006.

Pfaelzer, Jean. *Driven Out: The Forgotten War against Chinese Americans.* Berkeley: University of California Press, 2007.

Rediker, Marcus. *The Slave Ship: A Human History.* New York: Penguin, 2007.

Rénique, Gerardo. "Race, Region, and Nation: Sonora's Anti-Chinese Racism and Mexico's Postrevolutionary Nationalism, 1920s–1930s." In *Race and Nation in*

Modern Latin America, edited by Anne S. Macpherson, Nancy P. Applebaum, and Karin Alejandra Rosemblatt, 211–36. Chapel Hill: University of North Carolina, 2003.

Rippy, J. Fred. "Henry Meiggs, Yankee Railroad Builder." In *People and Issues in Latin American History: From Independence to the Present*, edited by Lewis Hanke and Jane M. Rausch, 110–16. Princeton, N.J.: Markus Weiner, 1997.

Rodríguez, José Baltar. *Los Chinos de Cuba: Apuntes etnográficos*. Habana: Fundacion Fernando Ortiz, 1997.

Rodríguez Pastor, Humberto. *Herederos del dragón: Historia de la comunidad china en el Perú*. Lima: Fondo Editorial del Congreso del Perú, 2000.

Romero, Roberto Chao. *The Chinese in Mexico, 1882–1940*. Tucson: University of Arizona Press, 2010.

Rouse, Wendy L. "'What We Didn't Understand': A History of Chinese Death Ritual in China and California." In *Chinese American Death Rituals: Respecting the Ancestors*, edited by Sue Fawn Chung and Priscilla Weggars, 19–45. Lanham, Md.: Altamira, 2005.

Salyer, Lucy E. *Laws Harsh as Tigers: Chinese Immigrants and the Shaping of Modern Immigration Law*. Chapel Hill: University of North Carolina Press, 1995.

———. "'Laws Harsh as Tigers': Enforcement of the Chinese Exclusion Laws, 1891–1924." In *Entry Denied: Exclusion and the Chinese Community in America, 1882–1943*, edited by Suecheng Chan. Philadelphia: Temple University Press, 1991.

Schiavone Camacho, Julia María. *Chinese Mexicans: Transpacific Migration and the Search for a Homeland, 1910–1960*. Chapel Hill: University of North Carolina Press, 2012.

Scott, James. *Seeing Like a State: How Certain Schemes to Improve the Human Condition Have Failed*. New Haven, Conn.: Yale University Press, 1998.

Shah, Nyan. *Stranger Intimacy: Contesting Race, Sexuality, and the Law in the North American West*. Berkeley: University of California Press, 2011.

Siener, William H. "Through the Back Door: Evading the Chinese Exclusion Act along the Niagara Frontier, 1900–1924." *Journal of American Ethnic History* 27, no. 4 (2008): 34–70.

Sinn, Elizabeth. *Pacific Crossing: California Gold, Chinese Migration and the Making of Hong Kong*. Hong Kong: Hong Kong University Press, 2013.

Siu, Lok. "Serial Migration: Stories of Home and Belonging in Diaspora." In *New Routes for Diaspora Studies*, edited by Sukanya Banerjee, Aims McGuinness and Steven C. McKay, 143–72. Bloomington: Indiana University Press, 2012.

Stanley, Amy Dru. *From Bondage to Contract: Wage Labor, Marriage, and the Market in the Age of Slave Emancipation*. Cambridge: Cambridge University Press, 1998.

Stevens, Todd M. "Brokers between Worlds: Chinese Merchants and Legal Culture in the Pacific Northwest, 1852–1925." Ph.D diss., Princeton University, 2003.

Stewart, Watt. *Chinese Bondage in Peru: A History of the Chinese Coolie in Peru, 1849–1874*. Durham, N.C.: Duke University Press, 1951.

Tsai, Shih-shan Henry. *China and the Overseas Chinese in the United States, 1868–1911.* Fayetteville: University of Arkansas Press, 1983.

Wang, Guanhua. *In Search of Justice: The 1905–1906 Chinese Anti-American Boycott.* Cambridge: Harvard University Press, 2001.

Weise, Julie M. "Mexican Nationalisms, Southern Racisms: Mexicans and Mexican Americans in the U.S. South, 1908–1939." *American Quarterly* 60, no. 3 (2008): 749–77.

Williams, Elizabeth Lew. "The Chinese Must Go: Immigration, Deportation and Violence in the 19th-Century Pacific Northwest." Ph.D. diss., Stanford University, 2011.

Woon, Yuen-fong. "The Voluntary Sojourner among the Overseas Chinese: Myth or Reality?" *Public Affairs* 56, no. 4 (1983–84): 673–90.

Worden, Robert Leo. "A Chinese Reformer in Exile: The North American Phase of the Travels of K'ang Yu-Wei, 1899–1909." Ph.D diss., Georgetown University, 1972.

Yen, Ching Hwang. *Coolies and Mandarins.* Kent Ridge: Singapore University Press, 1985.

Young, Elliott. "Regions." In *Palgrave Dictionary of Transnational History*, edited by Akira Iriye and Pierre-Yves Saunier. New York: Palgrave, 2009.

Yun, Lisa. *The Coolie Speaks: Chinese Indentured Laborers and African Slaves in Cuba.* Philadelphia: Temple University Press, 2008.

———. "Under the Hatches: American Coolie Ships and Nineteenth-Century Narratives of the Pacific Passage." *Amerasia Journal* 28, no. 2 (2002): 38–61.

Yung, Judy. *Unbound Feet: A Social History of Chinese Women in San Francisco.* Berkeley: University of California Press, 1995.

Zolberg, Aristide R. *A Nation by Design: Immigration Policy in the Fashioning of America.* Cambridge: Harvard University Press, 2006.

Index

Bennett, Jim, 261

Berry, John, 172–73

Bertillon inspections, 149, 150, 269

Black Atlantic, The (Gilroy), 3

Blanco-criollo (white-creole) racial type, 218

Boletín de Colonización (Havana), 86

Border crossings: catching illegal Chinese migrants and, 5, 141–42, 151, 172; Chinese migrant deaths and, 9, 161–62, 309 (n. 35); Chinese migrants' serial migrations and, 15, 99, 291 (n. 33); Gulf of Mexico and, 153, 179–88; passports and, 122, 123, 130, 147, 165, 186–87, 208, 209–11, 271, 316 (n. 47); unguarded borders and ports and, 130, 152, 160–61, 167, 169–70, 171, 172–73, 178, 191, 192; U.S. troops and, 178–79. *See also* Canada and Chinese migrants; Mexico and Chinese migrants; Smuggling; United States; United States and Chinese migrants; U.S. immigration bureaucracy

Border Patrol, 3, 132, 133–34, 172, 192, 245

Boston, 168

Bowen, Francis, 29–30

Bowring, John, 36–37, 40, 47

Bracero program, 277

Brandenburg, Broughton, 5–6

Braun, Marcus, 2, 12–13, 132, 201, 207; smuggling investigation and, 1, 4, 5, 6–7, 162–65

Brazil, 59, 62, 275, 276, 290 (n. 15), 299–300 (n. 109)

British Columbia, 14; anti-Chinese legislation and, 99, 104–5, 126; anti-Chinese sentiment and, 106, 129, 217–18; Chinese migrants and, 112, 121, 124, 140, 145, 284, 301 (n. 35); Chinese migrants to U.S. from, 155, 165–66, 167, 268; smuggling rings and, 261. *See also* Vancouver; Victoria, B.C.

British Emigration Board, 49

British Guiana, 29, 34, 49

British West India Committee, 36

British West Indies, 30, 32, 46, 49, 158, 292 (n. 26)

Brokering Belonging (Mar), 191, 265

Brown, Vincent, 64

Brownsville, 178

Bubonic plague, 199

Buffalo, 140, 169, 170, 264, 268

Buford, S. J., 170

Burlingame Treaty with China (1868), 91, 102, 155

Calexico, 109, 212

California, 14, 199, 213; anti-Chinese activities and, 102–3, 104–5; Chinese migrant legal cases and, 135, 136, 139; Chinese migrants to Cuba and, 32, 124; coolie labor conditions and, 46, 49, 60; coolie trade and, 33, 47, 48–49. *See also* Los Angeles; San Diego; San Francisco

Callao, 51, 89

Canada: Asian immigration and, 217–18; European immigrants and, 138, 139, 152

Canada and Chinese migrants, 9, 13, 292 (n. 26); anti-Chinese activities and, 104–5, 126; anti-Chinese sentiment and, 106, 117, 130, 217–18; anti-Chinese violence and, 129; as back door to U.S. and, 1, 99, 121, 152, 153, 155, 165–67, 170, 171, 174, 268, 307 (n. 1); Chinese benevolent associations and, 251; Chinese exclusion laws and, 10, 106, 168, 191, 213, 218, 247; Chinese interpreters and, 191, 265–66; contract laborers and, 90, 92, 93, 137; coolie trade and, 8, 32, 60, 90; credit-ticket mechanism and, 32, 46; deportations and, 139, 167; fraudulent documents and, 144–45, 147; free laborers and, 99, 112, 113, 127, 138, 171, 266, 267; head taxes and,

105–6, 126, 140, 168, 170–71; illegal entry and, 146, 156, 165–71, 191, 265–66; immigration policy and, 101, 117, 126, 130, 137–38, 152; kidnappings to Mexico and, 112–13; migrants in transit and, 158, 160, 161, 167, 184; naturalization and, 118, 119, 121; restrictions and, 99, 104–6, 168, 170–71, 191; Royal Commission investigation and, 103–4, 105, 117, 118, 170–71, 266; statistics and, 32, 106, 110, 111, 124, 169, 170, 171, 275, 276, 301 (n. 35), 310 (n. 47); unguarded borders and ports and, 160, 161, 167, 169–70; U.S. immigration policy and, 17, 99, 117, 163, 165, 167, 168–69, 170, 191, 253; from U.S. and, 104, 124, 135, 139; U.S. immigration inspection and, 132, 133, 179; U.S. immigration investigations and, 180. *See also* British Columbia

Canadian Pacific Railway, 104, 124, 145, 165; U.S. immigration policy and, 167, 168–69

Cananea, 203, 207, 208, 235, 239, 256, 261

Cañete Valley massacre, 77–79, 129

Cano del Castillo, Angel, 209, 211

Canton, 34, 35, 41, 48, 122, 293 (n. 36)

Canton-Chaochow Fellow Provincials Association, 242

Cantonese, xvi, 33

Canton system, 35

Cantú, Esteban, 210, 211–13

Cárdenas, Lázaro, 276

Cárdenas, Miguel, 252

Carranza, Venustiano, 207

Carrick, Fred, 264

Casino Chung Wah (Cuba), 249, 259, 274

Castilla, Marshal, 75

Castle Bruce, 183

Castro, Mauricio, 200

Castro, Raúl, 282

Cayaltil, 58

Central Mexican Railroad, 109

Chamber of Chinese Commerce of Cuba, 249–50

Chang, José, 4, 207

"Chapter in the Coolie Trade, A" (Holden), 22

Chaw Lin Hong, 180, 265

Chee Kung Tang (CKT, or Patriotic Rising Society), 250, 255, 256–58, 259

Chen, Eugene, 238

Chen, Helen, 159

Chen Chui Ping, 286

Chen Kwong Min, 206–7

Chenoweth, Harry K., 260–61

Cheung, Floyd, 255

Chiapas, 203–4, 220, 247

Chi Casio, Federico, 284–85

Chihuahua, 176, 177, 199, 224, 244, 246, 247

Chile, 78, 79

Chin, Ko-Lin, 279, 280

China: anti-Chinese violence in Mexico and, 198, 202–4, 207, 209, 210, 211, 212, 233–34, 235, 237–38, 241–42, 243, 247; Burlingame Treaty with U.S. (1868), 91, 102, 155; Chinese U.S. nationals and, 122–23; Cuba and, 43, 85, 206, 249, 259, 282, 284; emigration treaties and, 39, 51, 108, 109, 114, 207, 209, 212; mass emigration and, 32–33, 44; Mexico and, 98, 108, 109, 114; 1905 boycott on U.S. goods and, 149–50, 151, 253; 1949 Revolution and, 274, 284; 1970s and, 275; Peru and, 51, 98; today, 281, 282. *See also* Qing dynasty (1644–1912)

China Commercial Company, 92–93

China Commercial Steamship Company, 1, 109

Chin Bing, 180, 265

Chincha Islands, 64, 65, 85

Chin Chung, 145

Chin Coy, 180, 181

Chinese Americans, 155, 281, 308 (n. 7)

Chinese and Spanish Emigration Convention, 72

Chinese Consolidated Benevolent Association. *See* Six Chinese Benevolent Associations

Chinese Cubans, 186, 187, 274, 282, 283

Chinese Exclusion Act of 1882, 12, 32, 98, 99, 103, 106, 130, 131, 140, 143

Chinese exclusion laws, 9–10, 88, 274, 276; Canada and restrictive laws and, 10, 104–6, 168, 170–71, 191, 213, 218, 247; Chinese Immigration Act of 1923 (Canada), 106; Chinese merchants and, 149, 246, 253; Chinese Mexicans and, 118–19, 120, 121, 123; Chinese migrants not returning to China and, 156, 308 (n. 9); Cuba and, 9, 99, 126, 187, 205, 206, 213, 217, 247, 250; Geary Act of 1892, 120, 143, 148–49; illegal Chinese migrants and, 5, 8, 155, 171, 172, 192; Page Law of 1875 and, 102, 130; Peru and, 99; as protecting white workers, 98, 103, 126. *See also* Chinese Exclusion Act of 1882; Mexico and Chinese migrants; Smuggling; United States and Chinese migrants

Chinese immigrants. *See* Chinese migrants

Chinese Immigration Act of 1923 (Canada), 106

Chinese Law of 1849 (Peru), 56, 74

Chinese Law of 1861 (Peru), 65, 74–75

Chinese Mexicans: repatriations to Mexico and, 276; restrictions in Mexico and, 118–19, 208, 225, 235–36, 243, 258–59; U.S. Chinese exclusion laws and, 118–19, 120, 121–22, 123, 252

Chinese migrant networks, 15, 130, 143, 247; benevolent associations and, 249–50, 269–70, 284; Chinatowns and, 171, 182, 283, 287; Chinese political parties and, 17, 249, 250–51, 255, 256–58, 262, 269, 270; family associations and, 248–49, 266–69; smuggling rings and, 1, 260–66; tongs (Triad societies) and, 249, 255–56, 269

Chinese migrants: alienation and, 12, 290 (n. 22); as bringing in disease, 105, 106, 115, 116, 177, 199, 216, 229, 231–32; as businessmen, 115, 116, 119, 122, 125, 148, 149; deportations and, 136–37, 138–40, 141, 149, 167; deportation to China and, 140, 173, 175; fraudulent documents and, xvi, 144–45, 147–48, 151, 156, 187, 192, 261, 279, 308 (n. 7); as global phenomenon, 99, 300 (n. 7); legal cases and, 135–37, 138, 139, 148–51, 157, 170, 190, 207, 208, 225–26, 286, 313 (n. 130); middle-class and elite, 15, 16, 103, 291 (n. 35); naming and, xvi, 53–54, 142; naturalization and, 8, 15, 102, 118–22, 146, 270, 308 (n. 7); 1949 Chinese Revolution and, 274, 284; pathways of, mid-nineteenth to early twentieth centuries, 2–5, 10–11, 17, 99; photographs and, 143, 145, 147, 266; repatriation of bones and, 249, 251, 284–85; returning to China, 109, 139, 166, 200, 210, 246, 251, 308 (n. 9); sexuality and, 13, 15, 54–55, 57, 82, 87, 299 (n. 92); as sojourners, 9, 289 (n. 12); terms used for, xv–xvi; as transnational phenomenon, 10–11, 99, 300 (n. 8); women and, 102, 156, 308 (n. 7). *See also* Aliens; Canada and Chinese migrants; Chinese exclusion laws; Coolies; Cuba and Chinese migrants; Illegal aliens; Marriage; Mexico and Chinese migrants; Nation-states; Peru and Chinese migrants; Racism; Smuggling; United States and Chinese migrants; U.S. immigration bureaucracy

Chinese Nationalist Party (Kuomintang [KMT]), 249, 250, 255, 256, 257, 258, 259

Chinese National League, 261, 262

Chinese sexuality, 13, 15, 54–55, 57, 82, 87, 299 (n. 92)

Chinese Six Companies (Chinese Consolidated Benevolent Association). *See* Six Chinese Benevolent Associations

Ching Hoy Soon, 142–43, 144

Ching Wun, 125

Ching You, 121

Chin Lee, 182

Chinos (Chinese), xv. *See also* Chinese migrants; Coolies; Cuba and Chinese migrants; Mexico and Chinese migrants; Peru and Chinese migrants

Chin Yuk, 188

Cholos, 77–78

Chong Ruiz, Luis, 225

Chow How Tong, 284

Choza, Manuel, 123

Christy, William, 190

Chu chai tau (swineherds). *See* Coolie recruiters

Chuffat, Antonio, 204

Chung Sai Yat Po, 257

Cienfuegos, 216

Cimarrones, 75, 76

Cincinnati, Ohio, 266

Ciudad Juárez, 119, 176, 178

Ciudad Obregón, 236

Civil Code (Peru), 56

Clark, John R., 168–69

Clinton, Bill, 278

Club del Pueblo (Club of the People, Mexico), El, 220

Coahuila, 119, 247, 251, 252, 258

Coahuila Coal Mining Company, 252

Cócorit, Sonora, 203, 223

Code Noir of 1685 (France), 66

Cold War, 276

Colonos asiáticos (Asian colonists), xv

Colorado River, 213

Colorado River Land Company, 109, 214

Comercio, El, 47, 53–54, 216

Comité de la Costa Occidental (Committee of the Western Coast, Mexico), 243

Comité Directivo Nacionalista de la Costa Occidental (Nationalist Steering Committee of the Western Coast, Mexico), 243

Comité Nacionalista Antichino (Nationalist Anti-Chinese Committee, Mexico), 236, 238, 243

Commercial Corporation, 252, 254, 322 (n. 11)

Communism, 238–41, 257, 259

Communist Party of China, 259

Compañía Bancaria Chino y México, 254

Compañía Marítima Asiática Mexicana (Asian Mexican Maritime Company), 108

Conrado Silver, Rafael, 212

Consolidated Commercial Steamship Company, 199

Coolidge, Mary Roberts, 121

Coolie recruiters: deception and, 22, 40, 41, 42, 43–44, 45, 72–73, 294 (n. 65); kidnappings and, 35–36, 37, 40, 43, 45, 46; as not Chinese and, 33, 35–36; riots in China and, 35–36, 37–39, 40–41

Coolies: as aliens, 28, 61, 62, 130; auctioning and, 21, 51–54; branding and, 21, 47; Brazil and, 62, 290 (n. 15), 299–300 (n. 109); census and, 86–89, 93; as contract laborers, 8, 16, 46, 55, 57, 59, 91–92, 277, 294 (n. 80); contracts and, 41, 44, 45, 46, 48, 49–50, 58, 60–61, 65–73, 83, 86, 87, 89, 90, 91; coolie trade period, 9, 10, 16, 32, 34, 74, 75, 126, 274; deaths before arrival at destination, 22–23, 24, 26, 29–32, 44, 49, 53, 81, 84; deaths from disease, 22, 30–32, 292 (nn. 16, 17); deaths on plantations, 81, 84–85; defined, xv; end of coolie trade and, 44–45, 85, 89–90, 92, 93, 94, 102, 108, 128; vs. free black labor, 60–61, 69, 77; vs. free laborers, 16, 46–50,

59–60, 67–68, 72, 91, 92–93, 94, 294
(n. 81), 299–300 (n. 109); interpreters
and, 22, 23, 44; kidnappings and, 39,
40, 41–42, 43, 46, 72; manumission
and, 83–84, 85–86; marriage and, 65–
66, 81–82, 87; mutinies on ships and,
21, 22–28, 29–31, 36–37, 40, 44–45, 48,
49, 57, 58, 271, 291 (nn. 1, 10); nation-
states and, 27–28, 29, 50, 51, 57–58, 63,
67, 98, 296 (n. 112); newspaper views
of, 21, 46, 55, 60–62, 67, 74, 79–80,
82, 85, 92; as pirates, 26, 42, 48, 57, 58;
punishments and, 24, 25, 35, 41–42, 50,
53, 55, 57, 68, 72, 73–74, 76, 77, 79–80,
82–83; rebellions and, 21, 22–28, 44–
45, 75, 80, 81, 291 (nn. 1, 10); renaming
and, 21, 53–54; repatriation and, 51, 55,
86; resistance and, 21–22, 30, 41, 53,
80, 92; runaways and, 75, 76, 88, 89;
shipowner insurance policies and, 31;
ships and, 31–32, 39, 46, 48–49, 50–51,
57, 63, 74, 81, 84, 92, 94, 271, 272, 291
(nn. 1, 10), 292 (nn. 16–17), 295 (n. 94);
vs. slavery, 21–22, 39–40, 42, 47, 51–52,
55–57, 61–62, 64–66, 67–68, 69, 72, 73,
76–77, 93, 94, 127; social death and, 65,
296 (n. 12); statistics and, 32, 33–34,
292 (n. 25); stereotypes as victims and,
42–43, 51–52; suicide and, 22, 28, 31,
42, 46, 57, 65, 80, 83–85; as voluntary
emigrants and, 22, 33, 41–44, 45–46,
49–50, 51, 57, 72; women and, 87. *See
also* Canada and Chinese migrants;
Coolie recruiters; Cuba and Chinese
migrants; Peru and Chinese migrants;
Qing dynasty (1644–1912); United
States and Chinese migrants
Coolies and Cane (Jung), 59–60
Coon, Datus E., 173–74
Cooperativa Mexicana de Lavandería
Antiasiática (Anti-Asian Mexican
Laundry Cooperative), 229

Corral, Ramón, 199, 200
Corredores. See Coolie recruiters
Cotton, 214, 253
Covarubias, Ricardo, 214
Credit-ticket mechanism, 46
"Crimps." *See* Coolie recruiters
Criticism of the Cuba Report (William-
son), 94
Cruz, Donaciano, 175
Cuba: Afro-Cubans and, 204–5, 217, 218;
Asian immigration and, 88; racial
equality and, 14, 198, 205, 207, 217;
slavery and, 59, 63, 66, 68, 69, 76, 77,
86, 87, 94; Spanish migrants and, 11,
217; U.S. occupation and, 179, 205
Cuba and Chinese migrants: African
slaves and freemen and, 77, 94; anti-
Chinese sentiment and, 127–28, 207,
216–17, 273; census and, 85–89, 206;
Chinese benevolent associations and,
249–50, 251, 283; Chinese bones
and, 284–85; Chinese exclusion laws
and, 9, 99, 126, 187, 205, 206, 213, 217,
247, 250; Chinese government and,
43, 85, 206, 249, 259, 282, 284; coolie
contracts and, 46, 67, 68–73, 77, 86, 87,
93, 114; coolie deaths and, 30, 84, 88;
coolie labor conditions and, 16, 36, 41,
55–56, 60, 63, 65–66, 67–68, 73–74, 76,
79–80, 93, 94, 127; coolie manumission
and, 83–84, 85–86; coolie regulations
and, 8, 31–32, 55, 65–66, 69, 72, 74, 75,
80, 81–83, 85, 86, 87–88, 93; coolies to
Louisiana and, 46, 60, 90–91; coolie
trade and, 12, 33, 42–44, 54–55, 126,
130, 271, 272, 292 (n. 26), 294 (n. 72);
coolie trade auctions and, 51–52, 53;
coolie trade mutinies and, 22, 27, 29,
36, 37, 44–45, 49; free laborers and,
98–99, 126, 190–91, 206, 259, 265; illegal migrants and, 147–48, 259; immigration policy and, 101, 126, 130, 205;

independence wars and, 13, 14, 88, 127–28, 197–98, 202, 204–7, 217, 281–82, 315 (n. 30); merchants and, 122, 187, 190, 206, 259; smuggling to U.S. and, 1, 162, 163, 179–80, 183–84, 185–86, 187–88, 189, 190, 191, 261–62, 266–67; statistics and, 33, 110–11, 124, 180, 190, 206–7, 274, 276, 302 (n. 53); students and, 206, 274; sugar industry and, 32, 46, 68, 69, 80, 87, 126, 190–91, 206, 207, 250; tongs (Triad societies) and, 259–60; U.S. immigration policy and, 187, 188; from U.S. and, 32, 124, 206; to U.S. from, 32, 127, 159, 160. *See also* Havana

Cuba Commission of 1874, 16, 42–43, 72–73, 282, 294 (n. 72)

Cuba Commission Report, 43–44, 45, 53, 72, 82, 84, 88, 94

Cuban Congress, 205

Cuban Counterpoint (Ortiz), 273

Cuban Revolution of 1959, 284

Cuban Slave Code of 1842, 66

Cuban wars of independence (1868–98), 13, 14, 88, 127–28, 197–98, 202, 204–7, 217, 281–82, 315 (n. 30)

Culiácan, Sinaloa, 224, 230

Cunha Reis, Manuel B. da, 106

Cynosure, 180

Dambourges Jacques, Leo M., 254

Dana, Richard Henry, 51–52, 80

Dea Kay Sing, 147

Declaration of the Rights of Man and of the Citizen, 97

Delgado, Grace, 200, 214–15

Deng Xiaoping, 275

Detroit, 161, 170, 266

Día, El, 206

Díaz, Porfirio, 106, 114, 125, 175, 198, 238, 253

Dillingham, William, 104

Dillingham Commission (1907–11), 104, 137–38, 139

Dollar steamship company, 211

Don Juan (ship), 44–45, 49

Dragón Rojo (Red Dragon), 282

Dunton, John F., 146

Durango, 126, 181, 201, 220

Dutch in China, 36, 50

"Dying of Thirst in the Desert," 9

Eagle Pass, 118, 119, 171, 251, 252, 253

Eco de Yaqui, El, 223

Edelstein, Julius, 277

Effeminacy, 13, 57

Ejemplo de Sonora, El (Espinoza), 197, 202, 220, 258; cartoons and, 219, 223, 224, 225, 226, 228, 231, 232, 237; photographs and, 221, 230

Elías, Francisco S., 235, 236, 237, 243–44

Elías Calles, Plutarco, 209, 233–34, 235, 237, 240, 256

Elías Calles, Rodolfo, 237, 238, 244

Ellis, William H., 125–26

Ellis Island, 132

El Paso, Tex., 146, 171, 172, 176, 177, 178, 181

Eng Bow, 186–87

Eng Hock Fong Company, 93

Ensenada, 4, 5, 123, 172, 174, 175, 200, 246

Espenshade, Thomas, 281

Espinoza, José Angel, 199, 235, 243, 244, 256; *El ejemplo de Sonora* and, 197, 202, 219, 220, 221, 223, 224, 225, 226, 228, 230–31, 232, 237, 258

Estévez Infantil, Emilio, 186

Ettinger, Patrick, 171

Eugenics, 163, 205, 218–19, 224, 233, 247, 273

European immigrants, 12, 30, 42, 133, 138, 139, 152, 247; as illegal aliens, 130, 132, 163

Extranjeros (foreigners), xv

Extranjeros asiáticos (Asian foreigners), xv

Gulfport, Miss., 180, 261
Gum Tung, 183

Halifax, 182
Hanson, W. M., 180–81
Harper's New Monthly Magazine, 22, 23, 24, 25, 27, 28, 43, 165
Harper's Weekly, 5–6, 9, 61–62, 91, 291 (n. 1)
Havana, 172, 206, 216; Chinese Cubans today and, 274, 282, 283; Chinese migrant bones and, 284–85; Chinese migrants in independence wars and, 281–82, 315 (n. 30); Chinese political parties and, 250, 259; coolie trade and, 22, 26, 31–32, 36, 51, 53, 60, 80, 90–91; smuggling of Chinese to U.S. and, 1, 163, 179–80, 186, 187–88, 190, 266–67; smuggling rings and, 180, 187, 188, 261, 262, 265, 268; U.S. immigration inspection and, 179; U.S. immigration investigations and, 181, 188. *See also* Cuba and Chinese migrants
Havana Post, 206
Hayes, Rutherford B., 155
Hermosillo, 224, 243, 256, 261
Hgai Yick Ben, 187
Hing, Francisco, 225–26
Hoar, George Frisbie, 103
Hoey, William M., 261
Ho Jung Ley, 137
Hokkiens, 33
Holden, Edgar, 22–24, 25, 27, 28, 43, 291 (n. 1)
Holmes, Oliver Wendell, Jr., 136
Holocaust, 276
Homosexuality, 13, 87, 299 (n. 92)
Honduras, 262, 263, 274
Hong Kong: Chinese free laborers and, 92, 109, 112, 172; Chinese merchants and, 248, 251; Chinese migrant fraudulent documents and, 147, 148, 187; Chinese migrant networks and, 248; Chinese migrants returning to China

and, 251; Chinese migrants to Mexico and, 1, 4, 108, 109, 164, 199, 210, 267; Chinese U.S. nationals and, 123; coolie trade and, 29, 36–37, 40, 41, 44–45, 47, 48–49, 50, 69, 72, 92, 291 (n. 10), 292 (n. 25); repatriation of Chinese migrant bones and, 284
Hong Kong Daily Mail, 72
How, Frank, 261
Howe, Julia Ward, 84
Hsein Tso-Pang, 42
Huerta, Adolfo de la, 207, 212, 235
Huigan, 249
Hum Fook, José, 207, 208–9
Humiliation Day (Canada), 106
Hung League, 255
Hung Man Lew, 266
Huntington, Samuel, 273

Illegal aliens: Chinese contract laborers as, 93, 130; Chinese migrants after exclusion laws and, 130, 153, 192, 248; Chinese migrants as, 1, 2–5, 8, 12, 17; European immigrants as, 130, 132, 163; immigration policy and, 130, 131, 163; meaning of term, xv, 271, 273; Mexican migrants as, 8, 277; 1990s and, 278–79; as "wrong kind" of immigrant, 153, 193. *See also* U.S. immigration bureaucracy
Imagined Communities (Anderson), 272
Immigration Act of 1891, 135
Immigration Act of 1965, 276, 277–78
Immigration Bureau. *See* U.S. immigration bureaucracy
Imparcial, El, 244–45
India, 29
Industrial Workers of the World (IWW), 239, 263
Ingram, Rex, 234
Inspection Service (Mexico), 201, 209–10
International Railroad Company, 251–52
Irick, Robert, 36

Riley, William, 264
Rio Grande, 5, 178
Rising Tide of Color against White World Supremacy, The (Stoddard), 13, 271, 273
Robert Browne (ship), 36, 46
Rochín, Norberto, 258
Rodríguez, Abelardo L., 208, 212, 213, 258
Romero, Matías, 100, 106–7, 118, 124, 174
Romero, Robert Chao, 219–20, 224, 225, 283
Roosevelt, Theodore, 150, 153, 163, 193, 253
Royal Commission Report, 118, 170–71
"Runners." *See* Coolie recruiters
Russia, 50, 100, 240

Saco, José Antonio, 84, 85
Sai Qui Wing, 41–42
Salina Cruz, Mexico, 1, 4, 108, 164, 176, 177, 178, 204, 207
Salyer, Lucy, 135, 137
Sam, Charles, 123
Sam Hop Sing, 180
Sam Wa, 257
San Antonio, 119, 172, 181, 252
San Diego, 4, 123, 172–73, 200
San Diego Union, 174, 175
San Francisco, 143, 146, 148, 156, 251; anti-Chinese sentiment and, 102, 117; Chinese merchants and, 122, 125; Chinese migrant bones and, 284; Chinese migrants from Canada and Mexico and, 112, 155, 165, 173, 176; Chinese migrants in transit and, 107, 109, 157, 158, 172, 174, 186, 211, 246; Chinese political parties and, 256, 257; coolie trade and, 29, 36, 46; immigration bureaucracy and, 131, 132, 144, 189. *See also* California; United States and Chinese migrants
San Francisco Call, 125
San Francisco Chronicle, 200, 201
San Francisco Examiner, 172
San Hing, 114

Santos Fernández, Juan, 205
Sargent, Frank P., 179
Schell, A. P., 180
Schiavone Camacho, Julia Maria, 229
Seattle, 148, 177
Sea Witch (ship), 31
Sea Witch, The (Laing), 271, 272
Seeman, Melvin, 11–12
Select Committee on Chinese Labor and Immigration (Canada), 117
Sen Kow, 263
Servicio de Salubridad (Public Health Service, Mexico), 213
"Shadows, the" (group), 216
Shanghai, 40–41, 199, 241–42, 266
Shey Loud, 267
Shou Min, 261–62
Shu Gee, 268
Simmel, Georg, 8, 9, 272
Sinaloa, 198, 223, 224, 227, 234, 236, 237, 238, 242, 244, 246, 247, 256
Sing Tuck, 135–36
Sinn, Elizabeth, 284
Siu, Paul, 9
Six Chinese Benevolent Associations, 46, 112, 135, 148–49, 150, 173, 249, 260, 261
Slavery, 12, 69, 87, 271; abolitionists and, 21, 41, 51, 59, 63, 81, 84, 94; African slave trade and, 28, 30, 32, 42, 59; emancipation and, 56–57, 59, 60, 61, 90, 91; vs. free wage labor and, 59, 61, 63–66, 68; marriage and, 64, 81; purchasing freedom and, 66, 83, 86; slave codes and, 66, 76, 81. *See also* Coolies; Cuba; Great Britain; Peru and slavery; United States
Slave Trade Act of 1818, 28, 39
Smallcomb, Thomas, 174
Smith, John, 170
Smithe, William, 105
Smuggling: Canada and, 165–71; Chinese interpreters and, 176, 188–92; Chinese merchants and, 142, 147, 191–92, 254,

260, 265; Chinese seamen and, 182–83, 184; conditions of experience of, 161–62, 262–63, 268, 279; Gulf of Mexico and, 153, 179–88, 190, 262–64; 1990s to now, 278–80, 282–83, 285–86; routes taken and, 5, 160, 161–62, 169–70, 172–73, 181, 182, 184–85, 187, 192, 262–63, 279, 286–87; ship captains and, 173–74, 183–84, 262, 264, 265; smuggling rings and, 153–54, 174–79, 180, 187, 188, 192; statistics and, 160–61; tongs (Triad societies) and, 260–66; U.S. marshals and, 174, 175, 176. *See also* Cuba and Chinese migrants; Mexico and Chinese migrants; U.S. immigration bureaucracy

Socialist Party (U.S.), 239

Soldaderas (women soldiers), 227

Sonora, 164, 260, 261; anti-Chinese activities and, 115, 203, 208, 211, 219–33, 234–38, 257; anti-Chinese violence and, 129, 198, 199, 246, 256; Chinese exclusion laws and, 207, 214; Chinese migrant restrictive labor laws and, 235–38, 244; Chinese political parties and, 256, 257–58; *mestizaje* ideal of race mixing and, 218–19; miscegenation laws and, 225–33, 235; 1930s Chinese migrant expulsions and, 215, 234, 241–46, 247, 257, 276

Sons of England Lodge, 217

Sop, Manuel Jean, 208

South Africa, 13, 117

Southeast Asia, 32, 34, 292 (n. 25)

Southern Pacific Railroad, 251

Spain: anti-Chinese activities in Mexico and, 243; coolie contracts and, 50, 66, 69–73, 91; coolie labor conditions and, 75, 84, 94; coolie regulations and, 73, 75, 81; coolie trade and, 29, 31–32, 33, 43, 44, 49, 50, 72, 108; coolie trade regulation and, 37, 39, 49, 63; emigration treaties with China and, 98; Span-

ish migrants to Cuba and, 11, 217. *See also* Cuba and Chinese migrants

Spaulding, O. L., 121

Spence, Leonard, 262–63

Springstein, B. C., 261

Stanley, Amy Dru, 81

St. Louis Daily Globe Democrat, 242–43

Stoddard, Lothrop, 13–14, 271, 273, 278

"Stranger within Our Gate, The" (magazine article, Brandenburg), 6

Stratakos, Nicolas, 180

Strauss, Oscar, 109

Sugar industry: coolie regulations and, 73–74, 75, 89–90; Cuba and, 32, 46, 68, 69, 80, 87, 126, 190–91, 206, 207, 250; after emancipation, 90, 91; Louisiana and, 60, 90–91; Peru and, 65, 68, 69, 75, 79, 89–90

Suicide, 22, 31, 42, 46, 57, 65, 80, 83–85; as political act, 28, 84–85

Sumner, William Graham, 59, 66

Sun, Lou Yat, 261–62

Sunbeam, 183, 184

Sun Yat-sen, 217, 250, 254, 255, 256, 257

Supreme Court of Mexico, 225–26

Swatow, China, 31, 40

Syme, Francis Darby, 37, 39, 40

Syme, Muir and Co., 37, 38, 39

Syrian migrants, 1, 130, 152, 163, 210, 240

Taiping Rebellion (1851–64), 32

Tait, James, 37, 40

Tait and Co., 37, 38, 39

Tamaulipas, 124, 125, 181

Tampa, 179, 187, 188, 189, 190. *See also* Florida

Tampa Sunday, 186

Tampico, Mexico, 112–14, 115, 180, 181, 241, 252, 253, 265

Tang Horn, Louie, 267, 268

Tang Shue Wan, 176–77

Tapachula, 203–4

Tavares Mondo, José, 48, 49

Taylor, Richard, 176, 177, 178, 181–82, 188

Tcheng Loh, 234

Tea, Juan Pangtay, 122

Tello, Manuel, 211, 238

Tennessee, 92

Ten Years War (1868–78), 204

Texas, 142–43, 171, 172, 178, 181

Tijuana, 174, 175, 200, 240, 287

Times Mirror Company, 109

Tipton, SS, 262

To Die in Cuba (Pérez), 84

"Todo por la Raza" ("Everything for the Race/People," poster, Mexico), 224

Tongs (Triad societies), 199, 249; Chinese political parties and, 255–56, 269; expulsions and, 257, 258, 259; 1990s to now, 279, 286; smuggling rings and, 260–66; violence in Cuba and, 259–60; violence in Mexico and, 239, 256, 257–58

Toro de Once, El, 227, 228, 229

Torreón, 4, 5, 191, 252, 253, 254

Torreón massacre, 201–3, 204, 254

Torres, Luis E., 175, 200

Townshend, Frederick Trench, 55–56

Trachoma, 1, 163, 177

Tráfico, El, 115–16, 117, 218, 219

Trasivik, Daniel, 187

Treaty Convention (France, 1860), 35

Treaty of Amity, Commerce, and Navigation (Mexico and China), 209

Treaty of Tientsin (Great Britain, 1859), 35

Triad societies. *See* Tongs (Triad societies)

Trinidad, 184

Tseng, Marquis, 108

Tsungli Yamen, 108

Tucson, Ariz., 255

Tusan (tusheng), 283

Unión de Comerciantes Mexicanos de Fresnillo, 215

Unión Nacionalista Mexicana (Pro-Raza y Salud Pública) (Mexican Nationalist Union [Pro Race and Public Health]), 235, 243, 258

Union of Dependents of Small Food Retailers (Cuba), 216

United Fruit Company, 262, 263

United Press, 244

United States: Asian immigration and, 102, 160, 239, 277; European immigrants and, 130, 132, 138, 152, 163, 247; immigration policy and, 101–2, 137, 138, 208, 247, 304 (n. 4); Mexican migrant repatriations to Mexico and, 215, 219, 242–43, 247; Mexican migrants and, 5, 8, 9, 132, 152, 200, 277, 278, 304 (n. 4), 325 (n. 27); slavery and, 59, 66, 81. *See also* U.S. immigration

United States and Chinese migrants: anti-Chinese activities and, 102–3, 104–5; anti-Chinese sentiment and, 117, 120, 126; anti-Chinese violence and, 124, 129; Canada helping restrict and, 17, 99, 117, 163, 165, 167, 168–69, 191; Chinese departing from U.S., 155, 156; Chinese deportations, 136, 138–40, 141, 149, 167, 170, 173, 174, 286; Chinese deportations to China, 175, 187, 245; Chinese deportations to Cuba, 187, 188, 262; Chinese deportations to Mexico, 139, 181; Chinese entering illegally from Canada, 99, 155; Chinese entering illegally from Caribbean, 181–84, 262–63; Chinese entering illegally from Cuba, 1, 162, 163, 179–80, 183–84, 185–87, 189, 190, 191, 206, 261–62; Chinese entering illegally from Mexico, 5–8, 99, 155, 166, 171–79, 213, 245; Chinese exclusion laws and, 9–10, 32, 88, 98, 99, 115, 117, 118–19, 121–22, 123, 213, 247, 274; Chinese Mexican nationals and, 118–19, 120, 121–22, 123, 252; Chinese to Cuba from U.S., 32, 124, 206; end of coolie trade and, 90, 91, 92, 102; contract laborers and, 92, 109, 137, 213; coolie